Technical D

From the bottom up

By

Kevin Gurr

Disclaimer

All diving is potentially dangerous. Decompression diving especially is a 'dynamic' event, and even if guidelines such as those published in this book are followed, decompression illness, injury and even death my result. While the author has attempted to produce information in an up-to-date and accurate way, the reader uses this information combined with their own judgement at their own risk.

First Published by Phoenix Oceaneering in 2001

This edition published in 2004 by
Periscope Publishing Ltd.
33 Barwis Terrace
Penzance
Cornwall TR18 2AW

www.periscopepublishing.com

A CIP record for this book is available from the British Library

ISBN No 1-904381-20-0

Printed in England by Anthony Rowe Ltd
Eastbourne

Foreword

Tom Mount

Kevin Gurr has taken the overall world of technical diving and tied it into a neat presentation in this publication. I thoroughly enjoyed reading the advanced copy and it is evident that his knowledge and understanding of technical diving is a combination of practical experience and theoretical knowledge.

Kevin has a unique background as a pioneer in technical diving with expertise in deep diving, wreck diving, rebreather diving and cave diving. For those entering any form of technical diving today they should give thanks to Kevin for all his efforts in promoting this unique form of the sport, for his work with government organizations in coordinating their understanding of technical diving and seeing the vast difference between it and normal sport diving. At the same time identifying why it is not a conflict with commercial diving. Kevin was there when much of the diving world looked upon nitrox as 'snake oil' and technical divers as a bunch of brainless thrill seekers. Kevin helped them see otherwise.

I have had the privilege of knowing Kevin since around 1991 when we met first via phone calls, then at the first nitrox workshop at the DEMA show. Since that time I have worked with Kevin as a student, as a dive partner and as a co-author on numerous materials. We have co-taught programmes together, debated diving issues and helped form common ground on training issues with others that are still used in the IANTD syllabus today. In addition I value Kevin as a friend and a great innovator. He developed the very first Nitrox dive computer of which I was fortunate enough to own in 1993. In 2000 he once again stepped forward with the first fully available CCR and trimix dive computer. Leading the field just seems to be a part of Kevin's personality.

This work will undoubtly generate discussion on some of the approaches to particular issues. This is the norm with all technical diving endeavors, but all who are knowledgeable will agree, the content is exceptional and provides the safest practical approach to technical diving. Those entering technical diving for the first time are fortunate to have such a clearly written text and guide for learning how to conduct technical diving more safely. Detailed project plans and risk analysis add to the dimension of this work by providing insight on how to plan a dive or an entire project.

Kevin has managed to blend much of his already published work into one easily read and understood format. The book also encourages the diver to continue to grow, to avoid becoming stagnant, to learn and to contribute to the sport, just as he has.

This is a 'must read and apply' book for new technical divers and definitely a tool for all the experienced professionals out there.

Tom Mount February 2002.

Richard Pyle

More than a decade ago – before "Technical Diving" was conceived as such, before *AquaCorps* published its first issue, before any of the technical training agencies certified their first trimix diver (indeed, before the agencies really even existed) – there were scattered individuals around the world experimenting with exotic breathing gases and novel equipment configurations, in an effort to apply the mixed-gas diving techniques developed by the commercial and military diving to their own "recreational" diving needs. Without any forum of communication, most of these scattered individuals hardly knew of the existence of one-another, let alone shared ideas about equipment and techniques. Except for within certain localized close-knit diving communities, what little information exchange did occur, generally came through word-of-mouth – from the friend of a friend of a friend...

Around this time, I was desperately trying to find a source for reliable trimix decompression schedules. The only available tables (if you could even get your hands on them) were either based on heliox, or were custom "one-off"-type schedules that were rather expensive to have commissioned. I longed for the day when someone would develop a mixed-gas diving computer. Then I heard – through a friend of a friend of a friend – that some bloke in the UK had built exactly such a device. It was supposed to calculate decompression for any combination of oxygen, nitrogen, and helium – in real time – and was programmable, allowing different decompression models to be uploaded. The "bloke" who built it – was Kevin Gurr.

When you consider that such real-time mixed-gas decompression computers have only very recently begun to emerge on the market, you can't help but appreciate how far ahead of his time Kevin really was. But it didn't end with the mixed-gas dive computer. After a couple of years of correspondence, I finally got to meet Kevin in person at one of the first "Tek" meetings. There he showed me version 1.0 of his desktop computer program, "ProPlanner", which was not only among the first such programs available, was extremely well-designed, easy to use, and even included mixed-gas closed-circuit decompression capabilities!

I've had the pleasure of getting to know Kevin very well during the years since. In 1994, he and I spent ten days at Bill Stone's house learning about the Cis-Lunar MK-4P rebreather – an experience that still singularly ranks as the best and most useful learning experience of my entire diving career. We've spent many hours discussing all manner of diving equipment, practices, people, politics, and philosophy – especially during the many conferences we both attended during the early years of Technical diving. During one particularly memorable DEMA, Kevin and I snuck away from the meeting several days early to take the prototype of the Cis-Lunar MK-5P (for which Kevin contributed an enormous volume of design input) on its very first ocean test dives, down at Billy Deans' place in Key West. Oh, the stories I could tell!

From all of this, I've learned two things about Kevin that impress and inspire me the most. First, his bladder capacity exceeds that of any other human I've ever met. Second, and of somewhat greater relevance in the present context, the depth and breadth of his knowledge, experience, and wisdom about all manner of advanced diving activities is almost beyond comprehension. From his pioneering achievements in European wreck diving, to his explorations of numerous cave passages, to his grueling dive schedules in the tropical waters of Guam, Kevin is among the few in this field who has truly been around. And this is why you (the reader), and I, and future generations of advanced divers should count our blessings that Kevin has been able to harness his vast insight and lay it out for all of us within the pages of this book. Unlike many other books about advanced and technical diving, which often focus on one particular facet (e.g., physiology, rebreathers, cave diving, wreck diving, etc.), or are organized explicitly as a training manual, this one covers the spectrum.

When he asked me to write this Foreword, I figured I'd just do a quick scan of the draft book, and fully expected to see a review of what I mostly already knew. Instead, I found myself captivated and unable to tear myself away whenever I started reading a section. I've teased Kevin in years past about his "very British" writing style...but this time I have nothing but praise. From his spot-on descriptions of many of our mutual friends and heroes who helped pioneer Technical diving, through the insightful and important section on the woefully-underappreciated topic of Psychology, on to the highly detailed sections on equipment, gas physics and blending, dive techniques, physiology, first-aid, rebreathers, decompression, and even his personal account of the amazing *Britannic* expedition – Kevin nails it all, with helpful photos, graphics, and tables. I especially liked the section covering one of my particular areas of interest – In-Water Recompression (IWR) – a subject whose importance vastly exceeds the frequency with which it is covered in published form. How rare it is to find a book that scores high marks for both information content, and enjoyable reading!

Kevin has been around technical diving since before it began. He is a pioneer in the truest sense of the word. By all means, you should pay close attention to what he has to say. His words are backed by a level of understanding shared by very few others in our diving community. You may very well learn something from him that will some day save your life. I know that I already have.

Richard Pyle. February 2002.

Acknowledgements

I have pestered many people with the contents of this book throughout the three years it has taken to complete. I apologise to you all, you know who you are.

A small section of the text has been 'lifted' from IANTD training manuals I have written or co-written and my thanks are given to the Board of Directors for allowing me to reproduce it here. Thanks also to Leigh Bishop and Gerraint Foulkes-Jones for allowing me to reproduce their heliair tables.

All Britannic photographs are courtesy of 'Project Britannic'1997 and taken by Dan Burton. To my knowledge all other photographs are mine, with the exceptions of the surface shots of Britannic, which are courtesy of Simon Mills and the surface shot of the M1 submarine is courtesy of Richard Larn. There is also one photo taken by Kevin Denlay. Custom Divers, OMS and Poseidon all supplied equipment photographs.

Cover artwork is by Gavin Newman.

Published in 2001 by Phoenix Oceaneering Ltd.

Why write this book?
Since the early 1990's a new evolution of diving has affected the mass diving-public. A variety of descriptions have been used such as "technical diving", "extended range diving" and "advanced diving", but to name a few. As with any new concept it was initially met with awareness and even a certain level of discrimination.

Like all sports, diving is constantly evolving as new equipment and techniques are experimented with and new limits are extended. Very often these new 'concepts' are nothing more than old ideas re-visited with a fresh mind.

So why write this book? During several years of being involved with technical diving from its inception in the UK since the early 90's to its 'acceptance' by the air training agencies, I have observed many changes. I have witnessed (and been privileged to be involved in) many successful projects that pushed the boundaries at the time. There have been enormous developments in the tools for technical divers. Several 'experts' have informed us all how to 'do it', whilst many people have just gone out and 'done it', learnng through experience. Unfortunately, occasionally, a friend or colleague has paid the ultimate price for their endeavours; this is the nature of exploration and progress.

Whilst there is no single-way to undertake diving, (the sport and the environment are too dynamic) there are definitely several ways not to do it. This book is written as a collection of experiences by friends and myself in the industry who have earned some level of respect and reputation from their exploits and knowledge. It is designed to communicate simply and hopefully as practically as possible. No doubt there will be those who do not agree with some of the views expressed. That is their prerogative. As the author, my best advice is 'never take what you read as gospel'. Whilst it may have worked for the author at the time in his environment, it may not work for you in yours. Take on board what you read, try it and develop it as required. Knowledge is a precious thing - it has often been hard earned. You should analyse everything you hear and in the fullness of time generate your own decisions as a consequence.

This book is not a substitute for good formal (and practical) training. Treat this book as a guide, a collection of concepts and information with which to start work. This is not a finite reference work. That would be too impossible to generate and too arrogant to assume.

Safe Diving

Metrification
I considered for a long time how best to represent mathematical examples in metric and imperial units of measurement without generating confusion within the text. I decided to show all measurements using the metric system with any specific formulae that differ as a result, shown in both unit versions. Chapters with mathematical examples in them have the relevant conversions within the chapter. There is also a general conversion table in Appendix B.

Diving Pioneers

There are many contemporary pioneers associated with all aspects of diving, from Haldane father and son who pioneered decompression tables, to Cousteau who brought diving to the mass media. All of these have a place in history and have been discussed and documented many times.

This section is really a dedication. The following are my own personal modern pioneers. Some may think pioneer is too strong a word. These are people with whom I have become acquainted during many years. They have left their impression on myself and many others. They have shown us that the light at the end of the tunnel isn't just a train and by being involved in our endeavours have brought humour, friendship and knowledge without being egotistic, a rare trait. Unfortunately, some of these individuals are no longer with us.

Billy Deans
Billy is definitely a character larger than life when you meet him but only advertises himself through his deeds. Billy was just out there doing it when most of the rest of us were still trying to work out even what 'it' was. He lives in Key West, Florida and used to own a dive store/technical training centre there. If you lived outside the USA you either trained with Billy or Tom Mount. I had the privilege of working with both men. Billy introduced me to marine archaeology through the Pilar Project - a deep diving project in Guam to locate a Spanish Galleon that I later ran for two years.

If it could be done, Billy would find a way of doing it safely. That was his thing - safety first. I have never known anyone spout so many acronyms and sayings on the subject, but each one of them totally relevant. Billy had learned the hard way and lost friends. His whole diving philosophy was about not letting that happen again to anyone.

Billy dropped out of diving education after the 1998 Pilar season and is now a paramedic. He remains a close friend and I owe him a great deal.

Sheck Exley
Sheck was someone whome I only knew personally for a very short time, yet got to know better through his writings. I only ever met Sheck at the early US Tek conferences. We invariably ended up on the same decompression panels. He wrote Dr X, his decompression planning programme at about the same time we released Proplanner, the only other software available at the time being Z Plan by Corey Bergman who also was often at the discussions. Corey sadly died whilst practicing a body recovery in a dam in the Tennessee valley. He accidentally used the wrong gas at depth while using independent cylinders.

You would have thought there would be a little competition from another software author. Quite the reverse, Sheck was keen to share everything and discuss any problems. Sheck's books included, "A Blueprint for Survival" and "Caverns Measureless to Man" are on the diving 'must-have' list. Read them carefully. They contain a massive amount of history of why we do things the way we do for those of you busily reinventing the wheel.

Sheck died whilst exploring Zacaton Cenote in Mexico.

Dr. Max Hahn
Max Hahn was truly one of diving's modern pioneers. He worked with Bühlmann in the early years and later went onto generate algorithms for the first mass market dive computers.

Max once told me a story about his early diving experiences after World War Two. His diving started on ex-military Oxygen rebreathers in Germany's lakes. They had no knowledge about Oxygen toxicity. When I asked him how he knew how deep to go he replied, " we went down until we felt strange and them came up. We only did this excursion to depth once and then stayed shallow". Max was one of the most knowledgeable physiologists I have ever met, a very competent diver and someone who always had time even for the oddest question from the audience. I had the pleasure of teaching several classes with him, as a student. I'm not sure who learned the most. He unfortunately died in those same lakes in 2000 diving a rebreather.

Dr. Bill Hamilton
When I first encountered Bill in the early 1990's he was the only one who would give us a clue about extended range tables. He is an ex-fighter pilot turned Physiologist.

Bill developed the first available decompression software for use by deep divers. His programme DCAP was all we had that, and the tables he would generate for you if asked. I first used DCAP when we were doing experimental Rebreather dives at the Diving Diseases Research Centre in Plymouth with Dr. Maurice Cross in the late 80's. We needed to do a range of 100-150m heliox test dives and Bill had cut the tables. A combination of blind faith, lots of Doppler monitoring and a rebreather that thankfully had a manual over ride (the electronics kept failing), pulled us through and gave me an experience I would never forget. In a round about way Bill introduced me to technical Diving. I did not meet him in person until the first US Tech Conference in Houston, where nitrox was a dirty word and the diving industry was trying to ban it. Bill helped to chair a conference that paved the way for the acceptance of recreational mixed gas diving. He is still very proactive in this field and is on NAUI's Board of Advisors.

Jean Pierre Imbert
My first thought was, 'Who is this Frenchman telling us commercial diving problems have a relevance in our diving?' At the time JP's English was a little disjointed and hard to understand. He had worked for Comex in the 1980's and had helped find a correlation between surface decompression (completing the final phases of decompression in a chamber) and 'bends' inside the tables. This was the first detailed investigation into micro bubbles that had been presented to the diving public. It didn't give us any finite answers but sparked a chain of thought that made many of us start changing the way we dived. Since that time JP assisted our team with table generation for my 1997 Britannic project, he also attended one of my cave classes (with his girlfriend Patricia) in Florida and ended up a friend. We always seemed to be on the same speakers' list at various conferences. JP now runs IANTD France and is working on a new algorithm for diving, taking into account microbubble growth more effectively. He is active in generating extreme exposure tables for French cave divers.

Michael Menduno
Mike was the owner/editor of Aquacorp. The 'Tech diving bible' in the 1990's. The demise of Aquacorp was a sad loss. Mike is probably the first to admit he isn't a brilliant technical diver but he was the guy that got us all together. He organised the US TEK conferences. For several years it was just a meeting of minds. People saying "well I've been doing it this way for years and it seems to work. How about you?" A true melting pot of ideas which has formed many of the techniques and equipment we use today. Mike brought technical diving into the mass market and made the agencies and manufacturers listen. Through Mike's conferences I have made many lasting friends. I personally think we owe him a great deal.

Tom Mount
Aside from my own early experiments, Tom introduced me to 'technical diving'. IANTD was IAND. It was the only agency. You were taught in Tom's house and often ended up sleeping with one or two Rotweillers after a long day's diving. The only manual was Dick Rutowski's Nitrox Diver - everything else you learnt by example.

Tom is one of the survivors of the sport and hence one to be listened to. Tom was cave diving when most of the latter day 'guru's' hadn't even taken an open water class. On land, lectures often took the form of open discussion because we were all learning. In the water he was, and still is a task master. I'd never heard anyone scream underwater before. You knew when you'd screwed up.

He now has over 12,000 dives, many of them in caves. Tom has probably brought more education to would-be technical divers through his individual classes and through IANTD as a whole, than anyone else in the world.

Richard Pyle
I can't remember how it came about but Rich and I ended up on Bill Stones (designer of the Cis-Lunar rebreather) doorstep on an Autumn morning in 1994. Richard is an ichthyologist (in his own words 'fish nerd') who works at the Bishop Museum in Hawaii. The deal was that Bill would teach us how to dive his rebreather which was about to be redesigned for the recreational market. We walked into the garage and were presented with a red, somewhat slimy mess. On the floor were several rebreathers, in pieces, that had just been returned from Bill's latest expedition to the Huatala cave system in Mexico. "OK, put them back together" With a few words of wisdom, Bill went to his day job and we started building the units. Bill's logic being if we can build it we will understand it, a concept that I still pass on today. The following weeks were spent testing and diving the units. I have an endearing image of Richard in an Hawaiian shirt and shorts diving in a flooded quarry in Pennsylvania. I was cold and I had a wetsuit!

I got to know Richard quite well over the ensuing years. When the first Tech Diver Internet forum started he was very proactive, unselfishly giving advice to anyone with a problem, at times taking extreme 'flak' from others on the list. Richard is a very intelligent individual and has a vast amount of diving experience, he is a 'doer' rather than a talker but has no problems sharing his experiences, good and bad. His postings on rebreather survival are a must read for any budding rebreather diver. In the end Richard and I worked on the new Cis Lunar MK5 with Bill, eventually test diving a unit in Key West. Richard went on to work closely with Cis-Lunar for a few years, but remains a 'fish nerd' to this date.

Harry Railing
If you saw Harry in a crowd you would think 'military'. Talk to him and you just knew he was an officer in the Guards, which he once was. Harry was very 'proper' and a complete lunatic. One of the most 'fun' people I have ever met who just grabbed life and diving by the throat and shook it until he got out what he wanted.

An excellent diver, one of my first memories of him was on Tim Benito's boat as we motored to the Moldavia for a dive. Billy Deans was on board on his first visit to the UK and curious to see how British Tekkies performed. It was a bit choppy and we all got kitted up sitting on the floor of the boat. Billy was watching Harry intently as he strapped on various bits of wrecking paraphernalia. Billy, being his usual safety conscious-self looked down and asked Harry how long he would stay down on the dive. Harry, in his very British accent, replied, "Let's see how long the jolly old gas lasts shall we?". To this day Billy doesn't know if he was joking or not.

Harry was a student of mine on several occasions and became very active in the technical diving scene in the UK, helping out with our own TEK conference, occasionally and generally just being a good diving buddy. He eventually moved from London to Dorset with his wife and two children to 'get more diving in'. He sadly died in a rebreather diving accident in 1999. He was universally liked and respected in UK diving circles. Harry was famous for his Whisky Mixer Blender courses in the bar at UK TEK shows. He is sadly missed.

John Thornton
It is always cold in Scapa Flow and in March 1985 it was no different. My first trip to Scapa led me to meet John. A 6 foot 6 inch ex teacher turned dive boat skipper/scallop diver. The only way to warm up was either stay in bed or stick your hands in the engine water coolant tank. My first memory of John was of a madman finding out someone had found a battle ship navigation light and couldn't raise it. He strapped on a couple of cylinders (no BC) and leapt overboard into 45m of water. Ten minutes later he surfaced clutching the light with a fully inflated drysuit and a large grin. John was the first person to teach technical diving in Scotland. We became friends, he located and we first dived the Hampshire (Kitchener's grave) in 1993. John was an invaluable part of 'Britannic 1997' and has skippered and led many expeditions of his own. John's humour and personality are well known in the industry. He is still very active through his training/charter business 'Scapa Technical'.

John Saddington
My final 'dedication' is to John Saddington, a name few people will know. John is the ex-diving officer of Andover BSAC branch 942. Without John' I would not be here now. As a new diver he took me under his wing and taught me the basics of underwater survival. He and his small group of friends were one number short to make a dive team and I was going to make up the numbers. Through months of pool training, equipment failures, rough seas, sinking boats, freezing caravans and ridiculously early starts he turned me into diver. We all have our own John Saddington. I just wanted to thank mine.

Diving and especially technical diving has been said to be '40% physical fitness and 60% mental fitness', but what is mental fitness and how do we attain it?

As living beings one of our primary functions is to breathe in oxygen, which is used by the body to produce energy[1]. Energy fuels us and allows us to function. If we breathe correctly we function more efficiently. In short, we feel better, can exercise for longer, have a better resistance to disease and are less tired. With better breathing patterns we are able to work on our cardio-vascular fitness, using exercise as a tool. The more we exercise, the more efficient breathing machines we become.

Another important aspect of correct breathing is its ability to assist us when stressful situations occur.

Breathing is controlled by our autonomic nervous system, which is a subsystem of the central nervous system. Without thinking about it, we breathe, but if we do think about it we can modify the way we breathe. This is an important survival technique. This is where the link between mental and physical occurs; we can use our mind to control a physical function, breathing.

Getting ready for a deep dive

So how does breathing control stress? The answer is carbon dioxide or CO_2. CO_2 is the divers 'bad gas'. CO_2 affects our decompression strategy, nitrogen narcosis, oxygen toxicity and much more. For now let's concentrate on stress.

If we don't ventilate our lungs properly we may retain CO_2 and hypercapnia could result. An increase in CO_2 may be as a result of forced exercise or an immediate stressful occurrence. The body's response to an increased partial pressure of carbon dioxide is to modify its breathing pattern. Unfortunately breathing often only becomes more rapid and good ventilation is not established. Hence, a vicious circle begins, poor ventilation and ever increasing PCO_2's (partial pressure of CO_2). Eventually the mind looses control of the body, adrenaline is released into the system and our 'flight response' is activated and panic ensues.

So, achieving breathing control is the key. Many Eastern philosophies focus on mind control through breathing. Experienced explorers (not just divers) often employ techniques based on these thoughts. In some cases people use these to the extreme. It becomes almost a religion and it certainly heightens their survival response.

Telling new divers that they should practice Zen to improve performance will often be met with cynicism. Trainee technical divers are often the same. With time however and exposure to the environment, the diver sees the benefit of such beliefs and practices and will find his/her own 'middle ground'. A level of mental exercise that they feel is acceptable for their diving level.

Let's look at some simple breathing exercises.

Breathing

In the Western world we have lost the ability to naturally breathe correctly. We breathe from the chest instead of making use of the full diaphragm. Using the whole diaphragm is vital for divers especially during decompression as the majority of gas transport to and from the blood takes place in the lower part of the lungs.

Stand up, put one hand on the chest and one on the stomach. Now breathe in, focusing on the stomach hand doing the most of the movement. Breathe in to a count of five and out to a count of eight without holding your breath. This is an ideal breathing pattern. Extend this exercise to walking around and eventually diving. When coupled with exercise, not only will this improve your cardiovascular conditioning but will reduce gas consumption and improve

[1] See ATP page 102

your diving performance in general. Personally, I practice this technique when I've nothing better to do, such as when decompressing!

Using Goals

As humans we feel good when we achieve a goal. Goals can be simple, like completing a test, or complex, like completing an expedition successfully. The good feeling assists our ability to continue with an endeavour and plan for the next, often more challenging one. Many goals are subconscious., We naturally achieve them throughout the day by having a basic plan of what we want to achieve. Bigger goals require a lot of planning and may often be modified many times before completion.

Put simply, goals are important because they give us confidence in ourselves and our abilities.

Goals should be planned with the following constraints:

1. **They must be attainable**. It is futile planning to be an astronaut in two weeks if your current employment is an accountant.
2. **They must be measurable**. You must know when you have completed them and how successfully.
3. **They should be enforced**. Writing them in a prominent place is simplest. I use the back of my wardrobe door!
4. **They should be updated**. Once a goal is complete, start thinking about the next one to replace it.

Complex goals may have several stages, but each stage should follow the same criteria as above.

Quitting

Goals also enhance our ability to avoid quitting. There have been many instances in life where people have died when they just gave up. The classic example of the cave diver is always quoted. Where when lost in a cave with a depleting gas supply he chose to write to his family on his dive slate instead of searching for the exit, which in fact was only a few metres away and easily attainable. He drowned.

A simple way to improve your ability to avoid quitting is to do some simple form of physical exercise. When you feel like you want to stop....don't. Go that little further. Having set a mental goal and attained it, go that bit further. A example of this is when running and you feel like you cannot go on, make yourself do that extra little bit. Also practice power sprinting occasionally during the run instead of saving it all to the end.

Having set a mental goal and attained it; go that bit further!!

Applying Psychology to Training

Training is another key element which will improve our mental ability to survive as technical divers. Training is often taken for the wrong reasons, 'I need the ticket to get gas' etc. Unfortunately it is not uncommon for students to seek out the cheapest training available just to 'get it done'. This type of student is often not ready to learn and is not really sure why he or she is taking the training anyway other than for the above reasons.

There is no substitute for correct training from an experienced instructor. As a student it is your right to demand the best for your money. Seek out instructors by reputation and recommendation. That extra bit of knowledge an experienced instructor gives you may save your life. By committing to the correct training path you have already made a psychological decision to do it correctly.

Training is about taking onboard what your instructor tells you and perfecting it by repetition. Having completed the skill[2], there is always room for improvement. Try and complete the skill faster or add a level of complexity of your own. Another trick for survival training is if you have problems with a specific skill, that particular one should be the one to expose yourself to more than the others.

Training is not over when the course ends. On every dive, no matter how simple, you should practise a skill. Think up new skills of your own; anything that will improve your performance. All skills should be relevant to a survival situation or provide confidence when achieved.

Another aspect of successfully completing courses and repeated practising of skills is that our confidence builds. We perceive ourselves to be able to survive the incident for which the skill is designed. This is often exactly what happens as the repeated skill has formulated an 'autopilot reaction' or muscle memory. A response we naturally

[2] Skills list P 92

turn to under stress. The other effect of this is that having had a real incident and provided the correct response and survived, our confidence takes a major leap. Should the incident recur the response will seem more natural and the stress less pronounced. Slowly, with experience, we become more and more relaxed and more confident within the aquatic environment.

An example of how muscle memory training assists us can be found in many stories of experienced divers who have had underwater incidents. As the incident unfolds the experienced diver automatically selects the proper corrective action and the recovers from the incident. After the event, the diver realizes the gravity of the situation and has post-event stress. The reverse of this is the classic example of the inexperienced diver who has an underwater incident and reacts by panicking. Drowning and death often ensue.

Complacency

Training should be seen as a continuous event. Anyone who says they know it all and have done it all is a fool. I undertake at least one skill on every dive, no matter what the dive is. Never get complacent with training. Other than continuous low-level training, before any major expedition or dive you should embark on a strict training regime, from a physical fitness and skills aspect. Always look ahead to the next event and generate a training scenario for it. For instance if your next project requires the use of scooters, initiate a series of scooter rescue drills, such as towing a dead scooter.

In technical diving, practice definitely makes perfect!

Environment Experience

Another way of improving our confidence and helping the psychological aspects of training, is varying environment exposure. The physical environment in which we dive affects every aspect of what we do.

A new diving environment may affect our equipment configuration, decompression strategy and a host of other things. Hence, if we have the ability to experience a range of environments as divers, by necessity we will gain experience and new knowledge. More than any other factor, changing environments improves us as divers.

'Experts' with limited varying environment exposure should be listened to, for their often unique view on diving. Their view, however, should never be taken as applicable to all environments.

Developing an Attitude

Developing an attitude is an important aspect of becoming a good diver. The desire to 'get it right' should be paramount. Safety is the key issue. This is however often where complacency creeps in. Many divers have the attitude of 'well it hasn't happened to me'. It is often not until they or a close friend has a major incident that divers modify their safety ethics. This is human nature. Once you have made a rule, do not break it for anyone. Murphy's law says this will be the time it all goes wrong. **Remember – 'safety first'**.

Visualisation as a Tool

The next step to increasing our mental control is visualization. What does visualisation do for us in a way practical way? Visualisation can be used in two primary ways:

1. to gain an element of breathing control. Pre-dive visualisation for breathing control is used to reduce stress levels and control CO_2 generation. This can be coupled with bradycardial breathing[3] (facial immersion).
2. as a means of mentally rehearsing any problems. The technique calls for the diver to think of any problems that may occur. They then visualise a successful response to the incident. This positive visualisation not only reinforces our confidence but provides a prompt for our muscle memory. Should a negative response be envisaged it may be wise to abort the dive. There have been many instances where ignored negative feelings have resulted in an incident on the dive.

The Solo Diving Philosophy

If you are not happy getting in the water alone, do not dive!

A good philosophy to employ is the mental ability to dive solo. This says that if you are not happy doing this dive alone, do not get in the water, this doesn't mean you dive alone, it simply means your dive partner is there to share the experience and not as a diving 'crutch' if things go wrong. If you do elect to actually dive solo, entrapment should be your only worry. Hence, do not put yourself in the situation where entrapment may occur. Other than that there is nothing wrong with diving solo if you are properly trained and have the right equipment for the dive.

[3] See P.20 for technique

Looking at the other end of the scale, some sport divers become reliant on diving with their partner or 'buddies'. The 'buddy' concept is taken too far. The partner becomes a diving 'crutch' without which the diver does not feel safe and cannot function in the water. Diving with a partner should be a shared experience, each partner feeling confident in the other's ability to perform without relying on them in any way. If this is not the case then diving with a 'buddy' could well become dying in company.

How to Visualise
Visualisation begins with breath control. One technique is to think of any steady rhythm. By doing this our heart rate will follow it sympathetically. Imagining the second hand of a clock ticking, by breathing at the same rate, is one method or try and visualise a large ball bouncing on the horizon of the sea. Make your heart rate match the rhythm of the ball.

Bradycardial Breathing
This triggers our 'mammalian diving reflex' an ability left with us from pre-history. It is a way of slowing down our metabolism similar to that used by sea mammals on deep dives. Basically, the technique involves facial immersion, preferably in cold water. Breathe in, immerse your face and then breathe out through your nose into the water. Extend the 'out breathe' for as long as possible. Repeat the process for several minutes.

A way to 'test' this is to stand in a swimming pool. Without using the technique try and swim as many widths underwater on a single breath as possible. Now try hyperventilating and swim again. You will improve your distance. Try it after ten minutes of bradycardial breathing. As you swim do not think of each wall where you turn as a point. Envisage yourself swimming on through it. Notice the difference? Bradycardial breathing and visualisation are used together to reduce pre-dive stress and in the case of breath-hold diving, help us to stay submerged for longer.

Stress Management
In diving, stress often occurs when there is a sudden unexpected event and we feel threatened. Our initial reaction to stress is to modify our breathing pattern. We tend to breathe more rapidly. The side effect of this is CO_2 retention and a small release of adrenaline. Adrenaline is the chemical that triggers our 'flight response'". It gives us extra strength when we need it and heightens our awareness. This release of adrenaline will trigger panic if not controlled. Unfortunately, underwater, this is often followed by an irrational response. An example of this is the trainee diver who, when stressed, removes his or her mask and regulator in an attempt to breathe more easily and makes a bee-line for the surface.

Stop all activity, Breathe (concentrate on breathing out), Think about the situation and then Act.

The primary response to a stressful situation must be to regain breathing control. **Stop, Breathe, Think and then Act** is the desired sequence. After breathing control has been established, the next question to ask yourself is 'can I breathe?' If the answer to that is 'yes', all other problems are minor by comparison.

An essential requisite is to prioritise the incident and act accordingly. An example is the diver who finds his or her self caught in a net with a flooding mask, close to the end of their bottom time. The stresses involved are a physical pressure of entrapment and a time pressure as a result of a reducing bottom time and gas supply. The flooding mask should be a minor annoyance. The diver that lets stress run its course toward panic will probably tug at the net (making the situation worse), their mask will continue to flood, reducing vision. They may eventually run out of gas. The controlled diver will ask them self if they can breathe (the answer being 'yes'), un-flood the mask to enable the problem with the net to be seen. They may then elect to remove the entrapped fin from their foot to assist with disentanglement. Having cleared the fin, they will re-compute their decompression requirements and make future plans should their extended stay mean that gas supply will be a problem later in the dive.

Obviously having a dive partner should make the problem simpler as the partner can deal with the entangled fin much quicker. In any stressful situation, put your self mentally on the surface and work out what you would do there.

Types of Stress

Time Pressure	This is usually as a result of the diver having an unplanned bottom time that in turn affects their gas supply.
Task Loading	Usually this is as a result of multiple events happening at the same time, like the trapped fin and the flooding mask in an earlier example. Compound sources of stress like this one are the most dangerous.
Peer Pressure	Being forced into doing something by another, often this is someone whom you consider as a diving superior.
Ego Threat	Being of the opinion that your own skills and abilities are better than they actually are.
Physical Threat	Shark attack etc.

Reactions to stress may include the following:

Analytical Narrowing	The inability to do simple maths underwater. Looking at a dive timer and not being able to add the number two to the number on the screen.
Perceptual Narrowing	For example, having successfully navigated down a wreck, turning and making yourself believe you cannot retrace the task.
Slow Physical Response	An inability to perform simple tasks, either taking excess time or not completing it correctly

Symptoms of stress include:

Wide eyes	Victim becomes fixed with a wide stare, often accompanied by exaggerated breathing.
Dry mouth	Inability to salivate.
Fixation	Diver becomes fixated on a task. Repeated checking of equipment is common.
Upset stomach	Repeated visits to the toilet.
Nervousness	Withdrawn attitude

Whilst some of the above can be put down to minor pre-dive nerves, in many cases these symptoms, if left unchecked, will significantly reduce diver performance.

When encountering a diver with stress it is important to remain calm and offer reassurance them. Touch contact is an ideal method. Maintain eye contact and get them to control their breathing underwater. By showing them an exaggerated, slow breathing pattern, they will naturally try and follow it. Another technique is to distract the diver and point out something interesting to take their mind off their fears. Once the situation is under control, a safe exit from the situation may be undertaken.

I was teaching a cave course with Tom Mount once in Ginnie Springs. We had three students in the class. One of the students wasn't as fit as the others and had had a few of small problems throughout the course. It was the penultimate dive and one of the longest dives of the course. Tom was leading and I was at the rear with the diver in question in front of me. After about thirty minutes on the 'in route', with a fairly vigorous pace, the diver in front suddenly turned. His eyes seemed to fill his mask! This diver was either going through me or the roof. My reaction was to signal 'OK?' and try and smile. With that, he stopped for a moment, turned and then continued the dive. I breathed again!

On exiting I asked what had happened. He said he got out of breath and started to panic (instead of stopping the team and resting). His only thought was to exit as soon as possible. When he turned and saw me asking him if he was alright, he said that I looked so calm that he realised he actually was alright and was therefore able to continue the dive. Pre-dive stress or nerves is actually a good thing in moderation. It keeps us sharp. Even the most experienced divers experience it. The day you don't, something is wrong! Remember that whilst diving, many of the symptoms of stress may also be a result of nitrogen narcosis.[4]

<u>Training the mind is more important than training the body.</u>

---

[4] See P.150

Equipment Philosophies

Introduction

The equipment we choose to carry with us as divers can either improve our performance, hinder it or at worst be life-threatening. Equipment choice starts off as a hand-me-down from our diving peers. With time we add our own inventiveness. If we are wise we look long and hard at those around us close to the pinnacle of the sport and we learn from them.

Equipment choice is very personal. That is not to say everyone dives differently because their equipment is not the same, it is just that we all evolve our own systems and often become offended when it is criticised.

There is no one correct way to configure diving equipment. There are, however, several wrong ways. Hopefully, this chapter will guide you through the equipment minefield. Whilst a range of factors affect our equipment choice and configuration, certain basic principles and techniques are paramount to developing a safe system.

What Affects our Choice?

The prime movers of equipment choice and configuration can be categorised as:

Environment

- Without doubt the environment is one of the main reasons we may wish to change our equipment choice and configuration. Probably one of the biggest issues is wetsuit vs drysuit diving. This may not only affect our cylinder choice (steels or aluminiums for example) in an effort to reduce weight and therefore buoyancy, but warmer waters often bring better visibility, hence, a reduced need for lighting and less surface traffic (the busy waterways of the world tend to be in murkier water). The list goes on.
- Also, comparing cave and open-water diving, several equipment changes will take place.

Dive Objectives

- A dive requiring specific objectives may have specific equipment issues. Instructors often find this and carry additional equipment to support their students in times of minor emergencies. A 'with tools', working dive on the other hand is virtually limitless in its equipment requirements. One of the strangest pieces of equipment I ever put together was a proton magnetometre strapped to an Aquazep for deep-water precision artefact location. A very specific piece of equipment for a very detailed dive objective.

Phil Short piloting 'Scootermag'
A DPV with a magnetometre attached

Learning From Others

Whilst you should never be afraid to ask others about why they do things, one of the most dangerous things a diver can do is blindly follow another's philosophies without questioning them. As your equipment is your life support, it is vital that if you find something new which you think will improve your system, then test it first.

An example comes to mind of a diver on a course who had just 'surfed the net' and decided that a continuous loop harness (one without a shoulder quick release) was the only way to setup his system.

During the course, one of the skills was a surface rescue of an unconscious diver. This involved a tow and equipment removal to assist entry into a high-sided boat. It wasn't a nice day. The sea was running a 1 metre swell and it was a little windy.

> If the 'perfect' system is not suitable for your environment, modify it until it is, whilst maintaining the basic safety elements of the original idea.

The rescue went well until the towed casualty reached the boat. In an attempt to remove the harness, the casualty was facially immersed five times as the rescuer struggled with his harness. Also due to the wind affect on the boat and the focus of the rescuer (struggling with the harness and not maintaining watch on a moving boat), the casualty came dangerously close to impacting with the boat. Attempts to cut the harness failed due to wet webbing. Needless to say the diver refitted the harness with a reliable quick release. Whilst continuous loop harnesses do have a place in technical diving, this is a classic example of environment being the main driving force in this situation. Equipment choice is often a compromise. If the 'perfect' system is not suitable for your environment, modify it until it is, whilst maintaining the basic safety elements of the original idea.

Learning from those who have been 'in the field' is the classic way that good information is passed down. These people have learned by experience, by surviving situations which have forced them to make changes to their equipment. This is where your choice of instructor is vital.

If your instructor has not experienced the environment for which you aspire to dive within, they can teach you very little.

Something I have learned over the years (having dived with a lot of well respected technical divers from around the world), is that kit configuration is like a pyramid. Somewhere at the top is the 'perfect' basic configuration (specific tasks aside), which no one has. As the pyramid expands out below it, these are all the other levels of kit ideas and set-ups. The majority are the worst at the bottom of the pyramid. Like the pyramid, as you get nearer the top there are less variations. You will find that once you have attained a level of experience and made several kit adjustments, as you travel and meet other divers of similar experience their kit configuration will be similar to yours. You are on the same level and with patience and more experience the only way is upwards.

I have obtained some of my best ideas from students' initial concepts. They often have a fresh way of looking at things. I take their ideas, work with them, try them and sometimes discard them. Always remain receptive to new ideas no matter from where they originate.

What Makes a Good Equipment Configuration?

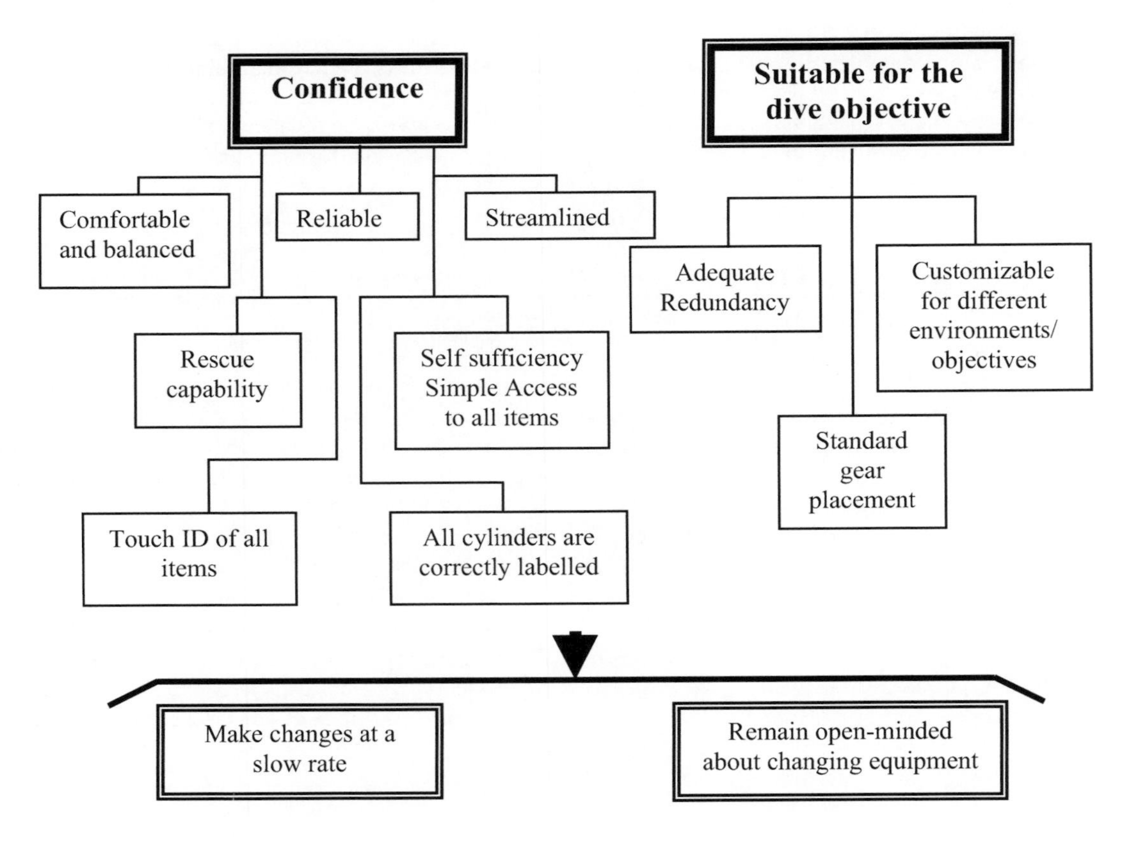

Looking at each box above in turn:

Confidence

In order for us to become confident with our equipment several things must occur.

1. Comfort and Balance

Unless we feel comfortable on a dive, our whole performance can be affected. Our equipment should almost feel like we don't have it on. A prime source of discomfort is the way we set-up our cylinders, both main and stage cylinders. This will be covered later. Weight should be evenly distributed around the system. If we have to wear a heavy item one side such as a canister light then we may need to add a counterbalancing weight on the other side.

Confidence helps you relax!

2. Reliable

Once positioned, items should stay where they are placed until required. In the longer term, items should not break unexpectedly. Putting a hand in a place and always touching the same piece of kit as well as being able to use it, is a very comforting feeling.

3. Streamlined

Streamlining does two things for us. Firstly it reduces our drag in the water and hence our swimming effort. Think of yourself swimming through the water and the water hitting your head, shoulders and diving cylinders (or rebreather) as you move forward. All the other equipment you carry should be behind or under these objects. Secondly, if we are streamlined we have less potential for entrapment as a result of 'dangling' kit. Whilst we should tuck everything away neatly it is vital we can access everything when required.

One good test is to sit on the bottom and take equipment out of all pockets and any other places you stow it. Anything that should be removed, remove it (obviously not main cylinders or permanently fixed lights etc.). Put these on the seabed in front of you, then put it all away again. If you can't replace everything, change the configuration.

4. Rescue Capability
Not only is it important in a stressful situation that you can get to all your own safety equipment, but should you become incapable of self rescue, then team members can also access the required areas and items of your configuration[5]. One way to ensure this is to have common kit configurations within a dive team.

5. Self Sufficiency
You should carry everything you need for the purpose of the task in mind. This primarily applies to safety items. Whilst it may be acceptable to share equipment to complete a working task, all personal safety equipment should be carried by the individual. Also, not only should you be able to touch everything easily, but you must be able to remove it and work with it as required. It is also important that you can actually stow it away again. Mis-stowed kit can cause problems later in the dive.

6. Touch Identification
The ability to instinctively know where everything should be is vital in a stressful situation. 'pat-down checks' prior to a dive are a good way to get used to where kit should be. Checking an item of kit's position occasionally on the dive is also a useful skill. If you lose something on a dive, a mid-dive equipment-check may give you time to do a quick search and find it.

7. Cylinder Labelling
More people have died or had near death experiences due to bad labelling and analysis protocol than any other reason in technical diving. Gas labelling and tagging is such a simple task that it often falls into the 'complacency' bin. Having done it a hundred times before, it's easy to forget. The rule must be 'trust no one', always ensure gas analysis and labelling is done or witnessed by you. Even if someone says "Well they just filled it with air", if multiple gases were available at the dive shop then you must analyse your gas. Once you have a consistent system, you will feel much more confident.

Suitable for the Dive Objectives

1. Adequate Redundancy
This is really about not carrying too much for the task in hand. Excessive equipment causes all sorts of problems (see under the *Confidence* section). Equipment clutter, bad streamlining etc.

As I change from open water wreck to Florida style cave diving. I remove my lift bags, EPIRB, Jon-line and delayed surface markers. I add reels (two to three are usually carried), an extra backup light (making two backups and one primary) and some cave markers. Everything else stays the same. This is for a basic cave dive.

The other side of this is where an item is defined as life support or, 'Primary[6]' equipment. This should be backed up but not excessively, so only carry two main cylinder regulators (I once saw as many as four!).

2. Customisable for Different Environments and Objectives
As with the previous example about moving from wreck to cave diving, it is important that when a change takes place, it does not mean a major reworking of the system (or touch ID becomes confusing). Changes from a dry to wetsuit diving environment should only mean a simple weight change and possible harness adjustment.

Whilst in a specific environment, if a new task is planned that requires an additional piece of kit to be carried, try and make sure it fits into the existing configuration as easily as possible. Again it should meet all the criteria under the '*Confidence*' section.

3. Standard Equipment Placement
Particularly when team diving, it is vital that everyone in the team can, in an emergency, quickly put their hand on a specific item in any other team members' equipment.

Having set up a good equipment configuration you should apply any new ideas slowly and methodically whilst maintaining an open mind to developments.

---

[5] See shoulder clip example on P.22
[6] Primary Equipment P.26

Primary and Secondary Equipment Concepts

How do we define what we must take on a dive as opposed what it would be handy to have? The concept of Primary and Secondary equipment is applied.

Primary equipment is defined as that which, in the event of a failure, may result in a life threatening event.

It should be borne in mind that when choosing Primary equipment, the diving environment will have an influence. An example occurs with cave diving. Whilst lights are certainly Primary equipment, in cave diving they are Secondary equipment (non life-threatening if lost) in most open water dives.

All Primary equipment is backed up with a redundant (2nd) unit.

Remember 'One is none and two is one'.

Secondary equipment is defined as that which will assist with the smooth running of the dive but its loss or failure will not endanger life.

An example here could be a reel and lifting bag for open water decompression diving. While the bags loss will make the decompression a little more stressful and diver location difficult, the diver should be able to maintain buoyancy and thereby decompress without it.

Classic Wreck Diving Primary Equipment List

In each of the cases below a second item will be carried.

- Main diving cylinder (second cylinder deployed as twin set/doubles)
- Primary regulator
- Source of buoyancy (extra BCD or a drysuit will be used)
- Dive timer or computer
- Cutting device

In Northern Europe and certain parts of the US and when deep diving I would add a torch to this list. The main torch being a fairly powerful one and ideally a canister unit. A reel and surface marker buoy (orange/red) would also be added in these conditions to alert the boat skippers (in rough seas) and surface traffic as to the diver's position.

Other than this everything else is Secondary (you only need carry one) and could include;

- Mask
- Fins
- Lifting bags
- Emergency surface marker buoy (yellow)
- Gauge torch
- EPIRB
- Mirror
- Jon-line
- Slate
- Compass
- HP gauge (manifolded cylinders only)

The above lists are just to provide you with a guide and the same concept can be applied to cave diving with obviously different priorities. ***The bottom line is - only carry what you need and avoid over redundancy.***

Where to Put It All?

In general, all Primary equipment should be accessible with both hands. This limits you to an area between the shoulders, forming a triangle going down to the naval.

We have talked about keeping equipment streamlined and the more we carry the more important this is. In general tuck equipment away. Tubes of neoprene are excellent at streamlining and protecting gear. Again imagine yourself swimming through water and the water first hitting your head, shoulders and diving cylinders. Prime stowage points out of the water flow are under the arms and underneath the cylinders.

In a few moments we will take a look at possible stowage specifics for each item.

Primary on the Right

Another philosophy I adhere to is everything I deem Primary is placed on my right hand side. This is mainly because I am right handed and naturally use my right hand in an emergency. Hence my main regulator and its shut down valve are on the right, my main torch and my main reel etc. From the right hand regulator also comes my primary inflation feed. I also carry my highest oxygen deco gas on the right. When diving closed circuit rebreathers, the oxygen addition is normally on the right so keeps it all **'Rich is Right'**.

> One good test is to sit on the bottom and take everything out of all the pockets and places you stow it. Anything that should be removed, remove it (obviously not main cylinders or permanently fixed lights etc.). Put on the seabed in front of you, then put it all away again. If you can't do it, change the configuration.

This 'Primary regulator on the right system', has no hoses crossing over behind my head. Everything from the right regulator first stage comes around my right side and so on for the left. A compromise occurs here. Cave divers have classically placed their main regulator on the left cylinder valve. This is because when they swim into a cave, if they bump the ceiling, it will be the Primary valve that will slowly shut, thus giving them warning of a slow gas shutoff. What they do not want to happen is to be breathing off the other regulator whilst the left post slowly shuts. They then have a gas emergency and switch to the left post for backup and the valve has bumped closed.

The reason I split everything right and left with no crossovers is I have seen confusion about shutting down the correct valve when hoses are crossed. As my system could mean my backup regulator could slowly close if I bump the ceiling, I ensure I reach back and check it after passing any restriction or after any ceiling contact. Also I periodically switch regulators during the dive just to check both are functioning correctly.

Equipment Checks

Whilst choosing the right gear is important it is just as important that it works! The first step here is a good maintenance regime, pre-dive equipment checks are also vital. A simple method of pre-dive checking is the S Drill.

S Drills are variable around the world but here is the basic system I usually use for open circuit.

The S (Safety) Drill

1. Open cylinder valves (I run mine fully open and one turn back to ensure I know which direction is off)
2. With a manifolded set of doubles/twinset, check the centre isolator is just open (one to two turns) to enable a rapid shutdown
3. Touch ID all equipment to confirm its security and position.
4. Check reels for tightness
5. Check torches operate correctly
6. Check all inflation and dump devices
7. Check (breathe from) all regulators (whilst looking at pressure gauges)
8. Check for leaks either on the surface and/or at 6 metres whilst decending

This can be expanded for differing situations. For instance, if I'm doing a long deco in a major shipping lane I do an EPIRB test fire (which needs to be coordinated with the Coastguard). Dive boats do break down! Modify your S drill as the environment/objectives dictate, but never do less than the basic one above.

With equipment checks it is important that you do not become distracted.

If you Break a Drill, Remake a Drill!

An instructor was preparing for a trimix training dive with two students. One of the students had forgotten one of his decompression cylinders. The instructor, being prepared for the usual foul-ups, had brought a spare. Its configuration was slightly different from what the student was used to, so the instructor exchanged it for one of his. Leaving his normal configuration of one yellow (nitrox) and one white (oxygen) compromised by having two white cylinders. Although both white cylinders were properly labelled, the initial colour ID was lost. The instructor analysed the gas in both cylinders and confirmed the analysis tags. He laid out the correct cylinder in front of the correct regulator and was about to attach them when the second student called him away for a minor equipment problem.

That corrected, the instructor returned to his cylinders and attached the regulators to the cylinders. The regulators (with cylinders attached) being touch ID'd for nitrox and oxygen were dutifully attached to the correct sides on the harness and the dive commenced.

All went well until the gas switch at 30 metres on the ascent. The instructor did not confirm the gas tag with anyone prior to switching due to minor problems with a nervous student. After one breath the instructor 'felt' something was wrong and immediately returned to bottom mix. A further confirmation of the gas tags on the cylinders revealed that the oxygen and nitrox cylinders were on the wrong sides with the wrong regulators attached. He had switched to oxygen!

The dive debriefing revealed that, after analysing and tagging his gas, laying out the regulators for attachment and being called away by the student, another student had decided to take a look at the instructor's regulators. When he returned them he swapped their positions in front of the cylinders. The instructor returned and put what he thought was an oxygen regulator onto an oxygen cylinder but actually attached it to the nitrox cylinder and hence the wrong side of the harness.

The lesson here is that, having lost the visual tag of a cylinders colour (having two white ones) he should have been especially careful about attaching the regulators to the right cylinders. As his personal set-up drill was interrupted he should have started the whole drill over again. **Break a drill, remake a drill.** As his SOP (Standard Operating Procedure) was broken by having to use two cylinders of the same colour, his vigilance on setting up the system should have been heightened. This, coupled with his inability to obtain gas confirmation prior to switching, almost killed him. All of this is easy to say with 20-20 hindsight but technical diving instructors are a high-risk category, often having to make judgement calls and modify their own SOP's for the students' benefit and the overall safety of the operation. In the words of Dr Bill Hamilton one of diving's pioneering decompression experts, 'shit happens!'.

Gas Identification

Main Cylinders

It is vital that all gas is labelled correctly. Many technical divers have died as a result of improper gas labelling. For main cylinders, which often experience different mixes, one suggested way is content tape. This is labelled with the mix and maximum operating depth and placed close to the cylinder neck. Additional labels such as date and mixers initials can also be added.

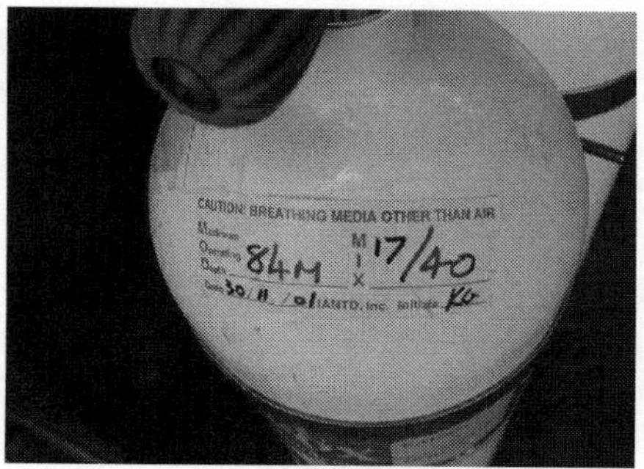

Content tape

Decompression Cylinders

A good start here is to colour code each cylinder. The basic groups are trimix, air, nitrox and oxygen. Personally, I count anything above 80% as oxygen and colour it accordingly. Each country will have different colour codes for identifying gases, some of them not applicable to diving. I use:

- Orange for any bottom mix trimix or when used as an intermediate[7] decompression gas
- Yellow for any nitrox
- Red for air
- White for 80%+

Diving in a range of depths in any given year, I cannot afford the luxury of a specific cylinder for a specific gas so this is where the content label proves useful. For instance, after making sure I have put nitrox in a yellow cylinder, I analyse it and attach a content sticker similar to the picture above. This sticker is placed near to the neck of the cylinder and facing away from me towards my dive partner when attached to my harness. This is done so that during gas switches we check each other's proposed gas switch before it happens. If I am solo diving I can easily reverse the tag so that I can see it more easily. This label is marked with the MOD (maximum operating depth) in large letters. Some teams elect to put larger car number plate style lettering on the cylinders in a similar position. This works well when on a project and when the identical gases are being used repeatedly.

Oxygen regulator guard

The next level of identification is the regulator. Touch ID of the second stage is one method. I personally opt to use all the same regulators for every gas so that in the field spares and servicing are no problem. Hence I lose this initial touch ID. I solve this by using an oxygen regulator guard (ORG) on my 80%/oxygen regulator. I also use coloured insulating tape to mark the second stage and write either trimix, air, nitrox or oxygen on the second stage, where other members of the dive team can see it in large white letters.

The final stage in gas ID is where it is positioned on the body. The philosophy as mentioned of '**Rich is Right** 'is applied. The highest percentage mix is positioned on the right hand side. If I am wearing two or more cylinders on one side, the highest is on top.

Decompression Gas on the Back

Some divers elect to carry more than two different gases on their back - one or two of bottom mix and one or more of decompression gas. This is potentially a very dangerous scenario even for the most disciplined diver. Having two regulators, even with touch ID and colour coding, easily accessible on the front of the body can, and has led to, confusion especially where narcosis becomes a factor.

I remember once being on a dive boat in Florida on an air dive to around 50 metres in clear warm water. One of the other divers on the boat had a back-mounted multi gas configuration with three regulators around his neck (two bottom mix, one deco mix). I asked him if he always dived that way. From our talk I gleaned he had substantial diving experience. Four weeks later the diver was dead as a result of switching to oxygen at depth. It was probably nitrogen narcosis that played a factor. I can see, however, how a gas failure and subsequent regulator switch in a stressful situation could also lead to confusion.

---

[7] See P.135 on intermediate trimix

Setting up Equipment

Introduction

This chapter will deal with the pro's and con's of differing equipment set-ups and also the types of equipment. The information is drawn from a large database of experienced divers I have known. This is not the be all and end all on the subject but at least it is a start. Whilst putting your own equipment together it is worth remembering to adhere to the ethic, **"Keep it Simple, Stupid" (KISS).** This means the simpler the system, the better you will be able to perform with it under stress and the less likely it is to fail. technical diving is not about carrying as much as you can, it's about carrying the minimum to survive.

Cylinders

There are two types - steel and aluminium. Both have different weight/volume characteristics and hence buoyancy. An example is that a 10 litre light weight steel weighs 11.3kg empty and is 2.3kg negative (heavy) in the water when full and 0.75kg negative when empty. The same volume of cylinder in aluminium weighs 12.9kg when empty and is 0.7 kg negative in water when full and 1.6kg positive (buoyant) when empty. You can see how this might affect the additional weight carried by the diver during the initial and final (after a proportion of the gas is used) parts of the dive.

On another extreme, large 20 litre cylinders while heavy when full on land are actually quite buoyant in the water when compared to 15 litre cylinders, purely because of their volume and wall structure. Hence, you actually need more weight with the larger cylinders.

Keep it simple!

Cylinders are the largest thing affecting buoyancy and therefore comfort and performance on the dive. As our diving goes deeper and longer, we may find ourselves having several configurations of decompression cylinders to help adjust for our additional weight and gas volume requirement.

Example

If I use a 15 litre steel twin set with a membrane drysuit, I can use 10 litre aluminium side mount decompression cylinders and trim out with an additional 2kg of weight (this is with a stainless back plate and a canister torch as well).

If I switch to the larger 20 litre cylinders I have to switch to 10 litre steel side mounts to maintain the same additional weight.

The bottom line is, 'You must experiment'.

Below are various tables representing the mechanical and buoyancy characteristics of several cylinder types. Buoyancy may vary slightly from batch to batch and from fresh to sea water. Cylinders exclusive to the US are quoted in Cubic Feet only. These specifications may alter as manufacturers change their designs. For exact specifications contact the manufacturers.

Notes:

1. internal volume is equal to Water Capacity (WC) [8]
2. only cylinders available in Europe and the USA have their specifications noted in metric and imperial.

Aluminium Cylinders

Luxfer Gas Cylinders

Capacity cu ft (litres)	Service Pressure psi (bar)	Outside Diametre in (mm)	Overall Length in (mm)	Empty Weight lbs (kg)	Internal Volume cu in (litres)	Buoyancy Full (Salt) lbs (kg)	Buoyancy Empty (Salt) lbs (kg)
13.2 (374.8)	3000 (207)	4.375 (111.1)	12.875 (327.0)	5.93 (2.69)	116.00 (1.90)	-1.7 (-0.8)	-0.7 (-0.3)
13.7 (387.1)	2015 (139)	4.375 (111.1)	16.500 (419.0)	5.40 (2.45)	172.00 (2.82)	+0.7 (+0.3)	+1.7 (+0.8)
19.9 (564.5)	3000 (207)	4.375 (111.1)	18.563 (471.4)	8.07 (3.66)	174.70 (2.86)	-1.4 (-0.6)	+0.1 (+0.1)
27.6 (782.0)	3000 (207)	5.250 (133.3)	18.000 (457.1)	11.38 (5.16)	242.00 (3.97)	-1.5 (-0.7)	+0.6 (+0.3)
30.0 (849.2)	3000 (207)	4.875 (123.8)	21.850 (554.9)	11.60 (5.26)	262.80 (4.31)	-1.0 (-0.5)	+1.2 (+0.5)
39.9 (1131.0)	3000 (207)	5.250 (133.3)	24.750 (628.5)	15.17 (6.88)	350.00 (5.74)	-0.8 (-0.3)	+2.2 (+1.0)
48.4 (1370.1)	3000 (207)	6.890 (175.0)	19.000 (482.5)	21.15 (9.59)	424.00 (6.95)	-2.4 (-1.1)	+1.3 (+0.6)
63.0 (1783.7)	3000 (207)	7.250 (184.1)	21.850 (554.9)	26.61 (12.07)	552.00 (9.05)	-2.1 (-1.0)	+2.6 (+1.2)
69.6 (1971.2)	3000 (207)	6.890 (175.0)	26.000 (660.3)	28.44 (12.90)	610.00 (10.00)	-1.6 (-0.7)	+3.6 (+1.6)
78.2 (2213.5)	3000 (207)	8.000 (203.2)	22.930 (582.3)	35.05 (15.90)	685.00 (11.23)	-3.6 (-1.6)	+2.3 (+1.0)
77.4 (2190.9)	3000 (207)	7.250 (184.1)	26.060 (661.8)	31.31 (14.20)	678.00 (11.11)	-1.4 (-0.7)	+4.4 (+2.0)
90.3 (2557.2)	3200 (221)	8.000 (203.2)	24.770 (629.0)	37.58 (17.05)	750.00 (12.29)	-3.6 (-1.6)	+3.1 (+1.4)
99.3 (2812.8)	3300 (228)	8.000 (203.2)	26.210 (665.6)	40.80 (18.51)	804.00 (13.18)	-4.3 (-1.9)	+3.2 (+1.4)

Catalina Cylinders

Capacity (cu ft)	Service Pressure psi (bar)	Outside Diametre (in)	Length (in)	Empty Weight (in)	Water Weight (lbs)	Internal Volume cu in (litres)	Buoyancy Full (lbs salt)	Buoyancy Empty (lbs salt)
100.0	3300 (228)	8.00	27.28	46.1	29.3	813 (13.3)	-7.5	0.0
77.4	3300 (228)	7.25	25.14	35.0	22.6	625 (10.2)	-5.8	0.0
60.0	3300 (228)	7.25	19.90	27.3	17.5	486 (7.9)	-4.9	-0.4
77.4	3000 (207)	7.25	25.75	31.6	24.4	679 (11.1)	-1.7	+4.1
67.0	3000 (207)	7.25	23.72	32.8	21.2	587 (9.6)	-5.0	0.0
53.0	3000 (207)	7.25	19.00	25.6	16.7	466 (7.6)	-4.0	0.0
40.0	3000 (207)	5.25	24.85	15.7	12.7	351 (5.7)	-1.1	+1.9
30.0	3000 (207)	5.25	19.98	13.7	9.6	266 (4.3)	-2.3	0.0
19.0	3000 (207)	4.37	17.12	7.5	6.0	167 (2.7)	-1.2	+0.2
17.0	3000 (207)	4.37	15.52	6.8	5.4	149 (2.4)	-1.3	0.0
13.0	3000 (207)	4.37	12.25	5.4	4.1	115 (1.9)	-1.4	-0.4
6.0	3000 (207)	3.20	11.00	2.6	1.9	55 (0.9)	-1.3	-0.9

---

[8] * ***Gas Capacity:*** *Values are calculated for PSIG and delivered volume (Van der Waals). For example a one litre cylinder at 0 psig (ambient sea level) has a delivered volume of 0 liters at 70F. 1 cubic foot = 28.316846592 liters.*

Low Pressure Steel

Pressed Steel

Volume (cu ft)	Service Pressure 10% Overfill OK (psi)	Outside Diametre (inches)	Weight (lbs)	Height (inches)	Buoyancy Full (lbs)	Buoyancy Empty (lbs)
95	2400 (2640 10%)	8.00	41.0	19.75	-4.75	-1.75
104	2400 (2640 10%)	8.00	46.0	23.94	-4.17	-1.00
120	2400 (2640 10%)	8.00	52.0	27.87	-3.80	0.0

OMS/Faber (In Europe)

* US LP cylinders are often re-rated as HP in Europe (232 bar)

Capacity cu ft (litres)	Service Pressure (psi/bar)	Height inches (mm)	Outside Diametre inches (mm)	Weight w/valve (lbs/kg)	Buoyancy Full (lbs/kg)	Buoyancy Empty (lbs/kg)
13 (2)	2640/180	14.0 (355)	3.9 (99)	5.9/2.6	-3.30/-1.5	-2.25/1
46 (7)	2640/180	23.0 (584)	5.5 (140)	17.6/8	-4.00/-1.8	0.00/0.0
66 (10)	2640/180	21.0 (533)	7.0 (178)	25.0/11.3	-5.15/-2.3	-1.67/-0.75
85 (13)	2640/180	26.0 (660)	7.0 (178)	31.0/14	-6.70/-3	0.00/0.0
98 (15)	2640/180	24.0 (609)	8.0 (203)	38.0/17.3	-7.73/3.5	0.00/0.0
112 (17)	2640/180	26.0 (660)	8.0 (203)	41.0/18.6	-8.00/3.6	-1.0/-0.45
125 (19)	2640/180	29.0 (736)	8.0 (203)	45.0/20.5	-9.50/4.3	0.00/0.0
131 (20)	2640/180	30.7 (780)	8.0 (203)	47.0/21.4	-10.31/4.7	+0.75/0.34

Heiser

Volume (cu ft)	Service Pressure 10% Overfill OK (psi)	Outside Diametre (inches)	Weight (lbs)	Height (inches)	Buoyancy Full (lbs)	Buoyancy Empty (lbs)
104	2400 (2640 10%)	8.00	N/A	N/A	N/A	N/A
120	2400 (2640 10%)	8.00	N/A	N/A	N/A	N/A

High Pressure Steel

Pressed Steel

Volume (cu ft)	Service Pressure 10% Overfill OK (psi)	Outside Diametre (inches)	Weight (lbs)	Height (inches)	Buoyancy Full (lbs)	Buoyancy Empty (lbs)
80	3180 (3498 10%)	7.25	32.50	19.88	N/A	-7.22
100	3180 (3498 10%)	7.25	38.70	24.01	N/A	-7.26
120	3180 (3498 10%)	7.25	45.30	28.64	N/A	-7.22

Seagate

Volume (cu ft)	Service Pressure (psi)	Outside Diametre (inches)	Weight (lbs)	Height (inches)	Buoyancy Full (lbs)	Buoyancy Empty (lbs)
80	3500	7.25	27.0	23.00	-8.0	-1.0
100	3500	7.25	33.0	27.25	-8.2	+0.5
120	3500	7.25	38.0	30.38	-1.0	+1.0

Buoyancy Testing

Put all of your equipment on and drain the cylinders to thirty bar. Now try and maintain a 3 metre decompression stop comfortably, adding or removing weight as required.

If cold is going to be a problem on long decompressions and you want to inflate your suit to offset this, rather than carrying additional lead for the whole dive, have some staged where it can be attached during decompression.

Manifolds
If you elect to use a manifold it should have a central isolation valve.....**end of story**. Bar manifolds are dangerous! A leak at any position can mean total gas loss. Independent cylinders are safer than a bar manifold when used with the 'rule of thirds'[9].

With manifolds a few simple rules apply:

- make sure you check gas analysis at each outlet, in case the centre valve was shut during filling or has failed.
- the centre valve should be just open during diving (1-1 & 1/2 turns). In the event of a shutdown being required this is speedily achieved. Angle the centre valve slightly forward to assist reaching it and to protect it a little. During the dive periodically check the valve has not closed.
- if you pick up a manifolded twin set, do so by each cylinder valve, not the centre of the manifold.

Some people choose to invert the whole set to assist with shutdowns. I personally believe this is only necessary if the diver has a disability. If you cannot reach over your head and touch the valves, change your configuration. Inverted sets give valve protection problems, entanglement problems and require custom length hoses to be manufactured.

Occasionally I see people with decompression cylinders also strapped to their back. Not only is this a bad idea from a gas switch confusion point of view, but should one of the extra cylinders have a regulator failure, it is not only difficult to shut the regulator down but swapping of a failed first stage between decompression cylinders (as is sometimes required) is virtually impossible, unless you get someone else to do it, which negates the self sufficiency ethic. They may not always be there! **Decompression cylinders strapped to the back with multiple regulators coming over the shoulders as a configuration has killed people and should be avoided.**

Putting them Together
Ideally, only steel band kits should be used to ensure the manifolds cannot distort. They should be periodically checked for tightness as the cylinders expand and contract during filling and vibration occurs during use and transport. I believe twin sets should be kept free of all encumbrances such as D rings and plastic boots. If your set is 'clean' and you enter a restriction, you can be certain you can then back out. There is no reason to strap anything to a twin set. I have never had or seen a situation where an item needed to be stowed in such a manner.

If your set is 'clean' and you enter a restriction, you can be certain you can then back out.

Side Mount Set-Ups
Side mount configurations have historically been used in cave diving, where the diver needs to have the smallest profile possible in order to get through submerged restrictions with minimal hindrance and damage to the cave. There are few commercially-available side mount rigs and as such divers have often 'invented' their own systems from standard equipment.

Any combined wing and harness system can be utilised. Soft pack versions like the Dive Rite Transpac are ideally suited to such an application, but even stainless steel harness/wing systems can be employed.

The first step is to attach the BC to the back plate. Use large washers to prevent the bolts from pulling through the material. The wing should be mounted as low down the back as possible as the bulk of the cylinder weight is placed around the hips. Lowering the wing provides better support.

Next, the wing needs to be secured or when inflated it will float up behind you. Various methods have been used here. As a minimum the BC should be anchored at the shoulders (you may have to sew on additional tags and Quicklink[10] them on) and near the hips. Using bicycle inner tube between points on the wing and around the back plate and harness should give the desired stream lining whilst allowing expansion when required.

Side mount systems give a truly independent gas source providing the regulators are regularly switched as each cylinder pressure reduces by one third[11]. Whilst side mounts are popular among European cave divers, many US divers also have a need for such equipment[12].

---

[9] See skills and drills on the following page
[10] A small removable link with a screw catch similar a chain link
[11] The Third's rule may be modified in certain environments
[12] For a detailed view on sidemounts visit *www.sidemount.com*

Manifold Guards

A very controversial subject. Initially introduced by cave divers to protect valves from ceiling impact especially when scootering. More recently introduced into open water diving. Some people use them with inverted cylinders, but in the main commercially available guards are not strong enough for this application.

I think in open water their design is probably of limited use when looking at the initial intention, to protect against knocks. Whilst they definitely still do this, they are more useful for the following:

- protection of the assembled set (regulators) during transit on boats
- as a means of assisting with a gas shutdown, particularly when heavy underwear is worn restricting movement. Simply reach over the head and grab the protector and raise the set those few extra inches
- as a way of carrying the set other than by the manifold

All of these have to be balanced against their ability to entrap line or wedge behind objects on a dive. Regulator guards do however have a place in cave diving with DPV's.

Remote Shutdowns

Affectionately known as 'slob knobs'. These provide the diver with the ability to shutdown a valve without reaching behind them. My own personal view is if you cannot reach, change the set-up, except in cases of disability. If you elect to use one you must remember that the screw locking the cable to the valve may need periodic adjustment (and maintenance, if steel) or one day you may be twisting like crazy while your precious gas is leaking away.

Decompression Cylinders

Badly configured decompression cylinders can be the prime source of dive discomfort. Their position on the body can affect trim drastically, drag, stress levels and hence diver performance. Decompression cylinders mounted anywhere other than on the harness (like on the back) can be problematic. Gas identification has already been cited. Also should a first stage fail, when it is inaccessible, swapping out for a working one is impossible. Rear mounted deco often means long HP hoses, something to be avoided with high FO_2's (failed long HP whips have caused oxygen fires).

Trimming out

With a balanced side mounted configuration lets first look at where to attach them to the harness. One 'D' ring on the hip and one slightly below the nipple are favoured positions that gives good balance whilst keeping the regulators out of the face. If you spread out your fingers and touch your hip and your nipple your little finger should be close to one and your thumb the other. This now gives you the 'D' ring separation distance on the cylinder its self. I like one clip near or around the neck and the second a hand span down the cylinder body. Once attached this tends to put the cylinder inline with the body when swimming, which is ideal.

Trimming out

Clips are attached with hard points; that is to say a stainless band and 'D' ring at the lower position (the 'D' ring is big enough to insert at least two gloved fingers in), a neck ring and either a quick link and shackle or webbing and shackle at the neck. Various other attachment methods are available but this **KISS** system has never failed me yet.

Regulators

Regulator choice is very personal and is based on the following;

- performance
- reliability
- serviceability

Looking at each in turn;

Performance
Performance is subdivided into how it actually delivers gas at depth characterised by its breathing resistance and how it 'feels' to the diver. Basically, a regulator is taken to depth and put on a breathing machine. The machine is then set up for a certain RMV (respiratory minute volume). This is normally around 50 to 60 litres/min, well in excess of what most divers breath under normal conditions. The inhalation and exhalation resistance is then measured and a work of breathing (WOB) graph produced.

Remember that if you are using a regulator for deep trimix diving its WOB will be improved by the use of helium. Manufacturers normally test their regulators with air. A regulator that works well at 10 metres on air will have a similar performance at 90 metres on 100% helium!

A regulators 'feel' can be affected by the shape of the mouthpiece and the way it delivers and exhausts gas. Some regulators start with a slow delivery during the inhalation cycle and then give it all at the end. Breathing cycle characteristics can generate an unpleasant feeling for the diver. If a regulator has user adjustments, it is essential to understand its function before using it. Comfort is important. Try several before making your selection.

Reliability
For me this is the main concern. My regulators may not have the highest specification in the world but they are reliable. This can only be discovered from recommendations by others and using it yourself. No regulator is perfect and each has its quirks. It is often divers themselves who find this out and then through feedback, manufacturers make improvements.

Serviceability
Another important issue is serviceability if you elect to work in remote locations or undertake a lot of diving. For expedition level work, something that can easily be serviced in the field is useful. Regulators that need much more than a low pressure gauge and a couple of allen keys to set up are a nuisance. I make all my regulators the same so that I can interchange parts as required.

Regulator set-up
With reference to main diving gas regulators, the important thing is 'think streamlined'. Hoses should flow down from the regulator behind your head, not poke out the sides like a Christmas tree. Normally the main regulator will have a second stage on a long (1.5-2m) hose and a LP (low pressure) hose for the suit or BCD (buoyancy control device), which ever is Primary inflation. I do not use hose protectors as they collect sand and grit. I like to be able to do simple visual inspections on hoses whilst assembling my equipment. The backup regulator will have a short hose to the backup second stage, a suit or BCD inflation and in my case an HP gauge. With a manifolded, isolated twin set, I only use one. Remember what you are trying to do is to cut down the number of failure points in a system.

Note the way the long hose wraps over the wing and the general hose flow

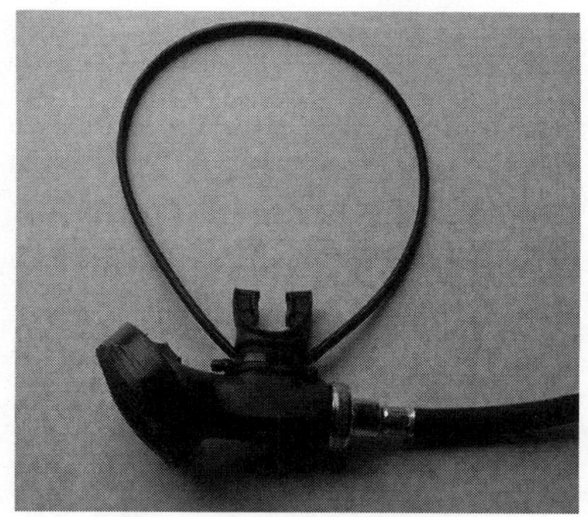

Second stage with necktie. Keep it as short as is comfortable

Any hose or 'O' ring you can remove is beneficial.

The HP gauge is a simple metal body gauge with no fancy boot/compass mount etc.

The inflation nipples on the LP hoses should all be the same. This allows for cross-patching in the event of an LP source failure. I have found the Schraeder style (found on most BCD's) to be the most reliable. There are few instances of them failing under pressure unlike some of the popular drysuit ones.

In my system the right hand regulator on the long hose comes round my right shoulder. This is the one I breathe off (more later). It has a brightly coloured front which says 'come and get me'. This is the one I donate. The backup short hose come round my left shoulder (possible on side exhaust regulators only) and its colour matches my suit. This second stage has a permanent tubing neck tie on it that cannot be removed. The neck tie is just long enough so that I can reach down and grab it with my mouth. I give this regulator to no one - it is my life support.

I am reminded of a story of why I like this system. I was wreck-diving with a student once who was using independent cylinders. Her backup regulator was on a snap in neck tie. During a shut down drill her primary regulator backfilled with water that for some reason she couldn't purge out. She had replaced her backup into its neck clip at the time and was attempting to purge the primary in her mouth. She got a little stressed and reached for her backup which had popped out of its neck tie and was floating behind her. I could see this and was ready with my hand-off regulator. In the panic that followed she lunged at me and tore my hand-off regulator out of my mouth. I had my back to the wreck at the time and during the lunge she managed to pin me to the wreck where I found my self unable to use my arms. Luckily I was able to drop my head and bite my backup into position.

Back to hose routing. From my right hand regulator the LP feed comes under my right arm and when drysuit diving clips into my suit. The left hand LP (BCD) and HP hose does the same on the left side. Each set has a small piece of bungee on the harness to locate it. This ends up with all LP inflation control and HP monitoring in the triangle area, previously mentioned. The left hand set of hoses is protected by a neoprene sleeve. The back of the HP gauge has space for an attached small primary knife.

Wherever possible I try not to use a clip to locate items where bungee will do (pure silicone tubing is best). The only clips on my kit are on my reels and side mounts. These are either piston or butterfly clips. In extreme cold and where the clip is visible and accessible I may use a snap shackle otherwise known as a 'suicide clip'. These can be major line traps and the only place I have used them in the past is on the neck of a decompression cylinder. They are a little easier to operate with frozen hands and are fully visible in this position. Do not use these where you cannot see them.

Decompression Regulator set-up

Aside from the labelling and touch ID issues already mentioned, the KISS[13] approach should again be applied. A first stage and single second stage are normally used. Where suit inflation is needed (in the case of trimix dives)[14]a single LP hose is used. The HP monitoring at the first stage should have as short a hose as possible. Often a 'button' gauge is used, hence there is no need for a hose. Not only are we reducing failure points with this system, but when high oxygen fractions are employed it is wise to reduce hose lengths in case of a hose failure. Should that event occur it is possible a rapid release of oxygen down a lengthy fractured hose could cause ignition as it accelerates and passes the fracture. This has occurred on at least one occasion.

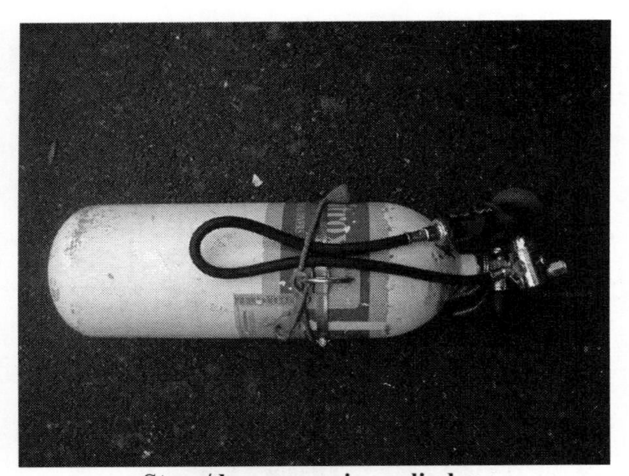

Stage/decompression cylinder.
Second stage is tied in with a bungee loop.
Note button HP gauge.

I normally line the base 'D' ring up with the valve outlet; thus the regulator itself is attached with the first stage between the diver's body and the cylinder, offering some protection. The second stage hose is then secured by bungee or car inner tube fixed around the cylinder. In cold climates large toggles are threaded onto the bungee to assist with hose removal and replacement with heavy gloves. The second stage is then secured close to the regulator head by means of bungee or a simple clip.

---

[13] See P.54
[14] See P.148

Long Hose vs Short Hose
This argument has raged for many years on Internet. Personally, I breathe the main regulator with a long hose. I do this because:

- having handed it off, I do not then have to convince the out of gas diver (who may be mildly stressed) that what they really want to do is change regulators again for the one in my mouth.
- an out of gas diver can instantly position himself/herself some distance from me and easily continue to swim - important if the incident happens during an ascent. This regaining of self-control assists with stress reduction.
- my long hose is the one I breathe. This is where most stressed divers will look for it, in my mouth. It's not so much your dive partner you have to worry about (who may know you put your backup in a little pocket under your arm). It's the guy who jumps you out of the blue. Believe me this does happen! As an added precaution I put my mask strap under my hood to prevent accidental dislodging during an emergency.

Advocators of the short hose argument (especially in the USA) are concerned with oral hygiene when you hand off the regulator you are breathing. In my view this is probably a secondary concern when the option is drowning and to my knowledge there is little evidence to support the concern.

Where to Wrap it
Another hot one. Most people have heard of the 'Hogarthian' wrap that originates from Florida cave diving. This is where the long hose comes from the cylinder, under one arm, up across the chest and around the neck into the mouth. Particularly long hoses are often tucked under a side mounted light canister to improve stowage.

Many people have adopted and are happy with this system.

Here are some alternatives:

Cylinder Stowage
One or two pieces of bungee are tied around one of the cylinders. The hose is then looped up and down between those bungees.

Pros:

easy to deploy

Cons:

difficult to re-stow
damage to hose may result if the cylinder/hose comes into contact with a wreck/reef
only easily deployable one side

Back plate Stowage
Again, a couple of small bungee loops are mounted on the back plate or harness, normally under one arm.

Pros:

more protected
fairly easy to deploy
re-stowable with practice

Cons:

may be uncomfortable
may compromise a side mount light canister mount. Often they will fill the same space.
only easily deployable on one side

Manifold Stowage
Bungee is again used on at least one point on the manifold, the long hose looping back and forth between the first stages.

Pros:

fairly easy to deploy

Cons:

not re-stowable
may become entangled with regulator first stages and slow any emergency shut-off procedures
multiple hose kinks may weaken the hose.

Wing/BCD Stowage
If the wing has constriction bungees, these can be used. If not, a simple modification can be made with a couple of small loops. This is the one I use. The hose comes from the right regulator down the side of the BCD and is tucked into one loop near the base of the wing, then it changes direction and comes back up the BCD. It then wraps around the back of my neck to my left shoulder and tucks into another loop. It then changes direction again, the final short length passing back around my neck and over my right shoulder around into my mouth.

Pros:

protected, because the BCD will collapse if I bump anything
easy to deploy and I can get either half or all of it out
deployable over the left or right shoulder
leaves the harness completely free for equipment attachment

Cons:

not easily re-stowable. I do a temporary Hogarthian wrap in the event of temporary deployment.
do not tuck it under too many bungees or it will not deploy easily

The main reasons I prefer the above to a Hogarthian wrap is it keeps my harness clean and I once saw a diver temporarily strangled when his Hogarthian wrap became wedged under his light pack as he was hit from behind in a restriction for a gas share by his partner. The long hose across his chest (when pulled by his partner) pinned his backup regulator in place. An interesting few seconds. Even if this scenario occurred with the BCD system you could reach back and just pull out more hose. Incidentally, I have noticed no adverse hose stress due to the bend radius the hose goes through as it tucks into the bungee.

As ever, it must be said that each set-up has merits in any particular environment. Experiment and then make your choice.

Lights
In general, lights fall into two categories, primary and backup. Primaries tend to be high-powered and relatively long lasting (90 minutes minimum). They either come with an integral battery pack or an umbilical to a remote battery pack. Backup lights are normally smaller, less powerful but (especially in cave diving) can be very long lasting. In open water, one primary and one backup light are used. In caves, one primary and at least two backups.

Primary lights can be categorised as follows.

Hand Held (non umbilical)
Pros:

fairly good light output
medium duration

Cons:

awkward to stow
singular use of a hand

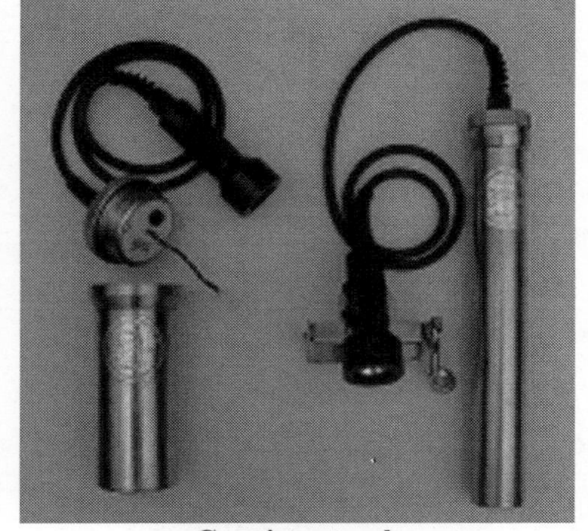
Cannister torches

Hand Held (umbilical)
Pros:

good light output
medium to long duration
multiple stowing possibilities
avoids singular use of the hand if Goodman handle is used.

Cons:

heavier, requiring adjustments to trim
large

Torch with Goodman handle

Otherwise known as canister lights these come complete with a cable (umbilical) to the hand held unit. The hand unit may incorporate the on/off switch. If not the switch will be found on the canister. The use of a Goodman handle releases the hand from just holding the light.

Standard umbilical lights use either tungsten or halogen bulb filaments. These offer a relatively white light output at a range of wattages (power output). Basically the higher the wattage, the brighter the light. This is (of course) at the expense of 'burn time' (duration). More recently, a new light source has become available through the automotive industry. Using a xenon arc system these are knows as HID or high intensity discharge lights. They offer a near perfect, white light source at a much reduced wattage, hence burn time is significantly improved. HID's are definitely the way forward for diving torches. Whilst canister lights may make it more awkward to focus and work in an area, one simple method is to loop the cable around your neck and allow the light to hang, providing light close to the required point.

Hat Mounted

Pros:

- gives complete freedom of hands
- multiple lights can be mounted
- allows lights to be easily focused at work point

Cons:

- low power
- may blind dive partner

Hat lights are popular with solo divers, especially in low visibility caves. This is probably their primary application. In good visibility and especially when diving with a partner, hat lights become unnecessary. A diver dazzled by another's lights can take many minutes to regain night vision.

Hat mount torch being used on a solo cave dive

Mounting

Primary Lights

Obviously non umbilical hand lights are simply held in the hand or allowed to dangle from their mounting clip. These are seldom used by technical divers due to their awkwardness.

Canister mounts are mounted as follows:

- on the base of the cylinders
  - popular with cave divers. The light is attached by 'D' rings to the cylinders. The light then hangs across the base of the cylinders. Care must be taken when sitting down. This is not really suitable for most boat applications due to the potential for damage.
- waist webbing mount
  - often used where large capacity battery packs are needed. The battery pack has a loop of webbing on it that threads through the harness waist strap. A weight belt buckle is used to keep it in place. With this configuration and when diving with two stages, both stages are mounted off of the same (opposite to the light) side.
- back plate mount
  - two steel bands are attached to the battery pack. The pack is then attached to the back plate by clips. Quick links (used to join chain) are often used. The pack sits under the shoulder out of the drag zone. Unless extremely large packs are used, stage cylinders can be mounted on the same side as the pack.

Backup Lights
Wreck divers often carry one backup light strapped to their shoulder, preferably in a neoprene sleeve. This is often used as a gauge reading or close working light in low visibility. Lights with a power switch rather than a screw top are best used to prevent accidental turn on or flooding underwater. Any additional lights are often stowed in the same place as when cave diving.

Cave divers carry at least two backup lights. Both attached by piston clips to the harness. They are held in place with neoprene sleeving or a simple bungee loop. The stowage point is normally the lower half of the webbing that runs from the shoulder to the waist.

Strobes and Light Sticks
While both have surface uses in an emergency, they also become very useful in low or dark visibility. Where shot or anchor lines are used when wreck diving, the light source is attached close to the bottom of the line to assist with the divers' return. Diver stowage will either be in a pouch or under some neoprene sleeving in the harness.

Determining Light Duration

It is important we know how long lights will last, especially when cave diving. Given that degrading battery packs and to a certain extent low temperature will affect performance, the following is a simple method to approximate duration.

Ohms Law
Where V is the voltage of the battery pack
Where P is the wattage of the light
Where I is the Amperes (current) used by the light

If we know the lamp wattage and the battery pack voltage we can find the current.

Hence: $I = P \div V$

If we have a 50 watt light and a 12v battery we have:

$50 \div 12 = 4.2$ Amperes

Therefore, if the battery pack is rated at 8.4 Ampere/hour the pack will last:

$8.4 \div 4.2 = 2$ hours.

Line Reels

Although inherently reels have fallen into two categories (those used for cave and those used for wreck), many people are now using the classic cave-style friction reels in open water.

Reel Use
Reels are used for assisting with navigation (laying a line in a cave or wreck), surveying (measuring distance and bearing) and as an aid to decompression. Reels are primarily categorised by the amount and type of line they carry and although friction reels will primarily be discussed here, it is worth briefly mentioning the other types.

Ratchet Reels
Popular amongst wreck divers. These reels are typically large (due mostly to the ratchet mechanism) which makes them difficult to stow. They normally carry approximately 50m of line which can be allowed to free run by depressing the ratchet handle. Line can then be reeled in by winding. If winding stops the reel spool will rotate back against the ratchet and lock. To let more line out simply depress the ratchet.

Up Line Reels
Popular with some East Coast American divers. The diver carries a large spool of bio-degradable line (sisal or similar). At the end of the bottom time the diver ties one end to the wreck or reef and while ascending, starts to reel out. At the decompression stop the reel is locked off. Once the decompression is finished the line is cut. Obviously on a deep dive these reels can become quite large and if used in tidal areas can generate problems with the diver acting like a pendulum and returning to the bottom unless excessive buoyancy is added. A line failure at this point could be disastrous and missed stops ensue.

Friction Reels
The most common type of reel for wreck and cave diving. They are equipped with either a central adjustable friction control or a screw clutch that works on the spool. When the lock is released it is easy for the reel to over run if the line is not checked, hence these reels need a little familiarisation before using them in anger.

General Guidelines for Reel Use
- when working with a reel, remember to lock the reel before attempting to tie a knot or loop the line around an object. In a large wreck or cave, dropping an unlocked reel could be disastrous.
- avoid unnecessary clips on the end of the reel line. Although they may attach the line to another quickly they can also come undone or even damage the other line. Tie a large loop in the end of the line so that the reel can pass through it, forming a loop.
- use a small plastic ball to prevent the line reeling back around the spool and/or a small loop of line to grip the line, especially when wearing gloves.
- as the line pays out, keep a finger on the reel to stop over-spooling the line.
- when returning the line to the spool, keep tension on the line by guiding it through your index finger.

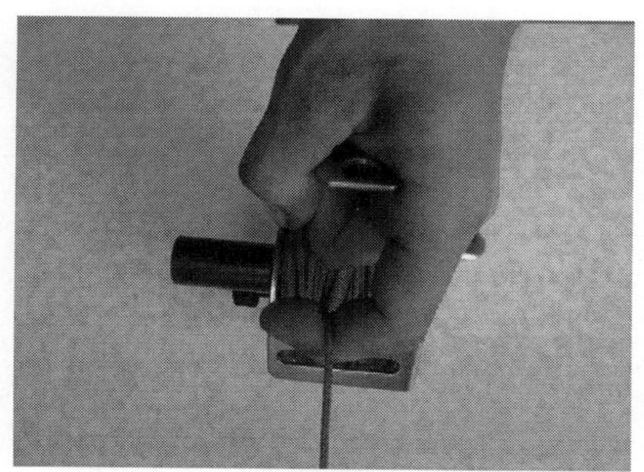

Line tensioner

Note plastic ball and loop

<u>**Reel Use**</u>
In cave diving reels are often categorized thus:

Primary Reel
- one with at least 50 metres of line, often used to run a line from the entrance to a permanent line. This type of reel is also used in open water as a main dive reel, possibly either to lay a guideline on a wreck or as a decompression reel. When used for decompression with a delayed surface marker buoy (DSMB) it may be deployed (dependant on depth) from the bottom or slightly deeper than the first decompression stop. Often when decompression diving a primary and a smaller backup reel will be joined together in case the first one jams when released. If deployed from the bottom, a safe alternative to this is to secure the primary reel to the wreck. Should a reel jam then occur the diver can lock the reel and attempt to free it or deploy their backup reel.

Safety Reel
- a smaller reel (25 metres) used only in an emergency, primarily when a search for a lost permanent line is required. In open water this could be the same as the backup reel.

Jump or Gap Reel
- a smaller reel again, often a finger reel with 10 metres of line or less. Used to run a temporary line from one permanent line to another. For instance a Jump reel is used when a side passage 'T's' off the main passage and a permanent line is also laid in it. The two lines (main and side) are not connected. The Jump reel is used to make the temporary connection[15]. A Gap reel is used when one permanent line ends and another begins a short distance away. The Gap line is temporarily laid between them.

Explorer Reel
- explorer reels vary significantly dependant on the distance of penetration/survey required and the environment within which it is taking place. Generally, they carry heavy duty line, sometime short sections (150m) on multiple reels or one big reel.

---
[15] See P.43

Jon-lines
Although technically not reel, a Jon-line can be a great decompression aid and is a good general tool underwater. Normally it is a 2 metre length of strong line with a piston or butterfly clip at one and a loop at the other. If decompressing in a current on a line attached to the wreck, the Jon-line is passed around the line and back through its own loop. Being of a smaller diametre than the shot line, it will lock in the larger ropes' weave. The clip is then attached to the crutch (scooter) ring of the diver's harness. The diver then hangs like a flag in the current. This is a very comfortable way to decompress, even in extreme current. Jon-lines are also useful when an emergency scooter tow[1] is required or whenever you just need a piece of string!

How Many Reels?
When cave diving a minimum of two reels will be carried (Primary and Safety). The same number applies to open water decompression diving, the Safety reel often being renamed a Backup reel.

Golden Rules
Reel Man
In any penetration dive the reel man is the first in and the last out. This rule should ***NEVER*** be broken.

Team Order
Team order is always maintained in a line following dive. This is only broken if there is an emergency in the team. In a light failure situation the diver with no light is shuffled to the centre of the team. In an out of gas scenario the distressed diver is allowed to lead the exit, thus controlling pace.

Line Rules
The following is offered as a basic guide to line laying and following, there are many detailed books[2] on the subject.
unless the situation demands it and the line is designed for it, do not pull on the line. Make an OK sign with your hand and use it as a guide if visibility deteriorates.
never swim under a line
keep a visual picture in your head of where the line is at all times. If visibility suddenly disappears you will have a better chance of finding it again.
as you swim along a line inspect it for damage and bad tie offs. Correct as necessary.
never run a slack line. It could lead to entrapment of you or other divers
never lay line under an obstruction. Imagine yourself following it out 'blind' (blacked out). Could you do it?
keep knots/wraps on the outside of tie points so that they can easily be followed in a blind exit.
assist the person running the reel by providing light at each tie-off or junction and if necessary swim ahead and take any slack out of the line being recovered.

Stowage
Reels should be stowed neatly and checked before use[3]. I prefer the system of having a hole at the bottom corners of my back plate. Each hole has a split ring through it with a small piece of bungee to make it sit upright. I can attach a maximum of two reels to each ring. In general, reels stowed anywhere else about the body become a hindrance, avoid the 'danglies' at all costs.

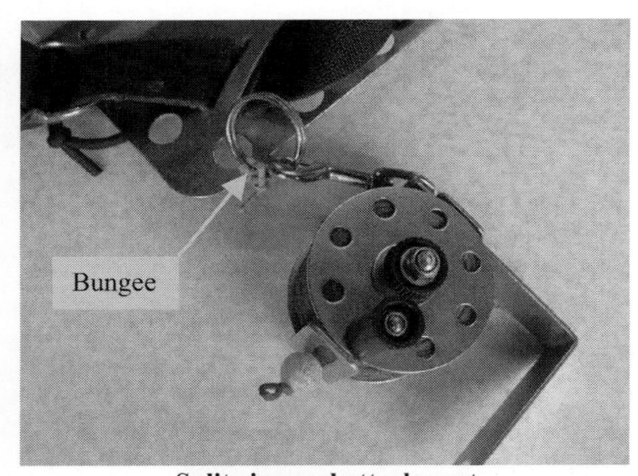

Split ring reel attachment

Types of Line
Lines used vary dependant on the application. Most diver carried reels (Primary, Jump, Safety and Deco) will use 1.5-2mm braided (not woven as this untangles easily when cut) nylon or similar line. This line is available in fluorescent colours that can be useful when identifying different divers/teams at a site.

---
[1] P.163
[2] See Bibliography
[3] P. 28

The type of permanent line laid in caves in the USA (like the main 'Gold' line in Ginnie Springs) is a larger more rugged line. In the UK and other low visibility cave environments, where the line may be used not only as a guide but to pull against, then 3-5mm polypropylene is often the line of choice.

Line Markers
Line markers fall into two categories;
permanent
normally with a distance from the nearest entrance marked on them. These can either be the classic triangular plastic marker or tape woven into the line.
temporary
carried and laid by a diver. Usually used to note the way out. For instance at a jump to another tunnel the jump from the main line will be looped around the marker that will point to the exit on the main line. Using the marker as a line anchor stops the jump line sliding up and down the main line. These markers will often be personalised with the diver's name or a specific feature (cut corner).
in some cases clothes pegs are used to mark a distance reached along a line. In some parts of the world cloths pegs are also used to mark the way out at a line junction.

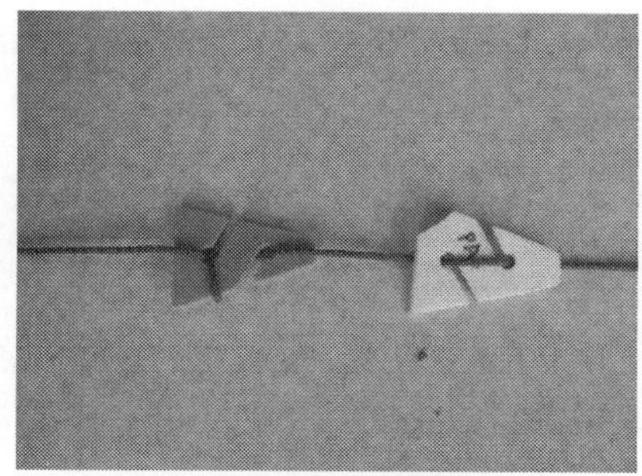

The marker on the left is tied in correctly to prevent it sliding

Line markers should be firmly locked around the line at all times. The number carried depends on the dive objectives. As a minimum, carry two on any penetration. Some divers elect to carry markers in a pocket whilst others clip markers onto a short piece of bungee with a knotted end, attached to one of the shoulder 'D' rings on a harness. I prefer the latter as it ensures fast and simple access.

Knots and Tying Off
Lines are often looped together and hence knots are not required. Where a tie-off is to be made to an item such as a loose rock or outcrop then a clove hitch is useful. Speed wraps where the line is passed around an object and then back under the line in a single wrap, are good for general line laying. There are many basic knots but as divers if you can tie a Bowline, a Clove Hitch and a Reef Knot these will cover most eventualities. There is an old saying 'If you can't tie knots, tie lots of knots'. This also sometimes works.

Snoopy Loops
Snoopy loops are a simple tool for belaying (tying off). It consists of a piece of rubber inner tube or bungee in a loop. This might be stretched over a prominent object or a rock (belay point) and the line attached to it, often with a cable tie or other securing method. Snoopy loops are often used where the line must be run in an area of passage where no permanent securing features can be found and a rock or lead weight is used after being moved into the right position. This method of laying line is popular among European cave divers.

Buoyancy Control Devices and Harnesses
Buoyancy control devices (BCD's) have in the sport diving realm in recent years been limited to Stabiliser (Stab) jacket styles. The buoyancy is split between the front and the back. This design often incorporates several pockets for kit stowage and the odd plastic clip for kit attachment. Where sometimes a large array of equipment is required to be carried, it is of limited use. Also, with heavier and more cylinders, attachment and damage to the system becomes a problem.

The alternative is a 'wing' and harness system. The wing is a 'U' - shaped bladder sandwiched between the diver and his/her cylinders giving anything up to approximately 50kg of lift (buoyancy). Wings generally fall into 'bondage' and 'Non - bondage' types. If a wing is a 'bondage wing' then it has loops of

Wings Stocks resplendent in a wing and harness

bungee around the bladder at intervals to force gas out once the dump valve has been operated. The bungee also ensures the wing stays close to the body. Bungees can also be tightened at strategic points to reduce inadvertent gas migration around the wing. The other type has no bungee and ensures a flat profile when little or no gas is injected into the wing. Whilst the 'non-bondage' wing may provide a low drag profile and reduce the possibility of entanglement, in certain circumstances it may 'flap' (moving through turbulent or high speed water) and thus generate drag in this manner. Again, your choice should primarily be environment-based. I find either adequate in most conditions.

Between the wing and the diver, often attached to the wing is the harness. Invariably it is made of strong 50mm webbing and looped through a plastic or stainless steel back plate. The back plate its self can be used to mount equipment[19] as well as the harness. Stainless back plates are used not only for strength but in an effort to reduce the amount of weight a diver will carry on a belt. Some divers sandwich plates together to further reduce, remove the belt weight or add a 'V' shaped lead weight between the cylinders. The harness will have strong 'D' rings attached at key points for equipment location and neoprene sleeving or bungee within which to stow equipment.

The harness also carries a small canvas pouch on the waist band. This has two pockets, one large and the other small. The smaller pocket is used to store frequently used items. In my case this is just a small, multi-page dive slate and pencil. The rear pocket carries a range of emergency gear stowed in the order I am most likely to use it. Starting from the top (most used), an orange SMB, a yellow SMB, a pair of wire cutters, a mirror, a spare Jon-line and a spare set of dive tables.

A typical harness layout is shown on the following page.

[19] P.39

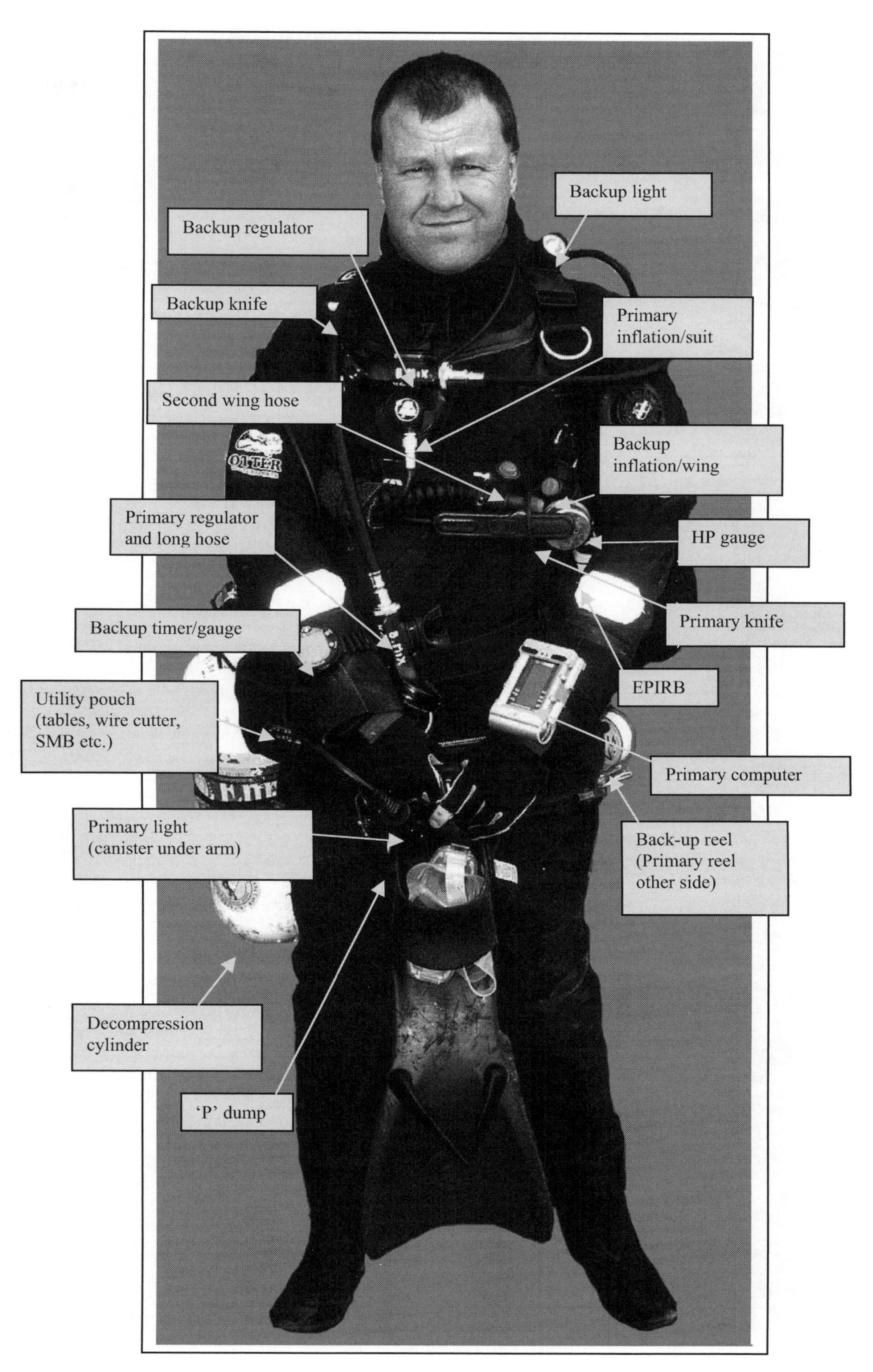
Backup light
Backup regulator
Backup knife
Primary inflation/suit
Second wing hose
Backup inflation/wing
Primary regulator and long hose
HP gauge
Primary knife
Backup timer/gauge
EPIRB
Utility pouch (tables, wire cutter, SMB etc.)
Primary computer
Primary light (canister under arm)
Back-up reel (Primary reel other side)
Decompression cylinder
'P' dump

Dive Timers/Computers

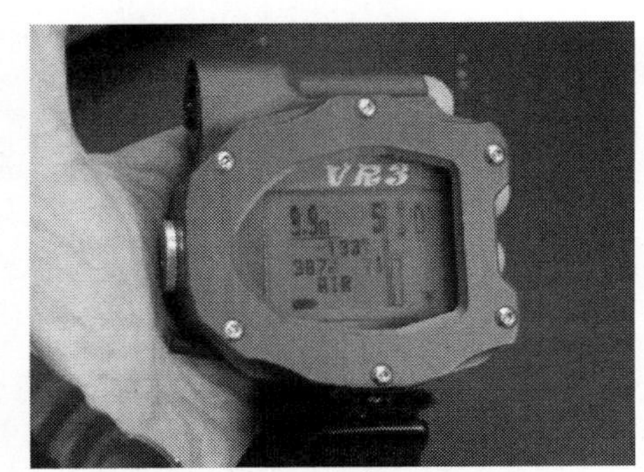
Switchable trimix computer

For diving requiring decompression, air computers become redundant due to their propensity to 'get bent' as the majority of extended decompressions require an elevated fraction of oxygen is used during the decompression stops. This ability to 'switch gas' is not found with air computers and hence the diver completes the required decompression before the computer. Air computers have a tendency to 'lock out' and remain in surface mode for anything up to 48 hours after such an event. Nitrox computers offer an alternative. Firstly, the non-switchable one (single gas) can be set to an elevated FO_2 and the decompression ignored, hence it is used in gauge mode. The high FO_2 ensures it will not violate but the decompression information is inaccurate, therefore tables are used. On most dives with a computer set to say 50% oxygen it will not 'bend' and can be used in a gauge mode without suffering lockouts. Switchable ones have a further advantage in that they obviously cope with the gas switch, some on a pre-planned set of rules (switch depth or time) and some, manually by the user. The latter is the preferred method.

When trimix or heliox diving in deep-water, most divers either take one or more dive timers or computers that have a dedicated 'gauge mode'", relying on manual tables for their decompression information. The alternative that has been available for some time now are trimix dive computers, some with up to ten gas switches, capable of dealing with any scenario.

The majority of timers stop counting at 99m in metric mode or 330ft in imperial. Some of the newer ones now go deeper. Before choosing a timer for deep-diving (or indeed any gauge) it is important to establish its accuracy. Digital instruments and their pressure sensing devices are governed by three constraints - the offset, the gain and the linearity inherent in the system.

The offset ensures it reads zero at zero (and if the gain is linear, 100 at 100) while the gain ensures it can go from zero to full-scale (its maximum reading) accurately. Linearity defines each reading in between is correct. When testing a timer/gauge you should not only make sure it is accurate at depth but also at several levels in between. A 1.0m accuracy at deeper depths and 0.5m accuracy at decompression depths is acceptable for most decompression diving or at worst case make sure it reads deep. If diving in extreme cold or heat these too can affect an instruments accuracy. In most cases, however, the instrument's have automatic temperature calibration built in.

It is essential to either have the instrument tested against a calibrated gauge or take down several depth gauges and find the ones that match closely to what you expect the depth to be. Remember when you do this, some gauges are calibrated in fresh water. For freshwater to saltwater conversions see Appendix B.

Don't forget that some decompression tables may be calibrated in either saltwater or fresh-water, so should be matched to the gauges. It would be far simpler if we all thought in pressure units (bar) and all instrumentation and tables were referenced to that.

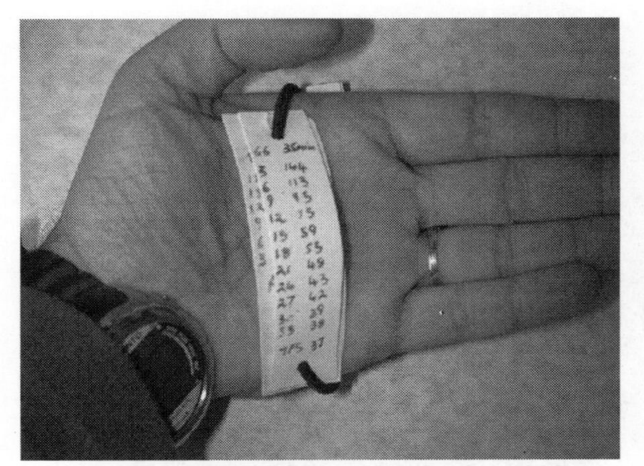
Runtime slate. Often used as backup tables

Slates

Slates come in two main forms - communications slates and decompression slates. Communication slates are either a single slate, small booklet of flexible plastic pages or a waterproof book. They are used for communication with other divers or possibly taking notes such as when teaching or surveying. A single word can certainly paint a thousand hand signals!! Some people prefer a hard wrap around wrist slate. I personally find this an encumbrance and prefer to keep my arms as clear as possible, except for a computer/timer.

Decompression slates are a simple plain slate on which the decompression or Runtime Schedule[20] can be written. These have a small piece of bungee attached that loops over the hand. They are normally stowed in a harness or diving suit sleeve pocket.

Instead of writing on the slate in permanent marker and then having to remove it with a solvent, an alternative method is to use masking or decorators' tape on the slate and then write on it in normal ballpoint pen.

Decompression Tables

In the air range a straight air table with an option to use 75% or greater at decompression is what the majority of technical divers carry as a backup set of tables. Even when you are shallow-range nitrox diving these basically get you out of trouble with a worst case decompression schedule (air), when a problem occurs.

EPIRB's

The Emergency Personal International Rescue Beacon or EPIRB as it is known is a device for signalling rescue vessels equipped with a receiver in the event of a diver becoming lost at sea. Many are available within a pressure proof housing normally submersible to 100 metres or more. EPIRB's operate on the standard worldwide distress frequency of 121.5 MHz. Approximate location distances are:

1.	Surface crafts	3 miles
2.	Oil rigs	5 miles
3.	SAR helicopters	10 miles
4.	Commercial/military aircraft	70 miles

When surfacing, the diver removes the EPIRB from its waterproof housing (most units having limited waterproofing to shallow depths) and simply loops the antennae around the neck. Some units have in-water activation once armed. It is important that EPIRB's are periodically tested. This can often be arranged with the Coastguard. Many units have a test facility. If the test is a live one, ensure the Coastguard is alerted before activation.

Other Signalling Devices

Several other forms of signalling devices can be used during diving. Some have multi purpose roles. For instance, a simple plastic mirror whilst useful for attracting attention on the surface (otherwise known as heliographs) offer an easy way of checking for leaks in a SCUBA system when submerged. In the case of solo diving this may be vital, the offending system being able to be shut down before major amounts of gas are lost. Lifting bags or surface marker buoys (SMB's) are often used to locate the position of a diver while they are decompression. Some SMB's are inflated prior to submerging and towed by the diver on a reel line. This technique is often used in areas with heavy shipping traffic, particularly during drift-diving. During wreck and any decompression diving a delayed SMB is often inflated from the bottom at some point during the dive, to indicate an ascent has started as well as the diver's position. Delayed SMB's often have simple non return valves in to prevent gas loss during heavy seas and are better suited than open lifting bags for this application. There is also always the danger that a boat skipper may attempt to recover a lift bag unaware that a diver is below.

Another use for delayed SMB's is to signal an emergency. For a dive being conducted without safety divers, a loss of gas may be critical. Some divers carry two SMB's of different colours. Often an orange one seen on the surface indicates the diver is well, whereas a yellow one or two together indicates a problem. The trained response of any surface team is to lower a cylinder of gas on a buoyed line (normally to the first decompression stop depth) appropriate for the dive being conducted. This buys the diver time until a safety diver or returning bottom diver can be re-launched to ascertain the problem. Slates can also be attached to SMB's to pass messages to the surface. If the surface crew wish to return a message, the slate is simply clipped to the line and sent back down. It is a very good idea to write your name on your SMB right at the top. Decompression techniques using SMB's and other systems will be discussed in later detail[21].

Whistles and strobes are other useful surface-signalling devices, especially if you plan to night dive.

---

[20] P.91

[21] P.155

Cutting Devices
The traditional diver's knife is a thing of the past. Normally, two cutting devices are carried. There are many high-quality but compact diver's knives available today. When choosing a cutting device, it is useful to define the entrapment hazards your type of diving may encounter. These could be:

- standard heavy fishing net
- monofilament fishing net
- electrical cables
- ropes and lines
- steel fishing tracer

The range of available cutting tools includes:

Standard Divers Knife
Normally manufactured of high quality stainless steel and will maintain a reasonable edge. If a slight serration is applied to the edge this is good at cutting ropes and lines.

Razor Knife
Basically a razor blade (or two) trapped in a plastic holder. Exceptionally good at cutting any netting and thin lines.

Surgical Scissors
Excellent on electrical cable but little else. Some surgical scissors will cut steel tracer line, webbing and fairly thick line. Lines or webbing which are saturated with water may give a problem.

Wire Cutters/Pliers
Good for wire and steel tracer but little else.

My personal preference is a small serrated titanium knife, a razor knife and surgical scissors if I am wreck diving. This combination seems to work in most instances. Titanium maintains an excellent edge but is very brittle (not to be used as a screw driver).

Masks
What is there to say about the humble dive mask? Quite a lot really, especially if we look at full face masks as well. The standard half-mask has been around since the beginning. We no longer employ the 'gold fish bowl' version in general diving, so what are the key points to look for when buying a mask?

- silicone construction will make it hard-wearing. Black or clear is good. I prefer clear as it is less like diving in a tunnel!
- low volume to assist with rapid clearing
- tempered glass
- a good strap. Some people replace the standard silicone one with a velcro and neoprene alternative which is more comfortable

Full Face Masks
Until recently there has really only been one full-face mask in general recreational diving use. This is the AGA Interspiro. Several other manufacturers such as Scubapro have released masks but for one reason or another they have not become popular.

Full-face masks come from a commercial background and were originally designed for diving in contaminated water or when using communication equipment, the latter being one of their major advantages over half-face masks.

Looking at the AGA first. This comes in two varieties, demand and positive pressure. As expected one supplies gas on demand (when you breathe) and one ensures there is always a slight positive pressure inside the mask (designed to keep contaminants out). The disadvantage of the latter is that if it does not seal properly then you lose gas. Most drysuit divers wear a hood with a smooth skin face seal to help reduce gas loss. When using the positive mask (which is the most popular). There is a lever on the mouth-piece that shuts off the regulator (to enable removal without gas loss). Close this, flip open the two catches on the lower neck straps and push the mask up and off your head.

As full-face masks provide a nice warm environment for the face, be prepared for a thermal shock. The best way to change to a regulator underwater is to pinch your nose as you remove the mask. This will help reduce the gagging reflex. Now fit your backup regulator and your spare mask (most people wear this on the back of their neck).

The AGA (and some other masks) have a flexible oral/nasal pocket that provides a seal of sorts around the nose and mouth. This helps reduce CO_2 dead spaces within the mask. By having the nose and mouth in the mask it is possible to breathe through the nose naturally. This helps prevent the dry mouth normally associated with regulator use. If you use a full-face with a rebreather, you may find that when you go in a heads-up position, the mask will vent around the top. Even more so, with rebreathers, a good fitting mask is essential.

Another mask available more recently is the Morgan 'Super mask'. This has an isolated top (eye) and bottom (mouth) section. The bottom part is fully removable by two simple clips or can just be hinged down to allow placement of a standard regulator second stage. This allows the diver to switch gases without removing the whole mask. Spare mouth sections can be attached to other first stages to ease gas switching.

Most full-face masks do not allow ear clearing via the standard nose pinch. The AGA is fitted with an adjustable block of rubber which is forced up towards the nostrils to make a seal. You then blow through the nose as normal. Some people can do this with just a swallow. Full-face masks do get a bit smelly, a weak Betadine™ solution or Dettox™ is sufficient to clean them.

In technical diving, gas switch blocks are often used with these masks so that multiple gases can be routed to the same regulator. This is a potential hazard in its self, especially if several gases are available on the same block via control valves. Any gas you are not using should be isolated on the block **and** at the cylinder valve until it is needed.

In general, full-face masks are best used where communications are required. I used them extensively on the Britannic project with our safety divers. The constant communication with the dive supervisor proved invaluable.

In the event of unconsciousness occurring underwater (oxygen convulsions etc.), full face masks give an obvious significant advantage. Full-face masks are also useful for conducting in-water recompression.

Navigation Aids

Whilst certain electronic aids are finding their way into diving circles (ultra sonic shot line detectors etc.) there is nothing more reliable than the humble compass. On completion of open-water training the compass is often forgotten as being a useful underwater tool. Compasses become especially useful again in cave and scooter diving.

A standard diving compass consists of the body with an engraved indicator or arrow. This is known as the 'lubber line'. It may take the form of a line across the centre of the glass. To take a bearing you site along this line. Some compasses have a window in the side (the sighting window) and does the same thing. Inside there is a floating disc or arrow. The top of the arrow or north on the disc will always orientate to magnetic north (which is slightly different to true north and which varies according to the area of the world in which you are situated). Around the outside of the compass is a rotating ring, marked in degrees.

A standard diving compass is not unlike a land compass in that north on the floating bezel will always point to magnetic north. With a compass in front of you and with North on the disc (or the arrow) aligned with the lubber line you are obviously facing north. The rotating outer ring can then be moved to make the 0 degrees or north marker line up with the other two. If you turn the compass to the left by 30 degrees the disc or arrow will appear to swing to the right (in fact it stays pointing north) and it will align with the 30 degree mark on the outer ring. This does not mean your heading is 30 degrees. Now twist the outer ring to the right so that the 0 degree marker is over the point on the arrow or bezel. Now read off the number on the outer ring which is over the lubber line. It should read 330 degrees. This is your heading. Looking in the sighting window will also give you this number, as the 330 at the bottom of the rotating bezel will line up with the bottom of the lubber line.

Remember compasses will be affected by anything that distorts a local magnetic field like a large ferrous object (steel cylinders) or possibly a scooter motor. I have watched countless students attempt to take a heading on a ship wreck!

Natural Navigation (Pilotage)
Whilst strictly speaking not a piece of equipment, natural navigation is still a vital 'tool' for a diver.

Experienced divers often talk of developing a sense of direction but even this cannot be relied upon in poor visibility. Natural navigation skills especially in caves and wrecks have saved lived. **The key is to remember what you have seen on the way in**. Not only will it assist your exit if lines have been lost or damaged but will reduce stress levels once a recognisable landmark has be re-established.

In wrecks and caves, prominent features make good landmarks - changes of depth, changes of bottom structure (mud to sand), rock structures in a cave and the sand ripples that run parallel to the shore when approaching a beach.

Over time the experienced diver automatically remembers landmarks and hence generates an awareness of their surroundings. Once attained navigation is no longer a major issue.

Surveying
Whilst not exactly a piece of equipment either, this seems a good time to talk about surveying. Surveying can be done in caves or open water, but why bother? Firstly, by taking the time to survey a site we become more familiar with it. This in turn increases safety should we become temporarily lost (relocating a landmark during an exit raises our confidence and improves decision making). By being aware of the sites depth profile we can accurately plan for decompression and gas requirements for our own or future expeditions. Also if you are trying to raise sponsorship for a project having a 'map' of what you intend to do is always beneficial.

Basic Methods
A survey is a balance of speed (going farther and getting more done) and accuracy. Initial surveys may require the former. Surveys use line so make sure you have those reel skills down before you even start or you will get nowhere. The process starts with a main survey line being laid in the direction of the survey (down the passage etc.). This line will be tagged at regular (3 metre) intervals. For simple surveying the diver will carry a survey slate, possibly a tape measure and a compass. The slate will be divided into four sections; one for the tag number (or distance from the start), one for depth, one for bearings and finally one for any notes.

To start the survey a primary 'survey station'" point is selected. This may be just inside the cave or at the start of an ope-water line. Start to fill in your slate. Now swim along the line until the survey line changes direction. This is the second survey station and the process is repeated. If the site has not changed direction for over 20 metres it may be prudent to split the survey leg and take a depth and distance reading anyway to improve the accuracy of your survey. It may be applicable to note landmarks at this stage. Dependant on the type of survey required it could also be necessary to measure the width or height of a passage as well using the tape measure. At the end of this survey period it is important to mark the end of the survey so that you or others can continue it later.

In open water the survey often involves laying line grids. If the work involves metal detectors to look for buried objects then several letter-coded base lines might be run. Depending on the site size and the visibility these will probably be a maximum of 10 metres apart. The grid is formed by crossing these lines at 90 degrees with a series of other lines, each coded again, making a series of 10 by 10 individual box sizes. Each box may be further subdivided. In some case very fine portable search grids will be overlaid on a certain spot for taking detailed written and photographic records. The important thing is that any point within the grid system can be pinpointed.

Remember it is easy to get distracted whilst surveying. Keep watching your gauges!

Compasses give the biggest errors in any survey. Remember, they are affected by ferrous objects (dive knives etc.). Take your time when sighting the compass. Errors can become compounded on long surveys. In certain caves even the rock structure can have an effect.

Once you have all the information make sure you get a hard copy as soon as possible. Pencil rubs off a slate very easily and hours of work could be lost!

This is the basics. For more information on surveying the reader is guided to the bibliography[22].

---

[22] Cave Diving by the Cave Diving Group of Great Britain

Diving suits

Wetsuits

For those of us lucky enough to live in warmer climes, the wet or semi-dry suit is a serious option even for extended range diving. The use of a secondary BCD is mandatory when gas diving with these suits, as the combined weight of the equipment will easily overcome the buoyancy of the suit[23].

Even in cold waters such as cave diving which involves an element of dry caving, then a wetsuit is the only real option. A classic example of this is British cave diving. Almost all done in wetsuits even though the water temperature is a static 6 degrees centigrade. Whilst long swims in this environment become uncomfortable they are interjected with short (and sometimes long) bursts of extreme exercise in both dry and damp conditions. A serious issue here is hypothermia[24]. This type of diving is always a compromise between manoeuvrability and staying warm. Also, because of the extreme abrasiveness of the environment, suits are often specially constructed to take wear and tear.

Drysuits

Dry suits come in two primary forms, membrane and neoprene. Membrane suits are constructed of several laminated layers. A waterproof one and an abrasion resistant outer. Some suits are constructed purely of a form of rubber, like early Naval suits. Drysuits keep you warmer in cold and temperate water at the expense often of manoeuvrability. Manoeuvrability is governed by the material and cut of the suit and the amount of underwear worn.

Neoprene dry suits are basically constructed of rubber with an inner and outer material protection, the rubber containing lots of small bubbles. They come in three basic grades;

Gas blown	where the majority of bubbles remain in tact. These offer the best warmth and highest buoyancy. Suits are often made from up to 8mm thick neoprene and offer little manoeuvrability.
Compressed	as above but with an element of compression applied during manufacture, reducing the quantity of intact bubbles. As expected, buoyancy and thermal rating is reduced but manoeuvrability is improved.
Crushed	little or no bubble structure remains. Manoeuvrability is high at the expense of thermals and buoyancy again. If material is compressed too much the cell structure of the neoprene can become damaged and the material leaks. This is characterised by small 'valleys' appearing on the inside material of the suit.

Membrane drysuits offer no significant positive buoyancy, lower thermal rating and excellent manoeuvrability. They are also often very hard wearing, pack light and dry quickly unlike their neoprene counterparts. For these reasons they have become the mainstay of extended range diving in temperate conditions. Their down side -low thermal rating - being compensated by intelligent underwear selection.

Manoeuvrability of any drysuit system is improved by the choice of entry zip. Back entry zips tend to restrict movement while using the arms due to the zips; rigidity. Front zips improve on this, providing the rear of the suit is designed to allow the back muscles to flex. Try spreading out your arms and measuring from wrist to wrist. Now cross your arms in front of your chest. Your back muscles have just expanded and significantly increased the distance. A good suit will cater for this. My own test is to crouch down and try and put both hand behind my back and touch the top of my spine. This is just about the worst position you can get into underwater. If the suit allows this (with underwear) then it is a good buy.

Pockets on suits (especially on the legs) are often excessive and present high drag profiles, thus increasing swimming effort and CO_2 build-up. Whilst leg pockets may seem like a good stowage area, even in full mixed gas (100m+) diving rig, all items of safety equipment have much better stowage positions about the body. Flat pockets with zips or velcro are ideal for backup tables and slates but that's about it. A wrist pocket for a run-time slate is also useful. If extra equipment such as bags have to be carried, consider placing these on stage cylinders or preferably the base of your backplate.

---

[23] P. 30

[24] P. 123

Thermal Underwear

It has long been recognised in the climbing fraternity that by using individual layers of clothing, heat loss is reduced. Slowly, this experience has bled into diving but we are still behind. Starting with the inner layers which are thin and designed to 'wick' water away (remove it), moving to the thicker outer layers which contain the bulk of the thermal protection Whilst heat is to be maintained it is vital that excessive moisture is removed as water next to the skin is 25 times more thermally conductive than air. Hence 'breathable' underwear is vital.

Underwear materials include;

Silk — probably the best inner underwear. Extremely good wicking and breathing properties but needs care and maintenance.

Mereklon — similar in properties to silk but more hard wearing

Thinsulate — comes in a range of weights, 100 gm normally being the lightest. The outer layers of a Thinsulate based undersuit are often constructed of Pertex which is a shower proof, breathable covering offering some abrasion protection. Ripstop Pertex is used to help reduce tears and is imprinted with tiny hexagons in inhibit tears. Thinsulate is a 3M product.

Holofil — basically a material used in sleeping bags but which has found its way into under suits. The material consists of strands of hollow fibres that help retain heat. It is extremely light and flexible and packs easily.

Suit Heaters

Supplementary heating has long been tried by divers, From simple battery-powered pads to chemical devices. Heated waist coats are preferred amongst some cave divers, borrowed from the motorcycle industry.

Whilst chemical pads are reusable and hence convenient they have a finite duration and care must be taken because some react to elevated partial pressures oxygen (as found in a drysuit at depth). People have been burned using such pads. Several people have tried to make a useful thermostatically-controlled pad system. Firstly, they take a lot of power (although generally they need only be switched on during decompression) and secondly they can produce hot spots. Kidneys are a chosen position for these pads, being an area of high blood flow close to the surface. Care must be taken though, as heat pads can actually aid hypothermia.

How we Lose Heat

If the body's core experiences a rise in temperature it attempts to dump heat. This is why hands and face etc. 'radiate' after exercise, it is the body's way of cooling down. Hence, if you put a lot of heat back in close to the core, if it is too much it will attempt to lose it by shunting it to the peripheries (hands and feet etc.). Whilst temporarily the hands and feet may feel warm, the core is cooling. At a certain point the core stops this as now it needs heat. It retains this by shutting down blood flow to the peripheries. Conversely, if the correct amount of heat is applied to the peripheries, some of this will get back to the core maintaining the heat levels. This is a much more efficient way of heating the body but difficult to perform on a diver. Dry gloves, thicker hoods and good Thinsulate socks help the problem. I have found that having an undersuit with integral socks (no elastic join) significantly helps foot warmth.

My Equipment Configuration - Open Circuit

June 2001.

Without doubt, diving in Northern European waters and especially the tidal channels of the UK, is among the most challenging in the world. I have dived all over the planet from the murky waters of the Yellow River in China to the limitless visibility of the Pacific, from Scandinavia to New Zealand and whilst my kit configuration is definitely a function of many hours spent in UK waters, I feel it's good to go anywhere.

The different disciplines of cave or wreck also leave their small mark, but generally speaking changes are minimal. The only exception to this is side-mount diving which requires a whole new harness! Even when rebreather diving I just bolt my back plate and wing onto the unit, hence my safety gear goes with it. I am constantly amazed by experienced divers who, when they buy a rebreather, seem to discard all their basic safety philosophies just because the rebreather comes with a different wing and harness.

Whilst there is no one perfect system. An interesting fact is that as you travel and meet other people who have been diving for a while, their configurations seem remarkably similar. Basically, if you are going to go decompression diving, whilst you may add more (and different size) cylinders for the deeper you go and the longer you decompress, the core kit is the same. Once you are decompression diving a rig's set-up is depth independent, you can still drown in six inches of water!

The basic principles of any rig are its buoyancy characteristics, streamlining and user-friendliness. These are inter-related.

On the buoyancy front the biggest decider is the suit. Neoprene and you have variable buoyancy characteristics as depth changes and often a lot of lead at the surface (even with certain side mounts). Membrane and you have a static weight characteristic at the sacrifice of minimal heat loss (with the right underwear). Membranes are often also more hardwearing. I use an Otter Super Skin, which is a membrane. It has one flat leg pocket (low drag) in which I keep backup air/75% deco tables. In the air/nitrox range they will always get you out, eventually! Personally I don't like the concept of stuffing reels and bags and other basic safety gear in big leg pockets. Aside from the drag problem, you have to remember to pack it each time. A simple harness pouch with it all in, always, is the best way. On my wrist is a small pocket for my main deco slate.

The suit has an attached hood to reduce flushing and a front zip to help with manoeuvrability. Neoprene over-seals reduce cooling at the wrists and provide UV protection for the seals.

Cylinders also affect buoyancy. Obviously you need to use bigger cylinders for deeper dives. 300 bar cylinders are a pain, just too heavy for minimal gas duration extension and you seldom get the complete fill anyway. Most of my diving down to 70 metres is done on twin 232 bar 12 litres cylinders. I trim myself so that with a single side mount and 1/3rd of my gas remaining in everything, I am comfortable at 3 metres. This means no lead, a stainless back plate and a steel torch canister are all I need. With the 12's, I find light weight steel 10 litres are the best side-mounts, both from a weight and gas duration standpoint. An empty 10 litre will still just sink, a 7 litre will float as they are usually aluminium. On the average 40 metre deco dive (say 35 mins bottom time) my stops will use a maximum of about 35 bar. This means I can easily get a weekend deco diving out of one decompression cylinder while maintaining rule of thirds. I can also use the same size cylinder down to about 100 metres as one or more of the decompression cylinders. Slightly bigger cylinders (15's) often need aluminium side mounts (10l's or bigger) as they are quite negative whilst 20's (with a much larger volume) need side mounts of steel because of the extra near empty buoyancy.

My manifold is any one with radial 'O' rings in the isolator bar (not compression ones) and with a small gas to valve seat interface hole to reduce valve turning pressure when full, this speeds the gas shutdowns. Try filling the cylinder to maximum pressure and see if the valve still turns easily. A good design will allow this and as long as you fill your cylinders with clean gas, it will stop debris clogging the valve and making it stiff.

My harness is a Custom Divers (CD). I like the harness because it allows me to easily cam band single cylinders onto it without using expensive accessories. This is good when I travel and have to use independent twin sets. It is also easily adjustable for switching from wetsuit to drysuit or from winter to summer underwear. The wing is a dual one because I do wetsuit dives occasionally and need the redundant buoyancy (dependant on what I am doing I may use a CD or OMS wing). The CD is not strictly a 'bondage' wing as the bungee doesn't go right round so it has a better drag profile (OMS do a non bondage wing as well now). If you do run a bungeed wing of any type, make sure you fully inflate the wing and pre-stretch the bungee before tying the loops in place. If you don't, it won't expand properly when you need it to do so.

The harness is simple with one shoulder release. The two top 'D' rings have little use other than to secure hoses and gauges in place. The ones slightly below your nipples are used for the top mount of the stage cylinders. Hold your hand out and stretch your thumb and little finger apart as far as possible. That distance is about the same as the distance between your nipple and your hip bone. The 'D' ring close to your nipple and the one on your hip are where the deco cylinder mounts, hence the same distance should occur between the neck of the deco cylinder and the base ring and piston clip (the base ring ends up just above half way up the cylinder). This has the affect of pushing the stage back towards your feet and trimming you more horizontally, which reduces drag and swimming effort. Using the nipple ring (possibly not a good term) keeps the valves out of your face and the triangle across your chest and down to your crutch clear for all your primary equipment (where both hands can reach it).

The top left shoulder of the harness stores a backup/gauge reading torch. Top right is a tiny net cutter (Dive Rite) both under neoprene sleeves. If completing a locked in decompression (attached to a shot line), I also tuck a 2 metre Jon-line in here under the neoprene sleeve. Lower left side of the harness is an EPIRB. This is replaced by a second backup torch when cave diving. Lower right is a compass and small mirror secured under neoprene. On the waistband I have a pouch with two pockets. The front pocket is for things I commonly use (writing notebook whilst teaching) on any dive. The back pocket is for emergency gear and is packed in the order of likley use so I don't have to dig for things. At the bottom is a pair of surgical scissors for net wire cutting on the bottom. Next is my emergency (yellow) SMB. This goes up when I have a major problem. Above that is a similar orange one which means 'I'm on my own but OK'. On top is a set of backup tables specific for the dive.

Attached to the base of the back plate is an OMS "Beaver Tail" where I keep two lifting bags. I don't use any bags that need a cylinder to inflate (not even the SMB's). They are too bulky and I have seen many students get to the bottom and having forgotten to fill the cylinder, have to go for the backup. The trick is KISS, 'Keep It Simple, Stupid'. A bag with a hole at one end will always reach the surface. My reels (minimum of two in open water, three when cave diving), are attached one on each side of the back plate to split rings in the lower left corner, away from the belt (hip) 'D' rings to avoid clutter. The rings are wrapped in bungee to enable them to spring out for easy reel attachment.

My canister torch (Custom Diver for general use or OMS Phantom light for filming/cave diving) attaches to the back plate under my right arm. The head is on a Goodman handle.

Regulators are all Poseidon Jetstreams. Although they are all the same, touch ID is maintained by putting regulator guards (a loop of bungee to stop breathing it accidentally) on high oxygen mixtures. They are also colour-coded and written on in big letters. I ensure they are all the same so I have common spares in the field and if I get a failure on a deep dive I can switch regulators on the cylinders and not have to put up with having a low performance regulator now being used at depth. Some people say Jetstreams are a 'wet breathe' and can easily free flow. The 'wet breathe' is basically a minor design fault. Simply wrap insulating tape around the outside edge (ring of holes) on the second stage. This will stop any lifting of the diaphram when diving in a current or scootering and prevent water turning the diaphragm over. To reduce the risk of free flows, when removing the regulator from your mouth, do so by pointing the mouthpiece down.

My main regulator tucks into bungee on my wing. I don't do a Hogarthian loop for reasons previously mentioned. You can pull the 2 metre hose out from any direction without it getting trapped and if I nudge the wreck it simply collapses into the wing and remains protected. The Jet streams, being handed, also allow me to keep everything off the left post coming around the left shoulder and everything of the right post around the right. This avoids confusion in a shutdown emergency, especially if you haven't developed that muscle motor memory yet! The backup regulator is on a short neck tie (make sure you can reach down and grab it with your mouth). All LP hoses are interchangeable (drysuit and wing). My HP gauge is a solid brass one with no boot and my main knife is strapped to the back. This keeps all primary life support gear in the triangle I mentioned. All hoses come under my arms for protection, except my second stage hoses.

With the exception of clips on my reels, that attach them to my back plate I have no clips on my rig (KISS again).

Deco cylinders\stages have the clips rigged as detailed earlier. The regulator hose is bungeed\inner-tubed in place and the second stage is fixed by a bungee loop to the cylinder neck. If I use a travel gas on deep dives where I need to switch to a stage on the way down and up, I may loop the second stage into a bungee on my chest 'D' rings. Otherwise it stays in the stage neck loop.

A final note on underwear. It is always a compromise between manoeuvrability and warmth. Put on your underwear and drysuit and crouch down. Now reach back and simulate doing a gas shutdown. If you can reach the valves, then the combination is satisfactory. I use a C-Bear Thinsulate with a weighting of around 100gm in the summer and 200gm in the winter. These are excellent suits. I have attached feet on mine that helps with periphery warmth. They are a good, breathable suit and coupled with very thin under clothes to wick any moisture off my body, work very well.

My Equipment Configuration - Closed Circuit

Basically the configuration is the same without the cylinders. I use a USN MK15.5 rebreather.

The main differences over open circuit are: my suit is fed from an external (side mount) cylinder that doubles as my open circuit bailout, I can switch this feed to my wing if needed. In the air range (approx. 50 metres) the external cylinder will be air and I use about three standard trimix bailouts down to 120 metres. I match these against the inboard diluent on a trimix dive so that the open circuit gas is the same as the diluent (to balance decompression) and I can decant from my open circuit into my diluent to top it up between dives if necessary be (ensuring I still have sufficient bailout volume).

Gas diving in Guam
MK 15.5 rebreather

On deeper trimix dives where multiple open circuit stages have to be carried for diluent switching/emergency open circuit use, (hence I will be negative) I will run my suit from one external cylinder and my wing from another. My primary bailout has a permanent neck tie for the regulator.

My rebreather has a wing, harness and stainless back plate just like my open circuit rig. All safety gear is in the same positios as on my open circuit harness. I see countless rebreather divers compromise this philosophy simply because they dive a rebreather...why? As I do not rely on any of my rebreathers gas for bailout etc. I can use all the gas for what it is intended, that is to stay down as long as necessary. All other gas is carried in external cylinders. The gas in these cylinders is calculated to get me to the next decompression ceiling or exit with nothing but a small stress reserve remaining. I do not run rule of thirds on these cylinders. If diving with a partner and he/she has a worst case failure in that their rebreather and their bailout fails (unlikely), then what I carry will get them out.

I never dive without a bailout cylinder even though I have over 500 hours to date on this unit and more on others.

The Leading Causes of Diving Accidents

The following is offered as a general guide. If you are unable to attain or adhere to these rules you are an accident waiting to happen.

Training

- must be a combination of classroom and practical in-water skills
- any one skill must be done to point of reflex action
- a good training regime should causes a positive behaviour change
- a lack of training is the largest contributor to accidents
- you, as the student, must be ready to learn

Failure to maintain sense of direction

- in caves - not following a continuous guide line
- in wrecks - not using a guide line or being totally familiar with the layout of the wreck site
- in open water - failure to reference and inability to use natural navigation
    - not only is the chance of being lost a threat but not being able to find decompression or stage cylinders is dangerous
- loss at sea on the surface

Gas

- on all technical dives use the 'Rule of Thirds' or applicable adjustments for the environment
- match gas supplies when diving cylinders of different capacities in two-person teams
- be disciplined to breathe normally in adverse situations

- carry more gas than you need. No one has died from too much gas to breathe
- remain within acceptable PO_2 limits. 1.4 bottom mix and 1.6 decompression mix
- keep a safe inert gas narcosis depth (30-40 metres)
- breath correctly to control CO_2 production
- use trimix on dives below 61 metres
- it is recommend to use trimix from 50 metres when diving overhead environments
    - reduce the depth in poor/stressful conditions

Risk
- decompression is not an exact science - be conservative
- consider the risk of all dives
    - distance, depth, complexity, equipment dependency, buddy team, etc should be catered for
- construct an analysis of the risk vs. the satisfaction of the dive
- maintain a proper attitude
- know your personal comfort zone and do not exceed it

Quitting
- divers die frequently because they simply quit trying
    - quitting is one of the responses to stress
- incorporate survival training into your exercise routine
- learn not to quit

Equipment
- the right tool for the right job
- have redundancy of life sustaining equipment
- get rid of the unneeded - be streamlined
- have a safe configuration
- a bad configuration may lead to uncomfort, entanglement or systems failure
- evaluate the required equipment and the best means of configuring it for safety, dependability and convenience

Team Selection
- a dive team should function as one - be a team not a team of individuals
- a dive team protects itself and keeps the team intact
- select team members you trust and that you know of their abilities/experience
- respect all team members capabilities and do not overstretch them through peer pressure

Stress
- stress contributes to most accidents
- it is usually the perception of an event that leads to adverse behaviour changes and then to the accident itself
- practising stress management drills. Be totally familiar with the environment and all emergency procedures. Stress is controllable, learn how

Skills Maintenance
- safety begins and ends with training
- personal training and skills maintenance is as valuable as formal training
- practise a skill on every dive
- periodically set up skill training exercises with your team members
- stay open minded, there is always something to learn

<u>Summary</u>

Your equipment and how you use it is a major factor in your ability to become a good diver. Learn from others, take your time and stay open-minded.

Gas Properties

Introduction

No diving text would be complete without a section on the gases we breathe, their properties and the mathematical laws that govern them. This, coupled with practical applications in the next chapter, will hopefully provide a good basis on which to build knowledge and understanding of the most basic principles of diving.

The Gases

Oxygen

Oxygen is a colourless, odourless, tasteless gas, the most plentiful element in the Earth's crust; its most important compound is water.

Oxygen was discovered about 1772 by a Swedish chemist, Carl Wilhelm Scheele, who obtained it by heating potassium nitrate, mercury(II) oxide, and many other substances. An English chemist, Joseph Priestley independently discovered oxygen in 1774 by the thermal decomposition of mercury(II) oxide and published his findings the same year, three years before Scheele's discovery was published. A French chemist, Antoine Lavoisier, first recognized the gas as an element (1775-80), coined its name, and explained combustion as a union of oxygen with the burning material.

Occurrence, properties, and uses.

The proportion of oxygen by volume in the atmosphere is 21 percent, by weight in seawater 89 percent, and in the Earth's crust 46.6 percent. (Certain recent figures suggest an even higher percentage of oxygen in seawater and in the Earth's crust.)

During respiration, animals and some bacteria take oxygen from the atmosphere and return it as carbon dioxide, whereas by photosynthesis, green plants assimilate carbon dioxide in the presence of sunlight and evolve free oxygen. Almost all free oxygen in the atmosphere is due to photosynthesis. About 3 parts of oxygen by volume dissolve in 100 parts of freshwater at 20° C (68° F), slightly less in seawater. Dissolved oxygen is essential for respiration of fish and other marine life.

Below -183° C (-297° F), oxygen is a pale blue liquid; it becomes solid at about -218° C (-361° F). Gaseous oxygen on Earth and in the lower atmosphere consists almost entirely of molecules of two atoms, O_2. Triatomic oxygen, O_3, called ozone, and monatomic oxygen, O, are more predominant in the upper atmosphere, where ozone shields the Earth from the Sun's ultraviolet radiation. Pure oxygen is 1.1 times heavier than air.

The chief source of commercial oxygen is the atmosphere, from which it is separated by liquefaction and fractional distillation. Of the main components of air, oxygen has the highest boiling point and therefore is less volatile than nitrogen and argon.

Medical applications of oxygen include use in oxygen tents, inhalators, and paediatric incubators. Oxygen-enriched gaseous anaesthetics ensure life support during general anaesthesia. Oxygen is significant in a number of industries that use kilns. Oxygen, in its liquid state, is also used to fuel rocket engines. As divers we use it in a variety of gas mixes to support life and help reduce decompression times.

Atomic number 8
Atomic weight 15.9994
Melting point -218.4° C (-361.1° F)
Boiling point -183.0° C (-297.4° F)
Density (1 atm, 0° C) 1.429 g/l

Nitrogen

Nitrogen is a colourless, odourless, tasteless gas that is the most plentiful element in the Earth's atmosphere, and a constituent of all living matter.

Daniel Rutherford, a medical student in Edinburgh, is usually credited with the discovery of nitrogen (1772) because he was first to publish his findings; but in England the chemists Joseph Priestley and Henry Cavendish and in Sweden the chemist Carl Wilhelm Scheele also discovered nitrogen about the same time. The French chemist Antoine Lavoisier first recognised the gas as an element and named it azote because of its inability to support life

(Greek *zoe,* 'life'). The present name (from 'nitre' plus the suffix '-gen,' thus 'nitre-forming') was coined in 1790 to indicate the presence of the element in nitre (ordinary saltpetre, or potassium nitrate, KNO_3).

Occurrence, properties, and uses.
Among the elements, nitrogen ranks sixth in cosmic abundance. It occurs in the Earth's atmosphere to the extent of 78 percent by volume, or about 75 percent by weight. Free nitrogen also is found in many meteorites; in gases of volcanoes, mines, and some mineral springs; in the sun; and in some stars and nebulae. In combination it is found in the minerals nitre and Chile saltpetre (sodium nitrate, $NaNO_3$); in the atmosphere, rain, soil, and guano as ammonia and ammonium salts; in seawater as ammonium (NH^+_4), nitrite (NO^-_2), and nitrate (NO^-_3) ions; in living organisms as complex organic compounds such as proteins.

Inhaled nitrogen dissolves slightly in the blood and in other body fluids. Under increased pressure, the amount dissolved is greater. The 'Bends', or decompression sickness, is caused mainly by bubbles of nitrogen (and other breathed gases) coming out of solution in the bloodstreams of persons such as divers, aviators and those who work in deep caissons on whom the air pressure has been reduced too quickly.

Commercially, nitrogen is prepared almost entirely by the fractional distillation of liquid air. Nitrogen, which has a lower boiling point (-195.8° C, or -320.4° F) than oxygen (-183.0° C, or -297.4° F), tends to evaporate first. On a small scale, pure nitrogen is made from its compounds; for example, by heating ammonium nitrite, NH_4NO_2, or barium azide, $Ba(N_3)_2$.

Chemically, nitrogen gas is quite inert, especially at ordinary temperatures. Owing to its inertness, nitrogen gas is utilised in the chemical industry as a diluent or as a blanket to exclude oxygen and moisture. The low temperature (and inertness) of nitrogen in the liquid state make it suitable for freeze-drying food and as a refrigerant when transporting perishable commodities. Liquid nitrogen also has proved useful in cryogenic research.

With oxygen, nitrogen forms several oxides, including nitrous oxide, or nitrogen(I) oxide, N_2O; nitric oxide, or nitrogen(II) oxide, NO; and nitrogen dioxide, or nitrogen (IV) oxide, NO_2. Many of the nitrogen oxides are extremely volatile; they are prime sources of pollution in the atmosphere. Nitrous oxide, also known as laughing gas, is sometimes used as an anaesthetic; when inhaled it produces mild hysteria. Nitrix oxide reacts rapidly with oxygen to form nitrogen dioxide, an intermediate in the manufacture of nitric acid and a powerful oxidizing agent utilized in chemical processes and rocket fuels.

Atomic number 7
Atomic weight 14.0067
Melting point -209.86°C (-345.8°F)
Boiling point -195.8°C (-320.4°F)
Density (1 atm, 0° C) 1.2506 g/1

Helium
The second lightest element (only hydrogen being lighter), helium is a colourless, odourless, and tasteless gas that becomes liquid at -268.9° C (-452° F). Only under increased pressure (approximately 25 atmospheres) does helium solidify. Below 2.17 kelvins, the isotope helium-4 has unique properties: it becomes a super fluid (its viscosity nearly vanishes) and its thermal conductivity becomes more than one thousand times greater than that of copper. In this state it is called helium II to distinguish it from normal liquid helium I. Chemically inert, helium does not form compounds, and its molecules consist of single atoms.

Helium was discovered in the gaseous atmosphere surrounding the sun by the French astronomer Pierre Jansen, who detected a bright yellow line in the spectrum of the solar chromo sphere during an eclipse in 1868. This line was initially assumed to represent the element sodium. The same year, Joseph Normal Lockyer, an English astronomer observed a yellow line in the solar spectrum that did not correspond to the known D_1 and D_2 lines of sodium, and so he named it the D_3 line. Lockyer concluded that the D_3 line was caused by an element in the sun that was unknown on Earth; he and the chemist Edward Frankland used the Greek word for sun, *helios,* in naming the element.

The British chemist, Sir William Ramsay, discovered the existence of helium on Earth in 1895. Ramsay obtained a sample of the uranium-bearing mineral cleveite, and upon investigating the gas produced by heating the sample, he found that a unique bright-yellow line in its spectrum matched that of the D_3 line observed in the spectrum of the sun. The new element of helium was thus conclusively identified. In 1903, Ramsay and Frederick Soddy further determined that helium is a product of the spontaneous disintegration of radioactive substances.

Helium constitutes about 23 percent of the mass of the universe and is thus second in abundance to hydrogen in the cosmos. Helium is concentrated in stars, where it is synthesised from hydrogen by nuclear fusion. Although helium occurs in the Earth's atmosphere only to the extent of 1 part in 200,000 (0.0005 percent), and small amounts are found in radioactive minerals, meteoric iron, and mineral springs, great volumes of helium are found as a component (up to 7.6 percent) in natural gases in the United States (especially in Texas, New Mexico, Kansas, Oklahoma, Arizona, and Utah). Smaller supplies have been discovered in Canada and South Africa and in the Sahara Desert. There are also large deposits in Russia.

The helium that is present on Earth is not a primordial component of the Earth but has been generated by radioactive decay.

Helium gas (98.2 percent pure) is isolated from natural gas by liquefying the other components at low temperatures and under high pressures. Absorption of other gases on cooled, activated charcoal yields 99.995 percent pure helium. Helium is used as an inert-gas atmosphere for welding metals such as aluminium; in rocket propulsion (to pressurize fuel tanks, especially those for liquid hydrogen, because only helium is still a gas at liquid-hydrogen temperature); in meteorology (as a lifting gas for instrument-carrying balloons); in cryogenics (as a coolant because liquid helium is the coldest substance); and in high-pressure breathing operations (mixed with oxygen, as in diving and caisson work, especially because of its low solubility in the bloodstream). Meteorites and rocks have been analysed for helium content as a means of dating.

Atomic number 2
Atomic weight 4.0026
melting point none
Boiling point -268.9° C (-452° F)
Density (1 atm, 0° C) 0.1785 g/litre

Carbon Dioxide

(CO_2), a colourless gas having a faint, sharp odour and a sour taste; it is a minor component of the Earth's atmosphere (about 3 volumes in 10,000), formed in combustion of carbon-containing materials, in fermentation, and in respiration of animals and employed by plants in the photosynthesis of carbohydrates.

The presence of the gas in the atmosphere keeps some of the radiant energy received by the Earth from being returned to space, thus producing the so-called 'green house effect'.

Carbon dioxide was recognised as a gas different from others early in the 17th century by a Belgian chemist, Jan Baptist van Helmont, who observed it as a product of both fermentation and combustion. It liquefies upon compression to 75 kilograms per square centimetre (1,071 pounds per square inch) at 31° C (87.4° F) or to 16-24 kg per sq cm (230-345 lb per sq in.) at -23° to -12° C (-10° to 10° F).

By the mid-twentieth century, most carbon dioxide was sold as liquid. If the liquid is allowed to expand to atmospheric pressure, it cools and partially freezes to a snow like solid called dry ice that sublimes (passes directly into vapour without melting) at -78.5° C (-109.3° F) at the pressure of the normal atmosphere.

At ordinary temperatures, carbon dioxide is quite unreactive; above 1,700° C (3,100° F). It partially decomposes into carbon monoxide and oxygen. Hydrogen, or carbon also converts it to carbon monoxide at high temperatures. Ammonia reacts with carbon dioxide under pressure to form ammonium carbamate, then urea, an important component of fertilizers and plastics. Carbon dioxide is slightly soluble in water (1.79 volumes per volume at 0° C at atmospheric pressure, larger amounts at higher pressures), forming a weakly acidic solution. This solution contains the dibasic acid called carbonic acid (H_2CO_3). For this reason, although CO_2 is denser than air, do not fill drysuits with it!

Carbon dioxide is used as a refrigerant, in fire extinguishers, for inflating life rafts and life jackets, blasting coal, foaming rubber and plastics, promoting the growth of plants in greenhouses, immobilizing animals before slaughter, and in carbonated beverages.

Ignited magnesium continues to burn in carbon dioxide, but the gas does not support the combustion of most materials. Prolonged exposure of humans to concentrations of 5 percent carbon dioxide may cause unconsciousness and death.

Carbon Monoxide
Carbon monoxide is a highly toxic, colourless, odourless, flammable gas produced industrially for use in the manufacture of numerous organic and inorganic chemical products. It is also present in the exhaust gases of internal-combustion engines and furnaces as a result of incomplete conversion of carbon or carbon-containing fuels to carbon dioxide. Carbon dioxide can enter divers breathing gases through the air intake on compressors or occur as a result of poor filtration/faulty compresors.

Carbon monoxide's toxicity is a consequence of its absorption by red blood cells in preference to oxygen, thus interfering with the transport of oxygen from the lungs to the tissues, in which it is required. Indication of carbon monoxide poisoning include headache, weakness, dizziness, nausea, fainting and, in severe cases, coma, weak pulse, and respiratory failure. Treatment must be prompt and includes respiratory assistance and the administration of oxygen, often with 5 percent carbon dioxide and sometimes under high pressure.

Carbon monoxide condenses to the liquid at -192° C (-314° F) and it freezes at -199° C (-326° F). It is only slightly soluble in water, and its physical properties closely resemble those of nitrogen.

Argon.
The first of the noble gases to be discovered, argon was named from the Greek word *argos,* 'lazy', because of its chemical inertness. In cosmic abundance, argon ranks approximately twelth among the one hundred or so chemical elements.

Argon is the most plentiful of the noble gases on Earth, comprising 0.934 percent by volume, or 1.288 percent by weight, of the atmosphere. The element is obtained from air by liquefaction and fractional distillation; although the boiling points of argon, oxygen, and nitrogen all lie within a few degrees of each other, efficient processing provides each gas in a purity of more than 99.9 percent.

In diving argon has been used as a drysuit inflation gas as it is denser than air and should help prevent heat loss. However certain naval trials suggest there is little to be gained by its use. Argon should not be breathed as it is exceptionally narcotic.

The Gas Laws

Ideal vs Real Gases
The Real gas law can be derived from the kinetic theory of gases assuming a perfect (ideal) gas. Real gases obey Boyle's law at sufficiently low pressures, although the product of pressure and volume (pv) generally decreases slightly at higher pressures.

An Ideal gas is a gas that conforms, in physical behaviour, to a particular, idealised relation between pressure, volume, and temperature called the General gas law. This law is a generalisation containing both Boyle's law and Charles's law as special cases and states that for a specified quantity of gas, the product of the volume (v) and pressure (p) is proportional to the absolute temperature (t); *i.e.*, in equation form, $pv = kt$, in which k is a constant. Such a relation for a substance is called its 'equation of state' and is sufficient to describe its gross behaviour.

The general gas law can be derived from the kinetic theory of gases and relies on the assumptions that;
1. the gas consists of a large number of molecules, that are in random motion and obey Newton's laws of motion.
2. the volume of the molecules is negligibly small compared with the volume occupied by the gas.
3. no forces act on the molecules except during elastic collisions of negligible duration.

Although no gas has these properties, the behaviour of real gases is described quite closely by the General gas law at sufficiently high temperatures and low pressures, when relatively large distances between molecules and their high speeds overcome any interaction. A gas does not obey the equation when conditions are such that the gas, or any of the component gases in a mixture, is near its condensation point.

For more information on the gas laws and their equations and usefulness, see the following chapter.

Maths: The tricky bit

While it is possible to dive without understanding too many formulae and principles, it is useful to know more about the maths of diving if you intend to push the limits. In fact it is virtually impossible to do some dives without a sound realisation of how to 'crunch the numbers'. Indeed, a thorough knowledge of such basics as the pressure laws is vital for safe mixed gas and rebreather diving.

The following is offered as a practical guide for the useful bits and a brief overview of the 'not-so-useful'.

Pressure.

Pressure is the amount of force applied per unit area. In diving, units commonly used for pressure are pounds per square inch (psi or lb/in^2), kilograms per square centimetre (kg/cm^2), bars, and atmospheres (atm). Approximately one atmosphere (dependant on weather conditions) is the amount of pressure or force exerted on all bodies or structures by the earth's atmosphere. At sea level, atmospheric pressure is equal to 14.7 psi, 1.03 kg/cm^2, 1.013 BAR, or 1 atmosphere. At higher elevations, the atmospheric pressure is less.

Pressure Equivalents

1 atm = 1.01325 bar = 10.337 metres (fw) = 33.9139 feet (fw) = 33.066 feet(sw)
1 bar = 0.986923 atm = 10.2018 metres (fw) = 33.4704 feet (fw) = 32.6336 feet(sw)

Hydrostatic pressure is the force resulting from the weight of water (or any fluid) acting upon a body or object immersed in water. Like atmospheric pressure, it is equal in all directions at a specific level or depth. The pressure increases as the diver descends at a rate of 1 kg/cm^2 per 9.75 metres of descent in sea water (sw) and 1 kg/cm^2 per 10 metres of descent in fresh water (fw).

The term *gauge pressure* is often used to express values such as cylinder pressure. For example, cylinder pressure is expressed in terms of units above atmospheric pressure. Cylinder pressure is also expressed in terms of bars (gauge). Some divers denote gauge pressures as 'bar' (lower case letters).

Absolute pressure exerted on a submerged body is the sum of atmospheric pressure and hydrostatic pressure. It is measured in pounds per square inch absolute (psia), bars absolute, kilograms per square centimetre (kg/cm^2 absolute), atmospheres absolute (ata). Some divers prefer to use the term BAR (upper case letters) to denote absolute pressure. 'Ambient pressure' is a synonym for absolute pressure and normally refers to the pressure surrounding or encompassing the body or object at the surface.

In diving, pressure values are often expressed in approximations. For example, even though one atmosphere is equal to 1.01325 bars, the terms are often used interchangeably (i.e., 1 atm = 1 bar). Divers often express equivalence between 33 feet of sea water (fsw) and 10 metres of sea water (msw) when 10 metres actually equals 32.81 fsw. These minor variations are of little consequence in diving because of the accuracy variables associated with depth and pressure measuring instruments used in diving.

Approximate pressure equivalents commonly used in diving

1 bar = 1 atm = 33 fsw = 10 metres = 14.7 psi

'Gauge pressure' refers to the difference between the pressure being measured and the atmospheric pressure. Most gauges are calibrated to read 'zero' at normal atmospheric pressure. Gauge pressure is converted to absolute pressure by adding 1.03 kg/cm^2.

For every 10 metres that the diver descends in sea water, there is a pressure increase of 1 atm (14.7 psi, 1 bar, or 1 kg/cm^2). Thus, at 99 fsw (30 msw), the absolute pressure is equal to four atmospheres (58.8 psia, 4 bar, or 4 kg/cm^2 absolute).

Absolute pressure in atmospheres or bars at a given depth may be determined using the following formula:

$$P_{(ata)} = \frac{D_{(fsw)}}{33_{fsw}} + 1 \quad or \quad P_{(bar)} = \frac{D_{(msw)}}{10_{msw}} + 1$$

where P is pressure and D is depth.

Usefulness. In a mixture of gases, the proportion of the total pressure contributed by a single gas in the mixture is called '*partial pressure*'. The partial pressure contributed by a single gas is in direct proportion to its percentage of the total volume of the mixture. The formulae associated with this principle are some of the most important to us as technical divers and will be discussed later in detail

---

Boyle's Law
This states that if the temperature of a fixed mass of gas is kept constant, the relationship between the volume and pressure will vary in such a way that the product of the pressure and volume remains constant. Mathematically,

$$pV = K$$

where p is absolute pressure, V is volume, and K is a constant. The temperature and mass are constant. Thus, at a constant temperature and mass the volume of a gas is inversely proportional to the pressure exerted on that gas. Consequently, when the pressure is doubled, the volume is reduced to one-half of the original volume. Boyle's Law may also be written:

$$P_1V_1 = P_2V_2.$$

To illustrate Boyle's Law, let us assume that a closed flexible container of air (i.e. rubber balloon) with a volume of 1 cf (28 l) at the surface is submerged to a depth of 33 fsw (10 msw). Using the above formula,

$$P_1V_1 = P_2V_2$$
$$1ata \ x \ 1cf = 2 \ ata \ x \ V_2$$
$$(1ata \ x \ 1cf) \div V_2$$
$$.5 \ cf = V_2$$

$$P_1V_1 = P_2V_2$$
$$1 \ bar \ x \ 28 \ \ l = 2 \ bar \ x \ V_2$$
$$(1 \ barx \ 28l) \div 2 \ bar = V_2$$
$$14 \ \ l = V_2$$

where P_1 is atmospheric pressure, V_1 is the volume at P_1 or 1 cf (28 l), P_2 is the pressure at 33 fsw (10 msw) in atmospheres, and V_2 is the volume at 33 fsw (10 msw). Note that the volume is changed by 50%.

Usefulness. In practical use you notice this most if you fill a lift bag or surface market buoy at two different depths. If you fill it at 10 metres (33ft) with one breath it may just reach the surface and be slightly inflated. If you fill it at 30 metres (100ft) with the same breath, at the surface it will be full. This is the reverse effect of that described above. So the effect is useful to note but the maths only really becomes useful when you want to fill a lifting bag and you need to know how much air to use. You need other formulae for this, these will be noted later.

Guy-Lussac's Law
States that the pressure of a gas at a constant volume is directly proportional to the absolute temperature. Algebraically:

$$\frac{P_1}{T_1} = \frac{P_2}{T_2}$$

where P and T are absolute measurements of pressure and temperature.

Temperature Conversion

$$°C = (°F - 32)\, x\, \frac{5}{9} \qquad °F = \left(\frac{9}{5}\, x\, °C\right) + 32$$

Charles' Law

Charle's law states that if the pressure of a fixed mass of gas is kept constant, the volume of the gas will vary directly with the absolute temperature. Conversely, if the volume is restrained in a rigid container (such as a scuba air cylinder), the pressure will vary directly with the absolute temperature. Algebraically:

$$PV = RT$$

where P is absolute pressure, V is volume, T is absolute temperature and R is a universal constant for all gases.

Usefulness. Neither of the above two are very practical but the phenomena best represents its self when cylinders are filled with hot gas and then they cool down and the pressure drops.

Daltons Law

Units for the pressure equations.

FO_2 or the fraction of oxygen. This is the percentage of oxygen in the mixture and in all the pressure equations is converted to a decimal fraction.

Example. 21% = 0.21.

P or absolute pressure at depth. (See the previous page for metric and US methods).

Example. 30 metres = (30÷ 10) +1 = 4 bar.

$P0_2$ or the partial pressure of oxygen in the mixture.

The three equations associated with Dalton's Law can be summarised as:

PO_2

<u>Equation 1.</u>

$$PO_2 = FO_2\ x\ P$$

Example:

What is the partial pressure of oxygen in EAN32 at 30 metres (4 ata)?

Answer: 1.28 bar

Usefulness. Equation 1 is used to find if a mix is safe to use at a given depth.

FO_2
Equation 2.

$$FO_{2(maximum)} = \frac{pO_{2(maximum)}}{\left(\frac{D_{(fsw)}}{33}+1\right)} \quad \text{or} \quad FO_{2(maximum)} = \frac{pO_{2(maximum)}}{\left(\frac{D_{(msw)}}{10}+1\right)}$$

It is important that the first decimal place of the answer is noted and will be used in the EAD formulae to be explained later. Example: If the answer is 0.362, then take 36.2% into the EAD formulae.

Example:
What is the '*best mix*' to use with a pO_2 of 1.45 bar on a dive to 30 metres?

$$FO_{2(maximum)} = \frac{1.45\ ata}{\left(\frac{99_{(fsw)}}{33}+1\right)} \quad \text{or} \quad FO_{2(maximum)} = \frac{1.45\ \text{bar}}{\left(\frac{30_{(msw)}}{10}+1\right)}$$

Answer : 0.362 or 36.2%

Usefulness. Used to determine the best mix to use on a dive at the chosen (safe) pO_2.

P **'Absolute Pressure' at depth**
Equation 3.

$$MOD = \left[\left(\frac{pO2}{fO2}\right)-1\right]33 \quad \text{or} \quad MOD = \left[\left(\frac{pO2}{fO2}\right)-1\right]10$$

Example:
What is the absolute maximum operating depth that EAN40 could be used on a dive?

$$MOD = \left[\left(\frac{1.6}{0.40}\right)-1\right]33 \quad \text{or} \quad MOD = \left[\left(\frac{1.6}{0.40}\right)-1\right]10$$

Answer: 30 metres or 99ft.

Usefulness. Equation 3 is more often used to determine the TOD or 'target operating depth' of the mixture or that depth at which the planned pO_2 will be experienced. The MOD or 'maximum operating depth' is then also calculated and noted as the maximum excursion depth in the event of an emergency. 1.6 will normally be taken as the MOD PO_2. 1.5 being the 'recommended' or TOD pO_2.

These are the "Big 3". **If you forget all else - remember these.**

All three of the pressure equations above can be generated using the pressure "T". Simply cover the item you are trying to find and the remaining two are either multiplied together (if on the same row) or divided (if above and below).

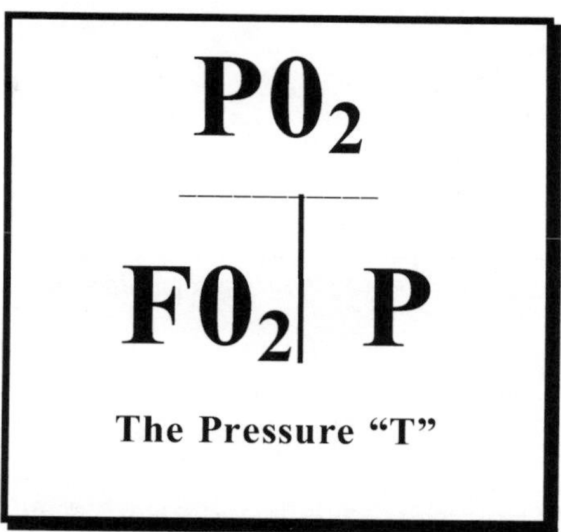

The Pressure "T"

Henry's Law.
Gas absorption is governed by *Henry's Law*, that states that the amount of a gas that will be dissolved in a liquid at a given temperature is almost directly proportional to the partial pressure of that gas. The term "amount" refers to the number of molecules or mass of the gas. When gas is in solution, its actual volume is negligible and there is no volumetric increase in the amount of liquid. Henry's Law simply expresses the effect of partial pressure on the amount of gas that will dissolve in a liquid. Solubility is also dependent on temperature and the type of liquid. For example, the solubility of nitrogen in oil or fat is about five times its solubility in water at the same pressure. The lower the temperature, the higher the solubility. This explains why a warm bottle of carbonated beverage forms bubbles more actively than a cold one.

Gas diffusion refers to the intermingling of gas molecules. In diving, Henry's and Dalton's Laws are considered when dealing with the diffusion of gas in the human body under pressure. The difference between the partial pressure (or tension) of a gas inside of a liquid (or container) and its outside partial pressure will cause the gas to diffuse in or out of the liquid and control the rate of diffusion. This pressure differential is frequently called the gradient. If a gas-free liquid is exposed to a gas, the inward gradient is high and the rate at which gas molecules will migrate into the liquid is high. As the gas tension in the liquid increases, the rate of diffusion decreases and eventually reaches an equilibrium, where the gas tensions in the liquid and outside the liquid are equal. The liquid is then considered saturated for a given pressure and gas. The subjects of gas solubility and diffusion are important in the study of decompression sickness and nitrogen narcosis.

Usefulness. Good if you are into decompression theory. Practically, not much use.

Equivalent Air Depth
EAD is used when we want to turn an air table into a nitrox table. If we are using a gas with more oxygen hence less nitrogen (nitrox) than there would be in air (21/79) at a given depth, then it recalculates at what shallower air depth the same partial pressure of nitrogen would be found.

Example:
If we were using a nitrox of 32% oxygen (68% nitrogen), the PN_2 at 40 metres would be 3.4. The same PN_2 using air is found at 33 metres. Therefore we can use a 33 metre air table when diving to 40 metres.

EAD can be calculated using the formula:

$$EAD_{(fsw)} = \left[\frac{(FN_2)(D+33)}{0.79}\right] - 33 \quad \text{or} \quad EAD_{(msw)} = \left[\frac{(FN_2)(D+10)}{0.79}\right] - 10$$

Where Fn_2 is the decimal fraction of nitrogen in the mixture and D is the depth in feet or metres of sea water. Let's assume that your analysation reveals that the mixture contains only 40% oxygen and you are planning to dive to a maximum depth of 100 feet/30 metres. Entering the value of .60 for the fraction of nitrogen:

You can now substitute the new values for depth and nitrogen fraction into the *EAD* formula:

$$EAD = \left[\frac{(0.60)(99+33)}{0.79}\right] - 33 \quad \text{or} \quad EAD(msw) = \left[\frac{(0.60)(30+10)}{0.79}\right] - 10$$

The equivalent air depth is calculated at 20.4 metres (67 feet). You would use a 21 metres (70 feet) schedule on the air table.

When analysed, the final mix must be +/- 1% of the planned value before recalculation of the EAD **MUST** take place.

Repetitive Diving and EAD

If the depth of the repetitive dive when calculated using EAD, is between two increments, use the ***shallower*** figure when calculating residual nitrogen time (this gives a greater RNT and is thus safer).

Oxygen Toxicity Maths

Both CNS (Acute) and Pulmonary (Whole Body) oxygen toxicity calculations are quite simple with a few basic rules. The physiology of oxygen toxicity is covered in detail in later sections.

Rules

- use the maximum PO_2 attained on the dive to calculate the CNS and OTU load for that gas and time.
- calculate additional loads for each gas switch
- if you use a single gas during the whole dive, only calculate the oxygen load for the decompression bottom time (BT). Calculating the oxygen load for a decreasing PO_2 ascent is not necessary.
- with multiple dives assume the OTU's just add together and use the REPEX table in Appendix A for multi-day missions.
- with multiple dives from a CNS standpoint assume the load decreases by one half every 90 minutes. Hence if a dive finishes with 100% CNS then 90 minutes later it is at 50% as a preload for the next dive and must be added to the next dives CNS load to give the total. Oxygen is assumed to have a 90 minute half-time and finer surface interval increments can be extrapolated.
- use 80% as a maximum recreational CNS limit. See decompression chapter for CNS management information.

After using Dalton's law to calculate the PO_2's at the relevant depths/gas switches on a dive simply use the CNS and OTU/minute table in Appendix A to calculate the total oxygen loads.

Archimedes Principle

This is the physical law of buoyancy, discovered by the ancient Greek mathematician and inventor Archimedes. The law stares that "any body completely or partially submerged in a fluid (gas or liquid) at rest is acted upon by an upward, or buoyant, force the magnitude of which is equal to the weight of the fluid displaced by the body. The volume of displaced fluid is equivalent to the volume of an object fully immersed in a fluid or to that fraction of the volume below the surface for an object partially submerged in a liquid. The weight of the displaced portion of the fluid is equivalent to the magnitude of the buoyant force. The buoyant force on a body floating in a liquid or gas is also equivalent in magnitude to the weight of the floating object and is opposite in direction; the object neither rises nor sinks".

A ship that is launched sinks into the ocean until the weight of the water it displaces is just equal to its own weight. As the ship is loaded, it sinks deeper, displacing more water, and so the magnitude of the buoyant force continuously matches the weight of the ship and its cargo.

Buoyancy is caused by ane increase in fluid pressure at increasingly greater depths. The pressure on a submerged object, therefore, is greater on the parts more deeply submerged, and the buoyant force is always upward, or opposite to the gravitational force; it is the net effect of all the forces exerted on the object by the fluid pressure.

Lead is so dense that its weight submerged is almost the same as in air. Aluminium on the other hand loses 38% of its weight in water. A diver loses nearly 100% of his/her weight because the body's density is nearly the same as that of water.

Usefulness
This is the one to use for lifting submerged objects. It allows us to calculate the weight of an object in water and thereby the lift required to raise it.

---

1. First calculate the weight of the object in air:

Weight in air (*Wo*) equals the density[25] (*po*) multiplied by the volume (*Vo*).

Let's assume we have a concrete block measuring 40 x 30 x 20 cm.

$$Wo = Po \times Vo$$

$$Po = 2430kg/m^3$$

$$Vo = \frac{40 \times 30 \times 20}{10^6} = 0.024m^3$$

$$Wo = 2403 \times 0.024 = 57.67kg$$

---

2. Next calculate the weight of the object in water. To do this subtract the weight of the volume of water it displaces from its weight in air. This is expressed as: weight submerged (*Wsub*) = volume of the object (*Vo*) multiplied by the difference between the density of the object (*po*) and the density of water (*pw*). As an equation:

$$Wsub = Vo \times (po - pw)$$

$$Wsub = 0.024 \times (2303 - 1026) = 30.64kg$$

($1026kg/m^3$ is the density of sea water)

Therefore, this submerged object weighs 30.64kg. To lift it will take at least 30.64kg of lift.

---

3. Next you need to calculate the volume of gas required to lift an object. Normally, lifting bags are rated by the weight they lift so this process is fairly simple. However, if you have an open container you are using to lift with, you may need to know how much gas is required.

One cubic metre of air will lift 1026kg. Hence one litre of air will lift approximately 1 kg at surface pressure. If the object was at 10 metres, then the volume of lifting air would need to be doubled (and so on as the depth increases as per Boyle's Law.). This final part becomes useful when you are trying to lift items using a SCUBA cylinder as an air source. This allows you to calculate how large the cylinder must be.

Example
An object requires 30.64kg of lift to raise it. It is in 60 metres of water. The lifting gas volume will be: 30.64 litres multiplied by the absolute pressure at 60 metres (7 Bar).

$$30.64x7 = 214.48 \text{ litres}$$

A 10 SCUBA filled to 50 bar has a free gas volume of $10x50 = 500$ litres

As the object only requires only 30.64kg this is more than enough.

---

[25] Specific gravity table is in Appendix B

Gas Management

As technical divers we primarily use what is know as the 'Rule of Thirds'" for calculating our gas requirements. For dives involving any decompression or any other form of overhead environment, this means we use 1/3rd going in 1/3rd coming out and we keep 1/3rd in reserve. Decompression and stage cylinders have a slightly modified version of this rule.

In cave diving we are not usually concerned with calculating the descent time and most gas calculations are done assuming the whole entrance swim is at depth. In deep open water dives it is vital we calculate the descent gas used separately, especially if different ('travel') gases are to be used on the descent.

This rule is only altered where excessive current or other environmental/physical hazards may speed up an entry or exit. With diving involving independent main cylinders (such as side-mounting) maintaining the 'Rule of Thirds' is achieved by first breathing one cylinder down to 2/3rd's of it's remaining pressure and then switching to the other cylinder. The process is repeated every third. After breathing each down by 1/3rd (leaving 1/3rd for the exit plus 1/3rd reserve) the diver will 'turn' the dive.

When rebreather diving the volume of gas carried in the bailout cylinder is calculated to be enough to exit on/swim up to the next gas switch plus a small stress reserve of approximately 15%.

In the metric system we reference our cylinders by the amount of water they can hold, known as the 'water capacity' (WC). This is not the volume of compressed gas in the cylinder. To find out the gas volume in the cylinder we multiply the WC by the fill pressure to give us the total gas volume. In the US system, cylinders are referenced by the total volume of gas they hold. This is measured in cubic feet (cu ft or ft^3). The cubic feet of gas a cylinder holds is also a measure of its fill pressure. Hence, a 72 cu ft cylinder only holds 72 cu ft at it's working pressure.

As a measurement 1 cu ft equals approximately 28 litres of gas. Armed with this and the other conversions in Appendix A, it is relatively simple to modify the following equations for use with the US system.

Terminology

Surface Air Consumption (SAC rate).
This is the total volume of gas we breathe per minute at surface pressure in litres or cubic feet

Respiratory Minute Volume **(RMV).**
The total volume of gas we breathe at a given depth. This is the SAC rate multiplied by the depth pressure in bar (absolute pressure).

Decompression Bottom Time.
Time from leaving surface to leaving the bottom.

Turn Point.
The point on the dive at which either one third of the gas is used or (in open water) one half of the decompression bottom time is reached.

Descent Time.
Time from leaving the surface to arriving on the bottom (open water).

To calculate our overall gas requirement we must first calculate our gas usage both at work and at rest. As new technical divers we should use an average of these two as our 'bottom mix' (SAC) rate. This can be modified with experience. The 'at rest' SAC rate can also be assumed to be our decompression gas (shallow water) breathing rate.

Using the following table you can calculate your SAC rate.

Surface Air Consumption in Free Litres For a Given Pressure of 10 bar

	Cylinder size in litres								
Depth	**1**	**3**	**7**	**10**	**12**	**15**	**18**	**20**	**24**
3	8	23	54	77	92	115	138	154	185
6	6	19	44	63	75	94	113	125	150
9	5	16	37	53	63	79	95	105	126
12	5	14	32	45	55	68	82	91	109
15	4	12	28	40	48	60	72	80	96
18	4	11	25	36	43	54	64	71	86
21	3	10	23	32	39	48	58	65	77
24	3	9	21	29	35	44	53	59	71
27	3	8	19	27	32	41	49	54	65
30	3	8	18	25	30	38	45	50	60
33	2	7	16	23	28	35	42	47	56
36	2	7	15	22	26	33	39	43	52
39	2	6	14	20	24	31	37	41	49
42	2	6	13	19	23	29	35	38	46
45	2	5	13	18	22	27	33	36	44
48	2	5	12	17	21	26	31	34	41
51	2	5	11	16	20	25	30	33	39

To use the table

1. Descend to a depth. Note how long it takes to use 10 bar at that depth.
2. Locate cylinder size and move down depth column to the test dive depth.
3. The result is free litres used on that dive, corrected back to surface pressure for the total time of the test.
4. Divide the number in the table by the time taken in minutes and decimals of a minute. This is the SAC per minute.

Example

1. Using twin 10's (20 litres) at 30 metres and breathing 10 bar would use 50 free litres of gas
2. Assume this took 2 minutes 30 seconds or 2.5 minutes
3. 50 divided by 2.5 = 20 litres per minute SAC

N.B With standard 232 bar cylinders this dive would not be possible.

Gas Calculation Definition Chart

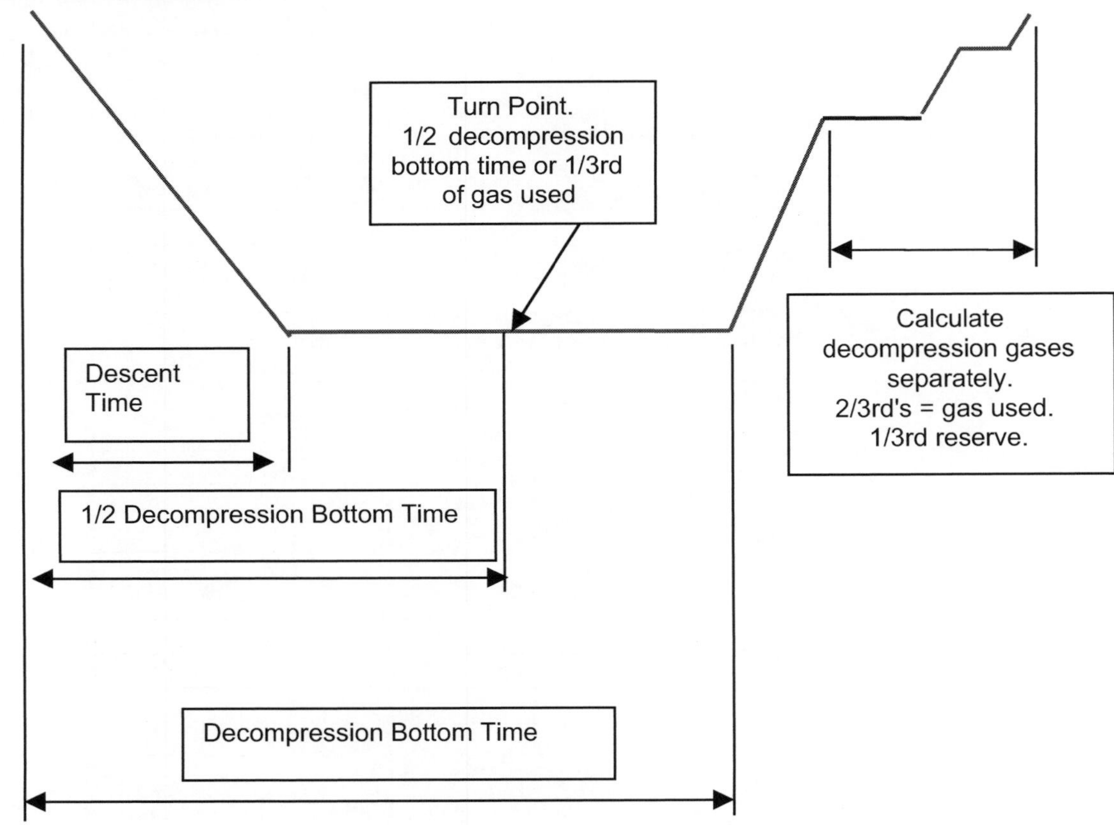

Summary

1. Know your SAC at a mean (half way between work and rest) rate
2. If a single gas is used for bottom and decompression gas, calculate decompression separately and add to the bottom gas requirement to give total volume.
3. If a separate gas cylinder is to be used for decompression, calculate the amount of gas required to do the decompression and multiply it by 1.3.
4. Either turn the dive on 1/3rd gas used or 1/2 of the decompression bottom time, whichever is sooner.

Stage Cylinder Calculations

Stage cylinders are defined as an additional gas supply which is required to extend a penetration or the bottom time of any dive. The normal rule applied is that one half (-10 bar) of the gas is breathed on the way in and then the cylinder ceases to be used. The minus 10 bar rule allows for a small stress reserve and to allow regulator operation at low pressures. The dive is then continued on the main cylinders to the 1/3rd used point. On returning to the stage (that is again breathed to the exit) the main gas cylinders still have a minimum of 1/3rd remaining as a reserve.

Stage rules may again modify with the environment.

Below is a simple table for calculating gas requirements for bottom mix.

Gas management Calculations. **This table is found again in the Tables appendix.**

	To Calculate	Example	Formulae
A	Depth	50m	
B	Depth pressure	6 bar	*A/10+1*
C	1/2 depth	25m	*A/2*
D	1/2 depth pressure	3.5 bar	*C/10+1*
E	Descent rate	20m/min	
F	Descent time	2.5 mins	*A/E*
G	SAC	20l/min	*From table*
H	Gas used on descent	175 litres	*DxFxG*
I	Planned Deco. bottom time	30 mins	
J	1/2 planned time minus descent time	12.5 mins	*I/2 – F*
K	Gas used on bottom	1500 litres	*BxGxJ*
L	Descent gas + bottom gas	1675 litres	*H+K*
M	L = 1/3rd. Hence Total =	5025 litres	*Lx3*
N	Cylinder size	20 litres	
O	Fill pressure	251.25 bar	*M/N*

Gas Matching

So having calculated our individual gas requirements, what happens if we dive with other people? Should we be concerned about their gas use? What if a situation arose whereby we needed to share gas? In open water this may not be too much of a problem as a direct ascent to the surface may be possible, but in an overhead environment this is definitely not possible. Now we could have a situation where two divers need to do a long sharing exit.

The real problem arises when two divers have widely different breathing rates or cylinder sizes. It is not necessary to match gas in multiple person teams (more than 2).

Let's look at this from first principles. For simplicity lets assume the breathing rate quoted is the breathing rate at depth (although this is obviously low in the example). **RMV at depth should be used if calculating from first principles although SAC rate or RMV can be used in the correction equation.**

Diver 1 (D1) has a 10L cylinder filled to 200 bar and has a breathing rate of 10L/min.

Diver 2 (D2) has a 12L cylinder filled to 230 bar and has a breathing rate of 15L/min.

If both divers penetrate until 1/3rd of their gas supply is gone, how many minutes will each have travelled into the cave?

D1 uses 66.67 bar (200÷3) on the swim in, which is 1/3rd of their gas.

D2 uses 76.67 bar (230÷3) on the swim in which is 1/3rd of their gas.

With a 10L cylinder D1 uses 66.67 x 10 = 666.7L of gas swimming in. If his breathing rate is 10L/min then he can swim in for **66.67 minutes** (666.7÷10).

With a 12L cylinder D2 uses 76.67 x 12 = 920.04L of gas swimming in. If his breathing rate is 15L/min then he can swim in for **61.33 minutes** (920.04÷15).

D2 will turn the dive first at 61.33 minutes. Therefore even though D2 has bigger cylinders and a higher fill pressure, he will turn first. **How much gas will D1 have left when D2 turns the dive?**

D1 will have penetrated for 61.3 minutes (D2's time). He will have used 61.33 minutes x 10L/min of gas = 613.3L of gas.

1. Given that **D1** has a 10L cylinder, the pressure used is 613.3L÷10L = 61.33 bar. As he started with 200 bar, he now has **138.67 bar left** (200-61.33).

What happens if D2 (with the higher breathing rate) now needs to share with D1 at this point (61.33 minutes into the dive)?

The exit is now at the combined breathing rate of 25L/min (10L + 15L) for the in penetration time of 61.33 minutes. This equals 25L x 61.33 minutes = 1533.25L used on the exit. This is now on a 10L cylinder (D1's). So to find the pressure used on the exit we divide 1533.25 by the cylinder size (10L). **Hence, 153.3 bar is needed for the exit**.

As seen at 1. above, D1 only has 138.67 bar left when he turns with D2. For both of them to exit at D2's time, will mean that they run out of gas during the exit.

So how do we match gas? The basic formula is:

$$\frac{\mathbf{D1+D2}}{\mathbf{D1+D1+D2}} = \textbf{the correction to apply to D1's gas supply}$$

This correction factor is multiplied by D1's cylinder pressure to calculate at what pressure D1 should turn the dive in order that both of them may make a safe exit in an emergency.

Therefore: $$\frac{\mathbf{10+15}}{\mathbf{10+10+15}} = \mathbf{0.714}$$

Now multiply D1's cylinder pressure by 0.714 = 200 x 0.714 = **142.8bar at the turn**.

So, if D1 turns at 142.8 bar now, the new penetration time for the team will be:

200-142.8 = 57.2 bar used by D1.

Therefore the new penetration time is 57.2 bar x 10L (cylinder size) = 572 litres of gas used during the swim in. If D1's breathing rate is 10L/min, the new in time is 572÷10 = **57.2minutes**.

So D1 has 142.8 bar left (the corrected turn point). Now D1 and D2 breathe off his cylinder for the return trip (57.2 minutes).

Total litres used is (10 + 15) x 57.2 = 1430 litres of gas.

In a 10 Litre cylinder this means the **pressure used is 1430÷10 = 143 bar.**

As D1 had 142.8 bar at the turn, they will run out right at the exit. This obviously is slightly impractical as stress has not been catered for or a slowed exit due to sharing, current etc. This correction equation calculates the absolute minimum. Be conservative, allow at least an additional 15%.

To double check, now run the correction equation substituting D1's numbers with D2's. If the pressure calculated is higher than in the first instance, then it is D2 who will turn the dive first at the new calculated pressure.

The positive thing about the correction factor equation is it can be used with SAC rate in min/min, bar/minute, cu ft/min or psi/min. The end result is the same. This equation can be put into a simple spreadsheet to simplify the maths. (See Appendix A for a SAC rate correction chart).

Gas mixing and handling

Introduction

Detailed training on how to mix and handle gas should be undertaken as part of a structured course. This chapter is not intended to provide that. Whilst 'home brewing' has been (and still) is carried out by a minority of the public, it is to be avoided wherever possible. There have been numerous frightening accidents, the results of which are sometimes horrific and totally avoidable. In the case of oxygen, the adage 'a little knowledge is a dangerous thing' certainly rings true. Expedition-level diving often requires gas mixing and oxygen cleaning to be undertaken in remote locations. Divers wishing to undertake such projects should go on a sanctioned course and in addition gain some practical experience (preferably with a dive centre) prior to undertaking gas handling in earnest.

Having been involved in gas handling for some years, in well equipped dive centres and 'in the field', this chapter is designed to dispel some of the common myths about gas handling and hopefully guide the reader to following a proper course of education before taking on the task.

Oxygen

We have already looked at the properties of oxygen in some detail in relation to physiology and physics. Oxygen itself is will not spontaneously ignite, at least not at pressures used in normal SCUBA diving. It will, however, rapidly assist combustion. There are basically three levels of oxygen combustion:

Oxidation

This is evident with steel and aluminium cylinders and is basically slow corrosion of surface metal. Most metals will corrode to some extent in an oxygen-enriched atmosphere. This does not mean that the gas has to be high in oxygen content. In fact, practical tests on both aluminium and steel cylinders at varying oxygen contents have shown no appreciable difference in corrosion at the differing oxygen percentages.

Oxygen fires

Oxygen supports fires. Once the oxygen is exhausted the fire is extinguished (try putting a lighted candle under a glass). If you supply an external source of oxygen the fire will continue. It is not the oxygen actually burning, it is the fuel.

Oxygen explosions

An explosion is just a rapid burning of a fuel. With oxygen most things can become a fuel. Some things burn more readily than others. An oxygen explosion is a rapid, often devastating event. Oxygen explosions can be extremely localised (in the case of one hyperbaric technician, an explosion in an oxygen line just left him without trousers but otherwise unscathed). Often the effects are more dramatic and fires follow.

The Fire Triangle

At normal SCUBA pressures three things have to be present for an oxygen fire to take place. Oxygen at some percentage must be present, a fuel (normally some form of hydrocarbon) must be present and a source of ignition (usually in the form of heat). Without all three the fire cannot occur. Any one of the three occurring in abundance increases the risk.

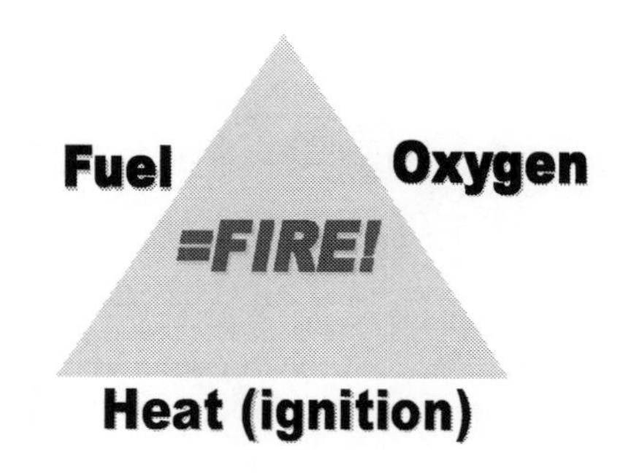

In the past, divers have filled cylinders and used valves with varying levels and pressures of oxygen without proper cleaning and have fortunately 'got away with it', often because one of the three conditions was not met in sufficient quantity. Unfortunately, as time passes equipment not cleaned becomes more and more contaminated as hydrocarbons build up. Users become lulled in to a false sense of security as nothing may have happened for years. Any gas facility technician will state that regular cleaning and maintenance of pipe work etc. is a must. Maintenance, often not being a diver's watchword and the unfortunate ethic of 'if it ain't broke, don't fix it' can lead to disaster.

Mixing Precautions

The rapid addition of oxygen causes turbulent flow and greatly accelerated gas temperatures that can result in fires. If the temperature is great enough, oxygen will react with almost any substance.

Always Open Oxygen Valves Slowly.

Nitrogen and oxygen are the main components of air. These two gasses have different molecular weights and may not mix immediately when filling. Using normal filling techniques is not necessary to 'tumble' or roll the cylinders to help mixing after filling, although high oxygen mixes may take longer to mix and tumbling can speed the process. Leaving mixes standing will allow them time to mix. In extreme cases, temporary gas 'layering' may occur where gases are non-uniformly mixed in the cylinder. This will result in varying oxygen concentrations during analysis. This effect is more pronounced when adding oxygen to cylinders with relatively high initial pressures. Once a gas is homogenously mixed it will not separate.

If in doubt allow time to mix and always analyse immediately prior to diving.

Oxygen Cleaning

Oxygen cleaning guidelines have been laid down by the technical training agencies and other regulatory bodies in various countries[26]. The method of cleaning is fairly standard as is the period between inspection and cleaning. Generally speaking, equipment is inspected once a year and cleaned if contamination is found. There is also a mandatory clean every two of years or in the case of cylinders when a hydrostatic test is due.

Equipment Requiring Cleaning

Although this is still under discussion in some countries, broadly speaking any item of equipment that is exposed to over 40% oxygen will require oxygen cleaning. ,In addition to this, all mechanical parts of the system must be suitable for use with oxygen. This area is a little 'grey' as just about everything will burn in oxygen. However, tests have been conducted that show certain plastics and metals are less prone to ignition than others at certain pressures and temperatures. These materials are then graded by their 'oxygen compatibility'.

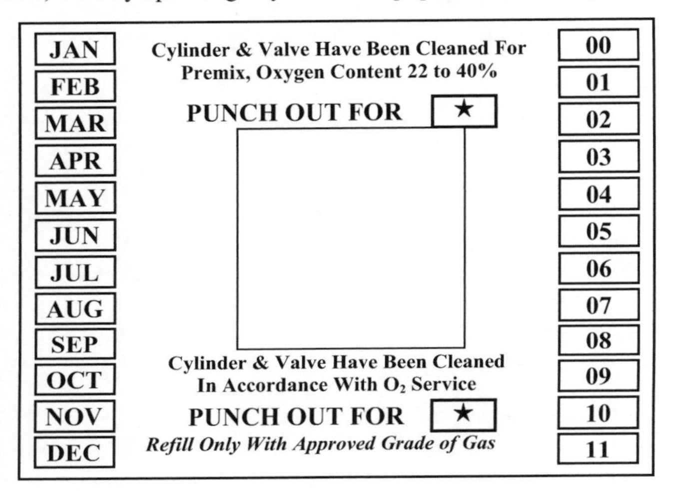

The 40% Rule

The 40% Rule is endorsed by OSHA, NOAA and most SCUBA training agencies. As long as the oxygen content of the breathing mixture entering the cylinder is 40% or less, then all SCUBA equipment can be used without oxygen cleaning.

Note: Usually during partial pressure mixing, pure oxygen is added to the cylinder at some stage; therefore all components must be in oxygen service.

Compatible materials found in SCUBA systems for use with Oxygen

Plastic/rubbers/greases

Nylon	Often used in valve seats
PTFE (low oil content)	Commonly known as thread tape
Pure rubber	Some diaphragms
Viton (used in 'O' rings)	A good material but wears easily.
Nitrile (used in 'O' rings).	Nitrile has been the standard 'O' ring component for many years with SCUBA equipment. In the early days of nitrox it was felt that this was not suitable and viton should be used. Eventually, additional tests were completed and nitrile was found to be sufficiently oxygen compatible for SCUBA pressures and temperatures. It is a better material and less prone to cracking in elevated oxygen percentages.
Halo-carbon grease	The preferred lubricant as opposed to silicone which is a hydro-carbon

[26] OSHA, NOAA. In The UK the British Standards Institute

Metals

High-grade stainless steel (316 grade)	Used in compressor pipe work and some regulator parts
Brass	Regulator bodies
Tungham	Used in compressor pipe work
Cupra nickel	Used in compressor pipe work

Cleaning Methods

There are many cleaning solutions on the market today that are hazardous, both physiologically and environmentally. If you are unsure about a solvent, check with the manufacturer. Certain materials may also be damaged by cleaning solutions. If in doubt, don't use the solution.

Solvents are good for different things. Some solvents will help remove greases while others prevent particle agglomeration and/or reduce the surface tension of the equipment on which you are working. Choose which solvent will do the job best for you. If you have any questions about the capabilities of a cleaning solution contact the manufacturer.

The Cleaning Process

The cleaning process is an important step to reducing fuels that exist within our fire triangle. As blenders, we must understand that it is impossible to remove all of the fuels within a system. Remember that even stainless steel will burn if it is hot enough. We need to know what actually exists that can act as fuel. Earlier, we mentioned that hydrocarbons make excellent fuels.

What exactly are hydrocarbons? Most everything is constructed of hydrocarbons - even many of the cleaning solutions that we use to remove hydrocarbons are made of hydrocarbons! What is very irritating about hydrocarbons is that many of them are difficult to see. As service technicians, we need to identify and remove as many of the possible hydrocarbons as possible. A short list of common hydrocarbons found in SCUBA systems include:

- Silicone grease
- Most oils
- Rust
- Metal filings
- Paint
- Hair
- Wood
- Paper
- Lint

Cleaning Solvents

Simple Green
MDA SD-13
Trisodium Phosphate (TSP)
Distilled Water
Blue Gold
Naval Oxygen Cleaner
Delta Omega Technologies DOT 111-113
BIOX

Equipment Cleaning

Before you disassemble and service any equipment the manufacturer must certify you as a technician.

Once qualified, the cleaning process involves a number of very straightforward steps:

1) Dismantle equipment
2) Inspect and prepare equipment for cleaning
3) Clean the equipment
4) Rinse and dry
5) Inspect
6) Re-assemble
7) Purge and flush

Dismantle Equipment

Use the manufacturer's specifications to break down the gear to its simplest components. Be sure to lay out the parts in a clean area and keep them organised. An untidy work area will result in the loss of parts and possible contamination. All disassembly must be done according to the manufacturer's instructions and always use the correct tools for the job. It is essential that the tools you use are also clean.

Inspect and Prepare

Begin by inspecting all of the components for damage, scratches, corrosion and wear. All parts that are to be replaced with O_2 compatible parts should be 'bagged', marked and recorded. These parts should also be returned to the owner of the equipment. Any parts that are damaged should also be replaced at this time; old parts are to be 'bagged' and labelled and again returned. You may now begin to prepare the equipment for cleaning by organising which parts need special attention for cleaning. Prepare appropriate solutions and apply the correct lubrications. A toothbrush may be used to remove any loose dirt, grime and grease.

Clean

There are some steps to cleaning and different ways to clean, depending on what equipment is available. Be sure to use the correct tools on the appropriate parts.

1. Soak all of the small parts in a mild or dilute solution or place in an Ultra sonic cleaner to remove corrosion and calcification. Ultra sonic cleaners are excellent for getting at sections of a part that cannot be accessed by hand or tool.
2. For cylinders use either a hot detergent bath or a lancing device with hot steam to remove grease. This will begin the process of eliminating much of the hydrocarbons.
3. Inspect all of the parts to determine if steps 1 and 2 should be repeated.

Mechanical Cleaning

Another method used to clean equipment is mechanical cleaning which employs different tools such as wire-brushes, grinding, swabbing, vacuuming, tumbling and a little elbow grease. Take great care when employing these methods as most SCUBA equipment can be easily damaged. Solvents and detergents are also used throughout this process.

Ozone Cleaners

The RGF/ISI multi-functional and portable sanitising system is capable of generating ozone and ozonised water for a wide range of sanitising applications. The RGF/ISI rebreather sanitising system has been specifically designed to simplify current cleaning and sanitising procedures for closed and semi-closed rebreather units. It is capable of destroying a wide range of organic and non-organic compounds without damaging sensitive components like sensors and electronics used in rebreathers.

Because ozone generators emit gases that are used for sanitising, it is able to reach into tight areas, nooks and microscopic gaps that regular cleaning cannot reach. In these areas, there is great potential for the accumulation of hydrocarbons, oil and mist particulate. In addition, the ozone from ozone generators combines with any residual moisture to form a cleaning agent whilst at the same time drying your equipment out. For heavy oil deposits, a pre-wash with detergent may still be required.

Rinse and Dry

In a prepared bath of clean distilled water, rinse all of the parts. It is recommended that from this point onwards you handle all of the parts with non-lubricated lint-free gloves. Make sure all of the parts are dried well before reassembling. Drying can be done with ovens and infrared lights, or by blowing with clean, oil-free, dry air. With cylinders, a final rinse with boiling hot water and then a clean air flush will quickly remove any moisture and prevent rusting.

It is important to not use blow dryers on floor-mounted cylinder stands for drying SCUBA cylinders. This is a popular method for drying cylinders, but can drive a great deal of contaminants back into the cylinder. The electric dryers generate heat and together with the electrical charges from their motors and the vacuum, draw dust, dirt and other organic and inorganic matter moves off the floor and straight into the cleaned cylinder.

Inspection

Thoroughly inspect all dry parts for residual greases and other contaminants whilst taking care to not re-contaminate your work. Be sure that the detergents are rinsed clean properly. White lights are ideal for general inspections and can be used in conjunction with inspection mirrors. Ultraviolet lights help reveal greases, hydrocarbon and organic oils that white lights can not pick up.

Re-Assemble

According to the manufacturer's specification, reassemble all of the components. Change all parts requiring annual replacement. Replace all of the components with oxygen-compatible parts. Where the specifications require lubrication, be sure to apply oxygen-compatible brands, such as 'Crystalube'. Be sure to maintain an oxygen-clean environment whilst working. You can easily re-contaminate your work.

Cylinder Labelling

The purpose of having properly labelled cylinders is to prevent divers from confusing the content of the cylinder itself. Certified mixed gas divers are invariably aware of the implications of diving a gas beyond its maximum operating depth. However, cylinders with higher nitrox mixes, decompression gases or oxygen may require specialised training and precautions, a level at which many divers are not qualified. Divers who are not nitrox certified may not even recognise a cylinder dedicated for nitrox as having anything other than air inside. Labels should be clear and easily recognisable.

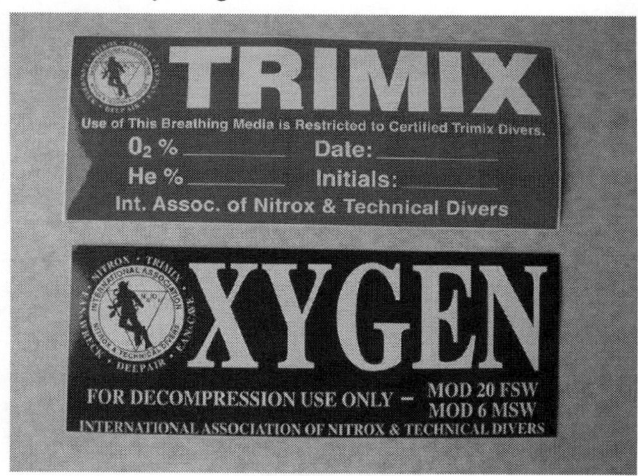

Cylinder labels

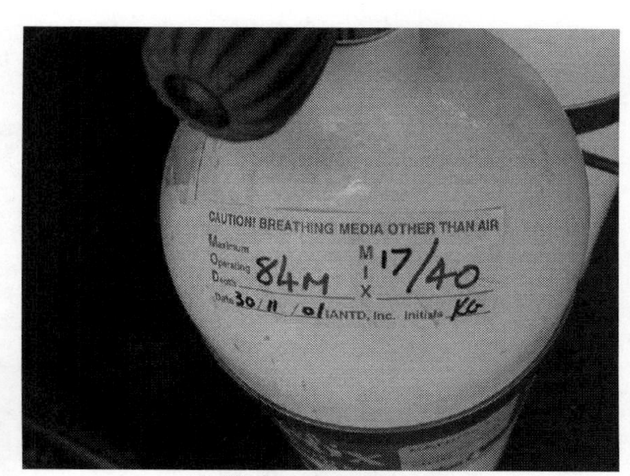

Cylinder content tape

Gas Purity

A brief note on gas purities. Most countries have 'diver' or 'breathing grade' pure gases. Never use 'welding' or 'industrial' gases, as although the gas may be of a high purity, the cylinders may not be regularly checked for contamination. Air for mixing with pure gases has been generally agreed to be acceptable when the hydrocarbon content is less than 0.1mg/m^3. **This varies country to country and really only applies to partial pressure mixing.**

Recommended Fill Rates*

Nitrox and Oxygen Fills 5 to a maximum of 7 bar per minute

(the slower the better)

Mixing Techniques

The majority of the world's recreational diving gases are mixed by partial pressure. That is to say oxygen (in the case of nitrox) is put into a cylinder to a certain pressure and air is added. Basically, partial pressure filling involves putting pure gases into a cylinder where they then mix. All other methods of mixing means that the SCUBA cylinder sees a mix of gases rather than initially a pure gas. Whilst partial pressure filling is extremely common, if it is not done properly it is potentially the most hazardous form of mixing.

Hazards can occur because of heat generated during the filling process. This is due to the speed of filling, flow rate being the issue. Whilst there is no finite standard for the speed of filling, oxygen rates as low as 5 bar (70 psi) are often quoted. As heat is primarily what we are trying to control, the speed will depend on construction of the filling system and the size of the cylinder. Hence, must be gauged on an individual basis. The higher the pressures of oxygen decanted, the greater the heat due to adiabatic compression.

Mixing Systems

The following is offered as a guide to system types and should not be used as a plan for building a system.

Mixing By Weight

Mixing by weight is a very reliable and accurate method of gas blending. It involves calculating the specific weight of a gas to obtain a desired mix. It is an expensive and detailed method and not suitable for dive shops or field operations.

Partial Pressure Blending

Traditionally, the cheaper way to blend gas, yet is also the most risky method as it involves a great deal of potential adiabatic compression. It is the primary method of blending technical nitrox fills or fills over 40%. It can be used in conjunction with a continuous flow blending system and with hyper filters in a double filtration system.

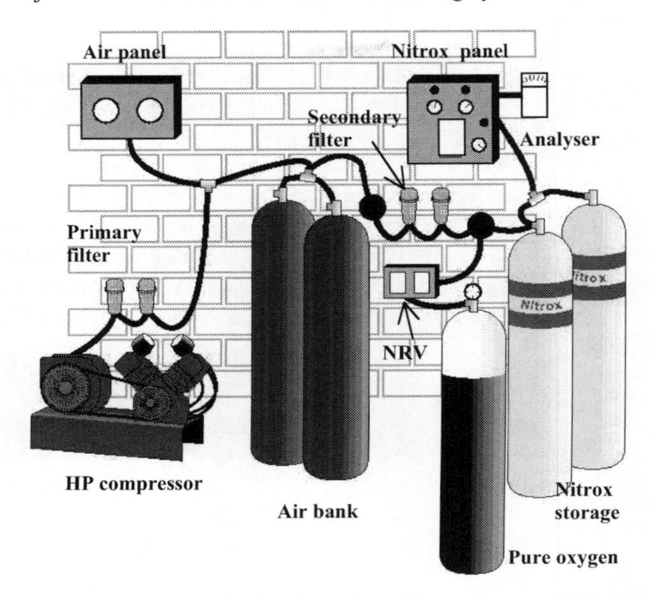

Partial pressure filling is based on proportional (by volume) filling. The proportion of each gas in a mix is directly related to its partial pressure.

Partial pressure filling relies on Dalton' s Law of partial pressures. As a minimum to actually partial pressure fill will require a *'transfill'* whip with needle valves for fine control. We use this whip to transfer a specific and predetermined amount of gas from a high-pressure source. Filling whips may be independent and attach directly to the cascade or storage bank, or they may be integrated into a distribution panel.

In a partial pressure system, compressed air is pumped through a second filtration system removing the hydrocarbons to within an acceptable limit. In most cases the primary filter is actually sufficient to ensure the gas quality. However, a second filter is added to reduce the effects of a possible single filter failure, the second one having its change-out period staggered against the first. This 'oxygen-compatible air' is added to the nitrox bank that has been filled with pure oxygen, possibly with the help of a booster pump system. Oxygen or nitrox is kept from flowing back into air banks through non-return valves (NRV). The percentage of nitrox desired can be adjusted by the addition of oxygen or air into the banks. Partial pressure fills, due to their slow and methodic blending, may require some time to mix. If your mix seems inaccurate, wait. Temperature, atmospheric pressure and humidity can also delay this process. Mixing directly into SCUBA cylinders should be done with extra care as the smaller the cylinder the greater the heat build-up. Adding oxygen to the cylinder first has the advantage that the oxygen is at relatively low pressure and that the mix is diluting all the time it is being filled.

Using a Nitrox Top-Up Chart
With partial pressure filling, a helpful tool is a nitrox top-up chart (see appendix A). This chart automatically adjusts the oxygen 'pressure to add' to make a mix. It takes care of the first three steps of determining your '*haves, wants* and *needs'*. The chart can also be used for scenarios that require a cylinder to be drained and also for pre-mixed banks of 40%.

Instructions:

1. Begin by finding the adjusted FO_2 of what you '*Want'* in the cylinder. Do this by finding your desired FO_2 in the left column and following across until you reach the working pressure of the cylinder.
2. Next, take the FO_2 that you presently have in your cylinder. Follow across the chart until you reach the current pressure in your cylinder.
3. Subtract Step 2 from Step 1. That gives you the total pressure of pure oxygen to add before topping with oxygen compatible air.
4. If your cylinder is empty, follow along the top row until you find the fill pressure and then look down the left column to the mix. Where the two meet is the amount of oxygen to add.

Real Gas Methods vs Ideal Gas Methods
We have to remember that different gases have different densities and will compress more or less than others. This will have an effect on partial pressure filling as it affects our partial pressure laws. It is what is referred to as 'real and ideal gas laws'. As an example oxygen is 10% more compressible than nitrogen or helium between 130 and 270 bar. In practice, this can mean errors of up to 10% on nitrox mixes and as much as 16% with trimix.

At higher pressures and temperatures, calculation methods involving 'Van der Waals Constants' or assumptions as given by Beattie-Bridgeman are used to accurately generate mixes using real gas equations. These theories look at the intermolecular forces and kinetic energy issues associated with the different gases.

Ideal gas methods state that, in an ideal world, the proportion of gases will not be affected by their different densities. In a continuous blending system, we can blend according to the ideal gas method because we do not proportion our gases by pressure, but usually through in-line analysing allowing us to automatically accommodate the difference. When we partial-pressure fill, we are blending by real gas methods and must account for the difference. In reality this is accomplished through experience and time. In practice, at normal SCUBA pressures, gas compressibility has a minimal affect other than with relatively high helium mixes.

Continuous Flow Blending
Traditionally, an expensive method of blending nitrox that required an oil-free compressor and an oxygen serviced system. Today, there are may continuous flow blending systems that have been developed and are inexpensive and efficient.

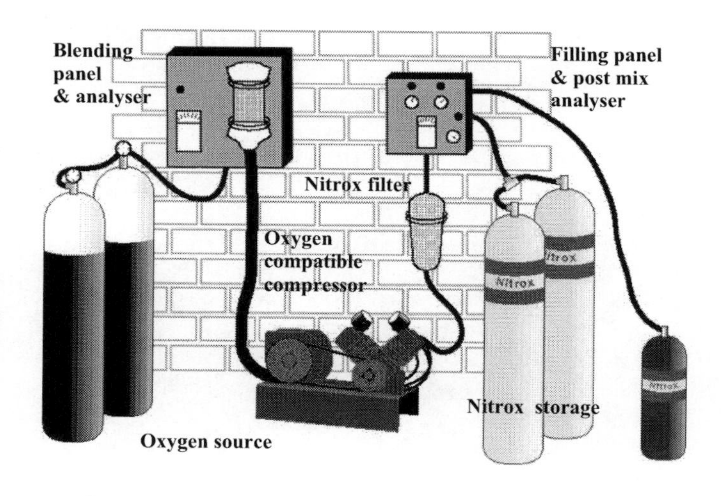

In a continuous flow system, air and oxygen are mixed together in the blending. The mixing occurs at ambient pressure before it is drawn into the intake of the compressor. The desired fraction of oxygen (FO_2) is maintained by monitoring the analyser and adjusting the oxygen injector (regulator) accordingly. Continuous low systems provide accurate homogeneous blends in short periods of time. An in-line analyser ensures accurate mixes through ideal gas methods. This system eliminates some of the risks associated with partial pressure filling, as it allows us more control of the oxygen being entered into the system. Continuous flow blenders can also augment high oxygen nitrox mixtures and provide easier ways to mix trimix by using this system to generate a 'base mix' as an additive to other gas mixtures.

Gas Separation

Gas separation systems separate the different gases that make up air. Specifically, they separate the oxygen from nitrogen. These systems provide an unlimited supply of oxygen and are ideal for remote locations and charter boat operations. They are, however, somewhat expensive and require you to modify a compressor system to oxygen service status.

By separating the individual constituents of a nitrox mix, we can quickly approach the desired FO_2 in fewer steps. Some systems such as the 'RGF/ISI infusion system' also incorporate a submerged compressor, keeping the gases cool and pumping quiet.

Types of gas separation technology that are available include;

- Membrane systems that incorporate differential permeability
- Oxygen generators pressure swing absorption (PSA)
- ISI "Accu-Blend" System

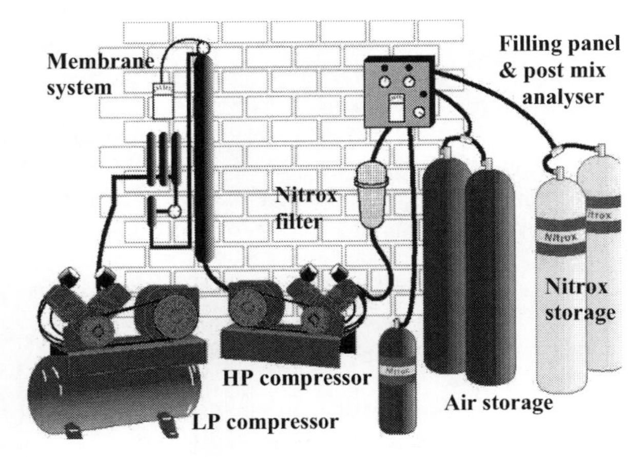

The differential permeability system replaces the pure oxygen supply purchased from gas suppliers. They must still be incorporated into a system capable of double filtration and compressors with oxygen compatible lubrication.

One example is the ISI 'Accu-Blend™' nitrox system from Infusion Systems, Inc. consisting of a highly reliable PSA oxygen generating unit driven by a high quality low pressure air compressor. The O_2 generating module removes the nitrogen from the ambient air using the pressure swing absorption technology (PSA). This generator can produce upto 90% pure oxygen. Gases expelled out of the generator are sent to a nitrox blending valve, where the desired nitrox blend is analysed and sent to a special submerged high pressure compressor. There, it is pressurised up to 300 bar. This unit is very reliable and also offers the ability to append an ozone generator to the unit to assist with O_2 cleaning.

Problems with Helium

Many inexperienced blenders seem to have trouble making trimix. These problems seem to become exacerbated when a higher percentage of helium is needed. There are two partial pressure ways to mix trimix:

The project filling station, a converted ambulance garage. 'Britannic 97'

Helium First

Without the aid of booster pumps[27] people often decant helium first because it is expensive. The main disadvantage of this is that they often do not allow the relatively high pressure of helium to cool before adding the other gases. Hence a speedy decanting of 100 bar of helium will often be 90 bar when cooled. In trimix, as the oxygen fill pressure is small by comparison, this can lead to significant mixing errors. It also means that oxygen has to be used at higher pressures.

Having filled a cylinder with a helium mix it is wise to check for valve leaks (due to helium's lower density) by filling the opening of the valve with water and looking for bubbles. This is especially true when storing mixes.

[27] P. 81

Oxygen First
Oxygen content is critical and if added first will be at low pressure. If this is added first, the bar reading will be fairly accurate as adiabatic heat will not have been generated. Helium can then be added and allowed to cool before adding air. Experienced blenders will apply their own gauge 'fudge factors' to compensate for heat generated at the speed they fill and will often add 10% or more to the bar readings to compensate and allow fairly rapid filling.

Oxygen Analysers
It is vital that all mixes are analysed prior to diving. No matter who has mixed it, if you are going to breathe it then check it. If you are analysing a set of doubles with a centre isolator, analyse both outlets.

Oxygen analysers are simple devices. An oxygen cell converts a partial pressure of oxygen to a reading on a millivolt metre. This reading is displayed as an oxygen fraction.

Calibration of the cells is normally in air. If high oxygen content mixes are to be analysed then it is better to calibrate in 100% oxygen as the cells can be slightly non-linear. Flow air (oxygen) over the cell, ensure the flow rate is low enough so that pressure does not build up on the cell face (as this makes a false partial-pressure reading). Set the analyser to either 20.9 or 100% accordingly, depending which calibration gas is used. If a group of divers is using an analyser, avoid the temptation to keep recalibrating. People tend to do this because when it is passed to the next person they see a high reading because the cell has not had time to stabilise and they assume the calibration has moved. If unsure, wait a few minutes before recalibrating or ensure a good calibration gas flow and start again.

Always adhere to manufacturers' instructions with regard to flow rate and analysis technique. Do not analyse when a low battery warning is showing on the analyser. Helium analysers are becoming popular and, although an expensive option, may be useful for larger operations.

Booster Pumps
What does a booster pump do? Put simply, it takes a low pressure gas and 'boosts' it to a higher pressure.

Booster pumps are arranged as single or a series of pistons. In the case of multi-stage units, pistons become progressively smaller, compressing the gas more and more. Each piston arrangement is known as a 'stage'. Boosters are often refereed to as 'scavenge' pumps. This is because certain configurations have the ability to reduce the supply gas cylinder to almost zero.

In diving, we normally use two stage units. These pumps are largely used for generating high pressures of pure gases such as oxygen and helium. However, trimix and nitrox has been successfully pumped using these systems. The issue here is contamination. Air associated with trimix must be from a pure air source or hydrocarbons will contaminate the pump. The next time you pump oxygen it could be disastrous. For this reason, pumps that compress mixed gas are either dedicated for that use or undergo more regular cleaning intervals.

Whilst booster pumps may seem to be the answer to all our gas problems, they must be used with extreme caution A few basic rules apply:

1. Never compress oxygen by more than a 6 to 1 ratio across each stage. In other words, if the oxygen supply cylinder is at 10 bar then the output of the first stage must not be allowed to go over 60 bar. In this case, the second stage would in theory have an output of 360 bar.
2. I recommend, for field use, that you do not let the final stage pressure go over 200 bar when pumping pure oxygen.
3. For the above reasons, the source gas pressure should not be allowed to fall much below 20 bar. The booster will start to slow down and labour as lower and lower pressures are reached.
4. Pump slowly, especially at high ratios. The output pipe will get very hot. An addition of a coil of pipe work (6 turns, 100mm diametre) at the output stage will significantly reduce this. High pump rates will also cause the drive stage to freeze (some freezing is quite normal).

Most boosters such as ' Haskels' are air-driven. That is to say an air source of around 10 bar is used to drive the pump. They will consume a lot of drive gas. A standard high flow SCUBA regulator (Poseidon Jetstream) can be used as the drive regulator. For short durations, boosters can be driven from SCUBA cylinders. On the 'Britannic' we had two boosters running flat-out, driven from a low-pressure compressor. For other projects such as our long term work in Guam we used a unit connected to the dive shops air bank. Boosters are a superb, portable way of getting around all those gas hassles that happen with expeditions, as well as being a good, general dive shop tool.

In recreational mixed gas diving we deal primarily with nitrox (air and oxygen), trimix (air, oxygen and helium), heliair (air and helium) and to a lesser extent heliox (helium and oxygen). There are various ways to manufacture these gases that would be covered in detail in a recognised blender course. In order that the reader may generate tables and spreadsheets, here is the maths.

(Note: In all cases for psi users, substitute the bar figure for psi.)

Nitrox

To calculate how much 100% oxygen to add to air to make a nitrox mix;

$$\frac{\textbf{Mix required} - \mathbf{0.21}}{\mathbf{0.79}} \times \textbf{fill pressure}$$

Example:
To make a 32% nitrox mixture at 200 bar

$$\frac{0.32 - 0.21}{0.79} \times 200 \text{ bar} = 27.85 \text{ bar of } 100\% \text{ oxygen.}$$

First add oxygen, then compress with air to 200 bar.
By making a spreadsheet using this formula it is possible to make a base and cross mix chart for nitrox[28].

Trimix Fill from Empty

Key. Phe = helium to add in bar/psi
Fhe = fraction of helium in mix
Pf = fill pressure
Fo_2 = required oxygen fraction
O_2p = oxygen to add in bar/psi

Step 1. To find Helium fill pressure.

$$Phe = Fhe \times Pf$$

Steps 2 to 5. To find oxygen to add.

$$\frac{\left(\dfrac{Fo2}{1-(Fhe)}\right) - 0.21}{0.79} \times (Pf - Phe) = O_2 p$$

Example:
To make a 17% oxygen and 40% helium gas mix at 200 bar.

Step 1.

$$\textbf{Phe} = \mathbf{0.4 \times 200 = 80} \textbf{ bar of helium}$$

[28] See Appendix A.

Step 2.

$$\frac{\left(\frac{0.17}{1-0.4}\right)-0.21}{0.79}\times(200-80)=O_2p$$

Step 3.

$$\frac{0.28-0.21}{0.79}\times 120=O_2p$$

Step 4.

$$\frac{0.07}{0.79}\times 120=O_2p$$

Step 5.

$$\mathbf{0.088\times 120=10.63\ \text{bar of oxygen}}$$

Trimix into an empty cylinder

Below is an alternative method, that helps to work out the 'equivalent narcotic depth' (END) and dive depth as a start point. Simply fill in the blanks by running the formulae in the right hand column. This sheet is found again in the Appendix A.

		Units	*Formulae*
A. Target Depth	=____	**Metres**	
B. Absolute Pressure	=____	**Bar**	**(A\10) + 1**
C. Target PPO_2	=____	**PPO_2**	**Check CNS Clock!**
D. Target FO_2 as a %	=	**%**	**(C\B) x 100**
E. Air Narcosis depth	=____	**Metres**	**Depth, using air at which Narcosis is apparent.**
F. Air Narcosis depth Absolute Pressure	=____	**ATA**	**(E\10) +1**
f. PPN_2 at depth E	=____	**PPN_2**	**0.79 x F**
G. Percent of nitrogen in mix	=	**%**	**(f\B) x 100**
H. PPN_2 at FN_2 in G	=____	**PPN_2**	**(G\100) x B**

Check for END. (H\0.79) -1 x 10 should = E.

I. Percentage of helium in mix.	=	**%**	**100-(D+G)**
J. Working pressure of your cylinder	=____	**Bar**	
K. Helium pressure	=	**Bar**	**J x (I\100)**
L. Nitrogen pressure	=_____	**Bar**	**J x (G\100)**
M. Total oxygen pressure	=____	**Bar**	**J x (D\100)**
N. Total air pressure	=	**Bar**	**L\0.79**
O. Pure oxygen pressure	=	**Bar**	**J -(N+K)**

Now fill helium to pressure in K, oxygen to pressure in O + K and air to pressure in J

This is a metric spreadsheet. To use in imperial change lines B & F for the US equivalent and change Bar to PSI.

Making a trimix – air top off

This is often used when a diver has residual trimix in a cylinder and plans to dive shallower on the following dive. In the case of air top off, the addition of air will raise the oxygen (assuming the original FO_2 was less than 21%) and nitrogen contents, thereby reducing the MOD and increasing the END. Often used when a subsequent trimix diver is shallower. Hence, giving a reasonable END and FO_2. The amount of air added can be balanced against narcosis and oxygen toxicity.

Key.
- Fhe = new helium fraction
- Ofhe = original fraction of helium in mix
- Ofp = original fill pressure
- Nfp = new final fill pressure
- GTA = gas to add to make new fill pressure
- FO_2 = new fo_2
- OfO_2 = original FO_2

Steps 1 & 2. $$Fhe = \frac{(Ofhe \times Ofp)}{Nfp}$$

Steps 3 to 5 $$Fo_2 = \frac{(0.21 \times GTA) + (Ofo_2 \times Ofp)}{Nfp}$$

Example: A trimix of 100 bar of 17/40 is topped with air to 200 bar. What is the new mix?

To find new helium fraction of the mix.

Step 1. $$Fhe = \frac{(0.4 \times 100)}{200}$$

Step 2. $$\mathbf{Fhe = 0.20 \text{ or } 20\% \text{ helium}}$$

To find the new oxygen fraction in the mix.

Step 3. $$Fo_2 = \frac{(0.21 \times 100) + (0.17 \times 100)}{200}$$

Step 4 $$Fo_2 = \frac{21 + 17}{200}$$

Step 5. $$\mathbf{Fo_2 = 0.19 \text{ or } 19\% \text{ oxygen}}$$

Heliair

This is used to make a trimix using just helium and air. Usually the oxygen level (FO_2) is set and the resultant END is accepted as whatever it comes out to be. Adjusting the final fill pressure will adjust the FO_2 and END.

Additional key. Hep = helium fill pressure
Fo_2 req = required FO_2 in the mix
Fp = fill pressure

Example: make a heliair with an oxygen content of 16% and a fill pressure of 200 bar.

$$Fp - \frac{Fo_2\ req \times Fp}{0.21} = Hep$$

$$200 - \frac{0.16 \times 200}{0.21} = Hep$$

200 – 152.38 = 47.6 bar of helium

Now find out the helium fraction in the mix.

$$Fhe = \frac{Hep}{Fp}$$

$$\mathbf{Fhe = \frac{47.6}{200} = 0.238 \text{ or } 23.8\%}$$

Alternatively, if we know the helium fraction (and END) we require, we can calculate the Fo_2. Having found this we can then use the first equation to calculate the helium pressure to add. Working backwards if we require a helium content of 23.8% (as above), what will the Fo_2 be?

$$Fo_2 = (1 - Fhe) \times 0.21$$

$$Fo_2 = (1 - 0.238) \times 0.21$$

$$\mathbf{Fo_2 = 0.16 \text{ or } 16\%}$$

Trimix Cross Mix
This is used when mixing one trimix on top of another. This calculates the extra helium pressure (Hep) and oxygen pressure (O_2p) to add.

Key.
Phe = helium to add in bar/psi
Ofhe = old fraction of helium in mix
Nfhe = old fraction of helium in mix
Opf = old fill pressure
Npf = new fill pressure
Ophe = old helium pressure in bar/Psi
Nphe = new helium pressure in bar/Psi
$Of0_2$ = old fraction of oxygen in mix
$Nf0_2$ = new fraction of oxygen in mix
O_2p = oxygen to add in bar/psi to make final mix
Hep = helium to add in bar/psi to make final mix

To find the new helium fill:

Step 1. $$Phe = (Nfhe \times Npf) - (Ofhe \times Opf)$$

Step 2. $$Ophe = (Ofhe \times Opf)$$

Step 3. $$Nphe = (Nfhe \times Npf)$$

To find the new oxygen fill.

Step 4 to 7 $$O_2p = \left(\frac{\left(\frac{Nfo_2}{1 - Nfhe} \right) - 0.21}{0.79} \times (Npf - Nphe) \right) - \left(\frac{\left(\frac{Ofo_2}{1 - Ofhe} \right) - 0.21}{0.79} \times (Opf - Ophe) \right)$$

Example: take a 17/40 trimix at 100 bar and make it into a 18/30 at 200 bar.

Step 1. $$Phe = (0.3 \times 200) - (0.4 \times 100)$$

$$Phe = 60 - 40$$

Phe = 20 bar of helium to add to the final mix

Step 2. $$Ophe = 0.40 \times 100 = 40 \text{ bar of helium in old mix}$$

Step 3. $$Nphe = 0.30 \times 200 = 60 \text{bar of helium in new mix}$$

Step 4. $$O_2p = \left(\frac{\left(\frac{0.18}{1 - 0.3} \right) - 0.21}{0.79} \times (200 - 60) \right) - \left(\frac{\left(\frac{0.17}{1 - 0.4} \right) - 0.21}{0.79} \times (100 - 40) \right)$$

Step 5. $$O_2p = \left(\frac{0.26-0.21}{0.79}\times 140\right)-\left(\frac{0.28-0.21}{0.79}\times 60\right)$$

Step 6. $$O_2p = (0.06\times 140)-(0.09\times 60)$$

Step 7. $\mathbf{O_2p = 8.26 - 5.56 = 2.7}$ **bar of oxygen to add to make the new mix**

To find the narcotic depth of any gas

Example.
What is the END of a 12/50 trimix when used at 100 metres

Fn_2 at 100m = 100 - (12+50) = 38% Fn_2

Using Daltons Law

$$Pn_2 = Fn_2 x P$$

$$Pn_2 = 0.38\times 11 = 4.18 Pn_2$$

Now find at what depth this PN_2 occurs in air

$$P = \frac{PN_2}{Fn_2}$$

$$\mathbf{P} = \frac{4.18}{0.79} = 5.29 = 42.9\,\mathbf{metres}$$

Summary
Gas mixing and handling should never be undertaken without correct training. Once trained, do not fall into the trap of thinking, ‘it will never happen to me’. Remain vigilant and never get complacent with analysis and gas labelling.

Too Many Toys?

In modern diving we have seen a mass of new 'gadgets' come to the market, some useful, some less so. Without doubt, as seen in a previous chapter, equipment configuration can make or break a dive. However, all the equipment in the world will not help a diver who is not practised with it. The following chapter provides a useful guide for skills to be developed.

Buoyancy Control

Sounds simple dosen't it? We all did it at basic diver level. A problem of diving with multi-cylinder configurations, scooters and especially rebreathers is that we begin again. Dependant on the dive, we will find ourselves carrying a great deal more weight. Careful choice of equipment will help minimise this. Let's start at the low end, a simple one side mount decompression dive with twin main cylinders.

My recommendation is, cater for the worst scenario. You completely lose or drain the side mount and you have to be maintain a stable decompression on the main cylinders alone. These will now get very low on gas. With wetsuits and certain dry suits there will be volume reduction in the suit material in deep-water (hence you feel heavier) and the opposite reaction when shallow. Exactly where you need to do decompression stops, you become buoyant.

The simple test is get in 3 metres of water in full kit with no more than 30 bar in the main cylinders (leave the side mount behind). Are you comfortable with this set-up? If not, add lead somewhere (if you have a harness consider adding another back plate) or change your gear i.e. use steel instead of aluminium cylinders, switch to a membrane drysuit etc.

Progressing that on to multi cylinder set-ups, a recommendation is to fill the cylinders with the same amount of gas as before and repeat the test again carrying one less cylinder than you actually require for the dive. This again allows for total loss or major gas reductions.

Take the time to trim out properly; bad buoyancy trim can, at best ruin a dive and at worst be very hazardous.

Ascents and Descents

Having got buoyancy right, now try ascent control. In wreck diving many people are 'line huggers'. They crawl up and down shot lines, paranoid of losing their grip. This is because they have no confidence in their buoyancy control.

Start by moving away from the line but keep using it as a visual reference. Stay within grabbing distance in case it all goes horribly wrong (remember practise this on a no-decompression dive!). Don't be afraid to use the 'up button' in deep-water, that's what the BCD/suit inflator is for (I generally try to trim myself so that I can do all buoyancy adjustments on my drysuit, hence I only have one thing to dump on the ascent). Start with small additions of gas. Do not fin hard as this is self-defeating, stirs up silt and generates CO_2. When it is time to dump gas, do it in small regular amounts, not one enormous one. On dives where I cannot trim out on the suit alone (lots of cylinders) I pre-fill the BCD at the surface to where I just sink and then use the suit for fine trim.

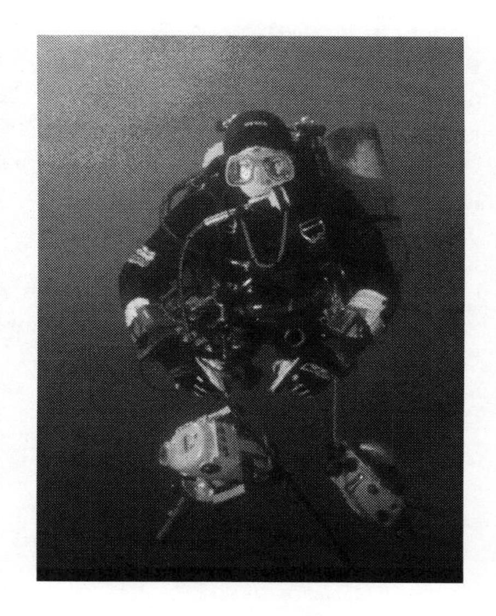

Dan Burton showing perfect buoyancy despite multiple stages and camera gear after a 120 metre dive.

Now try again using a delayed surface buoy (SMB) as a reference for the ascent. Do not hang under the bag. Float freely next to the line reel, try swimming around it when at a stop depth.

Having got all of the above under control, try a totally free ascent with no line reference (use your depth gauge) and simulate a range of decompression stops. On decompression dives many people make the mistake of thinking that 'getting on the gas' is the most important thing. It isn't - think buoyancy first. Get that right, then when your mind becomes preoccupied with other things (like checking regulators) you will not suddenly find yourself drifting down with oxygen in your mouth!

A final note on ascents: if you plan to do a long decompression dive for the first time with lots of stops, practise the stop part first. Check your run time accuracy, buoyancy control, gas requirements and thermal issues before you do it for real and find out the hard way.

Stowage

So now you can float around to your heart's content, but can you access all of the nice new gear you have packed? You looked good on the boat and you can touch everything, but can you access and stow it? Remember the test. In full equipment, sit in shallow water and take everything out of your harness and pockets. Lay it in front of you and now re-stow it (do it one piece at a time if some items float). Don't think if you can get it out that that's good enough. There will be times when it needs to be put away again tidily to ensure a safe exit from the dive. If you can't do it, change the position or stowage technique.

Decompression Cylinder/Stage Cylinder Drills

Having read and understood the equipment section and got your buoyancy right, stage cylinder removal and refitting should be easy. The reasons why cylinder handling skills are important is because should entrapment occur or speedy stage retrieval be required during long penetration dives (where stage cylinders are used to extend the penetration), you are able to cope quickly and efficiently.

Start with removing and replacing the stage cylinder whilst static. Remember to adjust buoyancy momentarily as you don and doff the cylinder. Now try again by dropping the cylinder and swimming past it. Turn back and refit it whilst still swimming without stopping. The trick is to have the cylinder balanced about the centre clip so that when you pick it up with one hand it remains almost horizontal and does not impede your swimming. Get the base clip on first and then the top clip, using one hand only.

Al Wright and Richard Lundgren Jon-lined in. Note the diver above has two stages on the same side due to carrying a heavy light pack as well.

Bag and Reel Work

The ability to use a decompression bag and reel is paramount if you plan to do decompression diving. These are usually only used when you have become separated from the main decompression system or are drift diving.

If more than one diver needs to deploy bags and there is a current, it is important to do it simultaneously or separation on the ascent may occur. To prevent a reel jamming and being wrenched out of your hand, it is a good idea to tie the reel into the wreck or reef if deployment from the bottom is required. If this cannot be done then clip two reels together,. If the first reel jams, the second can be released. In the majority of cases, especially on deep dives, it is better to ascend to just below the first decompression stop and then deploy a reel(s). Timely deployment may be important if a boat is trying to follow you.

Inflation of the bag should be with exhaled gas. Avoid purging a regulator into the bag, especially in cold conditions to prevent a 'free flow'. When diving with a rebreather, one technique is to hold the inflate and purge open on a BCD inflate hose at the same time and use this for filling. This only works if the BCD is not being used for buoyancy.

Run Time
Following a runtime schedule may not seem like a skill but when your general health depends on it you had better get it right! The tricky bit comes if it all goes wrong. The run time system is better than setting a stop watch for multiple stop dives as it allows you to quickly adjust a schedule and easily see where you should be in the depth/time timeline if you become distracted and momentarily forget.

Run Time Definitions
1. Bottom time (BT). Time from leaving the surface to leaving the bottom.
2. Time at first stop (TFS). Time from leaving the bottom to arriving at the first stop, rounded up to nearest minute.
3. Leave stop time (LS). Time point at which each stop is left.

On a run time schedule the bottom time, TFS and time leaving each stop are those highlighted.

Note. Most Bühlmann based decompression models assume the time at the stop includes approximately 20 seconds to move between stops.

Example

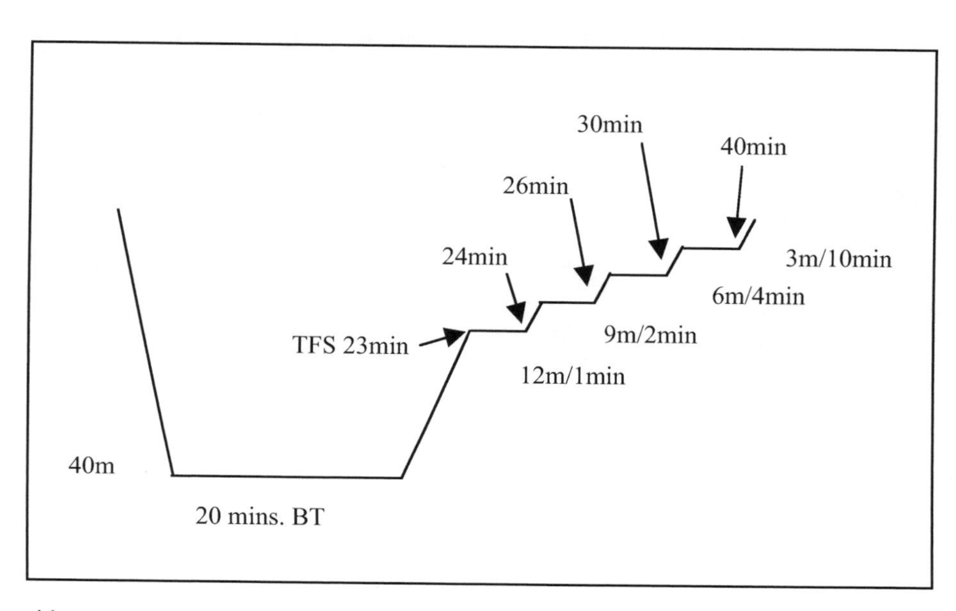

Things to consider:
- *I leave bottom on time but arrive at my first stop early.*
  - This is one of the most dangerous scenarios, you have had a rapid ascent and may have 'micro-bubble' problems that could manifest later in the dive. As a minimum wait at that depth until the run time has caught up and you are back on schedule. Personally I would undertake another minute or two at this stop before continuing if this had occurred.
- *I leave bottom and arrive late at my first stop.*
  - As long as your ascent is continuous and at a moderate rate (10 metres/minute maximum) then you need not adjust the schedule. Simply add the lateness to each stop leave time i.e. +1 minute.
- *I leave bottom early and arrive early at my first stop.*
  - Providing the ascent has been within tolerance then you may take the number of minutes you are early from the total run time
- *I leave bottom early and arrive late at my first stop.*
  - Again, as long as the ascent is continuous, simply add the lateness to the run time
- *I leave bottom late*
  - Obviously go to the next schedule

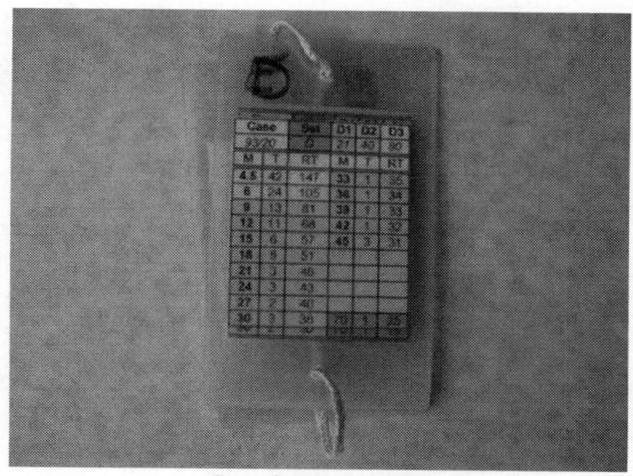
Laminated tables

On deeper dives, time control becomes much more

critical and divers must leave and arrive on time to ensure a safe decompression. This only develops with prastise.

Gas Shutdowns

Gas shutdown is probably the primary survival skill of extended range diving. This is a technique employed with manifolded twin cylinders. These cylinders are ideally fitted with a centre isolation valve (for reasons covered earlier). Whilst a non-isolated valve still gives the option to isolate one regulator first stage, a failure of a cross bar 'O' ring could be catastrophic. So assuming an isolated set of cylinders and in the event of rapid gas loss, the shutdown drill should be as follows:

1. Close the centre valve (it should be 1-2 turns open). This instantly saves one half of the gas irrespective of whether it is a cylinder 'O' ring, manifold 'O' ring or regulator failure
2. Now (assuming a regulator malfunction) you can close the valve for the malfunctioning regulator, having switched to the backup regulator. (If there was still gas left in that cylinder, you could still open the centre valve and gain more gas. Do not do this yet).
3. The drill now continues by opening the malfunctioning regulator and switching to it whilst closing the other regulator's valve.
4. Re-open that regulator's valve. Test both regulators are operating correctly and then re-open the centre valve.

Do not practise this drill on your own initially.
People sometimes get confused and turn off all their gas!

Once you are competent at the above try it whilst floating at a decompression stop and also whilst swimming. Many people initially find this skill difficult and say they cannot reach the valves. Unless you have a physical disability then it is simply equipment configuration stopping you. Try raising and lowering the cylinders. If you use a soft pack harness try a hard back plate.

Gas Sharing

Gas sharing simulates a total out of gas scenario. Start by separating from your partner by your normal swimming separation distance. Instruct him/her to remain still and swim up to him/her and commence sharing. Keep you regulator in your mouth but do not breathe in. Now do a shared swim for a few minutes horizontally.

Repeat the procedure but allow your partner to swim off at a normal rate. Finally, try again but this time exhale as you chase your partner. Remember, fining after your partner will generate lots of CO_2. Use 'pull and glide' techniques employing your arms as much as possible. Do not be polite about your request for gas. Take the regulator you need. Your partner should automatically go to his/her backup.

When you have mastered this technique, complete a horizontal share, followed by a vertical ascent. Remember, if you can breathe there is no rush to move off again once you have established the share. Deploy the long hose, get settled, control breathing and then make a comfortable exit.

As a minimum, this drill will show you how far to separate yourself from your partner on dives!

Respiratory Minute Volume

Not a skill as such but a useful tool in determining gas usage at rest and under stress. This is probably best done at about 30 metres, where narcosis starts to have an affect on most people.

Find a solid place to hold onto. Note the depth and start fining gently simulating a resting swim. Do this until you have used 10 bar on your gauge (or any other convenient number). Note the time in minutes **<u>and</u>** seconds it has taken to do that. Now complete the following maths:

My cylinder size is 22 litres and I used 10 bar of it; therefore I used 220 litres of gas (10 bar x 22 litres).

To use that amount of gas took 5 minutes and 30 seconds or 5.5 minutes.

Therefore; I breathed 40 litres/minute at a depth of 30 metres (220 litres / 5.5 minutes).

Corrected to the surface this is 10 litres per minute (40 / 4 bar absolute).

Now repeat the procedure but at a high work rate. The two answers you calculate should be the extremes of your gas duration. Initially use a figure close to the middle of these two for gas planning. Again, do not practise this alone. With experience you will be able to adjust this average figure downwards.

Lost Line
This is mainly useful in caves, but also applicable to wrecks and in some cases low visibility open-water diving where guide lines are used. Once the line has been lost, stop - do nothing. Try and remain in the same position. Do not sink to the bottom or rise. Do not turn around. If visibility (silt) is the cause, wait for it to settle for as long as possible. Control your breathing.

Now very carefully try to find something to tie one end of your safety reel onto. Following that, start a search in one direction. You should have a mental picture of where the line was when you last saw it. Try and stay at or slightly above that height during your search. Run out the reel for a distance slightly more than the estimated width of the passage you are in. If you can go any further you are running down the passage parallel to the line. In open water estimate the swim kicks to the line and then double it. Sweep with your other arm and try and protect your head. If you do not find the line, rewind the reel back to the start point and attempt a search pattern at 90 degrees to the last one. Try this at all four points of the compass. You should run across the line. If not, start again at a different height.

Lost Diver
In open-water a lost diver drill normally means searching for a few minutes and then surfacing (or moving up to decompression). In an overhead environment, if divers have become separated from a guideline they may need assistance to exit safely. Assuming torches are being used, the first thing to do is cup or turn off your light. Now look around for any other lights. It is unlikely they will have voluntarily turned off theirs. Do not move when you do this and make sure you are near the line. Now recalculate your gas supplies and ensure you have enough for a safe exit or possibly a short swim into the system. At each junction and at regular intervals, repeat the light procedure. If you see an unlined side passage and you suspect the lost divers may be down there, run a reel into the passage. Do not be tempted to just swim down it.

If you are a part of a large team, keep someone with you and send other pairs to search in different directions. Always send a team to the exit as the lost divers may find their way out and then the search can be cancelled.

Rebreather Skills.
The reason for the individual skills listed below is always the same. However, each rebreather has mechanical/electrical differences that infers the actual procedure may vary.

The causes are:

Hypoxic Loop.
Either a switch to a breathable open-circuit or a rapid injection of oxygen (or diluent if breathable at depth) is the remedy.

Hyperoxic Loop
Normally a rapid injection of diluent will be the remedy although on excessively high PO_2's (over 2 bar) it may be safer to switch to open circuit first and then flush with diluent after isolating the oxygen cylinder valve and/or controller. My recommendation is go to the source first (the cylinder valve). Some rebreathers (chest -mounted lungs) can be artificially pumped whilst in open circuit to simulate breathing and mix the gas. Back-mounted units can only be manually flushed whilst in open circuit.

Training on early Draeger units

Hypercapnic Loop
Excessive CO_2, probably as a result of a canister/absorbent failure. Whilst semi-closed mode (intermittent flushing) might work for a while, it is probably best to bailout.

Flooded Loop
Partially flooded loops may remain breathable for a while (you may have to change your swimming position). A full flood, or enough to cause a caustic reaction, equals a bailout.

Failed Electronics
Most units have a manual backup. Practise manual control regularly.

Open Circuit Bailout
I do this at the start of every dive so that it is an autopilot reaction. **If in doubt, bailout!**

Buoyancy Control
This is the skill people find most difficult as they often over fill the counterlung(s). Practise this first on static lines, followed by using a lift bag/SMB, then free floating. Be ready to use the wing a little more for trimming as you cannot use lung volume to compensate.

The actual execution of these skills may vary slightly rebreather to rebreather. Whatever the drills are, practise them all regularly (for more detail see Rebreather chapter).

Communications

Introduction

Communication in diving can take many forms, each having its own usefulness, dependant on the type of dive and environmental conditions. Whilst a 'picture might paint a thousand words', a few understood words definitely saves a lot of confusion. Many of the signals are 'standard' ones, often taken from the cave community. Some of the less standard signals are shown as an addition to these standards. Whatever you use, make sure everyone on the dive team knows them. The reader is guided to any cave diving manual for a full list of signals. This chapter will also discuss the different types of signalling systems and provide examples.

Communication Systems

Communication systems can be broken down into the following categories:

- Hand communication
- Rope communication
- Light communication
- Touch communication
- Written communication

As mentioned each of these has a use dependant on the dive or environment. Lets look at each in turn.

Hand Communication

Probably the most commonly used in diving. Often it is designed so that a single signal means an action or short sentence. Here are some of the not so common applicable to technical diving. With hand signals it is important wherever possible that all signals are single handed. This allows the other hand to hold a light to illuminate the signalling hand in low visibility or dark environments.

Counting

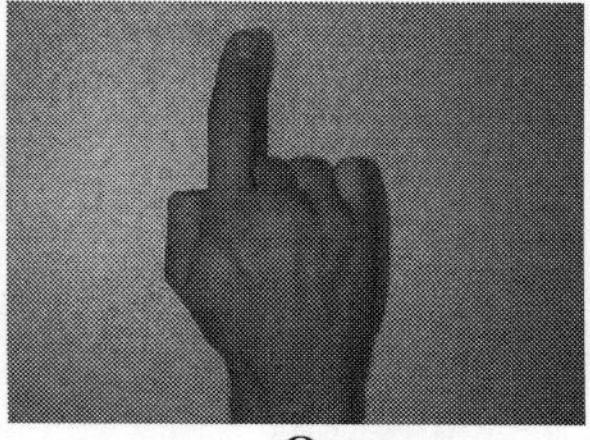

One

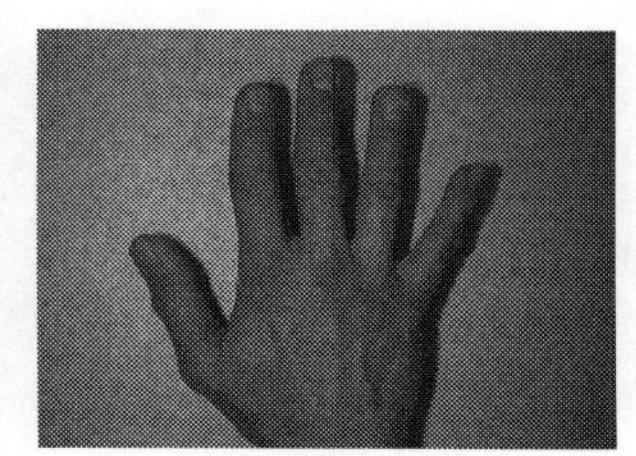

Five

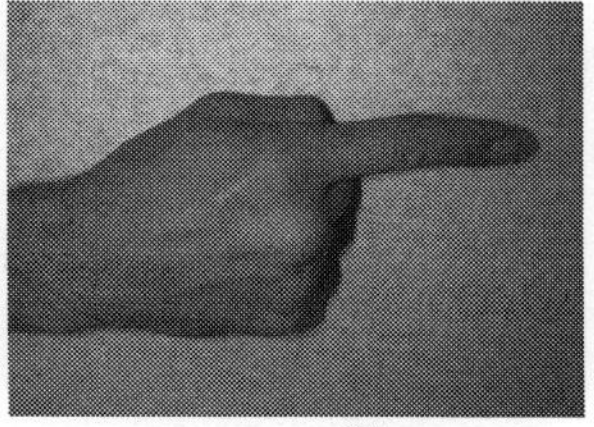

Six

To make the number ten (or any two/three digit number) just sign the digits individually. A zero is made like an 'OK' sign but bending the fingers into a fist with a hole in the middle. Six, seven, eight and nine are with the hand held sideways (nine is four fingers).

Decompression schedule

If you see this signal it means 'what is your decompression schedule?' This is usually replied first by signing the depth numbers and then the time at depth.

If you see the decompression signal followed by an 'up' signal (using the thumb), this means 'how much decompression is left to the surface?'

This signal, usually moved backwards and forwards, is used to indicate depth. You may wish a partner to level out at a certain depth. Use this and then give the depth in metres.

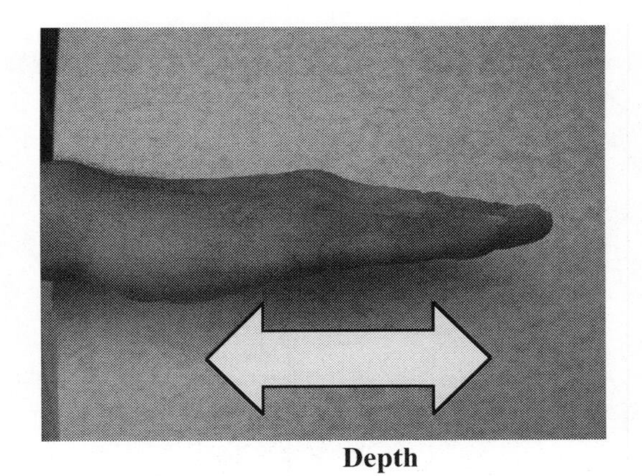

Depth

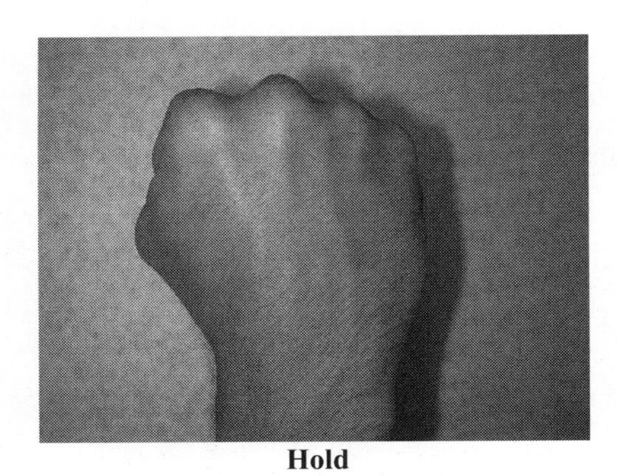

Hold

This signal means 'stop what you are doing' or 'I want to stop here'. It is the 'hold' signal. Often the fist is made with fingers facing out.

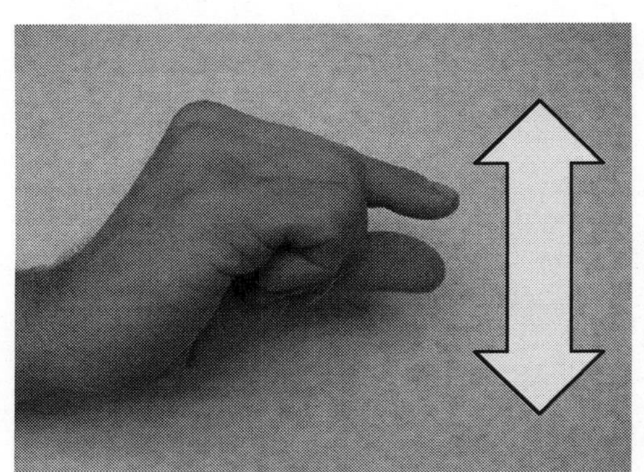

Small bubbles

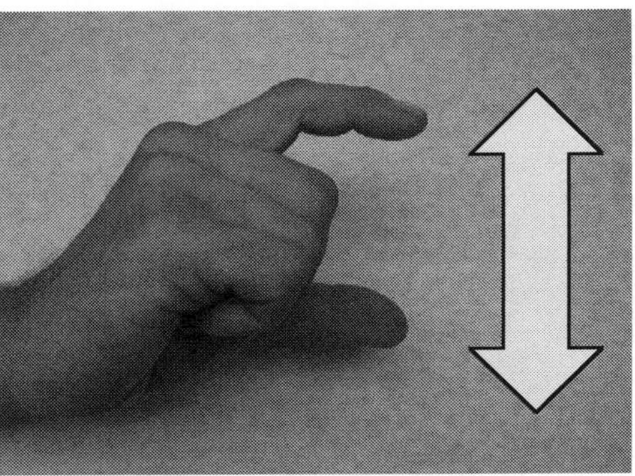

Large bubbles

Both of these are signals for a small and large leak. It is usually coupled with pointing to the offending item on your own equipment. The finger and thumb moves together and apart.

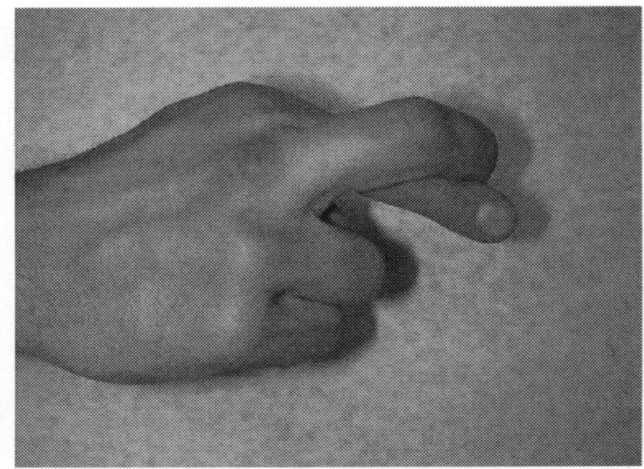

Line

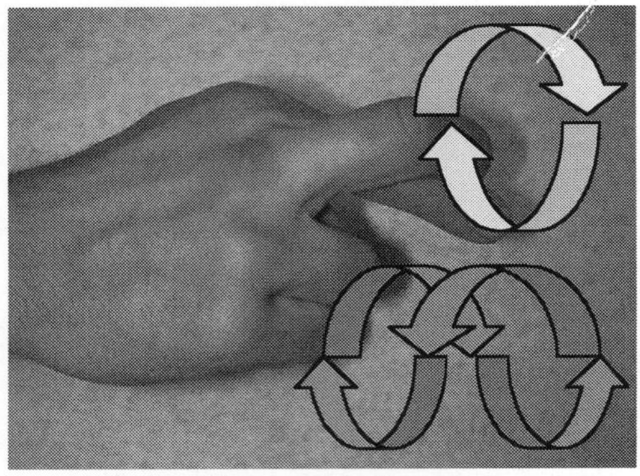

Continuous circle = reel
Figure of eight = tie a knot or tie off

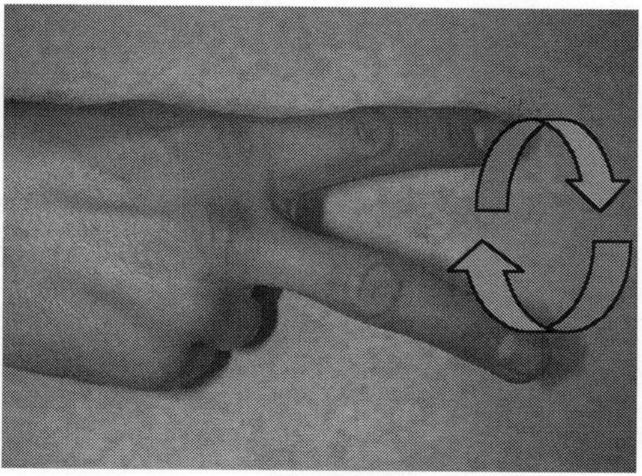

Gas switch

SMB

The 'gas switch' signal is usually performed in front of the mouthpiece and rotates back and forth by 180 degrees. The SMB signal may be followed by an 'up' sign to signal it is time to deploy. Normally the hand is raised up with fingers opening during the upward stroke.

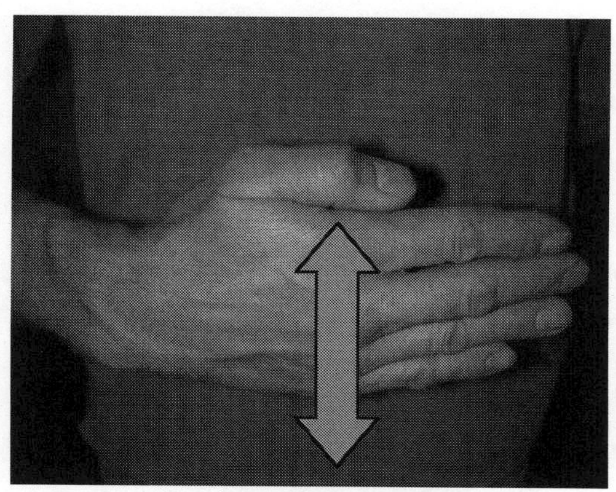

Any breathing problem

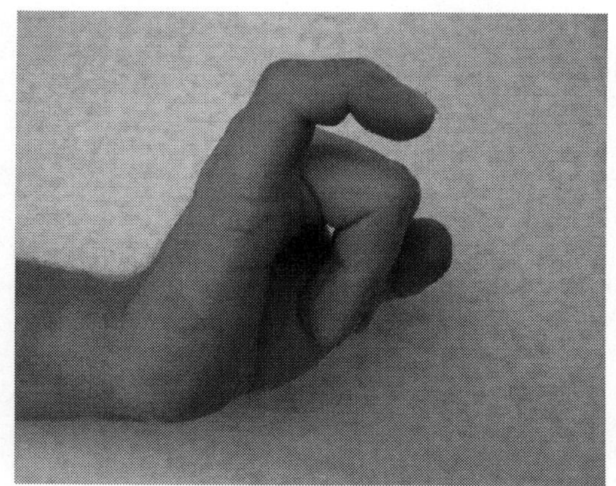

Question

The final two are a) any breathing problem, the hand moving back and forth from the chest, b) 'question' which would be followed by what is in question. For instance 'question' followed by pointing to a pressure gauge would mean 'how much gas do you have?'

Rope Signals

Usually, these are only used in commercial or base-fed sump diving (popular in the UK). They are also useful in emergencies when reduced visibility has occurred and divers are positioned about, or connected by a line. Primarily used when conducting searches such as a circle search where one diver stays in the centre of a circle and the other diver circles him/her holding an extended line. These signals are a modified set based on standard commercial diving signals.

One pull	'Are you OK?'	Reply is one pull. 'I am OK'.
Two pulls	'Stop'	Reply is two pulls. 'I have stopped'.
Three pulls	'Go down/move away'	Reply is three pulls. 'I am going down/moving away'.
Four pulls	'Come up/ move in'	Reply is four pulls.' I am coming up/moving in'.
Multiple pulls	'Emergency'	No response required. 'Investigate the problem'.

In Florida-style cave diving where there is a guideline, rope signals are seldom used as it is not wise to pull on the guideline. However, in low visibility sump-diving, lines are much heavier and rope signals again become useful.

Light Signals

Light communication is useful in wreck and cave diving. In fact, anywhere where it is dark but visibility is reasonable. A useful tip is not to shine the light at the person but where their light is focused as that is normally where they are looking. In cave diving, where you may be in a line of people, this generally means looking between your legs to spot the light of the person behind you and signalling at that point. Where their light shines is normally where they are looking. In cave diving all signals are rippled back to the rear of the group before again being rippled to the front. Do not acknowledge the signal back to the person in front of you when you receive it unless you are the last man in the team. When the signal again ripples from the back, pass it forward.

Signals are:

A wide circle	'Are you OK?'	Reply with same circle. 'I am OK?'
A slow movement left to right	'I need your attention'	No reply. Wait for further information.
A rapid movement left to right	'Emergency'	No reply. Wait for further information. Assume gas loss.

All other signals are highlighted by the light being shone on the hand doing the signalling.

Touch Signals

Used in low visibility between divers in a team. In cave diving usually the team will initially make contact with the guideline (not pulling on it but making an OK sign around it) and then with each other. The team will wait for a short period for a signal from the back, rippled forward, before moving off.

Signals are:

One squeeze	'Stop'
Push forward	'Go forward'
Pull back	'Go back'
Multiple squeezes	'Emergency'. Assume gas loss. If visibility is zero, do not remove the regulator from your mouth as the 'out of gas' diver will look for it there.

Written Signals

It may seem a little strange to include written signals here as most people can write, but some dives (especially working ones) may need a great deal of communication. Personally, I do not like arm slates and prefer a small loose leaf waterproof book or series of slate pages. I keep these in the harness pouch. They are wrapped in a single bungee loop and I also keep a set of backup tables between the pages. The pencil is one of those 'pop-up' lead pencils with multiple leads. The essential thing is to write clearly, abbreviating sentences if possible. An example would be 'found coins near coral head' instead of 'I found some coins near that coral head over there'. Clean the slate either with an eraser or scouring powder and a little water.

I have not really mentioned wireless communications in this book as it is seldom useful for deeper dives due to the problems with helium and voice distortion. A low-priced digital system has yet to come onto the market which would improve things significantly over existing analogue systems. Also, for good sound quality, you usually need a full-face mask which can be awkward from a 'bailout' standpoint. However, there are certain tasks where wireless communication is the tool for the job. So if you need communications shop around carefully and trial as many systems as possible before choosing.

Sound Signals

Only useful for surface support personnel. A reving engine or thunder flash can be used as a simple re-call signal.

Basic Physiology

Introduction

Whilst a basic understanding of physiology is useful for all forms of sport, most divers tend to avoid researching the details of human anatomy. With technical diving, a good knowledge of the body's workings will modify our treatment of ourselves, from diet to exercise. It is a useful knowledge tool and a subject of extreme importance. This chapter will outline the basic elements of human physiology and focus on how we can take care of ourselves and use our body wisely.

Cardiovascular System : Blood

In order for the body to stay alive, each of its cells must receive a continuous supply of food and oxygen. At the same time, carbon dioxide and other materials produced by cells must be picked up for removal from the body. This process is continually maintained by the body's circulatory system. The primary circulatory system consists of the heart and blood vessels, together maintaining a continuous flow of blood through the body. They deliver oxygen and nutrients to (and removing carbon dioxide and waste products from) peripheral tissues. A subsystem of the circulatory system, the lymphatic system, collects interstitial fluid and returns it to the blood. The heart pumps oxygen-rich blood from the lungs to all parts of the body through a network of arteries, and smaller branches called arterioles. Blood returns to the heart via small venules, that lead to the larger veins. Arterioles and venules are linked by even smaller vessels called metarterioles. Capillaries (blood vessels a single cell thick) branch off from the metarterioles and then rejoin them. The network of tiny capillaries is where the exchange of oxygen and carbon dioxide between blood and body cells takes place. The average adult has over 60,000 miles of blood vessels (arteries, veins etc.) in their body.

Body Fluids and Tissues

The human body is composed of many complex structural units which include cells, tissues and organs. These units and the fluids of the body (not including blood) compose 92% of the body. The cells are the body's microscopic building blocks. Cells group together and form tissue. Tissue is a group of similar cells with varying amounts and kinds of material filling in the spaces between them. Although there are only four main kinds of tissue (epithelial, connective, muscle, and nerve) there are many subtypes. Tissue groups form the organs and skin of the body. About 60% of the weight of the human body is water. Almost 40% of this is the fluid within the cells themselves. The rest, called extra-cellular fluid (the liquid between and around cells) is one part blood plasma and four parts interstitial fluid. Blood, about 8% of the body weight, flows continually through the interstitial fluid, nourishing, cleansing, and balancing it. This creates homeostasis. Homeostasis is when the chemical composition, temperature, and volume of the extra cellular fluid remains almost constant, fluctuating only slightly. It is important for the proper functioning of the human body.

Lymphatic System

The lymphatic system is not really a separate system of the body. It is considered part of the circulatory system since it consists of lymph, a moving fluid that comes from the blood and returns to the blood by way of the lymphatic vessels. Lymph carries some nutrients around the body, especially fat. It also distributes germ-fighting white cells. Lymph resembles plasma, but is more diluted and contains only about 5% of proteins and 1% of salts and extractives. It is formed from extracts of blood and other body liquids, called interstitial fluid or tissue fluid, that collect in the spaces between cells. Some of the interstitial fluid goes back into the body through the capillary membrane, but most enters the lymphatic capillaries, to become lymph. Along with this interstitial fluid, the lymph also picks up any particles that are too big to be absorbed through the capillary membrane. These include cell debris, fat globules, and tiny protein particles. The lymph then moves into the larger lymphatic vessels and through the lymph nodes, eventually entering the blood through veins in the neck region. The lymphatic system is thus a secondary transport system. Lymph has no pump of its own. Its flow depends on pressure from the blood system and the massaging effect of the muscles.

Respiratory System

The respiratory system is responsible for supplying oxygen to the blood and expelling waste gases (of which carbon dioxide is the primary constituent) from the body. The upper structures of the respiratory system are combined with the sensory organs of smell and taste (in the nasal cavity and the mouth) and the digestive system (from the oral cavity to the pharynx). At the pharynx, the specialized respiratory organs diverge into the airway. The larynx, or voice box, is located at the head of the trachea, or windpipe. The trachea extends down to the bronchi which branch off at the tracheal bifurcation to enter the hilus of the left or right lung. The lungs contain the narrower passageways, or bronchioles, that carry air to the functional unit of the lungs, the alveoli. There, in the thousands of tiny alveolar chambers, oxygen is transferred through the membrane of the alveolar walls to the blood cells in the capillaries. Likewise, waste gases diffuse out of the blood cells into the air in the alveoli, to be expelled upon exhalation. The diaphragm, a large, thin muscle below the lungs, and the intercostal and abdominal muscles are responsible for contracting and expanding the thoracic cavity to effect respiration. Ribs serve as a structural support for the whole thoracic arrangement, and pleural membranes help provide lubrication for the respiratory organs so that they are not chafed during respiration.

Digestive System

The digestive system is responsible for processing food, breaking it down into usable proteins, carbohydrates, minerals, fats, and other substances, and introducing these into the bloodstream so that they can be used by the body. The digestive (or alimentary) tract begins at the mouth, where the teeth and tongue begin the breakdown of food, aided by saliva, secreted by the salivary glands. The chewed food, combined with saliva, is swallowed and carried down the oesophagus to the stomach. In the stomach, food combines with hydrochloric acid which further assists in breaking it down. When the food is thoroughly digested, the fluid remaining (called chyme) is passed through the pylorus sphincter to the small intestine and large intestines. Within the long, convoluted intestinal canals, the nutrients are absorbed from the chyme into the bloodstream, leaving the unusable residue. This residue passes through the colon (where most of the water is absorbed into the bloodstream) and into the rectum where it is stored prior to excretion. This solid waste, called faeces, is compacted together and, upon excretion, passes through the anal canal and the anus. Along the way through the digestive tract, the pancreas, spleen, liver, and gallbladder secrete enzymes which aid in the digestive process.

Endocrine System

All the organs in the endocrine system are glands. They are unique from other glands, because they release chemicals known as hormones into general circulation. Other glands discharge their secretion into ducts and to a particular place. These glands are called exocrine. The organs of the endocrine system are located in widely separated parts of the body: in the cranial cavity, in the neck, in the thoracic cavity, in the abdominal cavity, in the pelvic cavity, and outside the body cavities. The hormones they release are important to body functions. They regulate basic drives and emotions, such as sexual urges, violence, anger, fear, joy, and sorrow. They also promote growth and sexual identity, control body temperature, assist in the repair of broken tissue, and help to generate energy.

The Nervous System

The nervous system of the human body is responsible for sending, receiving, and processing nerve impulses. It controls the actions and sensations of all the parts of the body, as well as thoughts, emotions and memories. Of all of the components of the nervous system, the brain is the primary component, occupying the cranial cavity. Without its outermost protective membrane (the dura mater) the brain weighs an average of 1.4 kilogrammes, comprising 92% of the entire nervous system. It is connected to the upper end of the spinal cord and is responsible for issuing nerve impulses, processing nerve impulse data, and engaging in the higher thought processes. The spinal cord serves as a sort of telegraph cable that allows signals to be sent to and from the brain to the structures of the body and received again in turn from them. The spinal cord is about 5mm in diametre, and is slightly flattened. It passes through the vertebral canal, created by the vertebral arches of the spinal column and sends out roots and branches much like a tree. These structures contain bundles of nerve fibres which extend all the way down the body innervating even the skin of the tips of your toes. A single nerve fibre consists of a chain of neurons. Neurons are the basic cells of the nervous system. They are responsible for receiving and transmitting nerve impulses and forming long fibres by linking together. They consist of a cell body, which contains a nucleus, with one or more axons and dendrites extending from the body. The dendrites are the multi-branched portions which receive impulses, whilst axons are the elongated structures carrying impulses away from the body of the cell. Billions of neurons are located in the body's nervous system. They are so efficient that a nerve impulse, such as a pain impulse, can be transmitted from the hand to the brain and back again to allow a reflex movement in a fraction of a second.

The Nervous System. Basic Elements

Nerves One or more of a bundle of signal carrying fibres which join the brain and spinal cord with other parts of the body.

Efferent nerves Take a signal to a region of the body.

Afferent nerve Returns a signal. The spine has both efferent and afferent nerves.

Plexus The term 'plexus' refers to a network of nerves or blood vessels. The nervous system features a number of these networks, where autonomic and voluntary nerve fibres join together. These networks include the brachial plexus (shoulder), the cervical plexus (neck), the coccygeal plexus (coccyx), and sacral or lumbosacral plexus (lower back). The plexus closely mirror the 'chakras' (energy centres) of Eastern philosophy.

Axion Nerves types which carry impulses away from the body of the cell

Dendrites Multi-branched nerve types which receive impulses and forward them to the cells

Ganglion A collection of nerve cells usually located outside the brain or spinal cord

Autonomic Nervous System

The autonomic nervous system is responsible for the self-controlling aspects of the body's nervous network and is under the control of the cerebral cortex, the hypothalamus and the medulla oblongata. Working in tandem with the central nervous system, the autonomic nervous system features two subsystems which regulate body functions such as involuntary smooth muscle movement and heart rate. These two subsystems are called the sympathetic and parasympathetic nervous system and their functions operate in opposition to one another, delicately balancing the bodily functions which they control. The sympathetic nervous causes fight or flight responses in moments of stress or stimulus, such as increased heart rate, saliva flow and perspiration. The parasympathetic system counterbalances these effects by slowing the heart rate, dilating blood vessels, and relaxing involuntary smooth muscle fibres.

Through thought and breathing control we can control the ANS (Autonomic Nervous System) to help reduce stress.

Parasympathetic Nervous System

The parasympathetic nervous system is also referred to as the craniosacral system. It features ganglia in the midbrain, in the medulla oblongata, and in the sacral region. The first two, the cranial ganglia of the parasympathetic system, pass impulses to the facial, oculomotor, gloss pharyngeal and vagus nerves. The sacral group of parasympathetic nerves originate at the second, third and fourth vertebrae and extend nerves to the bladder, the distal colon, the rectum and the genitals.

The nerves of the parasympathetic nervous system are responsible for conserving and restoring energy in the body ,following a sympathetic response to stress.

Sympathetic Nervous System

Viewed individually, the sympathetic nervous system, also referred to as the thoracolumbar system, features a series of nerves which branch out of the spinal cord between the first thoracic vertebra and the second lumbar vertebra. These nerve fibres join into a long trunk of fibres, called the sympathetic trunk, on each side of the spinal cord. Along the sympathetic trunk are enlarged clusters of nerve fibres, called ganglia. From these ganglia, a number of nerve fibres extend throughout the body's tissues. Many of these nerves create additional ganglia, such as the celiac ganglia and the mesenteric ganglia.

The sympathetic nerves are responsible for contracting involuntary smooth muscle fibres, viscera and blood vessels, speeding up the heart rate and dilating the bronchial tubes in moments of stress.

How we Make Energy. The Mitochondria

Mitochondria were first observed in the 1880's, but it took many years for scientists to understand the organelles function. Mitochondria are now sometimes referred to as the powerhouse of cells because these organelles release the majority of the energy obtained from food and make it available to the energy-consuming processes of the cell. Energy is generated from sugars and fatty acids. Specialized enzymes that trap energy from the breakdown of sugar are imbedded in the inner layer. Besides supplying energy, mitochondria also help control the concentration of water, calcium and other charged particles (ions) in the cytoplasm.

Mitochondria use oxygen to release the chemical energy stored in food. This process is called cellular respiration. The biochemical reactions of cellular respiration fall into two groups - the carbon pathway, in which sugar is broken down into carbon dioxide and hydrogen; and the hydrogen pathway, which transfers hydrogen to oxygen in stages, forming water and releasing energy. In the hydrogen pathway, the hydrogen's electrons pass through an 'electron transport chain' made up of enzymes[29]. The electrons give up part of their energy as they move from enzyme to

[29] An organic molecule which acts as a catalytic agent to facilitate or speed up biochemical reactions

enzyme. This energy is then stored in molecules of ATP[30] (adenosine triphosphate). In the end, 38 molecules of ATP (adenosine triphosphate) are formed for every molecule of sugar that is used up in respiration.

The number of mitochondria varies depending on the cell type and may constitute twenty percent of the cell, such as a liver cell, that has a high energy requirement. Mitochondria are the largest organelles in an animal cell, after the nucleus. They vary in shape, but many are sausage-shaped or filamentous structures surrounded by a double-layered membrane. The inner and outer membranes are separated by a fluid-filled gap. Mitochondria vary in diametre from 0.5 to 1 micrometre and in length up to 7 micrometres. Folds of the inner membrane, called cristae, project inward and subdivide the interior of mitochondria into a number of compartments. Mitochondria can change shape quite readily. They swell or contract in response to various hormones[31] and drugs and during ATP manufacture. This swelling and contracting appears related to the movement of water through cells and is particularly evident in the kidneys, through which 180 litres of water are filtered daily.

Mitochondria are also self-replicating. They 'reproduce' by splitting in half. The characteristics have led to the suggestion that mitochondria might have evolved from bacteria that once developed a close relationship with primitive cells and then lost the capacity to live outside the cell.

Another characteristic of human mitochondria is the fact that all of a person's mitochondria are descendants of those of his or her mother; no paternal mitochondria are present. This is unlike nuclear DNA which is equally derived from both parents. Scientists have long suspected that defects in mitochondrial genes could lead to inherited disease in the same way as defects in nuclear DNA.

Transport in and out of the Cells

The movement of substances in and out of cells is either a passive process or an active process (which in itself is energy consuming).

Passive transport requires no energy and can occur by simple diffusion. This is the passage of molecules of one substance from a region, where it is present in high concentration, to the molecules of another substance and forms a uniform mixture of the two.

Oxygen, nitrogen and other small molecules that can dissolve easily in lipids (fat) move readily back and forth across the cells bilayer. Some molecules such as glucose, or sodium and potassium ions, cannot cross the membrane on their own by simple diffusion. They need selective transport proteins or special channels to allow them in and out of a cell.

In active transport the cell works to bring molecules in and push them out. The energy needed for active transport is derived from molecules of a high energy phosphate known as ATP (adenosine triphosphate). The energy from ATP forms a 'pump' to transport ions. When ATP is broken down bio-chemically, energy is effectively released which allows three sodium ions to be pumped out of the cell through the membrane and two potassium ions to be taken in. Other substances are transported through the cell membrane in a similar fashion.

Cells also use another mechanism, called endocytosis, to move molecules into cytoplasm. Two types of endocytosis can occur - phagocytosis and pinocytosis. Phagocytosis (from the Greek 'phago' meaning 'I eat') is the process of ingestion and destruction of bacteria or other foreign bodies. Pinocytosis (from the Greek 'pinein' meaning 'to drink') is the uptake of fluid by a cell and pinching off of the plasma membrane. In both forms of endocytosis, a section of the surface membrane folds inward around the entering particle, then pinches off and carries the particle into the cell. The resulting sacs are called vacuoles.

The opposite process, exocytosis, occurs when vacuoles moving from the cell's interior fuse with the surface membrane and spill their contents outside of the cell. The method used to import or export substances depends on a combination of the transported item's size, chemical composition, electrical charge and abundance (concentration), as well as on its ability to dissolve in lipids.

---

[30] ATP a chemical which helps organisms convert glycogen to glucose.

[31] Hormones are complex chemicals which generate in one part of the body and circulate with the blood to another part where they control the function of an organ or a group of cells.

The Basic Dietary Elements

Carbohydrates

Carbohydrates provide energy for body functions and activity by supplying immediate calories. This is accomplished by the bodily transformation of carbohydrates into glucose, the main sugar in the blood and the body's basic fuel. Carbohydrates are stored in the liver and in muscle as glycogen. The body transforms glycogen in the liver into glucose for release into the bloodstream when it is needed for energy.

There are two general types of carbohydrates - simple and complex. Simple carbohydrates are sugars, glucose, fructose (both from fruits and vegetables) lactose (from milk) and sucrose (from cane or beet sugar). Complex carbohydrates consist primarily of starches as well as fibre that occurs in all plant foods. Complex carbohydrates are more beneficial for us than simple carbohydrates because complex carbohydrates have more nutritional value (they usually include protein, vitamins, etc.).

A high-carbohydrate, low-fat diet can reduce the risk for five of the ten leading causes of death, coronary heart disease, stroke, diabetes, certain forms of cancer, and arteriosclerosis (bone diseases). Fifty-five to sixty percent of daily calories should come from carbohydrates, with no more than fifteen percent of total calories from simple carbohydrates. Sources of carbohydrates include grains, nuts, potatoes, and fruits.

Protein

Proteins, composed of amino acids, are indispensable in the diet. They build, maintain and repair the body. Without dietary protein, growth and all bodily functions would cease.

The human body manufactures 'nonessential' amino acids, and requires ingestion of about eight or nine 'essential' amino acids. These can come from either animal or vegetable sources, such as eggs, milk, fish, meat, poultry, soybeans and nuts. High quality proteins, such as eggs, meat or fish, supply all essential amino acids needed in the diet and are called 'complete proteins'. The 'incomplete proteins' supply only a few of the essential amino acids and need to be eaten in combination with other protein sources for balance. A peanut butter sandwich is an example - the bread is rich in methionine and the peanut butter is rich in lysine.

As with most foods, too much protein in our diet can cause problems. Excess protein breaks down in the body for energy (after carbohydrates and fat are used) or, if not used, converted to fat. A diet high in animal protein increases the loss of calcium in the body. Also, excessive amounts of protein can produce dehydration, diarrhoea and may also aggravate liver or kidney disease. Only strength-building exercise, not more protein or supplements, will build muscles.

Fibre

Fibre is a large group of different chemical substances with a variety of physical properties, which are divided into two basic types - soluble and insoluble. There are five major forms - cellulose, hemi cellulose, lignin, pectin, and gums. Fibre is found only in plant foods which are passed through the digestive tract without being absorbed. Because it is not ingested, fibre performs valuable bodily functions.

Fibre helps move foods through the bowel more easily and aids in the elimination of wastes. A high-fibre diet may reduce the risks of cancer of the rectum and colon, and may lower blood cholesterol levels. Soluble fibre has been shown to produce a reduction in LDL[32] ('bad') cholesterol levels without decreasing the HDL[33] ('good') cholesterol levels. Soluble fibre can also retard glucose entrance into the bloodstream, an especially important factor for diabetics. Intestinal disorders, such as diverticulitis, constipation and irritable bowel syndrome, can be reduced by a high-fibre diet. People with gallstones, diabetes and obesity also benefit from a high-fibre diet. .

The daily intake of fibre is recommended to be about 20-30 grams a day. You can ensure an adequate fibre intake by eating a variety of foods (the less processed the better), eating more fruits and vegetables (unpeeled is preferable), drinking plenty of liquids and spreading out fibre intake by trying to eat foods high in insoluble and soluble fibre at each meal.

Insoluble fibre is found mainly in whole grains and on the outside of seeds, fruits, vegetables and other foods. Soluble fibre is found in fruits, vegetables, seeds, brown rice, barley, oats and oat bran.

---

[32] LDL Low Density Lipoprotein

[33] HDL High Density Lipoprotein

Vitamins
Vitamins are organic substances your body needs to function properly. They help process other nutrients and help to form red blood cells, hormones, genetic material and chemicals in your nervous system. We need very small amounts of vitamins - about 1/8 teaspoon a day. The recommended daily amounts (the RDA) are included with each vitamin description.

Fat-soluble vitamins are stored in the body but too much can become toxic. These include vitamins A, D, E, and K. Excess of water-soluble vitamins are eliminated by the body naturally. These include vitamins B1 (thiamine), B2 (riboflavin), B3 (niacin), B6, B12, C, folic acid (folacin), pantothenic acid and biotin. Other B vitamins include choline, inositol and PABA (para-aminobenzoic acid).

If you do not eat well-balanced meals and a variety of foods, a vitamin supplement may be useful. It should provide the recommended dietary allowances (RDA) defined by the government. (Because of the hazards of vitamin poisoning, 'mega' doses of vitamins should be supervised by a doctor). The RDAs are estimates of vitamins needed to meet the nutritional needs of most healthy people.

Vitamins and antioxidants are found naturally in many foods. Here are some examples;

Food	Contains	Benefits
Broccoli	Is an antioxidant and contains twice the RDA of vitamin C	Is an antibiotic and contains zinc and vitamin B
Carrots	Contains antioxidant betacarotene	Good for kidneys and liver
Garlic	Antibiotic	Reduces cholesterol and reduces blood pressure
Oats	Source of vitamin B	Relaxes nerves and blood pressure, may affect absorption of some minerals
Oily fish. mackerel, herring etc.	Source of omega 3	Protects against heart disease
Sunflower seeds	Source of vitamin E	Helps reduce exercise injury. Low vitamin E levels are a precursor to heart attack
Oysters and other shell fish	Source of zinc	Boosts the immune system
Oranges, leafy vegetables and other citrus fruit	Source of vitamin C	Reduces susceptibility to colds

Antioxidants help reduce the harmful affects of oxygen free-radicals. These accelerate the ageing process and damage LDL which transports 'bad' cholesterol. . It has been shown that cigarettes are a major source of free radicals and that regular doses of antioxidants reduce LDL damage levels.

Cooking can affect vitamins found naturally in foods. It is better to cook vegetables quickly, in as little water as possible; roast or boil meats; use cooking liquid in sauces and soups. 'Fortified' and 'enriched' foods are better than non-fortified and non-enriched foods. Fortified milk products have added Vitamins A and D which are lost when fat is removed. Enriched grain products have added wheat germ and nutrients that are lost during processing.

A Balanced Diet
Food contains proteins, fats, carbohydrates, water, vitamins, and minerals. Nutrition is the way our bodies take in and use food to maintain proper functioning and is the foundation of good health. Eating correctly is critical for the proper growth and functioning of our bodies. There is strong evidence that eating well can prevent several chronic illnesses or diseases.

The first principle to good nutrition is to eat a wide variety of foods, because different foods make different nutritional contributions to our diets. Keep a balance between calorie intake and calorie usage; in other words, don't eat more food than your body can use or you'll gain weight. The more active you are, the more you can eat and still maintain the balance. Also, foods high in complex carbohydrates and fibre, low in fat, and cholesterol-free (fruits, vegetables, grains and legumes[34]) should make up more than 50 percent of the calories you eat. The rest should come from lean meats and poultry, fish, and low-fat dairy products. This will ensure that you get the proper amounts of vitamins and minerals and help keep your fat and cholesterol intake relatively low.

[34] Bean or pea- like vegetables

There are several steps to be followed for a healthy diet.

1. Carbohydrates should represent at least 50 percent, with protein about 20 percent, of total caloric intake.
2. Keep your total fat intake at or below 30 percent of your total daily calories. Limit intake of saturated fat to less than 10 percent of fat calories.
3. If you need to lower your cholesterol level, maintain cholesterol intake at 300 milligrams per day, or less. Consume a diet high in complex carbohydrates.
4. Maintain a moderate protein intake. Eat a variety of foods.
5. Avoid too much sugar.
6. Limit salt intake to no more than 3,000 milligrams per day.
7. Maintain an adequate calcium intake.
8. Get vitamins and minerals from foods, not from supplements.
9. Maintain a desirable weight.
10. Drink alcohol in moderation.

Exercise

A large proportion of us do not exercise regularly. This is especially surprising because exercise can provide numerous benefits to diving: it can improve cardiovascular fitness; it can improve muscular endurance; it can increase energy; it can dramatically reduce the risk of coronary artery disease; it can aid in weight control; it helps lower cholesterol level and it can improve one's sense of well-being as well as raising self-esteem. In addition, risk factors associated with certain kinds of cancer can be modified by exercise and regular physical exercise can reduce mildly elevated blood pressure over the long term. Before starting on an exercise programme, check with your doctor.

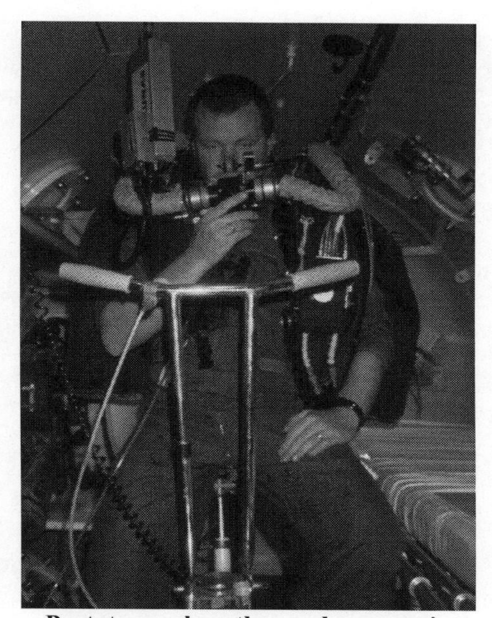

Prototype rebreather and an exercise bike at 50 metres. One way to work out!

Age is no barrier to exercise and its associated benefits. The more a person exercises, the better his/her chances to outlive his or her peers. Exercise contributes to longer life by reducing the effects of growing old. Regular aerobic exercise seems not only to help preserve neurological functioning into old age, but also potentially to enhance it in older people who have been sedentary for much of their lives. Staying physically active appears to be more important the older we get. Problems of aging, such as increased body fat, decreased muscular strength and flexibility, loss of bone mass, lower metabolism and slower reaction times, can be minimized or even prevented by exercise. Incorporating a relatively modest amount of activity in what was formally a sedentary life style derives a greatest surge in life expectancy. Remember, in order to get benefits from any form of exercise, it must become a long-term habit.

Exercise helps in weight loss and weight maintenance by building muscle tissue. The only exercise that burns fat is aerobic exercise. There is no evidence that exercise reduces or increases appetite. With regular exercise, though, calories burned should more than make up for any slight increase in appetite. Also, a programme of regular aerobic exercise may help lower total cholesterol and raise the HDL ('good') cholesterol[35]. Undertake exercise at least three times a week for thirty minutes per session to achieve benefits. However, there is a drawback. Exercise can affect blood cholesterol levels by temporarily causing a rise in cholesterol levels, by as much as 10-15%, for up to an hour after you've stopped exercising. Do not exercise just prior to having a blood cholesterol level test.

Variety in exercise is a key to staying fit. No single exercise adequately builds all aspects of fitness equally well. Having more than one activity to turn to also prevents exercise from becoming monotonous. Cross-training allows you to exercise more muscle groups than a single activity. Start slowly when you begin cross-training. The best method is to pair sports that train different parts of the body: swimming with cycling, rowing with running, etc. Split the total exercise time between the two activities, such as 20 minutes each for a 40 minute total workout.

---

[35] Found in animal fats, oils, egg yoke and the human body. Necessary for making vitamin E and some hormones (including sex hormones).

Benefits of exercise can be lost if you stop exercising altogether. If you merely reduce, however, you are often able to avoid or postpone the loss of benefit for at least several months.

Some tips for exercising:

- don't overdo it; discomfort isn't necessary ('no pain, no gain' is a myth)
- use adequate/appropriate footwear
- use controlled movements or slow down
- watch your form and posture
- don't bounce whilst stretching
- avoid high-impact aerobics
- warm up and cool down
- set realistic exercise goals; start slow and easy
- add variety (cross-train)

Warming up before exercising is the correct and best way to begin; stretching cold muscles can injure them. Regardless of any activity, it is essential to warm up first, then stretch. Warming up gradually increases heart rate and blood flow, raising the temperature of muscles and connective tissue and improves muscle function. It may also decrease the chance of a sports-related injury.

Warm up tips: a 5-10 minute warm-up is usually adequate (warm weather less time, colder weather more time); after exercise, cool down, slowing gradually; in cold weather, warm up indoors before going outdoors and finish by cooling down indoors.

Cold weather workouts require some allowances for the weather: don't overdress; wear several layers of loose-fitting, thin clothing; zip up; wear mittens instead of gloves; wear a hat or cap; wear shoes that offer good traction and shock absorption. Warm up and stretch indoors; drink plenty of fluids, as much water in the cold as in the heat; compensate for any wind; be on the defensive, remembering shorter daylight hours, etc; keep moving and wear sunglasses and sunscreen in hot climates.

Always remember: drink plenty of fluids, especially in hot weather, to replace fluids lost through sweating.

If you are 45 or older, consult your physician before beginning an exercise program. If you are 35 or older and have any risk factors for heart disease (recurrent chest pain, high blood pressure or cholesterol levels, smoking or obesity) consult a doctor. At any age, you should consult your physician if you have cardiovascular or lung disease or symptoms suggestive of these diseases.

Aerobics Exercise

A good level of aerobic fitness for divers is paramount. Exercise routines that generate muscle are of little use. Anything that keeps our gas transport system working at peak fitness is good. The best way to achieve this is aerobic exercise.

When an exercise lasts longer than a minute or two, the muscles obtain most of their energy from processes that require an increased supply of oxygen delivered to the muscles and tissues. These activities are called aerobic, meaning 'with air'. Aerobic activities include running, brisk walking, swimming, cycling, rowing, cross-country skiing, rope skipping and aerobic dance.

The most important element of physical fitness is cardiovascular endurance, this is the sustained ability of the heart, blood vessels and blood to carry oxygen to the cells, the ability of the cells to process oxygen and the ability of the blood to carry away waste products. Cardiovascular endurance is built up through exercises that enhance the body's ability to deliver ever larger amounts of oxygen to working muscles. The exercise must utilise the large muscle groups, such as those in the legs and most importantly, it must be sustained in order to achieve cardiovascular endurance.

When regularly performed, aerobic exercise helps keep elevated blood pressure at normal levels, reduces the risk of heart disease and can help control weight gain. There are also indications that it can raise the level of HDL ('good') cholesterol in the blood. An aerobic exercise regime can also have positive psychological benefits, such as increased self-esteem, lessened anxiety and even some relief from depression.

Pulse Rate with Exercise

As a guide to estimating how much we should exercise and just how fit we are we use our pulse rate as a guide. After exercise measure your pulse. If you are reasonably fit your pulse rate should equal 80% of the figure obtained if you take your age off of the number 180. Try and maintain exercise at this 80% figure. Remember 20-25 minutes is really the minimum exercise period for effective exercise.

Diving First Aid

The Incident

If an incident occurs a number of things need to be taken into consideration in order to provide effective first-aid. The scope of this chapter will assume that any casualties have already been rescued (or the incident has occurred) outside the marine environment. That is to say they are on dry land or on a boat.

The prime functions of any first-aid are:

1. **To preserve life**
2. **To prevent deterioration**
3. **To promote recovery**

Often known as the **'three P's'**

A generic accident management scenario would include:

- *Remove casualty from danger*:
    - Out of water
    - Away from shock hazard (isolate power source)
    - Away from heat source
    - Away from unstable structure
    - Away from machinery
- *Gather information:*
    - From the casualty
    - From others
    - Visual (situation) signs – something a first-aider sees or feels. Obtain symptoms information from patient
    - Think! Mechanism of injury. How could it have happened?
- *Ensure safety of other divers:*
    - If others still submerged, make arrangements for their safety
    - If a part of the same incident (especially DCI) but asymptomatic, then monitor carefully
- *Barriers for protection:*
    - Don gloves
    - Use mask
- *Casualty assessment:*
    - Start primary assessment
- *Apply applicable first-aid*
- *Alert emergency services*
- *Monitor the casualty*

Whilst most of the above is self-evident and common sense, the primary assessment is one of the most important aspects.

Primary Assessment

Response

The first step following an incident is to alert the casualty if possible and ascertain his/her state of consciousness. This is easily done by tapping the collarbone and elevating the voice to attract the casualty's attention. Do not shake them. If conscious, questioning can now begin to help ascertain the nature of the injury.
Levels of arousal can be assessed under:

Alert. Are they visibly alert and attentive?
Vocal. Can they be alerted by noise or voice?
Pain. Can they be aroused by pain (tap shoulder blade)?
Unresponsive. They cannot aroused.

ABC

The next step with both a responsive and a non- responsive casualty is to confirm the three primary functions. These are: **A**irway, **B**reathing, **C**irculation.

Airway
Ensure the chin is elevated and the neck extended (protecting the spine). The mouth and throat should be checked for obstructions. If any form of head or back injury is suspected do not tilt the head. Use a jaw thrust if possible.

Breathing
Listen and feel for breathing for at least 5 seconds. Look for rise and fall of chest.

Circulation
Check for the carotid pulse. Check both carotid arteries for pulse, in case of CAGE (cerebral arterial gas embolism) or stroke.

Bleeding
Next, look for and treat any major wounds. (*See section on 'Bleeding').*

Shock
Prepare for and treat potential shock. (*See section on 'Shock').*

The Secondary Assessment

Check for any medication\allergies\events
This can be checked using the acronym ;

AMPLE.

A Allergies check. Check for allergic tags.
M Medication check
P Past medical history
L Last ate or drank
E Events leading to the incident. Depth and time of dive. Ascent rate etc.

Pain
Locate painful areas

Repetition
Repeat primary assessment as required.

Vital Signs

Whilst conducting an assessment it is useful to know the normal vital signs one should expect from a person.

Pulse
Adult – 60 to 100 beats per minute and regular. A child's pulse will normally be faster.

Respiration Rates
12 to 20 per minute

Temperature
Place the back of your hand against your own forehead and cheek and the patients for comparison.

Tissue Colour
Found inside lower lip.
Look for cyanosis
Look for signs of hypoxia and CO poisoning

Resuscitation Techniques

Artificial Ventilation -Expired Air Resuscitation (EAR)

Expired air contains approximately 16% oxygen, which is sufficient to support life if no alternative means of ventilation are available. A preferred option is to use a pocket mask with an oxygen free-flow port. The rescuer is venting oxygen into the casualty with each breath. An approximate EAR rate is 1 breath every 5 seconds. Continually check for pulse.

1. Manual Ventilation

E.g. bag and mask. The bag should ideally have a reservoir and be fed from 100% oxygen.

2. Mechanical Ventilation

This can be performed with resuscitators such as the 'Helios Motivox' unit, which has a positive pressure ventilation mode that produces a peak pressure of 20cm H_2O. This is below the level that is likely to cause damage to the lungs. However, there must be proper training to use it.

External Cardiac Massage (ECM)

In casualties who have suffered cardiac arrest, i.e. the heart is no longer beating and no pulse can be felt, some degree of circulation can be provided by external cardiac massage. ECM will normally be combined with EAR. The combination of these two techniques is known as Cardiopulmonary Resuscitation (CPR).

CPR (EAR & ECM) Procedures

Single rescuer – 2 breaths to 15 compressions.
Dual rescuers – 1 breath to 5 compressions.

Defibrillators

Trained personnel only may use this technique; layperson courses and units are available.

Respiratory System Review

Whilst our physiology has already been covered in detail it is worth reviewing it as a part of this chapter.

Function
The primary function of the lungs is oxygenation of and removal of carbon dioxide from venous blood, returning from all other parts of the body. Strictly speaking, the respiratory system consists of airways, lungs and circulatory system because respiration involves the exchange of oxygen and carbon dioxide in tissues. However, it is practical to consider the cardiovascular or circulatory system separately.

Respiratory System Anatomy
The upper airway consists of the nose, nasopharynx, mouth, oropharynx, larynx, trachea and lungs.

The function of the nose and nasopharynx is 'warming'; humidification and filtering of inhaled air, and reclaiming heat and moisture from exhaled air. It also provides the sensation of smell. A large part of these functions is lost when breathing through the mouth.

The main functions of the larynx are to provide protection of the airway from inhaled solids and liquids and also production of the voice.

The trachea extends from the larynx and divides into two main bronchi. These in turn divide many, many times before terminating in air-filled sacks, called alveoli, where gas exchange takes place. There are 23 generations (divisions) of airways before reaching the alveoli.

Respiratory System Problems
Hypoxia and anoxia

Hypoxia is a low supply of oxygen at cellular level. Anoxia is a complete lack of oxygen. Hypoxia is classified as follows:

1. Hypoxic Hypoxia (anoxic anoxia)

The partial pressure of oxygen in arterial blood is reduced. This can be due to:

A. Reduced PO_2 in the inspired gas – e.g. altitude or breathing a hypoxic gas mixture at sea level.
B. As a result of impaired oxygenation of the blood, due to lung disease or a medical problem – e.g. pneumonia and lung collapse, pulmonary fibrosis, asthma and emphysema (these are causes of impaired gas exchange).
C. Due to impaired oxygenation of the blood from ventilatory failure – e.g. exhaustion, mechanical obstruction of the airway or increased breathing resistance.

2. Anaemic Hypoxia

Due to anaemia – usually not evident at rest until anaemia is very severe, but may limit exercise.

3. Stagnant / Ischaemic Hypoxia

Due to poor tissue perfusion. Although the blood may be carrying sufficient oxygen, insufficient blood is reaching the tissues – e.g. in shock due to haemorrhage.

4. Histotoxic Hypoxia

There is adequate oxygen delivery to the tissues, but cellular use of oxygen is impaired by a toxic agent – e.g. cyanide poisoning.

Treatment for Hypoxia/Anoxia

1. Ensure an adequate airway and support if necessary.
2. Give supplemental oxygen. Continuous high flow oxygen via a 'Hudson' mask with a reservoir is more appropriate in this situation as the patient may not be able to cope with the additional respiratory resistance imposed by a demand valve.
3. Call the appropriate emergency services.

Pneumothorax
Occurs when air (or other gas) enters the pleural space (between the lungs and the chest wall). This can either be through a hole in a lung or a hole in the chest wall. The lung on the affected side tends to collapse and the mediastinum may move towards the opposite side.

1. Closed Pneumothorax:
If the hole admitting air closes off again afterwards, only a limited amount of air can enter the pleural space. Unless the pneumothorax is very large, it does not cause much hypoxia and it may be symptomless.

2. Open Pneumothorax:
If the hole admitting air remains open, air moves in and out of the pleural space as the patient breathes (for example in a penetrating chest injury). If the hole is large, more air may move in and out of the pleural space than the lung. This causes hypoxia, hypercapnia and severe respiratory distress.

3. Tension Pneumothorax:
Occasionally, a hole may occur with a flap of tissue across it, acting like a flutter valve. This allows air to enter the pleural space, but not leave it. The pressure in the pleural space can rise above ambient pressure, causing a shift of the mediastinum to the opposite side, kinking of the great blood vessels and failure of venous return to the heart. This causes hypoxia and shock. Peripheral blood vessels become engorged and there is cyanosis and respiratory distress. The affected side of the chest may be over-expanded and will be hyper-resonant to percussion. The trachea may be deviated to the opposite side. This condition can be fatal unless air is released from the pleural cavity.

Pulmonary barotrauma (see decompression related disorders) can occur in divers who do not exhale sufficiently during ascent. Gas can escape from the lung into arteries (causing arterial gas embolism), mediastinum or pleural space. The change in ambient pressure and expansion of the gas in the pleural space can rapidly develop a severe tension pneumothorax.

Treatment of Pneumothorax
All patients with suspected pneumothorax require assessment and treatment in hospital. Appropriate first-aid measures are:

1. Ensure adequate airway and airway support if necessary.
2. Give supplemental oxygen. Continuous high flow oxygen via a 'Hudson' mask with a reservoir is more appropriate in this situation as the patient may not be able to cope with the additional respiratory resistance imposed by a demand valve.
3. Call the appropriate emergency services.

An open pneumothorax in the chest wall should be covered with a sterile airtight pad, which can be taped down on three out of four sides. This acts like a valve, allowing air to escape from the pleural space, but not re-enter it.

Life-threatening tension pneumothorax may need emergency drainage with a cannula placed into the pleural space on the affected side. This should be done by someone experienced in this procedure, such as a doctor or paramedic.

Collapsed lung
When a bronchus or bronchiole is obstructed, the gas beyond the obstruction will be absorbed and the lung segment will collapse. If the collapse is large, the mediastinum is pulled to the affected side (with accompanying tracheal deviation). Hypoxia and respiratory distress is likely to result. Lung collapse usually results from pneumonia or a foreign body in the lower airway, but is also caused by pneumothorax or haemothorax (blood in the pleural cavity).

Asthma

Symptoms of asthma include wheezing, coughing and a feeling of tightness in the chest (due to narrowing of the airways). R.A.D. Asthma – Reactive Airway Disease. Severe asthma attacks can be incapacitating and potentially life-threatening.

Some asthmatics are allowed to take part in sports diving. They should be well - controlled and not experience frequent attacks (i.e. not having to frequently use inhaled bronchodilators). They should not take oral bronchodilators or steroids, but regular inhaled steroids are acceptable. Asthmatics whose attacks are triggered by cold or exercise should not dive.

Most asthma attacks respond well to inhaled bronchodilators such as ventolin (salbutamol). If an attack is severe and prolonged, medical advice should be immediately sought. Asthmatic medication should be used on or by only the person for whom it was prescribed.

First aid assistance includes:

1. The patient should stop activity and rest
2. They should be sat up
3. Inhaler (if one is carried) – casualties only
4. Supplemental oxygen if necessary. This should be given by continuous high flow rather than demand valve.

Drowning

This is defined as 'suffocation by immersion'. In about 10% of cases, the first gasp of water when a breath is taken causes laryngospasm and death results from asphyxia, without any water in the lungs (dry drowning). In the remaining cases, the larynx eventually relaxes and water enters the lungs. There are theoretical differences between fresh water and salt water drowning, but these are not usually of any practical significance.

The initial goal in treatment of near-drowning is resuscitation:

A. Airway – clear of debris and open

B. Breathing (and supplemental oxygen) – artificial ventilation if necessary

C. Circulation – external cardiac massage if necessary

These patients are likely to be hypothermic and should be kept warm.

All patients who have suffered near drowning should be admitted to hospital, even if they have made an apparently full recovery, as there can be delayed and potentially life-threatening effects including pulmonary oedema (secondary or delayed drowning).

Hyperoxia

Although essential for life, oxygen in high concentrations is also toxic. In adults, there are two main types of oxygen toxicity. The first is subacute or pulmonary oxygen toxicity. This can be caused by concentrations of oxygen greater than 50% at sea level when breathed for many hours. When concentrations of 80-100% are breathed for more than 8 hours, irritation of the airways may result causing retrosternal pain (usually burning), cough and a feeling of shortness of breath. Exposure for greater than 24 hours can cause lung damage. The duration of exposure required to cause damage decreases as the partial pressure of oxygen increases and is therefore shorter with hyperbaric oxygen exposures.

Acute oxygen toxicity affects the central nervous system causing muscular twitching, dizziness, ringing in the ears, nausea and vomiting, convulsions and coma. This does not usually occur with partial pressures of oxygen below 1.8 bar. (1.8 is a non-submerged limit – 1.6 for immersion) As the partial pressure of oxygen breathed is increased, the duration of exposure required to produce symptoms decreases. Other factors can also shorten the exposure time required to produce symptoms such as exercise, hypercapnia, and immersion.

Patients suffering from either type of oxygen toxicity should be removed to breathing an oxygen partial pressure of less than 0.5bar as quickly as possible.

First-aid assistance includes:

Rest
Removal of any respiratory impediments
Supplemental oxygen by continuous high flow maybe necessary if DCI is suspected.
Only administer oxygen is the casualty is rested and alert and has ceased convulsing.

Hypercapnia
Retention of carbon dioxide is caused by insufficient ventilation for the amount of carbon dioxide that is being produced by the body. In divers this can be caused by an increase in breathing resistance due to gas density at depth or by faulty equipment. Initially this stimulates an increase in respiration. There may be a sensation of shortness of breath. If respiration remains insufficient, further CO_2 retention occurs causing confusion, decreased sensory acuity and eventually coma, respiratory depression and death. CO_2 'retainers'[36] as they are known, often experience headaches caused by hypercapnia.

In divers, carbon dioxide retention can also be caused by breathing contaminated gas or absorbent system failure (in rebreather apparatus). Divers in water suffering from CO_2 retention should stop exercising and rest, before beginning ascent. Divers exiting after a dive and showing symptoms of hypercapnia (normally a headache) are either CO_2 retainers, have faulty breathing equipment or have been stressed on the dive, the resultant breathing pattern generating CO_2 retention. This is normally characterised by a large usage of gas.

Treatment of patients on the surface suffering from CO_2 retention should consist of:

Rest
Removal of any respiratory impediments
Supplemental oxygen by continuous high flow if necessary

Carbon Monoxide Poisoning
In normal circumstances, oxygen is carried in the blood by combining with haemoglobin to form oxyhaemoglobin. The presence of haemoglobin allows blood to carry much more oxygen than it could do simply in solution. Blood with a normal haemoglobin count can carry approximately 21mls of oxygen per 100mls of blood at 1 bar breathing air. Without haemoglobin, under the same conditions, blood plasma can dissolve only 0.3mls of oxygen per 100mls. This is insufficient to support life.

Carbon monoxide binds to haemoglobin approximetely 220 times more strongly than oxygen, forming carboxyhaemoglobin, which cannot take up oxygen. Carbon monoxide is also toxic at a cellular level, affecting the enzymes involved in cellular oxygen utilisation. Carbon monoxide poisoning can thus fit into both anaemic hypoxia (as less haemoglobin is available to bind to oxygen, as in anaemia) and histotoxic hypoxia.

Symptoms:

Shortness of breath
Headache
Nausea and vomiting
Increased heart rate
Impaired judgement/conscious level
Unconsciousness and death

The classical 'cherry-red' colouring of lips and nail beds is usually not seen until carboxyhaemoglobin levels are very high.

Rest
Removal of any respiratory impediments
Supplemental oxygen by continuous high flow if necessary.

[36] Dr Ed Lanphier. USN Experimental Diving Unit

Circulatory System Review

Function

Blood transports oxygen from the lungs to the tissues where it is used and carbon dioxide in the opposite direction. The circulatory system also carries nutrients required by tissues and removes waste products to the organs that dispose of them (liver and kidneys).

Blood also carries various hormones, proteins and other chemicals required for normal body function.

Blood is: - Plasma (bulk transport medium)
RBC[37] (containing haemoglobin for gas transport)
WBC[38] (immune system)

Anatomy

Blood returns in veins from organs of the body to the vena cava and then into the right side of the heart (right atrium and right ventricle). From here it is pumped to the lungs via the pulmonary arteries. In the lung, blood is oxygenated and carbon dioxide is removed. From the lungs, blood returns to the left side of the heart in the pulmonary veins. The left ventricle then pumps blood into the aorta that feeds into all the arteries that supply blood to the body tissues. In the tissues, oxygen is given up to the tissues and the blood takes up carbon dioxide before it returns to the right side of the heart.

Circulatory System Problems

Wounds and Haemorrhage

Lacerations to larger vessels including pelvis and femur fractures can cause life-threatening haemorrhage. Blood loss should be stopped with direct pressure on the bleeding point if possible. Medical assistance should be sought immediately.

Pressure Points

A first-sider is limited to brachial (between upper and lower muscles of upper arm) and femoral (in groin) pressure point managment.

The basic process of first-aid is **Pad, Elevate, Pressure**.

Pad

Apply an absorbent dressing to the wound

Elevate

If possible raise the wound above the heart

Pressure

Pressure points slow blood flow to the site of the wound. In first-aid two can easily be used.

1. Brachial pressure point. Found on upper arm, press brachial artery against humorous.
2. Femoral pressure point. Found in groin. Press femoral artery against pelvis.

[37] Red blood cells
[38] White blood cells

Fluid Loss and Dehydration

Causes of fluid loss:

Blood loss (haemorrhage)
Sweat
Urine (immersion dieresis, cold induced dieresis)
Vomiting and diarrhoea
Respiratory (humidifying dry breathing gas)
Burns
Decompression sickness

Fluid loss and dehydration cause failure of the circulatory system and can cause shock. Hypovolemia is also caused by vasoconstriction.

Fluid replacement and re-hydration

1. Oral. Ideally isotonic water/salt/glucose mixture. Water is sufficient for mild dehydration.

2. Intravenous. In severe fluid loss, or for patients who are unable to take oral fluids, appropriate fluids must be given intravenously. This requires medical or paramedical supervision.

Shock

Shock is inadequate perfusion at tissue level. This results in inadequate oxygenation, provision of nutrients and inadequate removal of CO_2 and other waste products.

Shock causes:

Poor peripheral perfusion – slow capillary refill
Tachycardia (increased heart rate)
Thirst
Low blood pressure
Dizziness
Confusion
Coma and death

Shock should be treated with appropriate fluid resuscitation and treatment for the cause of shock. (A.B.C.s)

First aid treatment (in addition to A,B,C's) for shock should include:

Oxygen
Attend to any bleeding points
Keep the patient warm
Intravenous fluids given by personnel experienced in this procedure.

The standard first-aid treatment for shock in an EMS served environment includes not administering any fluids by mouth.

Decompression Related Disorders

Classification

Decompression Illness

1. **Pain only**
2. **Cutaneous**
3. **Serious:** Neurological
Pulmonary
Cardiovascular

Barotrauma

1. **Pulmonary**
2. **Sinus**
3. **Oral**
4. **Mask squeeze**

Causes

Decompression Illness – DCS & AGE

Decompression illness is caused by the evolution of dissolved gas into bubbles on or after an ascent. Whilst at depth, inert gas breathed at high pressure is dissolved into blood and tissues according to Henry's law, during ascent, ambient pressure is reduced and some dissolved gas must come out of solution. If the ascent is too rapid, this gas may form bubbles in blood and other tissues and these bubbles may cause symptoms.

Barotrauma

Barotrauma is caused by changes in volume of enclosed gas filled spaces in the body during ascent or descent. The ears, sinuses, teeth, gut and lung can all be affected.

Pulmonary barotrauma is caused by expansion of gas in the lungs during ascent. If the expanding gas is unable to escape (for example if the diver holds his breath), or the airway is partially blocked, pulmonary barotrauma (lung rupture) may result. Gas escaping from the lung by barotrauma may enter the pleural space causing a pneumothorax (which may develop into a tension pneumothorax with further gas expansion) or may enter the mediastinum, subcutaneous tissue or pulmonary venous blood.

If gas enters the pulmonary veins, cerebral arterial gas embolism (CAGE) is likely to result. This occurs when bubbles in arterial blood enter and block the circulation to the brain.

Diagnosis

Pain-only Decompression Illness

This usually manifests as pain in or around a joint, often shoulders, elbows and knees, but other joints can be involved. The pain is usually dull, aching and constant **and no position will provide relief, unlike a muscle injury**. It can vary from a mild 'niggle' to excruciating pain. Pain can manifest any time after surfacing up to and on rare occasions after 24 hours.

Cutaneous Decompression Illness (skin bends)

This is caused by formation of bubbles in cutaneous issue or cutaneous capillaries. It can manifest as a rash, a little like a nettle sting, often accompanied by itching. Another manifestation of cutaneous decompression illness is as an area of dark mottling of the skin called marbling (cutis marmorata), which looks similar to a bruise. This may be tender or painful. Cutis Marmorata is associated with neurological decompression illness and should be regarded as a serious sign.

Neurological Decompression Illness

This can manifest any time after diving but usually does so within an hour after surfacing.

Symptoms include:

Numbness and 'pins and needles'
Weakness of limbs, difficulty walking
Visual disturbances
Difficulty speaking
Dizziness and vertigo
Confusion, unconsciousness and fits

Cerebral Arterial Gas Embolism (CAGE)
Usually manifests during ascent or within a few minutes after surfacing.

Features include:

Visual disturbances
Numbness or pins and needles
Limb weakness, especially hemiplegia (weakness of arm and leg on the same side)
Confusion
Unconsciousness and convulsions

Pulmonary and Cardiovascular Decompression Illness
Bubbles in venous blood in small amounts are tolerated without ill effect. These bubbles are usually 'filtered' out by the lungs and the gas eliminated. In larger quantities though, venous bubbles may start to block pulmonary vessels. This produces shortness of breath, chest pains and coughing ('the chokes'). Obstruction of the pulmonary blood vessels can result in hypertension (shock) and in severe cases circulatory collapse.

In extreme cases, for example in explosive decompression or omission of a large amount of decompression, there may be formation of large amounts of gas in all vessels. resulting rapidly in shock, circulatory collapse and death.

Treatment of Decompression Illness

The definitive treatment of decompression sickness is recompression, but first-aid measures are important in ensuring a satisfactory recovery.

1. Resuscitation: attention to airway, breathing and circulation. Victims of severe decompression illness and CAGE may need artificial ventilation and ECM
2. Positioning: lie the casualty down flat, especially for serious decompression illness.
3. Administer oxygen
4. Administer fluids: orally, if the patient is able to take oral fluids, intravenously if appropriately trained.
5. Keep the patient warm
6. Arrange for evacuation to hospital / hyperbaric unit.

Oxygen Administration
Oxygen administration is an important component in first-aid for many conditions particularly:

Decompression illness and CAGE
Unconsciousness from any cause
Haemorrhage and shock
Pneumothorax and other causes of difficulty with respiration

In decompression illness, oxygen hastens the elimination of inert gas, reduces the size of any inert gas bubbles and helps to prevent more bubbles from forming. It may improve damaged tissues.

Speed of delivery is vital. The first 15 minutes after a symptom occurs may be critical.

Oxygen by Demand Valve
Patients with decompression illness who do not have any respiratory difficulty and who are able to tolerate using a demand valve should be given oxygen by this method, ideally with a facemask fitting. This will provide close to 100% oxygen. It also increases the duration of the supply cylinder, as it is a relatively efficient method of administration.

It is important to ensure that the mask is a good fit and that the casualty is not breathing any air from around the sides of the mask.

For some casualties, oxygen by demand valve is not appropriate because of the additional breathing resistance imposed by the apparatus.

Continuous Flow Oxygen
Unconscious (but breathing) casualties and those with respiratory difficulty will not tolerate a demand valve and should be given oxygen by a continuous flow system. This should consist of a cylinder with an appropriate reducing valve and flow meter with plastic oxygen tubing leading to a clear, light, plastic face-mask with a reservoir bag ('Hudson' type mask). With flow rates of 15litres/min, this system will deliver approx. 80% oxygen. The oxygen percentage will be lower if the flow rate is less (it is important to have a flow meter). Higher flow rates (18-20 litres/min) may be needed, especially in cases of barotrauma.

Cylinder duration is less with this system due to the higher total gas flow.

Oxygen Administration in Respiratory Arrest
Unconscious casualties who are not breathing require artificial ventilation. This can be done with EAR, mechanical ventilation with a bag and mask or with a 'power resuscitator'. One advantage of the latter two methods is that 100% oxygen can be given to the patient instead of 16%. The disadvantage is that they require additional training.

A self-inflating bag (e.g. ambubag) when fitted with a reservoir bag and connected to a continuous flow of oxygen of 10-15 litres/min, will deliver very close to 100% oxygen. In conjunction with a tight fitting facemask, this can be used to ventilate a casualty who is not breathing. Ventilation with a facemask is not always easy and requires some practice.

A 'power resuscitator', such as the Helios Motivox unit can also be used for this purpose. The peak inspiratory pressure is limited to 20cm H_2O, which is insufficient to cause barotrauma. It is important that the unit is in good working order and regularly serviced. Again, practise is required to maintain a patient's airway and use the unit effectively. This is beyond the scope of simple first-aid.

For most first-aiders a simple pocket mask with a supplementary inlet for oxygen is appropriate as it requires no extra training and will deliver approximately 50-60% oxygen levels.

Fluid Administration
Fluid administration is an important part of first-aid in decompression illness and can be useful in other conditions. Divers frequently have some degree of dehydration due to the effects of immersion dieresis, cold-induced dieresis and respiratory fluid losses (breathing dry gas). Intravascular bubble formation (e.g. venous bubbles) predisposes to fluid loss into tissues from the blood stream due to damage to the endothelial lining of the blood vessels. The easiest method of fluid administration is orally.

When to Administer Oral Fluids
Some form of fluid resuscitation should be given to all divers suffering from decompression illness. If they are able to drink then fluids should be given orally. This is not appropriate for unconscious casualties or patients who may be in danger of losing consciousness.

Ideally, oral re-hydration solution should be given. This is an isotonic solution containing sodium chloride and glucose. If this not available, water can be given.

Divers with decompression illness should be encouraged to initially drink approximately one small cup of fluid and then further smaller volumes until they start to urinate. Fluid administration should be continued until urine is clear. Caution should be used in divers with paralysis or loss of sensation as they may be unable to urinate and the danger is bladder discomfort and possibly rupture. **If they fail to urinate, stop fluid administration immediately**. In any event probably not more than 2 or 3 litres should be given without medical advice.

Oral fluids should not be given to casualties with haemorrhage and especially with shock as fluids are not absorbed well from the gut in this situation and these patients are likely to require surgery.

Intravenous Fluid Administration

This method of fluid administration is suitable for seriously ill and unconscious casualties. This is also the best way to give fluids to casualties with shock (e.g. due to blood loss) as fluid absorption from the gut is impaired in shock. Only suitably-trained persons should attempt this method of fluid administration.

The Skeletal System
The skeletal system is composed of:

Bone – There are 200 bones with three main uses;

- To support
- To protect
- To allow movement

The bones structure generally falls into one of three categories:

1. Long bones, such as the leg
2. Flat bones, such as the shoulder
3. Irregular bones, such as vertebrae

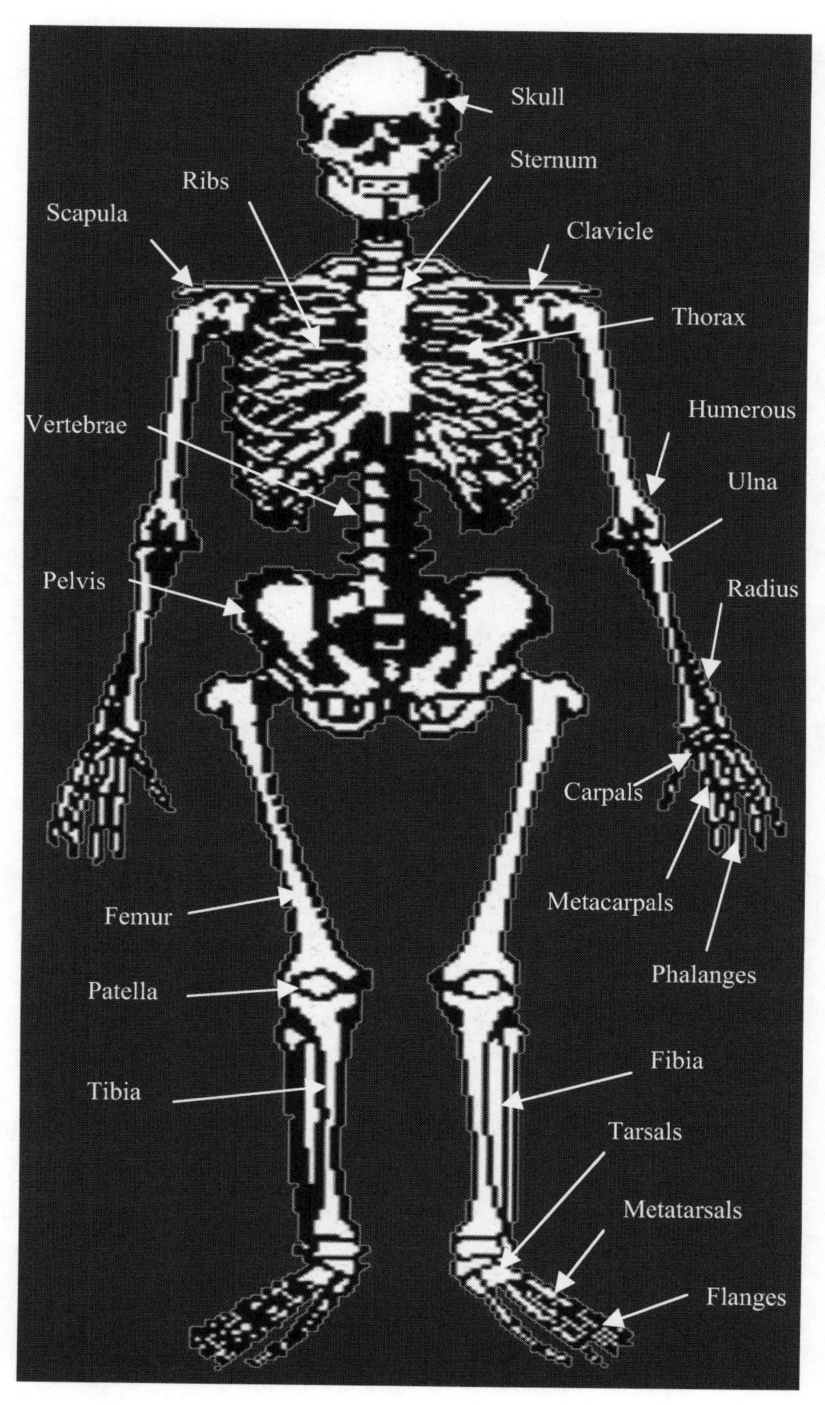

The bones of the skeleton can be separated into four main areas head, trunk, upper extremities and lower extremities. To enable the skeleton to move, a variety of joints complete the system. These include:

1. Fixed joints, found only in the teeth or cranial plate joints
2. Slightly movable joints found in cartilaginous plates between bones such as vertebrae.
3. Movable joints (synovial), include:
   - ball and socket e.g. hips
   - hinge e.g. elbow
   - gliding joints e.g. carpals
   - saddle e.g. wrist

Injury to the Skeletal System

Fractures
Defined as a break in the bone surface.

Causes – direct or indirect violence, muscular force or disease.

Classification of Fractures

Complicated – Bone breaks in two or more places. This may affect organs or blood vessels in the area of the break.

Impacted – Break ends driven into each other.

Depressed – Bone driven into a body cavity, such as in the skull.

Simple – A closed fracture – oblique, a break diagonally across the bone.

Transverse – A break at right angles to the bone.

Compound – Also open fracture, bone breaks through skin.

Greenstick – Partial break usually only in under 14 year olds.

Comminuted – Bone splintered into many small pieces.

Dislocation
Defined as the separation of a joint normally through force.

Areas affected, fingers, shoulder, elbow and ankle.

Other musculoskeletal injuries include tendon and ligament rupture, sprains, slipped disc and torn cartilage.

First-aid for Skeletal Injury

Fracture
Signs – The affected area may be deformed and swollen.
Tissue on site may be discoloured and with a compound fracture there will be a wound and possible bleeding at the site.
During injury assessment of the patient point, tenderness may be noticed.

Shock.
Symptoms - The patient will be in pain at the injury site.

For an EMS served environment splinting is often not required. A wounded area should simply be immobilised. Any constricting items such as jewellery should be removed and a cold pack can be used to minimise swelling.

In remote areas, splinting will be required. The splint should be well-padded and once in place circulation and sensation below the splint ties should be regularly checked.

Dislocation

Signs - The affected area may be deformed, swollen and discoloured.
A reduction or loss of function in the extremities of the affected area may also be noticed

Symptoms - Rhe patient will be in pain at the injury site.

In an EMS served environment DO NOT try to relocate the joint, as the risk of further damage to nerves, blood vessels and tissues is high. Simply treat as a fracture.

Head Injury

During injury assessment, head injury may be noted by the patient's response level[39] (ref. AVPU), wounds and deformity, bleeding from the ears, nose or internall bleeding, causing bruising of the eyes or behind the ears.

The patient may vomit and breathing may be shallow. For this reason ABC'S are critical.

Hypothermia

Features of Hypothermia

Mild hypothermia: Core temp 34-35°C

1. Shivering
2. Coldness/numbness of extremities
3. Cold induced dieresis, which can result in dehydration
4. Difficulty with co-ordination and fine movements
5. Lethargy and drowsiness
6. Amnesia of events whilst cold. Check situation where casualty is found i.e. cold wet or windy environment

Moderate hypothermia: Core temp 30-33°C

1. Drowsiness or unconsciousness
2. Fall in heart rate or irregular heart rate
3. Fall in respiratory rate
4. Shivering stops

Severe hypothermia: Core temp < 30°C

1. Semi-consciousness or unconsciousness
2. Muscle rigidity
3. Irregular heart rhythm and ventricular fibrillation
4. Below 25°C may appear dead. No pulse/reflexes, fixed pupils with no reaction to light or dark. 20.8°C lowest recorded survivable temp.

WITH A HYPOTHERMIC PATIENT THE FIRST AIDER SHOULD BEGIN AND CONTINUE FIRST AID EVEN IF PATIENT APPEARS DEAD (ESPECIALLY IF DROWNED).

Divers are susceptible to hypothermia because of:

Immersion in cold water
Respiratory heat loss – heating cold inspired gas and humidifying dry inspired gas
Wind chill post-dive

[39] P. 108

FIRST-AID Treatment of Hypothermia

Any movement of the patient must be avoided. Jarring may result in post immersion shock
Remove from cold
Keep horizontal during and after removal from the water
Protect from wind – blankets and sleeping bags
Body to body contact – skin to skin
Minimise heat loss from the head and evaporative heat loss:
This may involve removing wet clothing, but a large plastic cover combined with blankets or a sleeping bag will prevent evaporative heat loss without having to substantially move the casualty.
In severe cases where the heart has stopped, CPR will be necessary
Arrange transfer to hospital

Avoid using foil blankets next to the skin as water condensing on the blanket may drop onto the casualty and re-chill them.

Active re-warming should usually only be undertaken in hospital as it can precipitate ventricular fibrillation and cardiac arrest. In locations *very remote* from hospital assistance, the following method could be used for conscious casualties:

Keep the casualty in wetsuit/ drysuit, but take measures to prevent evaporative heat loss
Fill a bath with an initial temperature of ~36 degrees C
Immerse the casualty in the bath with the limbs elevated and outside the bath
Gradually increase the water temp to 40-42 degrees C

Re-warming should be with blankets and body to body contact.

Management of the Unconscious Patient - Summary

1. Safety first – ensure you are putting yourself in no danger and remove the casualty from danger if possible
2. 'Are you all right?' – tap the collar bone (do not shake the patient) and try to elicit a response
3. Call for / send for help (emergency services)
4. Lie the patient flat in a position where you can assess them
5. Start A,B,C's

A - Airway
Check that the airway is clear. Remove any material (e.g. vomit) from the mouth. Perform manoeuvres to open the airway such as:

- neck extension
- chin lift
- jaw thrust

Only do the above if you know no head, neck or back injuries have occurred – Think mechanism of injury!

B - Breathing
Check for breathing:

Listen for breath sounds
Look for chest movement
Feel for chest movement and breaths on cheek

If there is no breathing, then start artificial ventilation (EAR, manual or mechanical ventilation)

C - Circulation
Feel for a carotid pulse

If there is no pulse, start ECM

Once pulse and spontaneous breathing have been re-established, move the casualty into the recovery position (left lateral). Monitor breathing and pulse closely until help arrives.

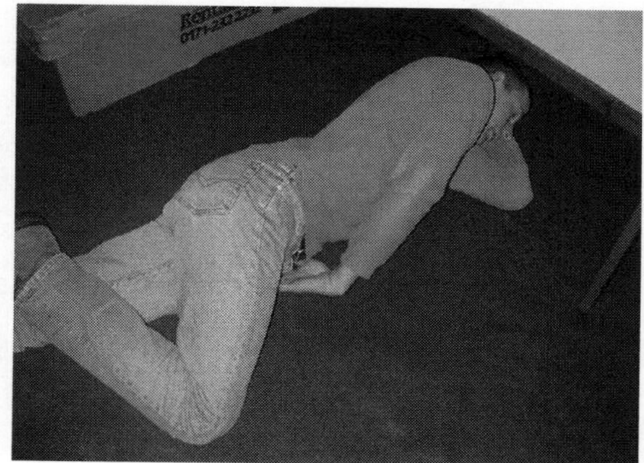

Recovery position
Note how the hand supports the head

Continue circle of care ~ A – B – C's

Continue to administer high flow oxygen to the casualty. Keep the casualty warm, call for help / await arrival of emergency services

Put the patient in the 'recovery position' – use a 'log roll', protecting the spine all the time

Decompression Theory and Techniques

Introduction

Many people become confused just looking at articles about decompression physiology. This chapter will hopefully clarify a few of the things we do know and investigate some of those we don't. Decompression physiology is far from an exact science at present and is often a mixture of fact and "what works, works". This chapter is written with that in mind.

Closed circuit decompressions will be covered in the rebreather section.

Let/s start by looking at some of the common terms we often read about and become confused.

Terminology

Tissue Compartment	First identified by J S Haldane. A tissue compartment is a theoretical group of tissues within the body which uptake (on-load) and release (off-load) gas at a certain rate. Uptake and release are also expressed as absorption and elimination.
Controlling tissue	The theoretical tissue which reaches super saturation first and hence controls the decompression at that depth.
Fast tissue	A theoretical tissue compartment with a fast rate of on-loading and off-loading of gas. An example of this is the blood.
Slow tissue	A theoretical tissue compartment with a slow rate of on-loading and off-loading of gas. An example is fatty tissue.
Halftime	Let's assume a tissue has a 30 minute halftime and is saturated at the surface to 1 bar. If we double the ambient pressure to 2 bar, then in 30 minutes the pressure within the tissue will be 1.5 bar. In another 30 minutes it will be 1.75 bar and so on.
Tissue tension	The partial pressure of inert gas present in a tissue
Lipid	Tissue with a high fat content
Aqueous	Tissue with a high water content
Saturation	A theoretical tissue is said to be saturated when the inert gas pressure within it is equal to the pressure of inert gas surrounding it. A tissue is said to be saturating when it is taking on gas.
De-saturation	As gas escapes from a tissue it is said to be de-saturating.
Super saturation	When the pressure reached within the tissue is greater than the ambient pressure. This occurs during ascent as the ambient pressure drops and the pressure inside the tissue increases as it cannot be released fast enough and the gas is trying to expand. This super saturation references a critical limit after which in theory, bubbles will form.
Tolerated overpressure	The level of super saturation at which, theoretical bubbles will occur. At this point gas can no longer stay in solution. Often expressed as an 'M' value.
Solubility	Different tissue types absorb more gas than others. Nitrogen is 5 times more soluble in fat than water based tissues. Whilst a gas may be highly soluble in a tissue (hold a large total amount) the rate at which it absorbs may be slow, as with fat. Nitrogen is more soluble than helium.
Diffusion	Diffusion is where high concentrations of a substance (gas) transfer to an area containing a low concentration.
Perfusion	Amount of blood flow or supply to an area. Certain parts of the body are more perfused than others like the brain.
Dissolved gas	A gas that is held in solution throughout the body.
Bubbles	Gases that for a variety of reasons have come out of solution.
Inert gas	We are primarily concerned with nitrogen and helium. Whilst these do not react with the body (they are inert) they can and do produce DCI
M values	The calculated partial pressure of gas in a tissue compartment that is safely allowed at a given decompression stop.

How the Body Deals with Gas

At 1 atmosphere (approximately sea level) breathing air, the body contains about 1 litre of dissolved nitrogen. This is equal to the partial pressure of dissolved gas in the alveoli, which is about 570mmHg or 0.75 ATA. At this time we are said to be saturated, our body cannot absorb any more nitrogen.

If either the fraction of nitrogen in the breathing gas increases (hence the partial pressure) or the ambient pressure increases (we submerge), which again affects the partial pressure of the mix when on SCUBA, the body will absorb (on-gas) more nitrogen again. If we hold at a steady depth, eventually we will again reach saturation where the partial pressure in the gas we breathe equalises with the bodies tissues partial pressures.

This process is allowed to happen because gas is dissolved through the lungs into the blood stream. As blood circulates and passes by tissues, if they (the tissues) have a lower gas tension (pressure) then some of the gas will transfer (diffuse) into the tissues. The blood now has a lower partial pressure of gas and as it passes by the lungs again it absorbs more gas, thus the process is repeated until the tissue tension equals that in the blood.

Tissue types absorb and release gas at different rates. This is partially dependant on the level of fat and the amount of perfusion. Tissues with high perfusion receive more blood and hence receive a greater supply of gas. Tissues with low blood flow may take longer to absorb gas. Exercise also speeds gas transport as the heart rate is increased to supply more blood, more oxygen and inert gas.

As temperature decreases, gas solubility increases. As temperature rises, solubility decreases and gas may come out of solution and form bubbles. Post dive heating (showers) has been shown to produce DCI.

Helium is slightly less soluble then nitrogen. Saturated tissues will hold less dissolved helium than nitrogen. This means decompression times will be shorter for saturated helium tissues. If solubility dominates for long exposures this should also hold true for short exposures (under 20 minutes) where gas exchange is limited by blood flow rates. For short bounce dives, nitrogen is a better gas because less will be absorbed.

As we ascend, the reverse of on-gassing starts to happen. The reduced inspired (breathed) partial pressure means that gas diffuses back from the tissues (with the higher partial pressure) to the blood and is carried out to the lung capillaries where it dissolves through the alveoli. If the ascent is too rapid then bubbles may come out of solution and block blood-flow around the lung capillaries. This in turn can slow down blood flow and reduce gas transport. Whilst bubbles of a certain size may be beneficial to off-gassing, large bubbles may distort and damage delicate tissues as well as slow down blood-flow.

There is a theory that suggest that bubbles can be so small as to bypass the lung filter and cross back through the heart to the arterial (oxygen rich) side of the blood system. These bubbles may grow (partly due to taking on more gas as they pass saturated tissues) and become lodged in the central nervous system. Work by Comex[40] in the North Sea supports this theory by showing proof of incidence of neurological DCI well 'within tables'. The bubbles were thought to have grown due to repeated depth excursions[41]. These bubbles bypassed the lung filter and became lodged in the central nervous system. These are now commonly called 'micro bubbles'.

The Bodies Natural Safety Margin

The human body uses more oxygen than it produces carbon dioxide. Carbon dioxide is more soluble, therefore more remains dissolved. The result is the total gas tension in venous (de-oxygenated) blood is less than the ambient pressure. This leads to a phenomena known as 'unsaturation'. Gas in venous blood is unsaturated by approximately 0.08 bar. This gives us a small safety margin during decompression as one can ascend a distance equal to 0.08 bar before gas tension begins to exceed ambient pressure, possibly causing bubbles.

Models

Decompression tables are simply models or estimations of how our bodies behave during diving. Below is a basic discussion of various models. What has become apparent in recent years is that the established saturation models like those pioneered by Haldane and Bühlmann are not enough, especially for deep decompression diving. Modern modelling basically falls into two categories: one attempts to cater for the affects of gas exiting out of solution in a controlled manner (saturation models) and the other models naturally, or otherwise, occurring gas bubbles (gas

[40] J.P.Imbert

[41] Bubble mechanics suggests that for a bubble to crush it is required to take it past the depth at which it was formed.

models). It is not the author's intention to discuss the various models in detail (there are many excellent books that can do this in far more detail)[42]. The purpose of this chapter is to remove some of the myths and provide practical advice on decompression safety. Whichever model you choose, make sure it is tried and trusted or conduct your own trials.

Solution Model

Professor A. A. Bühlmann was one of the first people to look at generating a decompression model for mass sport diving. There are many other unsung heroes such as Dr Max Hahn who took the basis of this work and worked with dive computer manufacturers (as did Bühlmann) to expand the thinking. The Bühlmann model used today assumes we have a range (16) of tissue compartments within the body which on-load and release gas at different rates. The decompression prediction assumes that during decompression, all gas is kept in solution. We now know this is not always to be the case as bubbles form on most dives. This 'pure' model is often insufficient for extended range diving.

There is practical evidence to suggest that the extended shallow water stops often associated with Bühlmann models are there as a necessity to control the onset of DCI after bubbles have been generated during the ascent. There have been many variations of solution models used, often by the military and the mass sport diving agencies. Statistically they 'work' but for extended range diving are proving to be somewhat lacking.

Bubble Model

Again there are a range of bubble models all basically assuming that bubbles are generated during an ascent and need to be controlled. As a result of this they often employ solution modelling as a base and attempt to try and predict the onset of bubbles. Models such as Dr. Bruce Wienke's Reduced Gradient Bubble Model (RGBM) focus on keeping bubbles within a safe size tolerance. Models like this are characterised by several deep-water decompression stops well below those of the established solution models. These deep-water stops control the growth rate of bubbles. By employing this profile it is possible to significantly reduce the shallow water decompression stops (when compared with solution models).

Practical application of these profiles were first noted by Hills, whilst studying pearl divers in the Torres Straits. He noted that exceptionally deep dives were conducted with minimal decompression by divers taking forced deep-water decompression stops to send up their catch.

Richard Pyle, an Ichthyologist from Hawaii also noted that he 'felt better' after taking a forced stop in deep-water to vent his catches swim bladders whilst returning from deep wall dives.

Stochastic Modelling

Worth a mention. Pioneered by the military, this is a database of thousands of dives and the resultant percentage and type of DCI for a given profile. From this a statistical model is generated and a prediction of DCI can be shown based on an equation. Tables are then generated.

The Models section of this chapter is a very brief overview of how the different models try to predict DCI. Readers are guided to the bibliography for more detailed reading on the subject.

Bubbles Basics

Hennessey and Hempleman were some of the first to look at the natural bubbles our body generates and theorised that they were a result of cavitation at the tips of the heart valves. These tiny gas bubbles were short-lived and dissolved back into solution within a few millimetres.

Unfortunately, as divers, we are absorbing gas all the time as we dive and some of this gas not only goes into solution but can add to these bubbles already in existence, making their survival distance longer. During an ascent, not only may gas come out of solution and form bubbles but any existing bubbles may grow. In the lung capillaries is where the bulk of the gas exchange takes place between the blood and inspired gas. Small bubbles may become trapped in the capillaries and are actually a very efficient way of getting rid of gas. However, if these bubbles are too small to become trapped, they may bypass the lung filter and find their way back to the heart, where they eventually return to the arterial (oxygen rich) side of the system. The arteries are at a lower pressure than the venus (de-oxygenated) side and hence bubbles may expand further. Unfortunately, the first stop for this bubble rich blood is potentially the central nervous system causing DCI.

---

[42] See Wienke, Bruce (Bibliography)

Pilar Project 2000. Phil Short recovering timbers, myself on the 'scooter mag'.
Photo Kevin Gurr

One of the first UK gas teams. Andy Judd, Alan Yeend, Phil Short, Alison Mason and myself.
Photo Ugo Losser

Family Day Out. Mandy and the girls. MK4 Cis-Lunar.
Photo Billy Deans

First Gas Dives in Scapa Flow. A 'young' John Thornton with me in the AGA. 1992

Cave Diving 1992. North Florida.
Photo Tom Mount

Pilar 1998. Andy Matroci and myself on the MK15.5's, Shaun Coles and the late Walter Canfield at the helm.
Photo Billy Deans

Britannic Bow Section. Project Britannic 1997. *Photo Dan Burton*

MK 15.5 plus metal detector. Pilar 1998.
Photo Billy Deans

Britannic 97. Al Wright and Richard Lundgren.
Jon lines in heavy current.
Photo Dan Burton.

Britannic 97. The 30kg plaque I laid on the wreck. It reads 'Jacques-Yves Coustuae. Pioneer Technical Diver. One of the many frontiers he touched. His example has enticed many of us to follow him and experience the silent world.' *Photo Dan Burton.*

Fontaine de Truffe, Dordoigne. France.
Photo Gavin Newman

Cova das Vallgonerva. Mallorca.. *Photo Gavin Newman*

Pilar 1998. Another use for a scooter.
Photo Pilar project

Britanic 1997. One of the three propellers.
Photo Pilar project

M1 project. Richard Larn, the dive team and myself, with the BBC film crew.
Photo Richard Lundgren

Pilar project 1998. "Tinker toy" our pulse induction metal detector system.
Photo Kevin Gurr

Britannic 97. Stern shot. Alan Wright is the dot in the middle.
Photo Dan Burton.

Pilar project 1997. Spanish silver coin recovery.
Photo Pilar project.

Britannic launching. The ship in the background is the Justicia now resting off Northern Ireland.
Photo Simon Mills.

Britannic 97. View from the bow to the bridge.
Photo Dan Burton.

Whilst all decompression theories assume that bubbles form either when the tissue tension v's ambient pressure is exceeded by any amount or by a certain ratio, the advent of ultrasonic bubble detection[43] has shown bubbles may form even when these limits have not been exceeded. Hence physiologists in recent years have tried to generate decompression models that predict the formation of these bubbles and their subsequent decompression. In practice it appears that a combination of solution and bubble theory is needed.

Bubble Mechanics

For a bubble to exist the gas pressure within the bubble must be equal or greater than the other pressures working on it. These crushing pressures are threefold:

1. the ambient pressure
2. the pressure of tissues pushing against the bubble
3. the surface tension of the bubble. The smaller the bubble, the greater the surface tension. Small bubbles may require large crushing pressures.

Several theories exist as to how bubbles form. Bubbles may possibly form between tissues when a mechanical stress has taken place and bubbles certainly form where turbulence or cavitation occurs.

Another theory suggests that we have bubble nuclei (microscopic pockets of gas) within the body. During diving these bubble take on gas and expand, causing problems during ascents. There is evidence to suggest that multiple days of diving may actually crush bubble nuclei. This has shown up as reduced Doppler scores for multiple days of diving the same profile.

Whichever theory or theories prove correct, the end result is bubbles coalesce (join) to form pockets of gas. Bubbles often distort, form a larger bubble to tissue contact area and form blockages. Bubbles then may place pressure on nerves and reduce blood flow to vital organs. They may even permanently distort tissue.

Once bubbles exist, if the ambient pressure reduces (you ascend) they expand. The gas inside the bubble is now at a lower pressure than the gas in the surround tissue. As a consequence more gas goes into the bubble, further expanding it. During bubble formation certain proteins are also released which in turn produce chemical mediators that can have affects such as thickening the blood, resulting in reduction of circulation.

Bubbles and the Immune System

Another unfortunate side affect of bubble generation is that the body's immune system sees them as a form of disease and attacks them. This is a complex and only partly-understood process. The immune systems response may go some way to explain why the onset of symptoms is sometimes delayed.

Blood consists of plasma which contains red and white blood cells, various proteins, platelets and other molecules. Plasma carrying oxygen and nutrients passes through capillary walls to supply the cells. Large molecules and red blood cells do not normally pass through the wall. When bubbles are present and generate inflammation, histamine is produced. This affects the wall of the capillary, making it more permeable. It may allow blood containing bubbles to pass through the wall. These bubbles that enter or formed within the interstitial spaces are too large to be re-absorbed and are then probably removed by the lymphatic system. Theoretically, bubbles in the lymph system can migrate to almost anywhere in the body.

Injured cells also release substances that attract platelets. These are designed to help localised clotting and plug any holes. Platelets themselves release a chemical which constricts the blood vessels. Pain and further swelling may ensue. Platelets attach themselves to bubbles forming larger blockages and restrict vital blood flow even more.

Dr Tristran Cope looking for bubbles

Bubble detection

A process known as Doppler detection is used to detect moving bubbles. The ability of a bubble to be detected is primarily dependant on its size. The smallest detectable bubbles are in the range of 20-25 microns. While Doppler is a good guide to decompression stress, as it does not detect stationary bubbles, the lack of a signal may not mean bubbles

[43] Doppler

are not present.

Doppler is the most common method in use for decompression studies. Ultrasonic frequency varies between 20,000Hz and 10Hz.The frequency used for bubble detection is normally 10Hz. The ultrasonic waves are strongly reflected at the gas liquid interfaces. The waves travel through body tissues, but are reflected by bubbles and bone.

The Doppler effect is only noted on moving bubbles, i.e. circulating and will therefore not pick up bubbles trapped in tissues.

Bubbles are represented as sound, picked up through headphones by an operator. The problems are distinguishing the bubble noise from sounds produced by the contractions of the heart, especially when active or shivering.
The equipment consists of:

1. transmitters to generate sound waves.
2. tranducers to convert waves to and from electrical impulses.
3. receivers to amplify the waves
4. speaker or headphones to present the results

Doppler has for some time been used as an aid in decompression table generation and many technical divers have used it in the field to modify profiles 'on the fly'.

Bubble counts are graded and scored. One such grading is the 'Spencer Scale'. Bubbles are graded from 0 (no bubbles) to 4 (constant bubble noise louder than the usual heart signal). In field use, bubbles are often recorded onto digital audio tape and sent away for scoring by a panel of experts.

Detection Points

Primary detection points are the pulmonary artery or the right ventricle of the heart found in the chest (precordium). This, however, can be a fairly 'noisy' detection area due to the function of the heart. The subclavian vein (below the clavicle in the shoulder) is also often used. With experience it is possible to pick out bubble noise against the normal 'whoosh' of blood flow as it is pumped by the heart. Start by logging subjects prior to diving, to get a reference sound. Readings should be taken immediately after surfacing and then again every 30 minutes or so. Peak bubble counts will normally occur between 30 and 60 minutes after surfacing. Most people will clear after 90 minutes if they have a low count on surfacing.

Testing for PFO.

PFO or patent formen ovale is a hole in the heart (which has not sealed properly from birth) between the right and left ventricle, hence de-oxygenated blood returning to the heart may bypass the lung filter and move over to the right (oxygenated) side of the heart. Therefore, bubbles bypass to the arterial system and potentially the CNS.

Approximately one third of the population may have a PFO of one form or another. PFO has been linked to incidence of DCI.

Detection is achieved by a cardiac echocardiograph with bubble contrast by the intravenous injection of saline with micro bubbles into the right heart. These are small enough to be trapped and removed by the lungs. Any bubbles that appear in the left heart indicate a PFO.

Carbon Dioxide.

CO_2 is probably one of our biggest enemies and the least taught at recreational level. As technical divers it is important we understand the mechanics of CO_2 and how it is generated and practise exercising stress-reducing skills[44] to reduce the potential threat from panic.

From the chapter on physiology we know the body produces carbon dioxide in the metabolic process. For every litre of oxygen metabolised, the body produces just under a litre of carbon dioxide. This carbon dioxide is produced at a cellular level and exits the cells via diffusion. Once in the blood the CO_2 is carried as bicarbonate due to its reactive nature. At the lungs there is a second diffusion and CO_2 exits with exhaled gas.

As CO_2 builds within the tissues it reaches a predetermined point which triggers the chemoreceptors. This, in turn, begins our inhalation. When diving, various factors alter these responses.

---

[44] see p. 20

Firstly, increasing PO_2 can make diffusion of carbon dioxide decrease. A bigger factor is any high partial-pressure of nitrogen. This has a depressing effect on the CNS. As the respiratory system is part of the CNS it results in a depressing effect on the breathing response.

As breathing response is slowed, CO_2 build-up occurs but without causing an increased need to breathe. (Many experienced divers have a very low gas consumption and others breathe incorrectly, such as skip breathing.) In this situation divers can be at a point where they do not ventilate enough CO_2. In diving, factors such as workload, cold and stress make the body produce more CO_2 which worsens the problem

U.S. navy research showed that breathing oxygen/nitrogen (nitrox) mixtures at depth increased CO_2 build-up whereas very little or no increase in CO_2 was found breathing oxygen/helium (heliox) mixtures. This is mainly due to the greater gas density of nitrogen based mixtures and hence increased work of breathing and CO_2 generation. A positive side affect is that less oxygen convulsions occurred on the less dense heliox mixtures.

Al Wright relaxing before a deep dive

Symptoms of excessive CO_2 include:
headache, sweating, dizziness, breathlessness (Dyspnoea) and visual disturbances. Carbon Dioxide is also a narcotic gas so narcosis experienced after rapid or hard fining descents may be partially attributed to CO_2 narcosis.

There is also a link between CO_2 build up and retention and DCI. During periods of high CO_2 production (such as when working hard) blood-flow to the tissues will increase to flush out the CO_2. More inert gas is transported (and absorbed) in the same time-frame. Problems arise later during ascent and decompression because tissues that have 'on-gassed' fast, at the high perfusion rate now 'off-gas' more slowly as the perfusion rate has dropped back to normal. Therefore, the extra inert gas cannot exit in solution and the tissues may over pressurise and bubbles form.

Some people naturally retain CO_2, purely due to their physiology, smokers, on the other hand, may retain up to 50% more CO_2 than a healthy non-smoker.

Ascent Gas Switches and Counter Gas Exchange.

Also known as isobaric counter diffusion. This can occur in one of two situations:

1. at depths of 200 metres plus, breathing helium mixtures whilst surrounded by a nitrogen atmosphere. This has occurred in chamber and bell dives and is not of concern to the recreational diver.
2. during decompression from non saturation helium-oxygen dives when the diver transfers to an air-breathing medium in the 30 metre range. This can cause extreme narcosis or true vertigo.

It has been noted in chamber dives where gas surrounding the diver is different from that being breathed, localised slight super saturation occurs where gas diffuses through the skin. For this phenomenon to occur, gases must have different physical properties. Examples in diving include, air and heliox and argon and heliox. Symptoms have been noticed with air and heliox at 90 metres which include, skin rash and itching, nausea, vomiting, vertigo and loss of balance.

It has been proven safe in trials to 180 metres that a diver can breathe heliox surrounded by air, but is at risk as shallow as 90 metres if the situation is reversed and air is breathed surrounded by heliox.

More relevant to the open circuit diver are inert gas switches. During deep gas switches the diver is placed in a counter gas exchange situation. Here the inert gas in solution within the diver is 'off-gassing' and the inert gas in the gas now being breathed is absorbed. The effects are the same but more limited due to the reduced amount of gas absorbed in the body. A more noticeable affect is when switching from a helium base to a nitrogen base gas and the 'narcotic shock' it can produce. One way to avoid the problem is to switch gas slowly, which can be achieved by swapping to the new gas for one breath then back to the original mix for two: followed by new gas for two and back to the original for one, before switching to new gas completely.

Omitted Decompression Procedures

Should decompression be inadvertently shortened or symptoms appear underwater during decompression. The following is offered as a practical first-aid procedure.

Note: 100% oxygen delivery at depths greater than 6 metres should not be undertaken without a full face masks and then only to a maximum of 10 metres.

Air / Nitrox- Omitted Decompression (Asymptomatic)

Repeat all stops deeper than 15 metres. Multiply the 10 and 6 and 3 metres stop times by 1.5. Surface, breathe O_2 and hydrate. If no symptoms, avoid diving for 24 hours.

Air / Nitrox- In-water (Symptomatic)

Descend two stops deeper than the stop, where symptoms started. Switch to the highest available PO_2. Wait 5-10 minutes, start ascent and repeat decompression procedure, evaluating symptoms at each stop. Extend stop if pain persists. Surface, breathe O_2, hydrate and medivac.

Mixed Gas - Omitted Decompression (Asymptomatic)

Descend two stops deeper than the first missed stop. Switch to highest available PO_2 (checking oxygen clock). Wait 5-10 minutes, start ascent and repeat decompression procedure. If no symptoms, avoid diving for 24 hours.

Mixed Gas – In-water symptoms (Symptomatic)

Descend two stops deeper than stop where symptoms started. Switch to highest available PO_2 (checking oxygen clock). Wait 5-10 minutes, start ascent and repeat decompression procedure, evaluating symptoms at each stop. Extend stop if pain persists.

It goes without saying that in an EMS served environment, DCI symptoms experienced on surfacing should be immediately treated with oxygen, hydration and immediate Medi-vac.

In-Water Recompression.

Note: 100% oxygen recompression at depths greater than 6 metres should not be undertaken without a full face masks and then only to a maximum of 10 metres. All recompressions should be undertaken with the casualty shackled onto a surface line and with a standby diver in attendance. Any in-water recompression should only be treated as a 'holding pattern' until medivac facilities are available.

Various options are available, all are emergency procedures to be used **only if EMS is significantly delayed or not available.**

In the past, divers have used air only to conduct a form of IWR. The outcome of these attempts has been varied. In some cases these have caused complete resolution but in others caused severe DCS for both diver and attendant. This 'hit and miss' nature prompted alternatives to be developed by Dr Carl Edmonds (Royal Australian Navy school of U/W Medicine).

Dr Cope testing an IWR rig

The Edmonds Procedure.

This is a pure oxygen treatment where the diver is taken to 9 metres breathing pure oxygen for a specified time. This can vary from 30-90 minutes depending on symptoms. The advantages are: breathing oxygen will take no further nitrogen into the tissues. This creates an increased nitrogen pressure gradient which will draw out nitrogen more rapidly present in tissues. Potential problems associated with deep (50 metres) air IWR, such as Narcosis and DCI for the attendant are removed. If the treatment must be aborted, divers can ascend directly to the surface as the treatment will incur no decompression. Due to the depth it is possible to conduct the treatment in sheltered water.

The US Navy Procedure.

This procedure is only for use when oxygen rebreathers are available and involves 100% at 9 metres for 60 or 90 minutes dependant on symptoms. This is followed by an additional 60 minutes at 6 and then 3 metres.

The Hawaiian Method.
A modified Australian method that includes a 10 minute descent breathing air to 9 metres greater than the depth at which symptoms disappear. This is not to exceed 50 metres, then back to 9 metres at a decreasing ascent rate where oxygen is breathed for at least 1 hour. Oxygen is then breathed on the surface.

Although all in-water recompression treatments have at some time been successful, they must be treated as an absolute last resort and should not be conducted without proper equipment and training.

In water recompression equipment list
The following is a basic list of the minimum equipment required:

- 'bell jacket' style harness with integral weights
- sufficient oxygen and air (break gas) for treatment. Usually, this will be 2 to 3, 10 litre cylinders of oxygen and one of air for a full Table 6[45] style treatment
- gas switch block coupled to a full-face mask
- a weighted line measured in 300mm increments
- communication system, preferably wireless

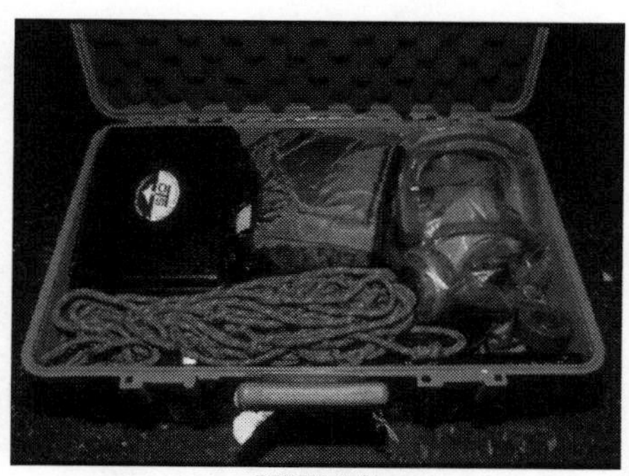

IWR kit

Post-Dive Rehydration
Post-dive decompression is as important as during the dive itself. Most people employ surface oxygen as a part of their decompression procedure. For extremely deep dives (especially where medi-vac is non-existent) and in addition to the standard surface oxygen usage a schedule of fluid replacement is added. One such technique has been pioneered by Jim Bowden and Ann Kristovich and used extensively on their deep cave explorations in Mexico.

Kristovich/Bowden Method
Any decompression schedule over 4 hours will include an IV for the surface deco period. Normal saline or lactated ringers are suggested. Glucose containing fluid is typically avoided if DCS is present. It is assumed that the diver's basic fluid needs are 4 to 6 litres per day. This requirement should be increased if the environment is warmer than 22 degrees Centigrade as more fluid will be lost through perspiration. This essentially means that a diver needs to have at least one litre of fluid for every four hour interval. All divers should be well hydrated prior to diving and ensure that their urine is clear and odourless.

The reason that IV is used post dive is because the fluid replacement then goes where it belongs, into the vascular system. Drinking a litre of fluid after a dive will not place a litre of fluid into circulation. A general rule is to administer the first litre as quickly as possible and begin a second litre at a rate of 200-300 cc per hour until the individual is urinating a clear and odourless urine. A person who is properly hydrated will excrete approximately 1 cc of urine per kg of body weight per hour.

Prior to this type of diving (10-12 hours of decompression), a pre-dive IV will be started to load the diver with fluids in advance.

Obviously this procedure involves some medical training. For most divers this procedure is impractical. Oral hydration is however just as important.

Decompression Techniques
For some time now it has been recognised that, quality as well as quantity of decompression is important. By quality we mean how decompression is physically conducted.

The following is a collection of science (if the analysis of DCI can be defined as such) commercially-attained knowledge and personal observations from a range of experienced divers.

In many cases any incident and especially DCI is a serious and frightening experience and the following is offered as a method of practical avoidance drawn from the above spheres of knowledge.

[45] Table 6 is a standard DCI treatment table

Fact, Fiction and Voodoo

The scope of this section is discuss the practical elements of mixed gas decompressions without going too deep into the science; partly so as not to generate confusion and partly because the science is still dynamic. For now, at least the philosophy of 'what works, works' is still relevant. Some of this has been covered in earlier chapters but is worth reiterating as a whole.

Over the years the art and science of decompression diving has evolved from almost folklore, through early experiments by pioneers such as Haldane, to eventually being taken up as virtual field trials by the mass recreational market.

In more recent years sport divers have had access to 'exotic' gas mixtures such as nitrox, trimix, heliox and heliair. In the case of trimix this has been used predominantly by divers simply extrapolating algorithms such as that developed by Professor Bühlmann for deeper depths.

Research over the years has come up with a variety of decompression 'models' designed to predict the decompression profile for a range of gases on any particular dive profile. The models themselves follow a range of theories, each trying to explain why divers suffer from DCI and how to avoid it.

Although a lot is understood about the mechanics of decompression, there is still much we do not know. As we are aware, the bottom line is bubbles. When we descend under pressure our bodies absorb gas. Looking at one of the classic solution models, it is assumed our bodies are divided into a series of 'compartments' which absorb and release gas at certain rates. If we stay submerged long enough, the partial pressure of gas in any given compartment will eventually equal the partial pressure of the same gas in the mix we breathe. This is known as 'saturation'.

As we ascend gas expands within the theoretical compartment. How far we can come up is defined by the amount of 'over-pressure' any one compartment can withstand before gas (in theory) comes out of solution, forms bubbles and potentially causes injury. This phenomenon of over-pressure is known as 'supersaturation'. For instance, whilst a compartment at a certain depth may saturate with a partial pressure of 1 bar, it may be able to withstand 1.5 bar supersaturation (a reduction in depth pressure that causes the gas within the compartment to expand to create a tissue tension of 1.5 bar) before theoretical bubbles are generated. A rise past this decompression ceiling (supersaturation over pressure) may cause gas to come out of solution and bubbles to occur. The length of time we spend at a decompression stop is controlled by how long it takes the compartment to 'off-gas' to a new safe level where a standard change in depth (often 3 metres) does not cause excessive over-pressurisation. Some computers allow for a sliding decompression ceiling rather than fixed 3 metres increments allowing the user to ascend in a smoother manner also known as 'flying the curve'. There is research to indicate that a progressive rather than stepped decompression may be more beneficial.

In theory (following the mentioned model) if we conduct the decompression within over-pressurisation limits our decompression will be 'safe'. Safe doesn't necessarily mean we are not getting 'bent' it just means we don't manifest sufficient symptoms to warrant treatment. A good indicator of decompression safety is how awake we feel after a dive. Post-dive tiredness is a sign of sub-clinical (not presenting classic DCI symptoms) DCI.

However, the control of bubbles using saturation modelling theories is insuficient. There is evidence to suggest that our bodies naturally generate bubbles as a result of cavitation at the heart valves[46]. The bubbles take the form of micro-nuclei which absorb gas during the dive. During an ascent, even though excessive over pressurisation (and bubble formation as a result of that) does not occur, the expanded nuclei may form bubbles.

Bubbles of a certain size are the ideal way of removing gas from the body, providing they become trapped within the lung's alveoli. If they are too small however (micro bubbles), they may pass through the lung and end up back on the arterial side of the circulatory system. Continuing ascents will then cause further expansion and excessive bubble formation in the CNS (central nervous system) and other vital areas resulting in DCI.

So how do we control these micro bubbles and exactly what is the optimum way to decompress from a deep, possibly mixed gas dive? It would appear that a combination of both models is what is needed.

From a micro bubble standpoint it has been noted[47] that conducting short decompression stops below the predicted first 'real' decompression ceiling can reduce the symptoms of post dive fatigue. The assumption is that micro

---

[46] Henessey

[47] Pyle and others

bubble growth is being controlled. Several physiologists have tried to predict these deep-water stops and their duration[48]. To date, there remains no commercially available algorithm which has been clinically trialled although many groups of extreme divers have their own empirical systems which 'appear' to work. The effect of these deep stops is to reduce the ascent rate significantly. It is worth noting at this stage that some classic solution models give bottom times which assume an instantaneous ascent could take place to the first decompression ceiling. Current thinking would seem to indicate that any form of rapid ascent is dangerous and rates of 10 metres/minute or less are more suitable even when combined with deep stops.

Taking the solution model first, what are the established rules for decompression from a deep trimix dive?

Helium is a 'faster' gas (absorbs quicker) than the other main component of trimix - nitrogen. Most trimix dives use large fractions of helium in a mix to combat narcosis. High helium contents have also been proven to reduce the probability of CO_2 retention[49] and its associated problems (oxygen toxicity, pH balance changes in the blood etc.). Due to its absorption rates, helium produces more decompression in short bottom times (less than 2 hours) than nitrogen. Hence, when looking at any compartment load at the end of a trimix dive bottom time, there will be more helium absorbed than nitrogen. As a result the first part of the decompression is designed to remove the helium. Helium, also being noted as a 'friendlier' gas from a DCI stress angle makes the use of large fractions of helium a much preferred option over heliair (often mixed as low helium fraction/high narcosis) and deep air diving.

A deep-water trimix decompression is completed in two ways. Firstly, if during the decompression the breathing gas can be substituted for a mixture weak (or non-existent) in helium, then suitable'off-gassing' of helium will occur. The trade off is that if the helium-less gas is breathed at depth (normally air or nitrox) then nitrogen may again be absorbed in some compartments. Dependant on the switch depth and profile chosen (narcosis aside) this may or may not lengthen the overall decompression. This is of secondary importance when we look at the ensuing problem providing a depth limit is established for this type of gas switch. Secondly, the breathing mixture should maintain a suitably high partial pressure of oxygen. The normal range of PO_2's should be kept within 1.6 to 1.0 bar. **Authors note**. *Down to approximately 0.70 bar is seen to be acceptable in practice for extreme exposure dives in order to reduce gas handling logistics (carrying/mixing multiple gases). However it is advisable to build in additional safety factors when the PO_2 is taken this low.* Taking air as an example, it has a PO_2 of 1.0 at approximately 37 metres, so if it was employed as a deep decompression gas, the switch to another oxygen rich gas should be made at around 37 metres. Keeping the PO_2's high again elevates the 'off-gassing' gradient during the predominantly nitrogen decompression portion of the dive.

Oxygen is the gas that supports life and is at the centre of a healthy metabolism. High PO_2 levels help produce an efficient decompression profile, providing they are balanced against oxygen toxicity.

In extreme deep diving intermediate trimix's may be employed. The advantages of using these are several fold. Firstly, they maintain the PO_2 within the afore mentioned acceptable levels. Secondly, they keep nitrogen narcosis at bay and thirdly, they provide ever-reducing levels of helium (and increased levels of nitrogen) which are needed to remove the high levels of helium saturated during the dive. The main question is where should this intermediate trimix concept be used? There appear to be several theories.

Some groups advocate using 'bottom mix' trimix up to the shallow stops (21 metres) and then switching to high levels of oxygen to complete the decompression, avoiding on gassing of nitrogen if lower FO_2 (high FN_2) gases were used at deeper stops. Whilst this appears to combat a problem of 'on-gassing' too much nitrogen, it does expose the diver to potentially high helium compartment over pressures, which themselves may cause symptoms of DCI. By using trimix in this fashion followed by high doses of oxygen in shallow water "are we treating rather than preventing DCI" using this concept?

A good decompression is probably a balance of two theories - of solution models and of bubble mechanics. The gas switch concept (trimix to 21 metres option) mentioned in the previous paragraph may actually generate decompression insult in deep-water (even if micro bubble stops are employed). The resultant high FO_2/shallow water deco section is used to treat the problem.

Is there another way to complete the decompression with potentially less stress on the diver? Possibly. Taking on board the concepts of adequate PO_2's, the inert gas switch and bubble mechanics, the following is offered.

---

[48] Imbert
[49] EDU

Assuming the body has generated micro bubble nuclei, these absorb gas during a dive. To control their expansion deep-water stops are employed. With the lack of an algorithm the accepted method of halving the depth between the bottom and the first stop and then completing a one to two minute stop seems applicable. This process is repeated if the depth between that micro bubble stop and the first real stop is greater than 10 metres. That allows the micro bubbles to come under control at this phase of the dive.

Now to oxygen. If the depth where the PO_2 in our trimix equals 1 bar is not too deep (from a nitrogen narcosis standpoint), then air or a nitrox (if toxicity allows) is suitable. The subsequent increased level of nitrogen in the new breathing mix is of secondary importance (providing it is used no deeper than around 51 metres) when compared to the oxygen level remaining at 1 bar or greater. If the depth is too great (from a narcosis standpoint) then an intermediate trimix high in oxygen (1.6 max.) and lower in helium can be employed. One note worth mentioning when using high PN_2 mixes is solubility. Nitrogen is more soluble than helium and any preformed bubbles will quickly absorb nitrogen. This is a good reason for using intermediate trimix's (creating small shifts in PN_2) coupled with micro bubble stops, rather than air.

With the new gas, which is low in helium, the 'off-gassing' gradient is now established. While some compartments may 'on-load' nitrogen, again for the short duration of these deeper stops, this is of minor concern. The next phase combines a range of gas switches with ever-increasing FO_2's to maintain the oxygen levels as discussed (1.6 to approx. 1.0) and control oxygen toxicity. The increasing FO_2's reduce the FN_2's and continue a suitable 'off–gassing' profile.

So is that the end of it? Probably not! Assuming our deep stops limited bubble-growth and our subsequent gas switch profile avoided gas coming out of solution, could micro bubbles again become a problem in shallow water? Probably. The critical depth range would appear to start at 21 metres (which is coincidentally the depth where the proponents of running intermediate trimix's switch to high FO_2 nitrox). In this area and up to 6 metres, practical experience[50] has shown a short extension of the decompression (10-20%) within this zone is beneficial, although this in some way may be negated by good bubble-controlling stops in deeper water.

It is worth also mentioning that gas switches need time to physiologically take place, hence a short time extension (1 to 2 minutes) should be added at each gas switch point.

This added to the final 'trick' of doing decompression at a minimum of 4 to 6 metres helps reduce supersaturation and bubble growth problems in shallow water and keeps the overall oxygen load under control.

[50] 'Britannic 97' and others

General Guidelines Covering all Dives

The following is offered as a list of 'do's' and 'don't's' for conducting technical (or indeed any) dives.

- analyse all gases prior to diving.
- ensure all gases are properly and visibly labelled prior to diving. Maximum operating depth should be especially visible on decompression cylinders.
- use 1.4 PO_2 on technical level exposures as a bottom mix PO_2 and 1.6 as a maximum decompression mix PO_2. This may vary with closed circuit rebreathers where 1.2 or 1.3 are more suitable long duration PO_2's.
- after a period of activity at the surface (kiting up) allow for a short rest period in order get breathing and heart rates back under control prior to entering the water. Experienced divers may use visualisation techniques or bradycardial breathing to achieve this. Stop whatever you are doing and breathe deeply for a period of time.
- during an descent, stop at 6 metres. Perform a leak and general equipment check. This wait time of an additional minute or so further allows the body to acclimatise to the new environment. Temperature and light level acclimatisation may take several minutes (up to 25 minutes for a major light level change). However, this brief stop will allow the cardio-vascular system to return to near normal rates.
- make a slow descent without excess exercise. Either free-fall or use hand-over-hand techniques with shot lines in tidal areas. Fining down the line will use a lot of energy and produce CO_2 which in turn predisposes us to narcosis and a range of other problems.
- having reached the bottom take another brief period to adjust equipment and attain correct buoyancy. All of these extra stabilising minutes are simply an attempt to return the body to a near surface functioning state so that it operates to maximum efficiency.
- during a dive, wherever possible use 'pull and glide'" techniques rather than heavy fining (with suitable respect for the environment). Use of the arms reduces CO_2 generation and breathing stress.
- if at any point during a dive a stressful situation arises – stop! Take 3 deep breaths (focus on breathing out), think and act in that order. Try and prioritise problems. Say "I have gas, I can breathe". There is now no urgency to commence an ascent. If at the end of the planned time something happens which slows egress, providing bailout schedules are (and should be) carried there is now no need to panic. In any emergency situation put your mind back on the surface and ask your self what you would do there in the same situation.
- if the depth of a dive is known, carry a schedule for the dive time and the dive time plus 5 minutes. If the depth is uncertain carry a schedule for the depth and a time and the depth plus at least 3 metres and the same time. Carry an additional schedule for the longest time and deepest depth assuming a decompression on bottom mix i.e. a loss of decompression gas (see suggestions for trimix schedules).
- always plan for the deepest part of the dive even if this portion is only 'a bounce'. i.e. if the wreck bottoms at 70 metres but most of the dive is at 68 metres, plan for 70 metres. Do this deep-water section early on in the dive.
- avoid saw tooth profiles, especially in relatively shallow water.
- maintain ascent rates of 10 metres/minute or less. Even from deep-water including micro bubble stops as required.
- as with a no-stop dive where it is wise not to return directly to the surface (as this is a calculated pressure ceiling) it is also wise not to return directly to the first decompression stop. One or two minutes spent waiting 3 metres below the first stop are beneficial when considering tissue over pressurisation and will have no noticeable affect on the remaining decompression.
- avoid unnecessary delays in deep-water on bottom mix, such as starting up a wall after the planned bottom time and then taking excessive time to stop and look without modifying your decompression schedule. Micro bubble stops of one to three minutes (dependant on depth) are not seen as excessive delays.

Surface oxygen after a 120 metre dive

- do not reduce stop times arbitrarily. Do not make assumptions on stop time reduction if using a non planned gas without first computing for the effects. In a team plan this would mean carrying a schedule for the worst gas scenario of the team (most deco.). A simple solution here is have the team match gas (use the same).
- when reaching the first stop and if using a time device which works in whole minutes, wait until the minute has incremented and then start the timing at that stop.
- if a stop involves a gas switch, start the stop timing after at least 3 to 4 breaths using the gas.

- maintain stop accuracy to +/- 0.5 metres, preferably in a horizontal position as this offers optimum comfort for long periods and helps maintain a centralised decompression level.
- after completing the final stop ascend half way to the surface and stop for a further 2 to5 minutes.
- whilst waiting for the boat to pick you up, stay on the highest available FO_2.
- upon entry into the boat after a long period of decompression, spend at least 5 minutes breathing your highest available FO_2 on the surface.
- hydrate with non acidic drinks at least 12 hours before a planned extended decompression dive. Hydrate again prior to the dive and immediately afterwards.
- avoid alcohol, caffeine and decongestants prior to diving.
- do not smoke especially immediately before and after a dive.

It should be noted that decompression is not a finite science and although some of the mentioned procedures may appear precise in their nature, they are only offered as a practical guide in the 'art' of avoidance of DCI.

Trimix Dives

Trimix is most commonly a combination of oxygen, helium and nitrogen. Trimix dives require specialist training in the use of decompression tables or software and often employ multiple decompression gases.

- apply general rules as above.
- where the FO_2 of the bottom mix is less than 16% avoid using it at or near the surface.
- on dives requiring a 'travel' gas (ideally where the bottom mix FO_2 is LESS than 16%) use the 'travel' gas down to a PO_2 of 1.6 bar. This 'travel' section may be programmed in as a part of the decompression profile or the assumption may be made that the downward travel is on bottom mix (from a tables standpoint) although travel mix (nitrox etc.) is used. This provides an extra level of decompression safety.
- on the ascent, switch away from helium as soon as possible. If possible, slightly before the planned first stop. On deeper dives intermediate trimix's may be employed to maintain the PO_2 whilst slowly reducing the Fhe.
- always include micro bubble stops.
- choose gases to minimise narcosis (MOD 40 metres) and minimise the drop in PO_2 on ascent (minimum 0.8 O_2). Gas switches should be made when these limits are met.
- apply 'air breaks' once your CNS limit has been reached. Resting decompressions (low CO_2's) greatly expand our O_2 tolerance. A better solution on deep trimix dives is to use trimix with a breathable PO_2 for the 'air break' period[51]. With high helium contents, the 'air break' time (5 mins) need not add to the decompression schedule as the majority of the shallow water decompression is removing nitrogen. Always ensure the 'break' trimix is breathable (not hypoxic) in shallow water.
- on high PO_2 decompressions, keep CO_2 generation to a minimum and conduct the majority of the final decompression at a PO_2 of 1.4 to 1.45.
- take submersible dive plans for depth and time scenarios, as above, with an additional schedule assuming a loss of the deep-water decompression gas. This will mean completing the deep stops on bottom mix. As a rule of thumb (on a simple two decompression gas dive) if you lost your EAN40 you would complete the stops on trimix doubling each of the times and then add approximately 20% to your oxygen/EAN 80 decompression stops. On trimix dives involving 3 decompression gases more detailed planning will be required.
- wherever possible dive as a team to ensure that spare gas is always available. Stage spare deep-water decompression gas at the first stop depth, especially in low visibility situations.
- plan for loss of high oxygen decompression gas by staging spare quantities. In open water any decompression gas loss can be catered for by keeping spare gas on the boat on a pre-set depth line and buoy systems. Have an agreed emergency signalling system to alert surface crew or safety divers when deployment is required.
- if a decompression gas is lost then subsequently recovered, start the current stop again on the initial (correct) gas schedule unless alternative on-line computations are available.
- employ team ethics wherever possible. This means employing decompression stations where conditions permit and staging emergency decompression gas especially for deep stops and in shallow water, if possible.

Gas Choice

With nitrox diving it is a fairly simple process to choose our bottom mix based on a safe working PO_2 (normally 1.4) and choose a decompression gas so that the bulk of the stops are carried out as near to 1.6 as a PO_2 as possible. Some deeper stops should possibly be completed on 'bottom mix'.

[51] This works because by the time shallow water has been reached, the majority of the Helium has 'off-gassed'. Breathing a high Helium/low Oxygen mix (minimum 16%) again does not adversely affect decompression and reduces our Oxygen load.

With trimix things are a little more complicated. Bottom mix is a choice of both PO_2 and now also END. Decompression gases begin with a 'best-guess' using decompression software (if you haven't already got hard tables). Generally gas switches during an ascent to either intermediate trimix or nitrox will occur at a depth where 1.0 to 0.8 as a PO_2 is again reached (although short stops in deep-water may again be on the previous mix). The only difference with heliair[52] against trimix is that a bottom oxygen PO_2 might be selected at the expense of a high END and vice versa as one is controlled during filling at the expense of the other (see appendix A). The following paragraphs is written as a guide to selecting the right gases.

A Final Note on Bubbles and Multi-Day Diving

In the air range it is an established practice to accept that multiple days of diving generate a residual load from an inert gas perspective. With high helium trimix diving this is not always the case as the 'faster' helium is often sufficiently dissipated prior to the dive end, leaving only a small nitrogen (and rapidly reducing helium) residual on surfacing. So, considering a saturation model standpoint, it is often applicable to assume no saturation pre-load on subsequent days of diving, especially if the overall dive trip is relatively short. This is certainly applicable in the 'recreational' trimix range (50-80 metres). Longer duration projects may need breaks in the diving to deal with inert gas pre-load.

The spoils of a good weeks gas diving

What about the bubbles? Whilst our body naturally generates micronuclei, it appears that regular compressions actually break them down and providing they are not given time to re-form, the noted quantity on subsequent dives is found to reduce. Are multiple days of gas diving actually beneficial from a bubble reduction view? It would appear so.

Problems with Oxygen

Oxygen would seem to be the answer to all our problems, the more the better. Hmmm perhaps not. Oxygen is toxic, narcotic, can cause temporary DCI and is a vasoconstrictor. What does this mean to us as divers? Oxygen is potentially twice as narcotic as nitrogen. The upside of this is that at the partial pressures of oxygen within which we normally operate (0.21 to 1.6). Oxygen narcosis is not a relevant issue. Nitrogen, which is breathed at far higher partial pressures, is the over-riding concern.

Vasoconstricting affects of oxygen are well documented. There is some evidence that the resultant reduction in perfusion (blood flow) may reduce off-gassing by as much as 20%. This, however, only manifests as a problem at PO_2's in excess of 2 bar.

Finally, how do we control the onset of an oxygen convulsion? Estimated times of breathing oxygen at elevated partial pressures have been documented for some time[53]. The percentage CNS method of calculating a CNS oxygen load has been used as a 'guide' for recreational divers and is suitable for 'recreational' mixed gas diving. Longer, deeper exposures however need a different approach to oxygen control. Several 'tips and tricks' apply:

- as with all diving related problems, stay well hydrated
- the established chamber treatment method of taking an 'air break' for 5 minutes in every 25 breathing oxygen helps reduce the onset of symptoms. This is often applied when the theoretical CNS exposure exceeds 150% or in some cases, when decompression stopd using oxygen begin. It is more beneficial to use a trimix as the 'break' gas.
- the majority of the elevated FO_2 decompression should be conducted at a PO_2 of no greater than 1.4 bar
- remain at rest with limited exercise during the high FO_2 decompression. This reduces CO_2 levels, the resultant vasodilatation in itself being a possible precursor to oxygen convulsions due to increased blood flow and delivery of oxygen

Gas choice is always a compromise between handling logistics, deco time, gas management, oxygen toxicity, safety and narcosis. Either carry lots of gases or be prepared to 'hang' around.

[52] Heliair. A mixture of air and helium only, no pure oxygen.
[53] NOAA Oxygen Limits

Typical Schedules for a 120 metre and a 70 metre dive.
PO_2 shifts detailed. **Stop times are for reference only.**

Depth	Time	B. mix	
120m	**25**	**11/60**	
Stop Depth	Time	Gas	PO_2
4.5	97	100	1.45
6	15	100	1.6
9	31	40	0.76
12	19	40	0.88
15	13	40	1
18	9	40	1.12
21	7	40	1.24
24	5	40	1.36
27	4	40	1.48
30	4	40	1.6
33	3	21	0.903
36	2	21	0.966
39	2	21	1.029
42	2	21	1.092
45	1	21	1.155
48	1	21	1.218
51	1	21	1.281
54	2	11/60	0.704
57	1	11/60	0.737
60	1	11/60	0.77
67.5	1	11/60	0.8525
75	1	11/60	0.935
90	1	11/60	1.1

Note marginal PO_2 at this depth. Intermediate trimix could be used, or air taken one stop deeper.

Depth	Time	B. mix	
70m	**25**	**18/40**	
Stop Depth	Time	Gas	PO_2
4.5	97	100	1.45
6	15	100	1.6
9	31	40	0.76
12	19	40	0.88
15	13	40	1
18	9	40	1.12
21	7	40	1.24
24	5	40	1.36
27	4	40	1.48
34.5	1	18/40	0.801
42	1	18/40	0.936

Oxygen. The Practical Bit

The past few years in technical diving have seen hot debates on whether to use pure oxygen or nitrox 80 (or similar) as a decompression gas.

What are the arguments?

- oxygen is more efficient as a decompression gas
- using oxygen also gives you a treatment gas on the boat
- filling with pure oxygen is more hazardous
- you need good buoyancy control to use O_2

I'm sure there are others but these seem to be the main ones. Let's look at each in turn.

From a straight math's point of view, yes you will do less deco using 100% O_2 if you use nitrox 80 instead of oxygen at the 6 metre stop and shallower. No doubt about it. However, one advantage of nitrox 80 is you can switch to it deeper. So quoting one of the standard decompression programmes like Proplanner, you can work scenarios where you actually do less decompression by switching to nitrox 80 at 9 metres! If you're in a cold environment this can make a major difference.

But hang time is only a part of the efficiency sequence. Pure O_2 is generally only pumped to 200 bar and often only then with a booster. How many shops have boosters? (OK you can stop counting now). So on serious dives you end up needing to carry more gas (oxygen). With nitrox 80, a 230 bar fill is no problem. Gas volumes are less of an issue.

Oxygen is obviously a major treatment for DCI. Without doubt 100% is best. On the other hand, any high O_2 % is better than a low one and unless you carry extra on-board oxygen purely for accident situations (which thankfully most people now do) there may not be enough left in a post-dive cylinder (which was only filled to 200 bar) to affect first-aid anyway. Obviously, the rule here is do not rely on a diving gas for first-aid, but if you have to use one, use as higher O_2 as possible.

Dealing with pure oxygen needs care, using any elevated O_2 at high pressure could be hazardous. Also, using a booster pump with pure oxygen isn't something the average 'tekkie' is up to. Care is needed with **all** decompression gases and the same safety rules should apply to any elevated oxygen mix. Make no special case for 80% or 100% - treat them all the same. There is obviously an issue of cleanliness. If you are only filling with O_2 then there is no contamination problem. If you mix with air (as in 80%) then contamination could occur. History has shown us that with regular oxygen cleaning and inspection this is a fairly mute point. However, care should still be taken to ensure your air source is as pure as possible.

The subject of gas-labelling is important. Whether it's 80 or 100% cylinders must be clearly marked, but not with just masking tape and a crayon! A large boldly marked tape with the MOD (maximum operating depth) and the gas content is mandatory. Position the label so that your partner can see it underwater and always ensure he/she checks it before you switch. It is also a good idea to colour code your cylinders. My high FO_2 deco mix is white and any nitrox is yellow. If you can afford it, then an even better solution is to have dedicated cylinders for different mixes, each permanently marked with the MOD of the mix.

Buoyancy control for any type of decompression diving must be a precise skill. If you 'yo-yo' your stops you will eventually get DCI. Whilst we notionally maximise the PO_2 of our breathing gas at 1.6 (6 metres on pure oxygen) some people advocate that using 80% provides a CNS safety margin. The reality is that at a resting decompression (low CO_2 build-up) we can greatly extend our CNS oxygen clock. Thus the depth control (from a CNS standpoint) is less of a problem. Most 'recreational' technical dives seldom exceed 100% oxygen load, so 80% or 100% is neither here nor there. Once you are doing really extended decompressions then you will be using air/trimix breaks anyway, which again extends the CNS clock.

Cave when compared to open ocean also makes a difference. Where in a cave you can sit on the floor or park in the ceiling and decompress, it is a lot less stressful than in the sea, as depth control issues are reduced.

Personally, the choice between 100% or 80% is about gas volume and the environment in which it is used. It is a lot easier to pump large volumes of 80% than 100% for the reasons mentioned. It depends on the dive logistics to define what you use. However, if you have access to surface supplied oxygen (large volumes) as I have had on many occasions, then it becomes the gas of choice. Decompressing under a boat on a nice fixed system or in a cave certainly lends itself to 100% oxygen use.

Whatever you choose is specific to the environment and logistics within which you dive. Either way you're probably right, but don't get slack on analysis and labelling; that's one thing that will finish your diving career very quickly!

Decompression Software

For some time there have been many types of decompression software available, allowing divers to plan a wide variety of decompression profiles to extreme depths. It is worth noting that the majority of early products were all based on Professor A. Bühlmann's work and as such were standard solution models. In the early 1990's divers took these programmes into the field and pushed them further and deeper. In fact far more so that any chamber trials conducted by the original physiologists ever went. In the main the profiles worked. More recently, a wider range of software has become available, some specifically focussing on the problems generated by micro bubbles. Be warned! Use a model that has a track record. Look for evidence of field trials or long-term use. Just because it gets you out of the water quicker does not mean it must be good. Several models have varying safety factors which can be user programmed. Talk with users and if possible the author. Find out what they use and remember it takes hundreds of dives to validate a schedule. Treat new information with caution.

DCI First Aid & Equipment

Arterial gas embolism (AGE) and DCS are the two most common diving related accidents. Symptoms may occur on surfacing or within 36 hours. Additional information can be found in various reference works.

The following is offered as a summary of the information already contained in the first-aid chapter and will cover:

General safety equipment:

Always carry:

- oxygen and 100% delivery system
- resuscitation equipment
- marine radio
- phone (if possible)
- emergency contact numbers
- water
- basic first-aid kit
- pen and paper
- diver recovery system (ropes/sling etc.)

Immediate First Aid

In any incident assume DCI until informed otherwise. First-aid for DCI is;

- keep warm and dry
- lay casualty flat
- stay calm, reassure the casualty
- administer O_2 IMMEDIATELY (first 15 minutes is critical)
- administer a small amount of fluids
- check urination periodically and continue to give fluids if urination successful
- note any changes
- contact emergency services
- prepare for medivac

Do Not:

- administer pain killers
- give fluids if casualty is unable to urinate regularly (25 minute intervals)
- delay in giving oxygen
- stop O_2 administration if pain worsens (allow for transient worsening[54])
- leave casualty unattended
- elevate to a higher altitude

Neurological Test.

The purpose of this test is to ascertain the extent of any DCI. Recording of this information will give chamber technicians a good idea of the casualty's previous condition and any improvements, on arrival at the recompression facility.

- ask questions:
  - where does it hurt.
  - when did symptoms occur; when was it worse?
- orientation:
  - does the diver know name and age, day and date?
  - do they know where thay are?
- does the diver appear alert?
  - eyes. Check eyes separately. Hold up fingers and ask the diver to identify different numbers.
    - ask the diver (from 0.5 metre) to follow one finger. First up and down and then side to side. Is the movement smooth and are the divers pupils the same size? Do both eyes track?
  - face. Ask them to smile; is muscle contraction the same both sides?
  - tongue. Stick out tongue; it should come straight out with no sideways deviation.
- muscle strength.
  - push down on shoulders whilst they shrug; is the pressure equal and strong?

---

[54] An increase in symptoms after a short time on oxygen

    - lay the diver flat and ask him/her to raise each leg and push against your hands. Are both strong? Use the same procedure for arms.
- sensory:
    - close diver's eyes and lightly touch points down each side of the body using a pointed instrument. Where do they not feel it?
- co-ordination:
    - stand the diver with feet together, arms stretched out front and eyes closed.
        - be prepared to catch the diver. Does he/she wobble or fall? Note if one arm droops.
    - ask the diver to touch his/her nose and your finger (0.5m away) rapidly, a few times.
- feet:
    - (Babinski Reflex). Take off diver's socks and run a pointed instrument up the sole. If the toes curl down, this is normal. If nothing happens, no conclusion can be drawn. If toes curl up, this is a reliable sign of spinal involvement.

With any DCI assessment it is important to look for and record any changes without causing the patient unnecessary emotional stress. When asking a question such as 'do you have pain?' ask for the answer on a scale of one to ten. Ask the same question again after a short period (say 15 minutes) and note any changes. Record all results and despatch them with the casualty.

DCI is no longer subdivided as Type 1 and Type 2 because it is recognised one may lead to the other. In general, DCI may start as joint pains or skin rashes and lead to minor or major neurological problems.

If in doubt, assume DCI and at the very least administer 100% oxygen. With all incidents contact the emergency services as soon as possible. Monitor the partner as well as the casualty and ensure they stay together throughout the rescue.

Speed of administration of 100% oxygen is vital. After **10 to 15 minutes of onset of symptoms** permanent damage may have taken place. Denying the onset of DCI is very dangerous. If you have any symptoms from mild pain, headache, nausea through to muscle weakness, do not hesitate - **ADMINISTER OXYGEN.**

If you feel 'funny', go on oxygen. It is virtually free, use it!

Minimal First Aid Equipment:

- 100% breathing grade oxygen and dual supply system.
- marine radio.
- a 'by size' selection of standard wound dressings.
- a selection of crepe bandages.
- assorted sterile adhesive plasters.
- 1 pair tweezers.
- 1 eye bath and ointment.
- 1 bottle aspirin.
- 1 bottle antiseptic fluid.
- resuscitation mask.
- 1 pencil and notebook.
- fresh water.
- 1 bottle vinegar (jelly fish stings).

Dehydration

Along side CO_2 retention and fast ascent rates, dehydration is one of the 'big three' when it comes to DCI avoidance and general well-being as a diver. Most people do not drink enough in daily life. As divers we often need to make a conscious effort to increase our fluid intakes pre and post dives. Failure to do so greatly increases the risk of DCI.

Dehydration lowers our blood volume. This means we are less able to cool our selves through sweating and the natural process of skin blood vessels dilating (red faced effect). At the same time, if we have to exercise, there just isn't enough blood. One effect is that blood pressure falls and the heart beats faster to compensate. As it pumps less and less blood it speeds up again. Eventually you may feel weak, overheat and faint.

Side-effects include blood plasma volume decrease, hence the blood becomes viscos (thicker) and blood-flow decreases in some areas. This may lead to a reduction in our ability to remove absorbed inert gas and therefore generate DCI.

How we lose water:

- through breathing, especially in cold climates where there is less water vapour in the air. Hot climates may be humid and consequently little heat is lost through breathing.
- heat and exercise causing us to sweat
- immersion especially in cold water[55]
- alcohol and caffeine suppress the anti-diuretic hormone which allows us to urinate more
- sea sickness
- lack of hydration at the start of a dive.

Without exercise, the following is a guide to water loss per day:

- temperate climates 2300ml
- hot climates 3300ml

Both of the above figures include sweat, fluid lost in solids and 350ml in insensible (mainly diffusion through the skin) fluid loss.

With exercise, water loss can increase to 6000ml. Your body compensates by reducing urine output. Based on these figures it is easy to see why fluid replacement, especially with exercise is important. Drinking regularly during exercise is an important factor in stabilising fluid loss.

For most exercise, water is as good a fluid replacement as anything. We obtain most of the other things we lose from our food. This includes salts known as electrolytes, a common advertising point in fluid replacement drinks.

Why Do We Need electrolytes?

Electrolytes are important for body function. They regulate several body processes such as fluid flow across cell membranes. Electrolytes help also propagate nerve signals, keeping you healthy and active.

Salt is an electrolyte when dissolved in water because it breaks up into ions which have one more or one less electron than normal and therefore are either negatively or positively charged. When we sweat we lose water and some electrolytes. If we did not do this we could become hypertonic (rich in electrolytes). Prolonged exercise generates significant electrolyte loss. If we only fluid replace with water we can dilute the body too much, a condition known as hyponatremia or water intoxication. This can lead to weakness and occasionally death.

Normal diving does not generate enough electrolyte loss to worry about. Replacement can be obtained through normal eating. In extreme heat and with pre and post dive exercise, a small amount of additional electrolyte replacement may be needed.

Other additives in drinks include carbohydrates. Basically carbohydrate is a fuel our body uses. By taking in carbohydrates we can delay fatigue and it can become a temporary meal replacement. Most fluid replacement drinks contain between 4% and 7% carbohydrates.

---

[55] page 148

Why Do We drink?

Our body has two main thirst sensors. The hypovolemic or 'low on water' sensor triggers as you lose fluids. If you use only water as replacement you may end up with too much, compared to electrolytes and your body will ask you to urinate to maintain the balance. If you rehydrate with electrolytes this will be avoided.

The second sensor is a 'high on electrolyte sensor' or osmotic thirst. Whenever you eat salty foods you feel thirsty. Salt is an electrolyte when combined with water. Now the balance tips the other way and you need more water.

Alcohol

Alcohol, although full of carbohydrate calories, cannot be metabolised like ordinary carbohydrate, and consequently is not a good energy source. It reduces the output of glucose from the liver (a primary energy source) generating fatigue. It is a central nervous system depressant and (like caffeine) suppresses the antidiuretic hormone (ADH) making us urinate and lose fluids.

Removing Fluids

Having hydrated sufficiently we often need to remove fluids during a dive. Assuming drysuit diving, one solution for fluid removal is adult incontinence pants. This works fairly well for short (2 hour) dives for most people. Wearing them under a pair of lycra cycling shorts stops it all from moving around! The next option is a drysuit 'P dump'. This is a simple valve in the suit leg. Some have a screw on end and some a 'pull dump' to release the urine. The best ones are pressure-balanced to the pressure inside the suit, so you can urinate at any depth. For men an adhesive condom is one of the best options for attachment but be careful not to kink the tube! For the ladies, I'm afraid I'm not qualified to give advice!

Kerk Kavalaris expecting the worst!

Summary

Dehydration is a condition of the body caused by loss of water and essential body salts and potentially a **major** contributor to DCI. Signs and symptoms of dehydration include dry mouth, decreased or absent urination, sunken eyes, wrinkled skin, confusion, low blood pressure and coma. The primary cause of dehydration is excessive sweating during exercise, especially in hot, humid weather, as well as persistent vomiting or diarrhoea from any cause, use of diuretics (water pills) or other drugs that deplete fluids and electrolytes, overexposure to sun or heat, recent illness with high fever, or chronic kidney disease. Possible complications of dehydration are blood pressure drop, shock or even death from prolonged, severe dehydration.

Dehydration can be prevented. Drink water in small quantities frequently during any exercise that causes excessive sweating. If you're vomiting or have diarrhoea, take small amounts of liquid with non-prescription electrolyte supplements, every 30-60 minutes. If you use diuretics, weigh yourself daily. Report to your doctor any weight loss of more than 1.5kg in one day or 2.5kg within one week. Weigh yourself before and after workout sessions. Skip the workout if a weight loss of 2% or more has not been regained.

Treatment for dehydration should be carried out under the advice of a physician. This usually involves bed rest and taking frequent small amounts of clear liquids (large amounts can trigger vomiting). Severe or prolonged cases may require hospitalisation for a time with fluids being taken intravenously.

Commercially available fluid replacers are not harmful and will not overload you with electrolytes or carbohydrates. They carry similar concentrations of electrolytes compared with your blood (they are isotonic and not hypertonic). They need not be diluted.

Thermal Considerations

Introduction

In certain parts of the world, cold often becomes the limiting factor on extended range dives rather than any decompression requirement, gas management or even CNS toxicity. The diving industry is only just beginning to catch up with the adventure sport industry (climbing etc.) in introducing new materials technology to keep us warm.

The Body's Thermal Mechanics

One of Newton's Laws states that energy is neither created nor destroyed, it is only transformed from one state to another. Humans are warm blooded (homeotherms) and attempt to maintain a stable body temperature. The human body has various insulations such as fat, muscles and a superficial skin layer. The insulating properties of fat remain fairly constant whilst the skin's insulation varies with blood flow. Muscles rapidly transfer heat when needed and have low insulation properties. We sense cold as a reduction in body core temperature.

The body generates heat as a result of shivering, exercise and chemically by boosting metabolism. In order to feel 'comfortable' we must maintain a thermal equilibrium, hence excess heat must be removed. A resting body consumes approximately 50 calories/hour/square metre[56] of body area and transforms this into heat. Of this generated heat, 24% is lost due to evaporation, perspiration and respiration; the remaining 76% is lost through radiation and convection[57].

The amount of heat our body loses is controlled by the following factors:

- body temperature
- outside air temperature
- density of insulation
- thickness of insulation
- insulating fibre diametre
- radiant parametres of the insulation

In order to remain comfortable the body must maintain a skin temperature of 33°C. This is a reflection of core temperature (37°C). The body maintains this temperature at the head (which can lose up to 30% of the bodies heat) and core at the expense of warming the peripheries (hands/feet etc.). If the core senses a drop in temperature it will shunt blood (and hence heat) away from the peripheries back to the core.

Another way the body conserves heat is by counter-current heat exchange. This is where veins and arteries closely intertwine (penguins feet are a classic example of this). Cold venus blood returning to the heart passes close to warm arterial blood, warming the venus blood before returning to the core. Certain groups of divers[58] are noted to have an increased ability to use this system. The control of body temperature is achieved by the hypothalamus (a kind of thermostat) situated in the brain.

Reactions to Cold

There are three ways in which the body responds to a drop in environmental temperature:

1. vasoconstriction of the superficial layer (skin). This reduces blood flow to the skin
2. blood vessel arrangements keep warmer blood nearer the core and reduce the amount of cold blood returning from the peripheries
3. another affect of vasoconstriction is to increase the insulating properties of the superficial layer due to the reduced blood flow

Excessive perspiration is a major contributor to heat loss as water transfers heat 25 times more effectively than air. This is why underwear that can remove moisture away from the skin is vitally important in any sport which requires bursts of energy followed by rest (a dive followed by a decompression).

---

[56] Known as 1 MET

[57] Convection is heat-loss through the gas/liquid medium around the body. Conduction is heat loss due to materials touching and transferring the energy.

[58] Korean breath-hold divers

Principles of Insulation

Whilst wetsuits certainly have their place in technical diving, the main area of concern for this chapter (which will be discussed in detail) is drysuit diving. As divers, thermal protection must be balanced against maintaining manoeuvrability. Another important factor is to regain heat should a temporary flood of a drysuit occur. To maintain thermal comfort a balance of three factors is required:

- rate of heat production
- insulation value of your clothing
- environmental temperature

Of these, the clothing's insulation value is the simplest to manipulate. Insulation works by trapping a layer of air/gas between the fibres (our body warms it by convection). The more air/gas trapped, the greater the insulation.

One of the most common forms of insulation is called Thinsulate™ made by '3M'. Thinsulate™ consists of microfibres that are less than 10 microns in diameter. That's ten times smaller than a human hair. This material is reported to trap more air in less space than any other insulating material. Many diving under suits use Thinsulate™ as a base with other materials making up the outer layers.

Thinsulate™ is a mixture of Olefin™[59] and Polyester™. It is graded depending on the mixture of these two and the overall weight. A good outdoor Thinsulate™ may have a ratio of 65% to 35% respectively of these materials. This 65/35 ratio Thinsulate™ is known as Grade C and is the type of material you should insist on as it is the best grade for diving. Diving Thinsulate™ is often sold in gramme weights, 150gm is a good summer grade (average water temperature 15°C) and 250gm is a good long duration diving or winter grade (average water temperature 6°C).

Thinsulate™ is quoted as 1 to 1.5 times warmer when compared with down (duck feathers) and twice as warm as many other insulating materials.

The outer covering employed on most under suits will be of a hard wearing breathable material such as Pertex™ or Ree-Tech™. These materials are constructed of a very fine weave, the distance between the strands being enough to let moisture out but stop water droplets from entering, proving to be shower-proof. The proximity of the strands also creates a capillary action that further helps to remove moisture. Moisture is drawn into the weave of the material where it evaporates and travels to the exterior. Pertex™ is often seen in a Ripstop™ variety, which due to a moulded pattern on the surface, reduces tearing.

The combination of the thermal inner and the breathable outer, results in a laminated construction. Be wary of laminated suits that have a quilted pattern stitched into them. The quilting causes compression of the thermal layer on the stitch line and 'cold bridges' (high heat loss areas) result. Tests with thermal imaging cameras have shown that certain quilted suits can lose up to 30% more heat than non-quilted[60].

Other Industry Terms:

Loft	the density of the product
CLO	a measure of warmth
Thermal weight efficiency	the ratio of CLO to weight
Compressibility	the degree to which the insulation will compress under pressure
Fibre blend	composition of the product

CLO Value

CLO value is used to determine the thermal efficiency of a material. One CLO has been approximated to the insulation value of a business suit and is based on the amount of activity, ambient temperature and the body heat loss figures (quoted earlier). You may find some garments may be rated in TOG. One CLO equals 0.645 TOG.

The American Society of Heating and Air-conditioning Engineers conducted tests to estimate the total effectiveness of an ensemble of garments worn by an individual. This was used to estimate the CLO value needed in different conditions to keep a body comfortable in a range of environments. As an example, for a skier under normal conditions, a CLO requirement for the ski suit of 2 is needed. Conversely, a soldier (mostly standing) in a cold-dry

[59] Olefin™ is a generic term

[60] 3M Insulation Projects tests

Arctic environment needs a CLO rating for his suit of 4.3. Unfortunately, to my knowledge, a diver has never been tested.

Inner Underwear

Whilst a Thinsulate™ type material is ideal to reduce heat loss and has good moisture removing properties, it may further improve things if another layer of a material like silk or meraklon™ is added to help remove any moisture from the skin (a principle known as 'wicking') and provide an additional air gap. Cotton fibres should be avoided as they trap moisture.

Meraklon™ was invented in the 1960's and was the first of the polyolefin fibres. A thin one-piece layer is ideal. Silk is as good or better, but requires more care when handling.

Another excellent alternative as a 'next to skin' layer is Polartec™. This a mixture of nylon and polyester. Some versions for activity sports also include Lycra™ to help provide some elasticity. This material typically has a 160 denier cordura nylon face for abrasion and wind resistance and a semi-velour polyester back to aid 'wicking' and comfort next to the skin.

Cold and Immersion.

Repetitive exposures to cold immersion progressively lower core temperature to a hypothermic level as the body does not have time to reconstitute heat. This means there is risk of core hypothermia on repetitive exposures regardless of thermal protection.

Breathing helium mixtures, gas entering the lungs will be colder than air as it loses its heat travelling from cylinder to regulator. However, when the diver exhales, gas leaving the lungs does not conduct heat from the body as readily as air. This is because there are fewer molecules to heat than with air. Therefore, air transmits more heat from the body than a proportional helium mix. Filling a drysuit with a helium mix will definitely feel colder than with air and is to be avoided at all costs because helium is approximately 6 times less insulating than air. Historically argon has been used as a suit inflation gas due to its increased density and insulation properties. Whilst this has been popular with technical divers, certain naval trials suggest the reduction in heat loss is minimal over air and argon gas is more placebo than cure.

With too few calories to fuel your body's needs, the body's metabolic heat production system shuts down. If the body has lost muscle through excess dieting or extreme repeat exertion without adequate calorie intake, then there is less heat storage capacity to combat hypothermia. Dehydration also decreases cold tolerance due to reduction in circulating fluid volume.

Tips and Tricks

- don't use cotton underwear
- keep your feet, hands and head warm (fitted hoods help prevent flushing)
- keep areas of high blood flow warm, such as kidneys and wrists
- do not restrict circulation (tight gloves)
- as a mimimum wear a base layer (silk etc.) and a mid/top layer (thinsulate/pertex combination)
- avoid underwear with stitching that penetrates all layers - this makes heat 'bridges'. On a thermal camera you will see heat being lost through the stitch lines. Quilted suits commonly suffer from this.
- avoid gaps in your underwear. Make it as much a one-piece as possible - attached socks help enormously
- between dives wear some form of 'wind stop' material such as Gortex™ over a wet or drysuit to prevent surface moisture chilling and conducting warmth out of the suit

Underwear is a science and should be treated as such. Demand information from your underwear supplier and not just glossy advertisments. A small shift in underwear philosophy could greatly improve your comfort level and maybe prevent hypothermia.

Diving Disorders

This chapter will cover the 'other' diving disorders. Those potentially less subtle and not covered in other chapters.

Animal Injuries

There are over 1000 marine vertebrates (and many more invertebrates) that are dangerous, venomous or poisonous to man. Obvious ones such as sharks, barracuda and crocodiles etc. are self explanatory. Suffice to say, in general do not provoke them and beware of territorial areas. Look out for behavioural changes, do not panic and thrash about. Exit the water as calmly as possible and be prepared to fend off the creature if it approaches. Eyes, snout and gills are sensitive areas which, if hit, may terminate an attack.

Behind you!

The wider variety of creatures we are primarily concerned with includes sea snakes, stone fish, stingray, jellyfish, cone shells, sea urchins and corals.

Sea Snakes

Basically, there are two groups – shallow-water coastal varieties which are bottom feeders and oceanic ones, drifting with the ocean currents. Sea snakes can be extremely venomous. Renal failure and other acute symptoms may occur and anti venom may be required. Most sea snakes are passive and attack is unlikely. In all cases, hospitalisation is necessary as symptoms may develop at any time within a 24 hour period.

Fish Stings

Animals such as stone fish, stingray and scorpion fish all fall into this category. In most cases symptoms are similar. The wound itself may be anaesthetised but hypersensitive in surrounding areas. Local pain will increase in intensity, possibly to an excruciating level. This will usually lessen after a few hours. In some cases swelling, vomiting, delirium and cardio-vascular problems may ensue. For stone fish in particular there is an anti-venom.

General first-aid is to lay the casualty down with the wound elevated. The wound should be immersed in hot (50 degrees centigrade) for up to 90 minutes, or until the pain subsides. The toxins are unstable and hot water helps to break them down. Clean the wound and attempt to remove any spines. Seek hospital treatment.

Jellyfish

Broadly speaking, all these creatures have some kind of tentacles that have stinging capsules or nemataocysts. The nemataocysts either 'stick to' or penetrate the skin, delivering toxin. Symptoms can vary from a mild itch to a severe systemic reaction. Blisters and ulcers may appear. Chest and abdominal pain may ensue. Of these animals, the sea wasp is probably one of the most venomous. A mild to excruciating pain can lead to coma and death in the case of a sea wasp. With mild stings the pain normally subsides within 12 hours. Again, with the sea wasp, death is often within ten minutes but survival prospects are good after one hour.

General first-aid includes soaking the area in white vinegar and gently removing any tentacles. Apply hydrocortisone lotion if available. CPR may be required. Seek medical treatment if symptoms are anything other than minor.

Cone Shells

Only some cone shells are dangerous to humans. Numbness and tingling may extend from the sting to the whole body. General paralysis may ensue. Visual and auditory problems can occur, generally within 10-30 minutes of the sting. Respiratory problems and cyanosis are also symptoms.

General first-aid for the conscious casualty includes immobilisation (lay prone) and a pressure dressing if the inflammation is limited. If the casualty is unconscious, CPR may be required and must be sustained until medical facilities are found. The casualty may be able to hear but not communicate. Good CPR may save their life. Seek medical treatment.

Urchins
One of the most dangerous is the crown of thorns star fish. Symptoms include nausea and vomiting. Hot water applied to any wound (or even a full bath) appears to help in most cases. Removal of the spines may be possible with care. In the majority of cases movement seems more beneficial than immobilisation as this breaks down the spines.

Corals
Symptoms range from mild irritation especially during washing of the infected area. Swelling and tenderness may occur with ulcers in extreme cases. First aid involves cleaning the wound and applying some form of antibiotic cream.

Poisoning
Poisoning can occur as a result of the ingestion or insinuation of a substance which produces a toxic effect. Well-known poisons, such as chlorine, are obvious. However, everyday substances like table salt or vitamins can be toxic if large enough quantities are consumed. The symptoms of poisoning include vomiting or diarrhoea, sweating, convulsions and loss of consciousness. If poisoning is suspected, IMMEDIATELY call your nearest Poison Control Centre. They will ask you to report the status of the patient and provide you with the location of your nearest hospital. Follow their instructions to the letter. If there is no Poison Control within your area, call for emergency medical assistance. Respiratory distress and cardiac shock may result in extreme cases.

Nitrogen Narcosis
The process which causes this is complex and not yet fully understood. Of the two major theories one relates to CO_2 retention and one nitrogen partial pressure. Although hypercapnia may not be the cause it does appear to increase the effects.

Looking at the partial pressure theory, as nitrogen is inert and hence non reactive within the body, any affects must be physical only.

Nitrogen is very soluble in fat and nerve cells have a high fat content. The effect could be similar to anaesthesia where gaseous anaesthetics impair the nerve transmissions between nerve endings and the brain. Nitrogen entering nerve cells could result in the same. One theory of how this may have an affect is called the myer-overton hypothesis and it states 'The degree of an anaesthetic's potency is relative to it's solubility in lipid' (fat).

The only way to prevent narcosis is not to deep-dive. Most divers experience some impairment past 30 metres. It often passes unnoticed and is merely a background feeling. Rapid descents to great depths can bypass this subtle effect and immediately bring on a feeling of great anxiety and even panic. Ascending a few metres can often alleviate any symptoms. Whilst we do not build a tolerance to narcosis we do become used to its symptoms and in some way may mentally adapt by completing tasks slower etc. Like anaesthesia, narcosis is dose-dependant and staying longer at depth actually worsens the symptoms.

Simple narcosis tests can be conducted to assess impairment. Take a slate, write 20 letters on the slate. Do five groups of four of the same letter. Write four B's, four K,s etc. Mix all the characters up. Now at the surface get a partner to time how long it takes you to tick off all of one letter (say the D's). Obviously the letter is their choice and not yours. Do not look at the slate or start the test until they say. They should time how long you take to complete it and how many mistakes you make. Now repeat this again at varying depths. Another interesting test is ask a diver to write his/her address at depth and look at handwriting degradation. I once had a student forget his address!

High Pressure Nervous Syndrome (HPNS).
Helium has a solubility in the lipid (fat) of 0.015 whilst nitrogen has a solubility in the lipid of 0.019. It would therefore be likely that the level of narcosis experienced at 10 Bar breathing compressed air would not occur until 43 Bar with a helium mixture.

This, however, is just maths. Test dives in 1965 to 180 metres and 240 metres showed a marked performance decrement. One difference to nitrogen narcosis is that the symptoms with helium mixtures began to improve after about one hour. This does not occur with compressed air. Another difference is that with helium mixes, motor skills are more impaired than intellectual tasks.

Helium mixes at depth excite the brain, whereas nitrogen mixes decrease the excitement of the brain.

The rate of compression greatly affects the onset of HPNS. With very rapid compression, symptoms can occur at relatively shallow depths. Avoidance of HPNS is achieved by very slow compression (150m per hour) or by stage descents. In 1970 divers were successfully compressed to 46 Bar by pausing their descent at 19, 31 and 40 Bar for 24 hours. Such methods are obviously not possible for open-circuit dives.

Trimix was first used for the experimental 'pressure reversal of narcosis theory'. Dives in 1974 to 330 metres with 10% nitrogen with rapid compression (33 minutes) showed no performance loss, no narcosis and no nausea, tremors or EEG changes. Nitrogen provided a 'buffer' for the HPNS symptoms.

Both Hasenmayer and Exley's deep cave explorations on heliox caused mild symptoms of HPNS manifested as a shaking fit. Later dives using trimix were symptomless.

HPNS has been noted in open circuit scuba dives between 120 and 200 metres again dependent on rate of compression (in this case descent rate). Another key variant in occurrence of HPNS is personnel variations in physiology.

Symptoms include muscle tremor, dizziness, vertigo, imbalance, nausea, intermittent somnolence (drowsiness or micro sleep) and loss of appetite.

Safety Divers

Historically 'safety' or 'stand-by' divers, as they are known in commercial diving, have been in the front line of diving safety. In the commercial diving world the stand-by diver often remains fully kitted for hours on deck waiting for an incident to occur, only being 'launched' when required.

With the advent of technical diving, especially with deeper and deeper wrecks and caves being explored using trimix, the safety diver has crept into the recreational diving world. So who is this group of divers, trapped between the surface and the draw of exploration being undertaken by those they protect? What does it take to be a safety diver and why would you ever want to be one?

As many trimix dives are undertaken without safety divers why do we need them?

Probability is the answer. The longer you stay submerged the more risk of incident. It's like if you walk in the middle of the street for long enough. You will get run over. Decompression dives can be long and complicated. More time spent submerged means nature has more time to ruin your day. Short projects or weekend trimix dives often 'get away' without using additional dive support such as safety divers, dive supervisors or medical technicians simply because they're not 'out there' long enough. That doesn't mean to say they will always remain safe. History tells us differently. Safety divers can at the very least improve your day and at best save lives. I have witnessed it on several occasions.

To be a safety diver takes as much skill and knowledge as it does to go to the bottom. Very often on extended projects, the most experienced members of the team elect to be the safety divers on the high-risk dives.

The skills list of a safety diver will include:

- service technician (for that exploding kit above and below the water)
- diver first-aid and an oxygen provider qualification
- an in-depth knowledge of the dive profile and what to do if it changes
- equipment capability (you will often carry as much or more cylinders and gear that any team member)
- the mental ability to work alone underwater
- a sixth sense of what will happen next
- boat skills - understand how the changing environment can affect boat/sea conditions and overall team safety
- cook/tea person
- insomniac

So safety divers need to be a bit more than 'one of your mates' who doesn't fancy going to the bottom.

What Does a Safety Diver Do?

Depending on the depth of dive (and team size) anything up to four safety divers can be easily used. I'll give a practical example of the work we did on the 'Britannic' in 1997. Due to the high current and shipping lane we had one safety diver who stayed on the boat. His job was to launch if any of the divers became separated from the decompression system or if someone needed to be recovered close to the surface. They would be equipped with a twin set of air with a 2 metre sharing hose and an emergency decompression line.

Miria Denlay
Safety diver. 'Britannic'97'

The second safety diver was to meet the divers at their deepest decompression stop. They would take any heavy equipment, such as scooters and cameras and clip them to a recovery line. They would also carry a twin set of the appropriate bottom mix (air if the stops were above 50 metres) and decompression gases the same as the dive team. They would stay with the dive team during the deep-water decompression and handover at the next gas switch depth (usually 30 metres) to the next safety diver. The 'deep safety' was the only safety diver allowed to get into decompression. After 'handing over' they would complete their decompression and return to the surface ready to take over a shallow safety diver role later in the six hour decompression.

The safety diver at 30 metres would stay out of deco and be in the water with the deep safety diver ready to take an injured diver directly to the surface (the deep safety only being able to ascend to 30 metres). They would carry a twin set of nitrox and the bottom diver's mid range deco gas and oxygen. This mid-range safety diver would hand over to another safety diver at the next gas switch (9 or 6 metres). This safety diver (and the shallow one) would have wireless communications equipment with a link to a surface supervisor.

Finally, the shallow stops would be covered by two safety divers rotating, as time permitted.

Basically, there is a safety diver in the water at all times and by staggering their decompression, a casualty can be taken directly to the surface at any time.

So, a summary of the work involved might include:
During the planning phase:

- Dealing with some of the logistics. This could range from ensuring fluid is available for a simple dive to defining and assembling sufficient gas quantities and its management for an extended operational period.

During preparation:

- Ensuring all equipment is in place and that support is correctly loaded; assembling any emergency equipment and verifying its functionality.

Prior to diving:

- Checking and tagging all decompression and dive gases.
- Assisting the divers to 'kit up'. Deploying of the decompression station and any in-water emergency equipment.
- Ensuring divers safely enter the water and all shallow water checks are conducted successfully.

During the Dive:

- At least one safety diver descends to the first gas switch point to ensure emergency gas is staged and functioning
- If possible, they wait until all divers have returned safely past the first gas switch point. The safety diver should then make sure all divers are safely on the decompression station prior to setting the station loose (if applicable).
- In a simple operation requiring two safety divers, one remains near the surface. In the event that a rescue has to be performed the 'shallow water' safety diver is best suited to this role. Also, if one of the team becomes separated this safety diver is deployed to define the extent of the problem and assist where possible (see other notes on deep and mid-range safety divers).

Post-Dive:

- Maintaining records. Assist the team with exiting from the water and de-kiting. Provide fluids and any surface gas for the team; stow equipment; help with an overall assessment of the operation and provide useful input for next time.

In short, safety divers are essential parts of the dive team and team members rotate through the safety diver role.

'Wings' Stocks being a caring dive supervisor

Dive Supervisor

The designated dive supervisor remains on the surface during all dive operations. The dive supervisor may elect to nominate a replacement dive supervisor from within the team at any point during diving operations if they have tasks to perform which will take them away from the deck.

The dive supervisor is in overall control of the dive and rigging operations. The dive supervisor in conjunction with the safety divers is in control of all record keeping and final equipment checks prior to divers entering the water. The dive supervisor also reviews any safety issue after the day's diving operation with the team. The dive supervisor is responsible for controlling all emergency situations.

Other Elements to Consider

Communications

The vessel must have VHF radios. In addition, short wave headsets are used between key members of the team during any rigging operations. This is ideal between the main vessel and any tender as they can be hands free units and provide an element of privacy. The operation will 'log-out' with the Coast Guard on leaving port and contact them when on-site providing details of the day's operation. Upon completion of the working day, the operation will log back in on arriving at port.

Kevin 'Admiral' Denlay
Dive supervisor 'Britannic '97'
Note the comms gear

Documentation

The dive supervisor will be responsible for keeping the daily dive log and completing a daily risk assessment plan.

(See Appendix B for typical dive logs.)

Introduction

As decompressions become longer and more complex, there is a need to use systems which improve individual and team safety and comfort. Long decompressions can be hazardous if conducted in shipping channels, tidal areas and cold environments. The decompression itself, as a additional hazard, can necessitate long uses of high oxygen mixtures. Well-constructed and planned decompression systems significantly reduce the risk.

When To Use a Decompression system

A good guide is, any decompression that requires multiple decompression gases and/or is more than approximately 30 minutes long (meaning that single or pairs of divers surfacing on marker buoys would become significantly separated) requires the use of a decompression system. Let's look at the problems in turn.

1. **Multiple decompression gases:** the use of multiple decompression gases usually means long and possibly deep dives. In certain situations (especially on trimix dives where deep-water decompression gases are needed) if a diver loses a deep-water decompression gas he/she may not be able to complete the decompression on their remaining gases. In open water this normally applies to dives over 80 metres in depth (given 'recreational[61]' bottom times). Hence, some kind of decompression system is used to stage safety gas for this phase of the dive. Better still, this scenario is further covered by using safety divers who carry additional gas.

Decompression station Britannic '97

2. **Long decompressions:** long duration decompressions, especially in tidal waters, means that individuals deploying surface marker buoys (SMB's) to decompress under will become separated. This is a hazard for three reasons:
   a. in the event of any one (or several) divers having an incident and surfacing, the boat skipper may just be in the wrong place at the wrong time and assistance may not be rendered quickly enough. Also, should an incident occur, the skipper may be forced to leave the vicinity with injured divers making the probability of loss of the remaining divers still in the water high.
   b. in surprise adverse weather, divers can become lost
   c. in shipping channels, large vessels may try and avoid another boat but individual divers will not be seen on a boat's radar.

Decompression Stations and Habitats

The function of a decompression station or habitat is to provide a stable platform on, or within, which the team can complete the decompression phase. Advantages and disadvantages of such systems are:

Advantages:

- a place to stage emergency equipment
- allows the team to stay together in a tidal environment
- provides a visual reference to assist with buoyancy control (stations)
- allows the team to exit (or partially exit) the water (habitats)
- provides extra safety in the event of an oxygen incident or where oxygen durations need to be extended. Habitats because the casualty is dry. Stations because casualties can be assisted by the other divers or recovered by the safety divers.
- reduces the effects of cold (habitats)
- provides a common communication point

---

[61] 30 minutes max

Disadvantages:

- high level of individual discipline required to act as a team
- divers have to be able to return to the shot/anchor line/station
- habitat set-up may be complex

Varying environmental conditions require different adaptations to the decompression station concept. Three basic layouts of decompression stations will be discussed as well as simple and complex habitats, although there are others.

System 1

Use area -
Low to medium tidal flow, good in water and generally good surface visibility. Small or large dive teams. Possibly heavy shipping traffic.

Method –
This system normally involves the support boat being tethered into the wreck/reef on a fixed single point bow mooring. The boat then deploys a weighted drop-line under the stern of the boat which joins a horizontal line or bar at 6 metres connected to the bow mooring line. In good visibility, where a return to the mooring line is simple, decompression cylinders may be staged on this 6 metres line or at a point on the mooring line where they will be first needed. The boat may also provide surface supplied oxygen or indeed any decompression gas. In current, divers may use Jon-lines to clip off to the mooring line.

One alternative to the single weighted drop line for larger groups of divers is to assemble a solid trapeze which is suspended on its own buoys and tethered to the boat. The base of the trapeze is again attached to the main down line by another horizontal line.

Guam '98. The search for the 'Pilar'. Jon-lines in heavy current

Safety systems -
Each diver carries an inflatable surface marker should they lose any of the lines. A dual colour-coded system is used one for 'alone but OK' (orange) and one for 'Help. Need gas etc' (yellow). Unless a return to the mooring line is guaranteed, divers will always carry all their own gases. Divers should carry some form of surface signalling device (flares\EPIRB).

System 2

Use Area -
High tidal flow. Low in-water visibility. Possibility of poor surface conditions. Small or large dive teams. Possibly heavy shipping traffic.

Method -
The main buoy line is sunk (shot or grapnel) to the site with a large surface buoy. The boat is not fixed to this line and works as a safety boat at all times. At the end of the dive the anchor or shot is retrieved and tied up the line several metres and hooked in place allowing the line to free-float with all divers using it as a visual reference. With trimix diving, safety, travel or deep-water decompression gas may be staged at various gas switch points.

Safety systems –
Each diver carries an inflatable surface marker should they lose any of the lines. A dual colour-coded system one for 'alone but OK' (orange) and one for 'Help. Need gas etc' (yellow). Divers will always carry all their own gases. Divers will carry some form of surface signalling device (flares\EPIRB). The surface vessel will carry emergency gas to be deployed on measured and buoyed depth lines, (dependant on the dive plan) in the event of an emergency

buoy being deployed. Slates can be attached to buoys for additional information. Boat must be equipped with radar and radios.

System 3

Use Area –
High tidal flow. Low in-water visibility. Possibility of poor surface conditions. Small or large dive teams. Possibly heavy shipping traffic.

Free float deco bar. English Channel

Method -
The main buoy line is sunk (shot or grapnel) to the site with a large surface buoy. Two 9 metre lines with a buoy at the top and a weight (2-4 kg) at each base. Each line will have loops every 3 metres. The lines are joined as in a trapeze with a movable bar (2-3 metres long). This station is attached to the main buoy line by a 'jump' or 'travel' line. Dependant on the amount of tide expected, this line will be 6m or longer than the point to the deepest decompression stop, allowing for the angle on the line due to the tidal effect. With trimix diving safety, travel or deep-water decompression gases will be staged as appropriate. Adaptations to this system for larger groups may include several down-lines and a triangular bar system.

Safety systems -
Each diver carries an inflatable surface marker should they lose any of the lines. A dual colour-coded system one for 'alone but OK' (orange) and one for 'Help. Need gas etc' (yellow). Divers will always carry all their own gases. Divers will carry some form of surface signalling device (flares\EPIRB). The surface vessel will carry emergency gas to be deployed on measured and buoyed depth lines, dependant on the dive plan, in the event of an emergency buoy being deployed. The boat must be equipped with radar and radios.

System 4

Use area –
Good underwater and surface visibility. Low volume surface traffic. Small teams. Minimal decompression.

Method -
Each diver or pair is allowed to deploy their own surface marker as the decompression starts.

Safety systems –
Each diver carries an inflatable surface marker should they lose any of the lines. A dual colour coded system one for 'alone but OK' (orange) and one for 'Help. Need gas etc' (yellow). The surface vessel will carry emergency gas to be deployed on measured and buoyed depth lines, dependant on the dive plan, in the event of an emergency buoy being deployed. Divers will normally carry some form of surface signalling device (flares\EPIRB).

Team Management
With systems 2 and 3 above and in extreme tidal areas, team management is vital. If team members are late arriving back at the station the current may be so strong as to drag down the surface buoys and therefore sink the station. Should this situation occur the only option is to deploy the individual surface markers (orange) and commence solo decompressions. To ensure team members return to the station within a safe tidal window, it is vital that tidal conditions are assessed and a team plan devised. The key is to define what is often known as a 'cut-off time' or the time point in a run time schedule when the jump line will be disconnected from the main line, thus allowing the station to free float. This can either be a fixed time of day in the team plan or a time point in the runtime schedule of the last pair to enter the water (i.e. entry plus 30 minutes). Each team member signs in on a slate positioned where the jump line joins

Alan Yeend using a delayed SMB

the main line. Should the majority of divers return within the time and other team members not yet be returned, the 'on station' team has the option to disconnect the jump line at the station end (rather than descending again) at the 'cut-off' time. Each team member must be able to navigate back to the line or be prepared to use a line reel.

Members not managing to return by the 'cut-off' time will realise this and simply deploy their markers and not waste energy or gas trying to return to the station.

There may be several adaptations to this system. Whichever is employed, teams are advised to practice all eventualities before settling on a system.

The above systems are primarily focused on open-water use. Cave or quarry dives have their own specific problems but generally involve the staging of gases and emergency equipment at fixed points. The use of any system that requires a return to a fixed point should employ visual markers such as strobes, reels or lights attached near the bottom to ensure a safe return.

Emergency Procedures

The main point of using any decompression system is to avoid team separation and improve safety. However, this does not always happen. To help reduce further problems as a result of separation, decompression 'drop stations' are used.

Drop Stations.

These are used when an emergency signal is seen from a diver at the surface. These are usually a specific colour (yellow) SMB or two SMB's together. The drop station will be a line as long as the deepest planned gas switch. The line will have on it at least a cylinder of each of the deep-water decompression gases tied on at the maximum operating depth (MOD) of each gas. Cylinder valves will have been pressurised and turned off to prevent free-flows. In some cases the shallow decompression gas will also be on the line, but usually as there is more time to correct a problem when shallow, this safety gas will be carried on the boat and only dropped if the safety diver deems it necessary, or if an additional pre-arranged signal is seen. Too many cylinders make the drop station unwieldy and prone to tangling.

Often the drop station is 'launched' with a safety diver descending with it to ascertain the problem. Whatever the problem the first assumption should be a gas failure and the station is always launched.

This system covers individual becoming separated from the main up-line or divers using individual SMB's.

Safety Boats

Where decompression systems are employed that require the vessel to be locked in to a down line and station, then a 'safety boat' should also be used. This is a small, fast vessel capable of following and recovering drifting divers and in an emergency being able to take a casualty to shore or the nearest medi-vac point. The checklist for a safety boat might include:

Radio
First Aid Kit
Oxygen resuscitation equipment
Diver recovery system
Emergency drop station with appropriate decompression gases
Navigation equipment (for relaying position)
Drinking water
Standard boat safety gear such as flares, tools etc.

Habitats

Dependant on the climatic conditions, extended decompressions (where there is either cold or a risk of oxygen toxicity) should involve decompression habitats where the divers may partially or totally exit the water to complete the decompression phase. Habitats can be simple affairs that allow a portion of the diver to exit the water (almost like an up-turned bucket) or more complex arrangements that allow a complete team of divers to totally exit the water[62]. Habitats reduce the possibility of hypothermia as well as help control the risk of drowning should an oxygen convulsion occur.

---

[62] Dr William C Stone. The Wakulla Springs Project.

Habitat construction can be a detailed science especially when one is designed for open water use. If a unit is to be constructed that is capable of allowing a team of divers to fully exit the water, this will take considerable engineering skill and resources. A list of problems that face the'would-be habitat designer' might encompass;

- **Total internal space required**. This defines the buoyancy the construction will experience (Archimedes principle). This may vary from a few kilos of uplift to several tonnes. To give the reader some idea, a habitat capable taking 6 people may experience an up thrust of some six tonnes and (ignoring construction and personnel weight) need six tonnes to hold it down. If it cannot be tethered then suitable ballast will need to be sunk.
- **Ruggedness and strength of construction**. The materials used must be suitable for the force exerted per square metre when the construction is filled with air. Also, if the habitat is to be deployed for a period of time, it must stand up to the rigours of the environment.
- **Deployment**. The larger and more complex the arrangement, the more the risk of damage or even loss during deployment and retrieval.
- **Equipment staging and gas supply**. The system may need detailed mounting systems to take primary and emergency gas supplies as well as other equipment.
- **Venting**. To reduce the risk of fire and other gas related problems, the habitat needs to be continually flushed with fresh air. Positioning and running of compressors capable of this may prove difficult especially in the open ocean.

Habitats have become popular with cave divers, mainly because exploration cave dives tend to be very long and the environment is more static than the open ocean, making habitat deployment and anchoring relatively simple. In cave diving the types and size of habitats vary considerably. From the large-scale Wakulla Project[63] unit to upside down plastic waste bins often found in places like the Emergence du Russel Cave system in France, each is correct for its task.

---

[63] The Wakulla Springs Project book is an excellent reference for would be habitat designers. See Bibliograpgy.

Diver Propulsion Vehicles

What is a Diver Propulsion Vehicle?

A diver prolusion vehicle or DPV is a motorised underwater vehicle capable of carrying one or more divers to and from an underwater location. In the past, DPV's have been both air and battery powered. Simple sport units are capable of towing a single diver behind the motor/propeller unit. More complex military ones can carry up to four divers on and around the unit. The first military unit developed by the Italians in World War One was 8 metres long and based on the aft end of a German torpedo!

In 1935, the Italians again developed a new DPV or 'human torpedo' using an electric motor for the first time (early ones were air powered). This increased range and speed. Modern sport DPV's are all battery-powered and possess several unique features compared with their earlier military counterparts.

Why Bother with DPV's?

With the extra effort required to run and maintain a DPV, why are they so popular with technical divers?

- cave divers regularly use DPV's to extend the range of their cave exploration often carrying more than one into a system.
- any divers working in deep-water or where breathing effort is increased use DPV's to reduce general fatigue and stress.
- wreck divers and even archaeologists use simple DPV's to remove sediment and assist with artefact location.
- cameramen and videographers use DPV's as a means of getting closer (or keeping up) with their subjects as well as a mounting platform for equipment.
- support divers use DPV's to stage equipment for deep penetration teams.
- DPV's are just good fun, especially (in my opinion) when combined with a closed circuit rebreather!

**Camera and light Aquazeps
M1 project**

Benefits and Risks

Going farther still means you have to get back! Especially in a cave dive, going in to the system a long way means coming out a long way!

Benefits	Risks
• Reduced exertion o Less CO_2 buildup • Reduced gas consumption • Energy conservation • Increased travel • A good general tool • Fun	• Getting complacent with level of penetration • Not correcting gas rules • Lack of finning means cold becomes an issue • Equipment failure procedures become more complicated • Higher maintenance levels • Never forget where you are!

Proper training and practice will ensure your DPV becomes a fun tool to enhance your diving safely.

Types of DPV's

Basically, there are three types

- tow behind. usually short, simple single battery units. Often single speed.
- Basic ride-on. Often dual or multi-battery units. More complex controls.
- dual units. Two large ride-on's connected together. These massive units have complex controls (joysticks) and are often loaded with heavy survey equipment or extra gas supplies.

Construction Do's and Don't's

The Body

Bodies are either plastic (PVC) or metal (usually aluminium). The type of construction will limit the durability and operating depth. Both are relatively easy to repair.

The Propeller Shroud

The design of the shroud is such that water is channelled to improve the propeller's thrust and provide protection for the unit and pilot. Damage to a shroud should not be taken lightly. Repair should be as soon as possible. At best, a damaged shroud will reduce speed and worst, throw the prop shaft out of alignment and flood the unit.

Switch Gear

Most DPV's have a 'deadman switch' which when released automatically stops the motor. Holding the switch for prolonged periods can generate fatigue. Many divers lock the 'deadman' in place with bungee or straps. This has increased risk but reduces stress. As most switches are of the magnetic reed variety, another method is to tape or place a magnet on/into a glove. If your hand moves, the DPV stops.

Some DPV's even have variable speed controls.

Batteries

Batteries come in various types; all are rechargeable and need special handling. Always adhere to the manufacturer's charging guidelines. During use and whilst charging, batteries produce hydrogen which is highly explosive. Catalysts can be used in the battery compartment to convert this to water and make it safe. Flooding will cause rapid discharge and produce hydrogen. Always be careful when opening a battery compartment. Never do so near a naked flame.

Always be careful when opening a battery compartment.
Never do so near a naked flame.

Battery Care:

- charge as soon as possible after use
- recharge annually when not in use
- do not overcharge
- keep away from heat and direct sunlight
- do not store discharged
- check burn time with a practical test after prolonged storage and before any deep penetrations

Tips and Tricks

Dive planning using DPV's is not dissimilar to normal free swimming planning. However, often things happen faster at speed and dead DPV's can themselves become hazards.

Rule 1

Have a reliable, well maintained DPV. Place small absorbent sponges in vital areas to suck up small leaks. Make sure your own equipment is safely stowed, check reels and any danglies regularly throughout the dive.

Rule 2

Stay neutrally-buoyant at all times. Make sure your DPV is properly trimmed. I make my ride-on Aquazep slightly nose heavy. With tow-behinds, make sure the prop wash is directed under the body. With a ride-on, use a crutch lanyard to your harness scooter ring. Do not put excessive weight on the 'T bar' or 'cruise seat'. All of this helps to keep you correctly streamlined.

Rule 3

Don't go at warp 10 just because you can! Speed reduces your battery life/penetration. Speed puts stress on you and the unit (scootering with multi-stages at speed or even worse. a rebreather isn't fun for long).

Increased speed also means you have less time to react to natural hazards. Reduce speed in low visibility and small passages. More speed equals distance faster and more possibility of becoming separated and lost. Learn to walk before you run!

Phil Short trimmed out. The white loop on the front is a metal detector

Rule 4

Be mindful of getting lost. It is easy to motor along taking in the scenery and then realise you don't know the way home. Use natural/compass navigation regularly.

Rule 5

Be mindful of current. It may not feel bad whilst on the DPV but if you have to swim back, that becomes another matter. In open water, if using the DPV during an ascent up a line, do not allow your self to get too far down current. You may have to swim to the line at any time. Circling ascents and descents are better or ascend up the line with the DPV switched off and carried like a stage.

Rule 6

Do not allow your DPV to override your safe dive plan. Always assume it will fail at the worst possible time and plan accordingly.

Rule 7

When team-diving DPV's, look after each other. You may see the hazard but your partner may not. Also, make sure your surface team knows how to handle your DPV and stow it safely. There is nothing worse than finishing 4 hours of decompression and surfacing to a wrecked DPV someone has handed into the boat improperly.

Rule 8

Keep your DPV skills up to date. Practise before any major dive, especially towing.

Rule 9

In open water carry a lift bag so that you can quickly send a damaged DPV to the surface. Make sure the boat crew know what it looks like so that the DPV can be removed from the water ASAP. Saltwater kills DPV's, quickly! Do not park DPV's on the bottom in swell conditions. Make an underwater scooter park by inflating a small bag and tying it 2 to 3 metres off the bottom. Now attach your DPV to it, clear of the bottom.

Rule 10

Always wash your DPV in fresh water, especially the prop shaft. Regularly check for signs of wear and small traces of weed/line on the shaft. Never run the shaft dry for long periods. Store your DPV with as many 'O' rings removed as possible.

Deployment and Recovery

DPV's are relatively fragile especially in the wrong hands. I have already mentioned educating support crew and the use of underwater scooter parks. Some models such as the Aquazep benefit from fitting crash bars to protect the handles which are the weak point. As a general rule never pick a DPV up by its handles. Never jump in carrying your DPV, it could damage the seals at best and at worst damage you!

Hand in your DPV, have it carried to the start of the dive by a support diver or have it lowered on a buoyed line. In open water with limited support personnel I will sometimes deploy the DPV on a buoy and then jump in near the buoy. Pick up the DPV and scooter to the wreck down line.

When recovering a DPV from a deep dive it is often a good idea to get rid of it early in the decompression. Have a safety diver bring down a recovery line and clip it off. Arrange for either wireless communication or rope signals to be employed to recover it asap. On simple dives, clip it off to a surface buoy while you climb back in the boat, then recover it. That way you can be the one recovering the DPV or at least supervising the recovery.

DPV Specific Safety Kit

Additional items that may not usually be carried might include:

- manifold guard to protect valves against impact at speed
- spare mask for high speed loss (or put the strap under your hood) or damage
- lightweight plastic helmet
- lift bag for recovery and parking
- an EPIRB/strobe in open water, for when you've gone that bit too far!
- A'jon-line' for towing
- extra instruments for mounting on the scooter (timer/compass)
- heavy duty cutters for line/wire

Make sure you can reach all safety gear with one hand. You may be driving with the other!

Other points to remember include: if you notice a change in propeller noise or speed STOP IMMEDIATELY! Check the prop and shaft for entanglements. Try and remove them by hand (having previously isolated the power) first before diving in with a knife.

If your DPV starts to run away either try and jam it under a rock, in the ceiling or if on an open-water ascent just let it go. If the runaway is controlled then ride it out as far as you can.

Swimming a 'dead' DPV out is not always a smart thing to do, go back the following day and retrieve it.

Skills and Drills

1. do a full workshop session. Make sure you know how everything works. Get a electro/mechanical picture of the DPV in your mind. Generate a dive preparation check list.
2. do a shallow dive getting your trim right and maintain neutral buoyancy at all depths. Try spiralling ascents and descents as well as controlling buoyancy following a line with the scooter clipped off as a stage. Always isolate the power before clipping a scooter off. Try various speeds.
3. run a pre-planned compass course estimating time and distance travelled. On a timed run (out and return) make allowances for current to navigate back to the start point.
4. swim for 200 metres with a dead DPV in a horizontal direction.
5. practice three tow techniques:
   drop the dead DPV and tow by grabbing your partners manifold
   drop the dead DPV and tow grabbing their fins
   tow using a 'Jon-line'. Crutch/scooter ring to scooter ring is best for this method (stay on dead DPV).

Now complete all three above whilst gas sharing. Establish a good signalling/awareness routine to cope with changes during the tow.

In summary, for many of us, DPV's are the 'weapon of choice'. Coupled with a closed circuit rebreather, the possibilities are endless, but remember 'he who dies with the most toy's still dies'. As with all extended range diving, know your own and your equipments' limitations and have fun. Try pulling that first barrel roll and you'll know what I mean!

Operational Safety

Safety should be something we are all concerned about. With technical or extended range diving, where the diver is more likely to stay submerged for longer periods of time, there is a higher risk of problems occurring. A simple analogy might be: 'if I stand in the street long enough I am more likely to get run over'. The longer a diver remains underwater the more the effects of equipment reliability - diver error and environmental changes become an issue. Complex dives often involve extended decompressions, depth outside of the accepted sport limits, large amounts of gas and support equipment as well as sophisticated dive platforms such as boats and underwater habitats. The following is offered as a general guide to questions to be addressed when planning such dives.

To define a safe operating procedure we must first look at several specific issues:

1. the type of dive and it's associated hazards
2. risk
3. safety planning
4. dive platforms
5. safety divers
6. rescue management and equipment

Types of Dive

The range of dives available to recreational divers is almost limitless. Over recent years the concept and scope of recreational diving has expanded into the realms of what has become known as technical diving. So there is recreational diving and there is technical diving, but what is the difference? Divers are often diving for fun past the recreational norms of 40 or 50 metres, so depth is not necessarily the issue. It is now fairly common in certain parts of the globe to see divers hiring boats to take them out into 70 metres of water and do a 'recreational' trimix dive. So where does recreational diving really stop? Should the analogy be that as long as the diver is doing it for fun it is still recreational diving irrespective of depth and time submerged? What makes diving 'technical?'

Some expeditions get very *technical*. Chamber being installed. 'M1 project'.

Perhaps the difference is based on the functions of time and exploration. Exploration is going somewhere no one else has been before (which generates its own risks) and extending submerged times at any depth exposes us to risks outlined above. Taking open water diving as an example, this generally means going past the sport diving limits (40 metres+) and/or spending significant time at any depth, hence generating a considerable decompression obligation.

So a description of technical diving might be:

'Technical diving is a range of knowledge, skills and suitable equipment which, when combined correctly, allow recreational divesr to increase their safety whilst underwater. This information may be employed in either shallow or deep-water, may be used to safely extend the divers submerged duration well into the realms of extended decompressions and is often used as a tool for exploration'.

As readers are in the main interested in technical diving, this type of diving will be the focus. It is not to say that any dives planned would not benefit from some of the topics discussed in this chapter, of course they would.

Put broadly types of dives include:

1. Shore dive
2. Boat Dive
3. Cave Dive

Entrance to St. George cave. Dordoigne Valley. France

Whilst all types of diving (especially at a technical level) are generally similar; cave-diving should and does command the most respect. Many of the techniques employed in technical diving were first used in caves.

The cave environment is both fascinating and challenging; both from a mental and a technical standpoint. Caves, although initially appearing benign can soon turn into a diver's worst nightmare. As such, cave diver training is some of the most rewarding. If you think you are a good open-water diver, take a cave class! Cave diving is not the same the world over. Cave diving in the UK is a million miles apart from cave diving in Florida. However, most of the basic skills employed are generic and are covered within this text. **Do not stray into caves without the correct training.**

Diving Hazards

Items 1 & 2 can be subdivided in to 'reef' or 'wreck'. All dives can obviously be fresh or salt water and may be at altitude or at night and there are a variety of different cave dives. Looking at each one in turn (and in order to identify the risk involved) let's list some of the hazards.

Type of Dive	Scenario	Hazard
Shore - Reef	Entry/exit point	Physical injury
	Current	Swept away from safe egress
	Marine life	Physical injury
	Boat traffic	Physical injury
	Sea state	Physical injury, inability to safely egress
	Weather	Changing sea state, reduced surface visibility
	Gas failure	Drowning
	Underwater visibility	Loss of dive partner
Shore - Wreck	All of the above	All of the above
	Entrapment	Drowning or other physical injury
Boat - Reef/wreck	All of the above	All of the above
	Underwater visibility	Loss of line to surface
Cave/wreck penetration	Line loss	Inability to find exit
	Silt out	Inability to find line or partner

The above is a table of some but not all of the general hazards (both physical and environmental) which might occur. This should be completed for the specific dive being planned and where necessary, corrective actions defined for any high risk scenarios.

Risk

Looking at all of the above, the overall risk for each item can be defined as a combination of the probability of any event occurring and how life threatening it is. As all dives involve risk, they should have varying levels of safety planning. In some cases such as gas supply failure where the probability of failure is potentially low (due to reliable regulators) but the life threatening potential is extreme - the combined risk is high and hence detailed safety plans should be made. In another situation the probability of losing a safe egress from a shore dive in bad weather is fairly high but the potential for rescue and hence the life threatening factor might be low, making the overall risk minimal.

In general, low-risk dives normally have their safety requirements covered by standard diving equipment and practises such as those often employed on a normal recreational dive. High-risk dives need specific emergency plans for any highlighted hazards. So how do we assess risk and define which scenarios need more planning than others?

Generate a Table to Assess Risk.

Probability of a hazard occurring should be graded as:

1. not likely
2. possible
3. probable

Life threatening factor should be graded as:

0. no risk
1. low
2. medium
3. high

For example, looking at the table below, in the first example a diver uses a single high quality regulator and a loss of gas is the defined hazard. This regulator however has a low failure probability of 1, but if it does fail (as there is only one) the potential for loss of life is high due to drowning etc. Hence the overall risk is high (4). In this instance the most practical safety plan for this scenario would be to carry a backup or redundant regulator. The same type of assessment can be made for the other examples and a safety plan generated.

Scenario/Hazard	*Probability*	*Life Threatening factor*	*Overall risk*
Loss of gas	1	3	4
Loss of boat	1	2	3
Loss of partner	1	0	1

In summary:

- define each hazard
- define the probability of the risk occurring
- define how life threatening it is
- grade the probability and life-threatening factor to define the overall risk
- plan for the specific safety procedure to instigate should the combined risk score be 3 or above

As all dives do involve risk the need to execute them must be balanced against that risk and the potential reward. In some cases the reward is worth the ultimate risk. The focus of this chapter is to make you think about the hazards and define which require detailed safety planning to reduce the overall risk.

Risk is reduced by proper planning, training and equipment.

Safety Planning

Having defined the hazards which require detailed safety planning (scoring 3+) it is important to review the environment's affect on those hazards, after which a safety plan may be generated.

The world's diving environments are not only varied across the globe but may vary from day to day and even hour to hour at any one site. Each type of dive has its own specific environment due to its location. Especially in open water, dives that require extended decompressions or long submerged durations may be affected by a range of changing environments. It is important to plan for these changes and include them as part of a risk assessment.

As the dives' environment and any physical hazards affect our overall safety, let's now include both of these in our safety plan and define possible corrective action to reduce any risk. This will be completed for a range of dives.

Shore Diving

Hazard	*Safety Procedure*
Difficult access/egress to site	Carry kit in stages\employ 'Sherpas' Use ropes and slings.
Ocean swells	Submerge ASAP to identify underwater hazards. Deploy exit line and floats. Use shore cover personnel.
Ice	Always use line to surface and shore personnel. With thick ice, ensure surface cover has safety-cutting equipment.
Bad surface visibility	Carry surface signalling equipment. Sonic alerts or EPIRB'S work in most instances.
Bad underwater visibility	Use buddy lines and compasses
Boat traffic	Use surface marker buoy
Nets and lines	Carry cutting equipment
Current	Where long dives are planned in a tidal area, tidal planning to predict an egress point is vital. Shore and probably boat cover will be needed. Drifting divers should always use a surface marker.

Shore diving generally requires that a diver has good navigational skills especially when ocean diving along cliffs, where specific access\egress points are limited. Where drift dives are to be performed with an extensive floating decompression, ensure boat cover is adequately equipped.
With all diving, but especially where land is to be crossed, remember: always respect the environment and landowners' wishes.

Boat Diving

Hazard	*Safety procedure*
Rough seas	Deploy diver pick-up and kit drop lines with buoys tethered to the boat. Do not attempt to egress in full kit.
Current	In the event of being swept away carry signalling equipment, flares, EPIRB'S, sonic alerts etc. Plan for a lost diver drill and search pattern at a predetermined time point where the divers should have surfaced.
Other boats	Never surface without a marker or being on your boat's shot line
Entrapment	Avoid penetration. Check structures for safety before entering. Dive with a partner who may be able to assist
Nets and lines	Carry cutting equipment
Poor underwater visibility	Use strobes or reels on the down line to ensure a safe return.

Cave Diving

Hazard	*Safety procedure*
Current	In extreme cases work against the flow going in. Test for changes in current and tidal effects before entering. Lay strong lines. Correct planning should prevent tidal problems.
Low in water visibility	Always use continuous exit lines. Remain in touch contact.
Collapse\entrapment	Dive as part of a team. Do not enter unsafe structures.

We have looked at a range of dives and their possible hazards. We have defined the probability of a hazard occurring and the life threatening potential if it happens. As well as defining the risk we have looked at how the environment may produce its own problems and how to plan safely to reduce those problems.

It is worth noting at this point that the three most common causes of diving fatalities can be definedd as:

1. **not planning for proper gas reserves ('rule of thirds') especially on penetration dives.**
2. **not carrying a truly redundant gas source.**
3. **not using a continuous guide line to the exit on penetration dives.**

Dive Support Platforms

Dive platforms can be subdivided into those that remain on the surface and those that stay submerged during the dive. In the simplest form these range from shore safety personnel, the boat, through to decompression stations and habitats. Shore personnel must be aware of the team plan, carry safety equipment such as oxygen and ropes and slings and have good communications (phone/radio).

Surface supplied oxygen being used with a fixed mooring. The large sled is a diver-towed underwater metal detector. 'Pilar' project 1998.

Boats

Let us first define the functions of a boat in a technical diving operation. Briefly, these can be listed:

- safe transport to and from site
- protection from the elements
- accommodation
- a dive-support platform
- a rescue platform

The first three categories of the above list are almost always defined by the physical size of the boat. Boats as operational platforms tend to fall in four size-related categories. These categories will also define the range of the vessel and possibly its suitability for a specific operation.

Type	*Construction*	*Size*	*Suitability*
Dory/Boston Whaler	GRP or aluminium	Up to 6 metre	In-shore open boat work. Can be used for small team technical operations
Inflatable	Rigid or soft-hull inflatable	Up to 9 metre as a sport boat	In shore and off shore work. All levels of technical operation.
Day boat	GRP, wood or steel	Up to 15 metre approx.	As above
Live aboard	As above	Generally up to 25 metre	As above plus expeditions

Whilst each of the above may be suitable for technical operations, each has its own problems. Because weather will often decide the range and type of diving undertaken on the smaller vessels, larger boats also generate problems in strong weather particularly with diver egress. Even though larger vessels may take divers comfortably to site in strong weather, diver safety may still be compromised during the entry and exit phase because of poor ladders/high sides etc. In short, anything much above a force 5 on the Beaufort scale will preclude safe diving. Extended decompressions in strong seas also become uncomfortable unless precautions are taken[64].

The 'M1' submarine. A converted landing craft was used for this 80 metre dive project

Accommodation will only normally be found on the larger live on board/expedition size of vessels. Find out as much about the boat as possible prior to chartering. Three things that can make a trip miserable above all others are poor or inadequate food, inability to rest comfortably and poor sanitation. All of these also affect team safety.

Boats as Dive Support Platforms

[64] P. 155

The boat is used to deliver the divers to and retrieve them from the water, to allow an area for kiting and de-kiting, to provide protection while they are submerged and to transport equipment specific to an operation. The following is a list of practical suggestions to overcome some of the associated problems.

'M1' project team and film crew.
Divers: Phil Short, Rich & Iggy Lundgren and myself.
The historical expert was Richard larn. Russel Cately ran the chamber.

Entry and Exit.
Smaller vessels allow the diver to roll backwards to enter the water and once in, clip on additional equipment and cylinders (if boat space is limited). Exit at worst will involve removing the equipment prior to returning into the boat. This is especially true of the inherently stable inflatable technology. Larger vessels may have a similar entry method although stern entry doors are becoming more popular and do provide more safety and less potential for physical injury with multiple cylinder set-ups. With larger vessels, re-entry to the boat will often be via some form of ladder. Whilst side ladders are extensively used in some countries, on non-cathedral hull boats (where the pitching of the vessel can be extreme) this type of exit can be hazardous. In general, stern platforms provide for a much more stable base for entering and exiting the boat. In any event one of the safest ways to re-enter any vessel is to remove excess equipment prior to so doing. Two proposed methods for achieving this are;

1) Use a small support boat (inflatable) to retrieve heavy equipment (side mounts etc.)

2) Deploy a kit retrieval line. This is a long line (5-10 metre) with brass rings positioned along it and a large float at one end. The other end is tied to the stern of the boat, preferably at a high point away from the propeller using floating line. If surface conditions are slight, simply return to the line, remove one side mount clip at a time and clip it to the line (this stops accidental dropping and loss of the cylinder).

If conditions are severe, undo the rear side mount clip whilst still submerged (at the last stop) rather than in the surface swell. Attach one clip at a time to the line to prevent loss. Pull your self back to the boat using the line, allowing the skipper/support crew to retrieve the cylinders. If twin sets are to be removed, provide a firm anchor point on the set by which it can be lifted (not the manifold). Some boats may have winches to assist with this.

Kiting and de-kiting
Whilst kiting areas on smaller boats may be limited, on larger vessels there can often be too much space leading to confusion on the boat. Boat loading plays a crucial role especially if an emergency occurs. In summary:

- ensure personnel team equipment is accessible in the order of which it is to be used. The first pair of divers in the water should have their kit nearest the kiting area or exit point.
- ensure that all safety equipment is easily accessible and make space to treat a casualty
- where possible make a separate kiting up to travel area for equipment. In rough seas equipment tends to move around and should be firmly locked in a stowage area to prevent damage. It is often far safer to fully rig equipment on land prior to loading and then firmly secure it in the boat rather than trying to assemble and test it in a pitching sea. This also reduces the number of kit bags required (freeing valuable space). Simple benches or a central table make good kiting areas once on site, empty bags being stowed underneath.
- if support divers can be used, employ them to kit team members. If they are not available, educate your boat skipper!
- when re-entring the boat, de-kit as quickly as possible and stow equipment.
- employ team planning to reduce pre-dive stress. Each member has an assigned task and each pair helps the previous pair to dress in and out.

Operational Checklists
A vital part of operational safety is ensuring that all equipment is loaded prior to leaving base. In order to achieve this it is prudent to generate checklists. The following is offered as a typical checklist that might be employed.

Personal Equipment	***Boat Equipment***	***Emergency Equipment***
Cylinders	**Shot lines**	**Surface oxygen**
Regulators	**Navigation gear**	**First-aid kit**
Suit inflation system	**Decompression station**	**Casualty recovery eqpuipment**
Harness and wing	**Emergency deco. gas**	**Fluids**
Primary light	**Radio/cell phone**	
Backup lights	**Anchor**	
Primary reel	**Tools/spares**	
Backup reels	**Kit recovery lines**	
Dive computer		
Backup dive timers/gauges		
Dive tables		
Run time tables		
Communications slate		
Emergency buoys		
Marker strobe		
EPIRBS/flares/sonic alert		
Lift bags		
Knife		
Net/line cutter		
Tools/spares		
Suit and underwear		
Fluids		
Mask/fins/gloves		
Compass		
DPV		

Similar checklists can be generated for shore and cave-diving activities.

Protection whilst submerged
Whilst the dive is being conducted, it is the boat's function to protect the dive team. Whilst the vessel its self can offer physical protection from other sea users by employing such things as radar and communications equipment. Its ability to do this for the whole team relies on the divers acting as a unit. In tidal areas it is just not acceptable that extended decompressions be carried out on an individual basis where there is a possibility that the group will become fragmented. Separation of the team is hazardous for the following reasons:

- the boat cannot offer protection from other vessels for all team members
- as weather and sea states change, divers may become lost
- if a pair of divers or an individual has a problem, the boat may not be in the right place at the correct time
- if separated pairs of divers or individuals have problems, the boat cannot be in two places at once
- in emergencies, organised team help is more efficient that 'buddy' assistance

The only real answer to this problem is the use of decompression stations or habitats as described in a previous chapter.

Whichever boat platform is used there are several golden rules which should not be broken:

- never leave the boat unattended
- carry a 100% oxygen supply system
- carry a medical kit
- carry communications equipment (radio, phone, flares etc.)
- as a minimum carry a compass and/or more suitable electronic navigational aids

Helicopter Rescues.
Important points to remember are:

- remove all obstructions (aerials etc.) from pickup point.
- always follow the pilot's instructions.
- never touch the winch man, lines or stretcher until a ground wire has touched the boat or sea. There is a risk of electric shock.
- do not attach any lines from the helicopter to the vessel.
- do not haul on the winch line.
- attach detailed written information about the incident to the casualty.
- position the boat into the wind at an angle of 30 degrees off the port bow. You may be asked to slowly motor (5 knots).

In the event of a lost diver scenario the dive boat should mark the last known position prior to leaving the incident site.

Insurance.
International medical insurance to cover diving incidents and any subsequent treatment can be covered by taking out Divers Alert Network (DAN) insurance. DAN can also advise on chamber locations and rescue facilities.

Conclusions
The safety planning of any single dive or series of dives may range from the simple to the extremely complex. Remember, define the hazards, assess the risks, plan for the specific scenarios and stay in practice.

'One of the best weapons in your arsenal is you, providing you are a prepared and practised logical thinking diver.'

Rebreathers

Rebreathers are not new. However, until recently they have only been within the grasp of the military and sophisticated commercial operations. Advances in electronics, manufacturing techniques and the branching move from traditional 'air' diving into 'technical' diving, have led to renewed interest in rebreather technology. When used properly by qualified individuals, rebreathers provide significant advantages over open circuit SCUBA, especially for extended range diving. Dramatically lower gas consumption, optimisation of gas mixtures to minimise decompression time, near-silent operation and reduction in heat loss are a few of the benefits. The value of these benefits must be balanced against the operational complexities and maintenance requirements inherent to rebreathers.

Early History
The first practical use of a re-circulating oxygen system was devised by Henry Fleuss in 1878. In 1880, he demonstrated the practicalities of such a system in flooded tunnels. The first true chemical carbon dioxide absorbent material, barium hydroxide, was used in 1881 by Khotinsky and Lake to remove excess CO_2 from an experimental rebreather system. In 1905, Fleuss was again experimenting and developing submarine escape apparatus. In 1912, Draegerwerk demonstrated a submarine sled equipped with rebreathers that provided 2 hour durations.

During World War II, the Italians used oxygen rebreathers to attack shipping in Gibraltar harbour. The British Commandos responded with early nitrox units which offered increased depth capability and thus attained major advantages over their Italian counterparts.

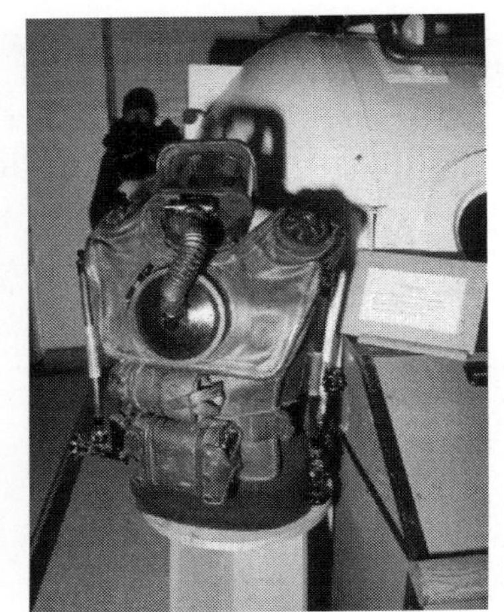
Military oxygen rebreather

Recent History
From World War II we move on to 1969 and the 'Electrolung'. Designed and developed by Walter A. Starck, III and John Kanwisher, the Electrolung employed the earliest form of electro-chemical oxygen sensor. Next came the Biomarine CCR1000, the predecessor of the Carleton Technologies MK15/16 (used extensively by the US Navy) but more recently finding a place amongst technical divers.

In the commercial world, rebreathers were primarily designed as bailout equipment from deep bell-dives. Manufacturers such as Reimers, Comex and OBS all pioneered these systems, some of them being used to depths of 530 metres as in the Comex HYDRA VIII experiments conducted on hydreliox (hydrogen, helium and oxygen).

Several recreational units now exist and many are in every day use.

There can be no doubt that technical and educational support is now available for the use of rebreathers in a recreational market place.

Types of Rebreathers

What is a Rebreather?
A rebreather consists of a breathing loop from which the diver inhales and into which he exhales. All modern rebreathers share certain basic components: a mouthpiece connected to two breathing hoses (one for inhaled gas, the other for exhaled gas); a system for adding oxygen to the breathing loop; a system for removing CO_2 from the breathing loop; and a collapsible bag or 'counter-lung' (to make up the volume of gas inhaled or exhaled by the diver). Oxygen is injected into the loop to replace that which is metabolised by the diver, and CO_2 exhaled by the diver is removed by a chemical absorbent material. Because the majority of the exhaled gas is retained in the loop rather than exhaled as bubbles, rebreathers allow for much greater gas efficiency (longer durations with a given quantity of gas) than SCUBA.

Counter-lung size is a critical aspect of any rebreather design, because it must be sufficient to accommodate the full volume of gas the diver inhales and exhales on a single breath. Many rebreather designs incorporate two counter-lungs in the breathing loop - one for inhale and one exhale. Because the counter-lung expands as a diver's lungs compress, the total volume (displacement) of the diver and rig remains almost constant. Therefore, unlike open circuit SCUBA diving, there is no change in buoyancy during the diver's breathing cycle.

There are three types of rebreather: p*ure oxygen*, c*losed circuit*, and *semi-closed circuit*. Each type has different capabilities and limitations.

Pure Oxygen Rebreather

Pure oxygen rebreathers, or simply 'oxygen rebreathers', have long been used by the military (as in the early 'pendulum' units[65]) for covert operations although they are more often used in surface operations (firemen etc.) They are usually simple, small chest-mounted units that incorporate only one gas (100% oxygen) in the breathing loop. As oxygen is metabolised by the diver and CO_2 is removed by the absorbent, the volume of gas in the loop is reduced. This reduction in volume causes the counter-lung to collapse and triggers an addition valve which replaces the metabolised oxygen. Excess gas is vented via a check valve. Because there are no inert gases, there is no decompression obligation when using oxygen rebreathers. However, due to oxygen toxicity concerns, this type of rebreather has a finite depth limit, normally 6 metres.

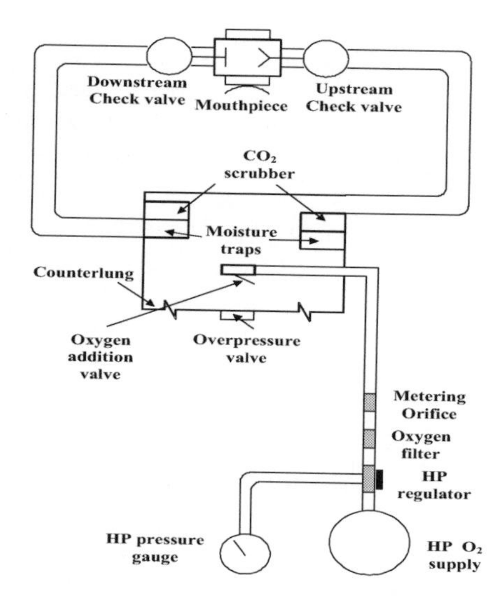

Oxygen Rebreather.

Semi-Closed Circuit Rebreather

Semi-closed circuit rebreathers generally work by feeding a pre-planned oxygen-rich mixture into the breathing loop. The percentage of oxygen in the mixture is determined by the working depth (the mixture is chosen so as to not exceed a PO_2 of 1.5 bar or less at that depth) and the required inspired oxygen fraction, is calculated from the flow rate of the unit and anticipated oxygen consumption of the diver. These systems broadly fall into two common categories according to the way they replenish the consumed oxygen.

The first type continuously injects oxygen-rich mixture via a flow orifice which may be adjusted by the diver. These are generally classified as **active** systems. Because the injected mixture contains an inert gas (or *diluent*), semi-closed circuit rebreathers are not restricted to depths of 6 metres or less. However, the diluent portion of the mixture is not metabolised by the diver (as the oxygen is) so the loop volume continuously increases as the oxygen-rich mixture is added. Consequently, this type and in deed all semi-closed circuit rebreathers must periodically vent-off excess gas, which typically occurs about every fourth or fifth breath (in the case of constant flow systems). Gas usage estimates for this type of semi-closed circuit system vary but are commonly about one-third that of open circuit SCUBA.

The second type of semi-closed circuit unit employs oxygen-rich mixture injection linked to the divers' RMV or work-rate. Known as **passive** units they generally only add gas when required. Control devices ranging from compound counter-lungs to ratchet and gear systems[66] are employed. These systems generally conserve more oxygen and can even lengthen the life of the absorbent.

---

[65] Pendulum rebreathers employ a single hose leading to the absorbent cannister and rely on the diver completely exhaling to remove all the CO_2 from a single breath.

[66] Interspiro ASCS military unit.

An additional feature sometimes found in both types of system incorporates an additional supply of pure oxygen. During portions of the dive when a constant depth will be maintained, the addition of the oxygen-rich mixture can be disabled and the system then uses the counter-lung to actively add pure oxygen by means of a ratchet or bellows acting upon an addition valve as the counter-lung collapses due to metabolism (as in the pure oxygen rebreathers). Thus, semi-closed rebreathers can function as closed circuit (but not electronically controlled) rebreathers, when the depth is held constant.

Because semi-closed circuit rebreathers of the first type are the most common, they will be discussed in detail here.

In semi-closed rebreather systems wherein PO_2 control is not linked to work rate, PO_2 variations can be a problem. The variation in PO_2 is important for three reasons:

- the final inspired PO_2 of the diver is vital to avoid hyperoxia or hypoxia.
- variations in the PO_2 (or more specifically, variations in the diluent gas partial pressure) make decompression calculations difficult.
- incorrect adjustments of the flow rate system (which affects the inspired PO_2) greatly affect rebreather duration (i.e., gas consumption).

In a semi-closed circuit rebreather, the metabolic (oxygen consumption) rate of the diver and/or the mixture flow rate[67] of the unit are critical in determining the inspired fraction of oxygen that the diver breathes.

The three basic factors to consider in semi-closed circuit (active) rebreather oxygen management are:

- oxygen fraction of the supply gas
- volume flow of the supply gas
- oxygen consumption of the diver

In order to maintain inspired PO_2 within safe limits, it is important to understand the mathematics involved with calculating the fraction of oxygen inspired by a diver using a semi-closed rebreather. The inspired oxygen fraction can then be used in conjunction with the ambient pressure (i.e., depth) to determine inspired PO_2. In reality, the calculations for modelling actual gas concentrations in the breathing loop are very complex. However, for practical applications, it is useful to make several assumptions in order to simplify this task:

1. the total oxygen from the supply cylinder equals the sum of oxygen metabolised by the diver and oxygen lost during periodic loop venting (i.e., a "steady state" system). Loss of oxygen from mask clearings or leakage will be considered negligible.
2. the volume of inert gas absorbed by the diver's blood and tissues will also be considered negligible (with respect to the volume of inert gas in the breathing loop and oxygen-rich supply cylinder), as will the volume of CO_2 and other trace gases in the loop.
3. the loop volume (including diver's lungs and counter-lungs) remains constant.

The following definitions are used:

$\mathbf{Q_S}$	= supply (input) flow of the oxygen-rich mixture.
$\mathbf{Q_V}$	= vent flow of the exhausted loop gas.
$\mathbf{V_{O_2}}$	= volume of oxygen consumed by the diver.
$\mathbf{F_SO_2}$	= fraction of oxygen in the inlet supply flow.
$\mathbf{F_IO_2}$	= fraction of oxygen inspired by the diver.
$\mathbf{V_S}$	= total volume of the oxygen-rich supply
$\mathbf{D_S}$	= duration of the oxygen-rich supply
l/min	= litres per minute

(**NOTE:** Values of $\mathbf{Q_S}$, $\mathbf{Q_V}$, $\mathbf{V_{O_2}}$ and $\mathbf{V_S}$ are calculated in one-atmosphere equivalent volumes.)

[67] As RMV linked systems only inject gas on demand, then work rate rather than flow rate defines the amount of Oxygen in the loop. Constant flow systems rely on both work and flow rate. Hence, the mathematics of constant flow systems will be detailed as above.

In a 'steady state' system, the input of gas into the loop of a semi-closed circuit rebreather, $\mathbf{Q_S}$, is divided between the volume of oxygen consumed by the diver ($\mathbf{VO_2}$) and the volume of gas vented from the loop ($\mathbf{Q_V}$), such that $\mathbf{QS = QV + VO_2}$ or, conversely:

$$\mathbf{QV = QS - VO_2}$$

The volume of oxygen in $\mathbf{Q_S}$ and $\mathbf{Q_V}$ is a product of the flow rate of the total mixture multiplied by the fraction of oxygen in the mixture.

Hence:

Inlet oxygen volume = $\mathbf{QS \times FSO_2}$

Vent oxygen volume = $\mathbf{QV \times FIO_2}$

NOTE: Depending on where in the breathing loop the gas venting takes place, it is very likely that the fraction of oxygen in the vented gas will be somewhat less than the inspired oxygen fraction, $\mathbf{F_IO_2}$. However, for the sake of modelling steady-state semi-close circuit rebreather gas dynamics, this calculation of vented oxygen volume will suffice.

In a semi-closed circuit rebreather, all the gas in the inlet flow goes out through the vent except for the oxygen consumed by the diver ($\mathbf{VO_2}$), as represented by the following equation:

$$(QS \times FSO_2) = (QV \times FIO_2) + VO_2$$

Because we are trying to find the inspired fraction of oxygen ($\mathbf{F_IO_2}$) and we can set the supply flow $\mathbf{Q_S}$ but do not know the vent flow $\mathbf{Q_V}$, we can substitute $\mathbf{(Q_S - VO_2)}$ for $\mathbf{Q_V}$ (from the previous equation), and rearrange to read:

EQUATION 1:

$$FIO_2 = \frac{(QS \times FSO_2) - VO_2}{(QS - VO_2)}$$

This is known as the steady state *semi-closed equation.*

Example:

The supply mixture for a semi-closed circuit rebreather is EAN-36 ($\mathbf{F_SO_2}$ = 0.36), and the flow rate, $\mathbf{Q_S}$, is set to 30 litres/min. A diver, experiencing a moderate workload, metabolises oxygen at a rate of 1.0 litre/min. What is the actual inspired fraction of oxygen?

$$\mathbf{F_IO_2 = \frac{(30 \times 0.36) - 1}{(30 - 1)} = 0.338 \text{ or } 33.8\%}$$

Because oxygen metabolic rates depend on diver workloads, the $\mathbf{VO_2}$ can vary considerably from a low of about 0.3 litres/min for a resting diver, to as much as 3.0 litres/min or more for a diver undergoing extreme exertion. Thus, with the same EAN-36 supply mixture flowing at the same 30 litres/min rate in the example above, the $\mathbf{F_IO_2}$ can range from as high as 0.35 to as low as 0.29, depending on how much the diver is exerting.

One way to elevate the $\mathbf{F_IO_2}$ to levels more closely approximating the percentage of oxygen in the supply mixture is to increase the input gas flow rate ($\mathbf{Q_S}$). For example, by doubling $\mathbf{Q_S}$ to 60 litres/min (maintaining EAN-36 as the supply mixture and 1.0 litres/min as the rate of metabolic oxygen consumption) equation 1 yields an $\mathbf{F_IO_2}$ of 0.35 (or 35%). Unfortunately, however, the increase in $\mathbf{Q_S}$ results in a corresponding increase in $\mathbf{Q_V}$, and consequently a *decrease* in the duration of the gas supply ($\mathbf{D_S}$):

EQUATION 2:

$$D_S = \frac{V_S}{Q_S}$$

With a given oxygen rich supply cylinder, if Q_S is doubled, D_S is halved. It is important to note, however, that gas supply duration is independent of depth. Therefore, **semi-closed circuit rebreathers become more efficient relative to open-circuit as dive depths increase.**

> **With semi-closed circuit rebreathers, it is also important to note that there is a minimum value of Q_S that is needed to avoid hypoxia.**

To allow safe direct ascent to the surface at any time during the dive, the minimum acceptable F_IO_2 is 0.20 (20% oxygen). Thus, the minimum value of Q_S should be calculated based on an F_IO_2 of 0.20 and the maximum value of V_{O_2} for the maximum workload possible during the dive.

NOTE: All prospective semi-closed circuit rebreather divers should become familiar with their own oxygen metabolism rates under a variety of workload conditions.

Substituting these values into Equation 1, we get the following:

$$0.20 = \frac{(Q_S \times F_SO_2) - \text{Maximum } V_{O_2}}{(Q_S - \text{Maximum } V_{O_2})}$$

With a gas supply mixture containing an oxygen fraction of F_SO_2, the minimum safe flow rate (Q_S) can be calculated by rearranging the above equation to read:

EQUATION 3:

$$Q_S = \frac{V_{O_2 max} \times (0.20 - 1)}{0.20 - F_SO_2}$$

Example:
A diver plans a dive to a maximum depth of 40 metres with a maximum PO_2 of 1.4 bar and the expected metabolic oxygen consumption rate is 1.0 litres/min. The oxygen-rich supply is contained in a 6 litre cylinder filled to 200 bar. The maximum metabolic oxygen consumption rate for this diver under heavy workloads is 2.4 litres/min.

a) What is the minimum safe flow rate for the oxygen-rich supply gas and what would be the inspired oxygen fraction at that flow rate?

To achieve a maximum PO_2 of 1.4 bar at a depth of 40 metres, a supply gas mixture of EAN-28 is used (calculated using Dalton's Law). With an assumed maximum metabolic oxygen consumption rate of 2.4 litres/min, we calculate the minimum safe supply gas flow rate using Equation 3:

$$Q_S = \frac{2.4 \times (0.20 - 1)}{0.20 - 0.28} = 24 \text{ l/min}$$

b) What equivalent air depth (EAD) should be used for decompression calculation?

To calculate the EAD, we need to calculate the F_IO_2. Using Equation 1, with Q_S set to 24 litres/min and V_{O_2} set to 1.0 litres/min, the inspired F_IO_2 is calculated as:

$$F_IO_2 = \frac{(24 \times 0.28) - 1}{(24 - 1)} = 0.25 \text{ or } 25\%$$

As noted earlier, the EAD of EAN-25 at a depth of 40 metres can be calculated as:

$$\frac{(1 - 0.25)}{0.79} \times 40 = 38 \text{ metres}$$

or decompression calculations, an air table of 39 metres would be used.

NOTE: Even though the F_IO_2 is less than 0.28, and thus the inspired PO_2 at a depth of 39 metres is less than 1.4 bar, the maximum PO_2 exposure (oxygen toxicity) for semi-closed circuit rebreather dives should be calculated based on F_SO_2, not F_IO_2. This is because at low metabolic rates the F_IO_2 will approach the F_SO_2, and also because many semi-closed circuit rebreathers utilise the oxygen rich mixture as an emergency open-circuit bailout supply.

a) How long will the oxygen rich gas supply last?

Multiplying the capacity of the EAN-28 supply cylinder (6 litres) by the pressure (200 bar) yields a total supply volume (V_S) of 1,200 litres. Using a minimum Q_S value of 24 litres/min, we can use Equation 2 to calculate the duration of the supply gas:

$$D_S = \frac{1{,}200}{24} = 50 \text{ min}$$

Suppose the diver in the previous example wished to maintain a higher F_IO_2 of 30% at the same work rate.

d) What should the flow rate (Q_S) be?

This can be found using Equation 3, substituting 0.20 for 0.30, and substituting the expected V_{O_2} for the maximum V_{O_2}:

$$Q_S = \frac{1.0 \times (0.30 - 1)}{0.30 - 0.32} = 35 \text{ l/min}$$

e) What is the duration of the EAN-32 supply at this new flow rate?

Using Equation 2:

$$D_S = \frac{1{,}200}{35} = 34 \text{ min}$$

Divers using semi-closed circuit rebreathers should always remember the following:

- flow rate settings are critical for gas management.
- the minimum flow rate needed to maintain an F_IO_2 of at least 0.20 (20% oxygen) should be calculated using the expected *maximum* oxygen metabolic rate (V_{O_2}).
- decompression calculations (i.e., EAD values) should be calculated using the expected *actual* oxygen metabolic rate (V_{O_2}).
- the maximum operating depth (MOD) and oxygen toxicity clock should be calculated based on the fraction of oxygen in the *supply mix* (F_SO_2).

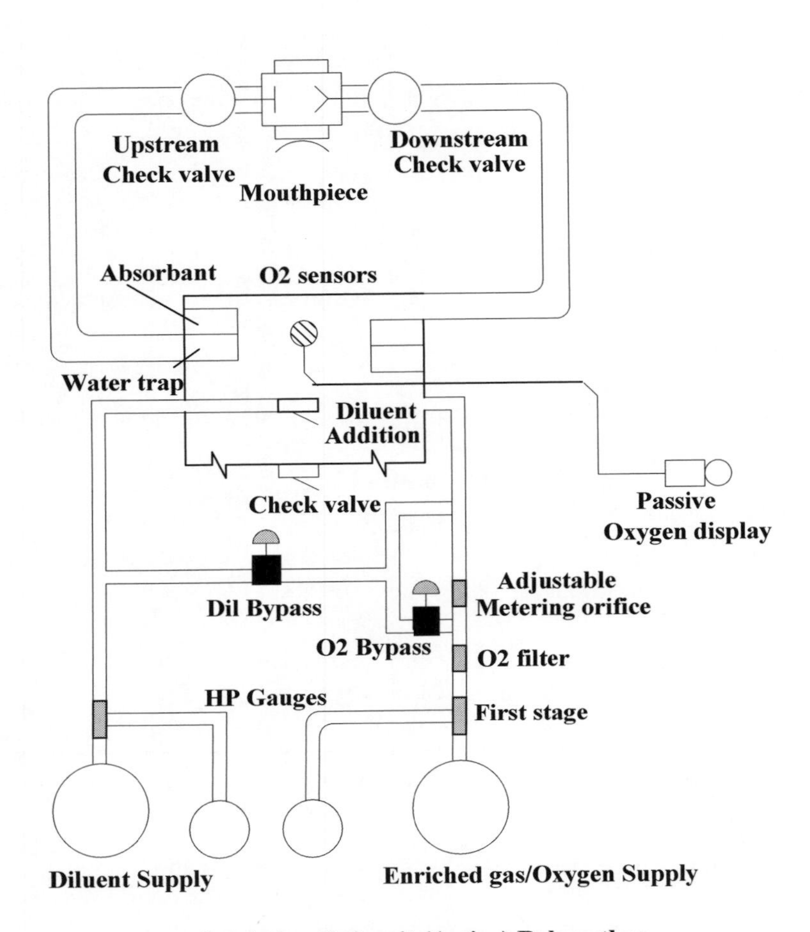

Semi-closed circuit (Active) Rebreather.

(**Note:** Diluent supply and O_2 sensors may not be included dependant on the units operational parametres.)

Passive Semi-Closed Circuit Rebreathers
Whilst the more common active semi-closed systems have been discussed in detail above, it is essential to mention is the new generation of **passive** addition systems. The concept of passive systems is not new[1]. Advantages of passive systems over their active counterparts can be defined as:

- as the addition of gas is linked to the divers RMV, then wastage is minimised. A maximum efficiency of 80% compared with open circuit SCUBA is quoted.
- the compound (interactive) depth compensated counter-lungs employed in the unit allow for a much more accurate tracking of the desired $\mathbf{F_IO_2}$. A figure within 3% of the desired $\mathbf{F_IO_2}$ is quoted.
- although not common, it is obvious that passive systems have a firm role to play in recreational diving and any diver considering buying a semi-closed unit should consider all the options.

Closed Circuit Rebreather
Closed circuit rebreathers differ from semi-closed circuit rebreathers in two ways. 1). gas is not periodically vented from the breathing loop (except during ascents); 2). the $\mathbf{F_IO_2}$ in the breathing loop is dynamic (changes with depth) such that a constant oxygen *partial pressure* (PO_2) is maintained instead of a constant oxygen fraction. Closed-circuit rebreathers are also characterised by having separate oxygen and diluent (e.g., air, EANx, heliox, trimix, etc.) gas supplies. The oxygen addition system is regulated by electronics connected to oxygen sensors and an electrical oxygen injection valve and/or manually instead of a constant mass-flow or passive addition system.The addition of diluent is a manual or automatic process, usually relying on the collapse of the counter-lung forcing an injection valve open (thereby automatically adding diluent as the volume of gas in the counter-lungs decreases). The electronic control systems often provide very detailed information, especially if real-time decompression calculation is included with the unit. The user has the ability to select the operating PO_2 or '**set point**'", and in some cases actually change this on the dive to enhance decompression efficiency. Because monitoring the PO_2 in the breathing loop is so critical for ensuring a safe breathing mixture, most closed-circuit rebreathers incorporate several oxygen sensors and a secondary 'passive' (used as a backup should the electronics fail) display of the measured PO_2.

Closed-circuit rebreathers are inherently more complex than semi-closed circuit rebreathers and require that more attention be paid to keeping the inspired PO_2 within safe limits. However, they also provide greater advantages over semi-closed circuit systems because they use considerably less gas (due to the lack of periodic venting) and because the maintenance of a constant PO_2 provides significant decompression advantages.

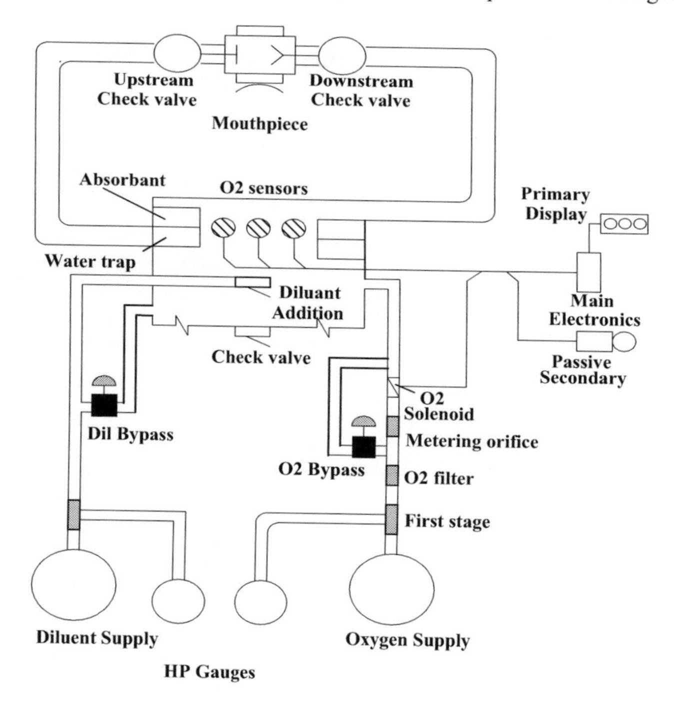

Closed-Circuit Rebreather.

[68] FENZY.

Each type of rebreather -- oxygen, closed-circuit, and semi-closed circuit -- has its own set of advantages and disadvantages. The intent of this section is not only to enlighten readers as to the operation aspects of rebreathers, but also to be able to recognise which type of rebreather suits their needs best.

Closed and Semi-Closed Circuit Rebreathers - General Concepts

Overview

Basically, all rebreathers are designed to conserve as much gas as possible and can be extremely efficient in doing so. Closed-circuit systems are most efficient. and differ from open-circuit SCUBA in two major ways. First, with the exception of ascents, there is no venting of the breathing loop of a closed-circuit system. Second, whereas open-circuit maintains a constant *percentage* (fraction) of oxygen in the breathing mixture at different depths, closed-circuit maintains a virtually constant *partial pressure* of oxygen throughout the dive. This latter discrepency has several important physiological ramifications.

Semi-closed circuit systems are somewhat intermediate to closed-circuit and open-circuit SCUBA. Although they conserve gas by recirculating the exhaled breath and removing CO_2, they periodically vent off excess gas that builds up in the loop. Also, like open-circuit SCUBA, these systems maintain a generally constant *fraction* of oxygen in the breathing mixture throughout the dive. The maximum operating depth of the gas (based on maximum PO_2) is planned in advance.

Example:

Imagine a person breathing 100% oxygen at sea-level. The ambient pressure (and thus, the pressure within the lungs) is 1 bar. The partial pressure of oxygen (PO_2) of the breathing mixture in this case is also 1 bar. If the same person was breathing air (21% oxygen, 79% nitrogen) then the PO_2 would be 0.21 bar, and the partial pressure of nitrogen (PN_2) would be 0.79 bar.

(**NOTE:** Although one bar is not precisely equal to one ata, they may be considered equivalent for discussions of diving physiology.)

If a diver breathed 100% oxygen at a depth of 30 metres, where the ambient pressure is 4 bar, then the PO_2 would be 4 bar (highly toxic). If the person breathed air at the same depth, the PO_2 would be 0.84 bar (0.21 x 4), and the PN_2 would be 3.16 bar (0.79 x 4).

Closed-Circuit Rebreathers and Partial Pressure

The need to fully understand the physics of gas partial pressures is of vital importance to all rebreather divers (even more so than for open-circuit SCUBA divers). In a closed-circuit rebreather, the electronic control system maintains the partial pressure of oxygen at a constant value, which is commonly known as the 'set point'. When the oxygen sensors detect that the PO_2 within the breathing loop drops below the set point, the electronic control system triggers a solenoid valve that injects additional oxygen into the loop. Hence, the PO_2 of the breathing mixture is kept constant throughout all portions of the dive. The remainder of the gas volume in the loop is taken up by diluent, which may consist of one or more inert gases.

Example:

Imagine a diver using a closed-circuit rebreather at a depth of 30 metres, where the ambient pressure is 4 bar. If the oxygen set point is maintained at 1.4 bar by the system, then the partial pressure of the Inert gas diluent is therefore 2.6 bar.

When a diver ascends to 10 metres the ambient pressure reduces to 2 bar. Because the PO_2 in the loop is still maintained at 1.4 bar the diluent partial pressure is now only 0.6 bar.

Closed-Circuit Rebreathers and Decompression

It is partial pressure of the inert gas within the breathing system that determines the decompression obligation. Thus, in order to minimise decompression penalty, it is best to minimise the inspired diluent partial pressure, which is achieved by maintaining the PO_2 at its maximum (within oxygen toxicity limits). When using open-circuit

SCUBA, the *percentage* of oxygen is constant, which means that the PO_2 is at its maximum only during the deepest portion of the dive. During all shallow portions of the dive (including decompression stops) the PO_2 is below maximum. To increase decompression efficiency, some divers using open-circuit SCUBA switch to different breathing mixtures on ascent to keep the inspired PO_2 high. However, due to logistical constraints, such diving is generally limited to two or three different decompression breathing mixtures, so the inspired gas mixture is optimal only at two or three points in the dive profile.

Example:

Imagine a diver on open-circuit SCUBA at a depth of 30 metres using EAN-35. The ambient pressure is 4 bar, so the PO_2 is 1.4 bar and the PN_2 is 2.6 bar. In a closed-circuit rebreather using nitrogen (air) as a diluent, with an oxygen set point of 1.4 bar/ ata, the PN_2 and PO_2 are the same as the above example at the same depth.

As the diver ascends on open-circuit SCUBA to 15 metres, where the ambient pressure is 2.5 bar, the PO_2 is 0.875 bar and the PN_2 is 1.625 bar. At the same depth on a closed-circuit rebreather with an oxygen set point of 1.4 bar, the PN_2 will have fallen to 1.1 bar. Hence on a closed-circuit rebreather the PN_2 at this depth has been reduced by 0.525 bar, or approximately 32%, and the decompression efficiency is greatly increased.

Because closed-circuit rebreathers maintain a constant PO_2 (thereby minimising the overall inert gas exposure) they can dramatically reduce the decompression obligations for a dive when compared with an open-circuit SCUBA dive of the same depth and duration. Some rebreathers even have the capability to increase the PO_2 and/or changing diluent gas composition at any time during the dive, minimising decompression even further.

Because semi-closed circuit rebreathers maintain a relatively constant *fraction* of oxygen in the breathing loop, decompression schedules must be calculated the same way they are for open-circuit SCUBA. Furthermore, because of the potential variability in the $\mathbf{F_IO_2}$ inherent to semi-closed circuit rebreathers (due to variations in work rate and gas supply flow rate) decompression calculations must incorporate an extra degree of conservatism.

Bill Stone surfacing after a 24 hour dive on his prototype Cis-Lunar rebreather. No it wasn't Champagne!

Basic Respiratory Physiology

Although about 21% of the air inhaled by a person at sea level is oxygen, not all of this oxygen passes through the alveolar membranes into the blood. In fact, only a relatively small amount of the inhaled oxygen is utilised (the actual proportion used depends on a variety of factors, but is generally less than about one third to one quarter of the amount inhaled). The majority of inhaled oxygen is exhaled during normal breathing. About 80-82% of oxygen absorbed by the blood during respiration is converted by metabolic processes into carbon dioxide. This carbon dioxide is eliminated from the body during each exhaled breath.

During most conditions, the urge to breathe is almost entirely triggered by the need to rid the body of carbon dioxide, and only to a much lesser extent by a need for more oxygen. Consequently, *respiratory rate* (number of breaths per minute) is determined largely the rate at which carbon dioxide is produced during metabolism and not by the concentration of oxygen in inspired gas. An increase in the concentration of inspired oxygen does not significantly reduce the respiratory rate at a given level of exertion.

Respiratory rate, in conjunction with the volume of gas ventilated with each breath, determines the *respiratory minute volume* (RMV). The RMV, therefore, is a measure of the total volume of gas ventilated during a single minute. The length of time that a particular quantity of breathing gas will sustain a diver using open-circuit SCUBA is determined by the RMV (which, for a given person, is determined by the rate of carbon dioxide production) and the depth (or, more specifically, the ambient pressure). The concentration of oxygen in breathing mixture has virtually no effect on the RMV. Because of this, open-circuit SCUBA is inherently inefficient as a means for supplying oxygen to a diver, because most of the oxygen is lost in the form of exhaled bubbles. Because more gas molecules are exhaled with each breath at greater depths (but RMV remains relatively constant), open-circuit SCUBA becomes even less efficient as the depth increases.

Rebreathers greatly enhance the efficiency of oxygen supply utilisation, because exhaled oxygen is recirculated, rather than lost in exhaled bubbles. In the case of closed-circuit systems, almost all of the oxygen carried by the diver is made available for metabolic needs (the only wasted oxygen is the amount vented during ascents, mask clearings, or other leakage). Furthermore, almost none of the inert gas in a rebreather is wasted, because the same inert gas molecules continue to flow around the breathing loop throughout the dive. Semi-closed circuit rebreathers are not as efficient for gas utilisation as closed-circuit systems; however, they are considerably more efficient than open-circuit SCUBA. In all Closed and most semi-closed circuit rebreathers, the volume of gas consumed is essentially independent of depth. Consequently, the greater the depth, the more efficient rebreathers are when compared to open-circuit SCUBA. Because of these factors, rebreathers generally require much smaller gas supplies, or, conversely, allow much longer durations with the same gas supplies. It should also be noted that certainly closed-circuit rebreather durations are dependant on *metabolic rates*, not *breathing rates*. Rapid breathing may not reduce the duration of a rebreather gas supply; conversely, skip-breathing or excessively slow breathing may not prolong it. Our breathing rate is nature's way of providing an estimation of metabolic rate. This is why passive semi-closed systems have RMV linked addition. However, it is not a finite link. Hence, the above explanation.

Gas Toxicity

Although covered in other chapters it is worth reviewing them again specifically. Rebreathers allow for greatly increased gas utilisation efficiency and (in the case of closed-circuit systems) increased decompression efficiency. There are a number of problems which may become apparent when equipment malfunctions occur or when divers engage in bad diving practices. In general, most of these problems involve inadequate maintenance of a life-sustaining gas mixture in the breathing loop.

In many cases, specific problems are comparatively minor for open-circuit SCUBA divers but may be fatal to rebreather divers. Fortunately, most rebreather designs incorporate a variety of safeguards to reduce the likelihood of such problems occurring. However, no amount of clever engineering or component redundancy can completely ensure that the gas mixture in the breathing loop will always remain sufficient to sustain life. Therefore, it is of utmost importance that all rebreather divers fully understand these problems and repeatedly practise appropriate emergency procedures to be able to cope with them.

Where as the breathing gas composition on open-circuit SCUBA dives is *constant* and predictable, the gas composition in a rebreather loop is *dynamic*, changing throughout the dive.

Asphyxia

If a diver breathes in and out of a closed bag, CO_2 levels will rise and oxygen levels will be depleted (due to metabolism). These conditions lead to an increasing shortness of breath, known as *dyspnoea*. If this process continues, the end result will be unconsciousness and ultimately death. The breathing difficulties are primarily caused by the increased CO_2 levels and death results from insufficient oxygen. Thus, although the increasing CO_2 level in a 'closed bag' environment is what induces discomfort and affects breathing patterns, it is the depletion of oxygen that is of greatest concern.

Hypoxia

Whereas the problems associated with *hyperoxia* may be familiar to experienced open-circuit SCUBA divers, *hypoxia* is not as frequently a concern. Hypoxia is defined as insufficient concentrations of oxygen at the cellular level, such that the cells cannot function normally. The brain cells are the most susceptible to hypoxia, unconsciousness and death being the end result. Hypoxia is a major concern when using all rebreathers, and perhaps the single *greatest* concern for closed-circuit systems.

Hypoxia is especially hazardous not only because of potentially fatal consequences, but also because, like oxygen toxicity, there is seldom any warning. In a rebreather with a malfunctioning oxygen injection system, the onset of hypoxia may be very gradual. An extremely observant diver may notice subtle symptoms such as uncoordination, euphoria, and the inability to think clearly and/or perform simple tasks prior to unconsciousness. Such symptoms may be evident if the inspired PO_2 drops to 0.15 bar or less and unconsciousness invariably results if the PO_2 falls below about 0.10 bar. If a diver suffering from hypoxia is not resuscitated quickly by the administration of an oxygen mixture, the ensuing loss of brain function will cause failure of breathing control. If air or enriched air is administered prior to breathing failure, then a full recovery will ensue. Because of the low margin for error, hypoxia symptoms can *very easily* pass unnoticed and because an increased sense of euphoria and reduced mental capacities may impair a diver's ability to take corrective action, it is extremely important that rebreather divers ensure that the gas mixture in the breathing loop remains well above hypoxic levels. Although semi-closed circuit rebreathers are generally considered less likely to cause hypoxia than closed-circuit systems, hypoxia is a major concern in *any* recirculating breathing loop.

Hypoxia is a major concern for rebreather divers because it can lead to unconsciousness and death without warning.

Hyperoxia

Hyperoxia is defined as excess concentrations of oxygen at the cellular level. Most humans can normally withstand oxygen partial pressures of up to 0.35 bar for indefinite (extremely long) periods. If inspired-oxygen partial pressures exceed 0.5 bar for extended periods of time, the onset of oxygen toxicity will result in either or both of its' recognised forms. Above a PO_2 of about 1.0 bar and at comparatively short exposure times, the onset of symptoms becomes less predictable and more severe. Although a variety of symptoms have been reported, extreme hyperoxia may induce severe convulsions. Although oxygen-induced convulsions in and of themselves will not kill, a convulsing diver who is not wearing a full-face mask will, in all probability, drown. Convulsions are not reliably preceded by warning symptoms and are therefore particularly dangerous. Factors that may affect the probability of an oxygen-induced convulsion are many and varied, but the most important factors include actual PO_2, duration of exposure, level of exertion and cumulative oxygen exposure.

Although measurements of cumulative oxygen exposure should be familiar to all qualified enriched-air nitrox divers, they will be discussed specifically with respect to rebreather applications. Tables in Appendix A show oxygen exposure limits for a single dive upon which the percentage CNS calculations are based. Time limits define the maximum duration of a single exposure to a given partial pressure of oxygen, above which central nervous system (CNS) oxygen toxicity symptoms may occur. Appendix A shows OTU or pulmonary/whole body oxygen values over single or multi-day exposures. These values are based on the REPetitive EXposure system or REPEX method developed by Dr. Bill Hamilton.

Divers using open-circuit SCUBA or semi-closed circuit rebreathers experience maximum inspired PO_2 values only during the deepest portion of the dive. The inspired PO_2 in a closed-circuit rebreather remains constant throughout the entire dive, regardless of depth. If the oxygen set point is set relatively high so as to minimise decompression requirements, the %CNS exposure often becomes the limiting factor of closed-circuit rebreather dive duration. On multi-day diving missions, OTU limits may be the limiting factor. Decompression advantages of high PO_2 set points must be balanced against cumulative oxygen exposures.

With closed-circuit rebreathers, where the inspired PO_2 remains relatively high throughout the entire dive, CNS oxygen exposure may be the limiting factor of dive duration.

When using a closed-circuit rebreather, the actual PO_2 in the loop may temporarily deviate from the oxygen set point under certain circumstances. Deviations may occur during normal operation whilst the system attempts to compensate for PO_2 fluctuations, or as a result of malfunctions in the oxygen addition system. Sudden depth changes may have profound effects on instantaneous inspired PO_2. As the ambient pressure rises during the descent, the partial pressures of the gases in the breathing loop correspondingly increase. If the oxygen set point is relatively high (e.g., 1.6 bar), the momentary rise in PO_2 could be dangerous. Most rebreathers will automatically compensate for depth changes by adding an appropriate amount of diluent gas to the loop, thereby preventing the PO_2 from grossly exceeding safe levels. Nevertheless, momentary PO_2 'spikes' may occur, therefore the breathing loop of a closed-circuit rebreather must be carefully monitored. During ascents the reverse problem occurs. A drop in ambient pressure results in a reduction of the loop gas partial pressures. If such drops occur faster than the oxygen addition system can compensate for, hypoxia may result. This is a potential concern for both closed and semi-closed circuit rebreathers.

For the above reasons, **the oxygen set point on a closed-circuit rebreather should not exceed a maximum PO_2 of 1.4 bar**, and **the oxygen fraction of the supply gas for a semi-closed circuit rebreather should not be less than 25% at normal workloads for the bottom phase of the dive**. Whenever possible, lower set points on closed-circuit systems and more oxygen rich gas supply mixtures on semi-closed circuit systems should be used. Higher oxygen set points may be useful during decompression on certain dives. This must, however, be balanced against dive duration and workload.

Hypercapnia
Hypercapnia (an excess of carbon dioxide at cellular level) can become a serious problem in any form of closed circuit breathing system. Because the exhaled gas in a rebreather is recirculated through the breathing loop, excess CO_2 generated by metabolism must be removed. This is achieved by passing the loop gas over a chemical agent, or 'absorbent' that binds to CO_2 molecules. The absorbent, often referred to as the CO_2 'scrubber', is usually contained within some sort of canister or chamber.

Over time, as the CO_2 binding sites on the chemical absorbent become saturated, the absorbent loses its ability to remove CO_2 from breathing gas. The length of time a CO_2 scrubber lasts depends primarily on the rate of CO_2 production from metabolism, the ambient temperature, and the amount and type of absorbent used. If the absorbent starts to reduce in efficiency, if improper packing of the absorbent material leads to *channelling* of breathing gas, or if the absorbent material gets wet, the resulting increase in CO_2 levels may lead to hypercapnia.

Increased levels of CO_2 are primarily responsible for breathing stimulus. Ambient air has approximately 0.033 % (0.00033 bar) CO_2, which is sufficient to provide the stimulus. A PCO_2 increase to as little as 0.02 bar will show a marked rise in breathing rate (dyspnoea). If the PCO_2 exceeds 0.1 bar, symptoms of confusion and drowsiness become apparent. When the PCO_2 exceeds 0.15 bar, symptoms may include difficulty in breathing, rigidity and muscle spasms. Prolonged exposures to increased levels of CO_2 can ultimately lead to unconsciousness. Severe symptoms of hypercapnia (including lost consciousness) can usually be quickly reversed with flushing of fresh gas into the breathing loop. Other symptoms of hypercapnia, such as headaches, nausea and sore chest muscles, generally take longer to resolve. Skip breathing, resistance in breathing equipment and excessive work rates will compound any problems.

Hyperventilation
Hyperventilation is not a form of gas poisoning, but rather a term often used to describe overly-rapid breathing or excessive lung ventilation. Hyperventilation can lead to problems if it results in rapid breathing without sufficient ventilation of the lungs (i.e., short, shallow breathing). A somewhat less common problem is hypocapnia, an excessive reduction in CO_2 levels (due to over ventilation), which may induce symptoms similar to hypoxia.

Oxygen Metabolism
In a pure oxygen rebreather, the length of time a diver may stay underwater (ignoring oxygen toxicity) is dependant only on the rate of oxygen consumption as there is no inert gas in the loop to lead to any decompression obligation. In mixed-gas rebreathers, the draining of the diluent cylinder during multi-level dive profiles and the ensuing inert gas decompression penalty will usually limit the time submerged far more than the oxygen supply. However, with practice and on dives with few depth fluctuations, oxygen metabolism may be the factor limiting rebreather duration. Oxygen consumption rates at various levels of work are shown below.

Zero exertion	**0.3 litres/min**
Rest	**0.5 litres/min**
Moderate work	**0.9 litres/min**
Heavy work	**2.0 litres/min**
Extreme work	**3.0 litres/min**

Oxygen Metabolism Rates.

Example:

Imagine a diver is using a closed-circuit rebreather configured with a 2 litre oxygen cylinder pressurised to 200 bar.

a) How long will the oxygen supply last at a moderate work rate?

The total volume of oxygen equals 400 litres. Ignoring oxygen lost during ascent and from mask clearings or other leakage, the supply will sustain the diver for:

$$\frac{400}{0.9} = 444 \text{ minutes or } 7.4 \text{ hours}$$

(**NOTE:** Because oxygen metabolism depends only on exertion levels, the duration is independent of depth.)

b) How long would the same cylinder last if breathed on open-circuit SCUBA at a depth of 10 metres, assuming a surface consumption rate of 20 litres/min?

Each breath at 10 metres contains twice the amount of gas as a breath on the surface and a cylinder will last half as long:

$$\frac{400}{20} \times 0.5 = 10 \text{ minutes}$$

c) What volume of oxygen would be required to sustain a diver at 10 metres, with a surface consumption rate of 20 litres/min, for 7.4 hours?

$$20 \text{ l/min} \times 7.4 \text{ hr} \times 60 \text{ min/hr} \times 2 = 17{,}760 \text{ litres}$$

Rebreather Functionality and Design

General Rebreather Design

All rebreathers consist of a breathing loop, which includes a mouthpiece, a counter-lung (a collapsible bag that expands as a diver's lungs compress during exhalation, and collapses as the lungs expand on inhalation) a CO_2 absorbent housing (sometimes referred to as the 'stack' or 'canister') and some method of adding both oxygen and inert gases, either combined or individually. Most closed-circuit rebreathers also incorporate some sort of electronic control system.

When discussing the flow of gas through a rebreather loop, the terms 'upstream' and 'downstream' are used to refer to the relative position of certain items in the breathing loop. Exhaled gas travels through the breathing hose on the downstream side of the mouthpiece, usually into a counter-lung. From there, the gas usually flows through some sort of water catchment system, then through the CO_2 absorbent in the canister and then back to the upstream side of the mouthpiece. Some systems include a second counter-lung upstream of the mouthpiece.

The design of the mouthpiece, counter-lung(s), canister, and breathing hoses greatly affects the breathing characteristics of the rebreather. The '***work of breathing***' required to circulate gas through the breathing loop is critical to the well-being of the diver, and affects not only the amount of CO_2 generated but also the ability for the diver to adequately ventilate during stressful situations or heavy workloads. A level of breathing resistance that is acceptable for short periods of time may cause dyspnoea or more serious conditions over extended durations. Because RMV (Respiratory Minute Volume) is approximately 25 to 30 times the rate of oxygen consumed, a diver metabolising 1 litres/min of oxygen will cycle 25 to 30 litres of gas through the breathing loop. To minimise the amount of energy expended by the diver in cycling so much gas through the breathing loop, the resistance to gas flow through the loop must also be minimised. If breathing resistance is too high, a diver's RMV may fall below what is necessary to remove metabolised CO_2 from the circulatory system, and hypercapnia may result. An increased breathing resistance also produces an increased *work of breathing* and higher CO_2 levels. This problem is compounded with increasing depth because breathing resistance increase as gas density increases.

The construction and functionality of various components are critical factors determining overall breathing resistance. These components differ considerably with each type and manufacturer of rebreather.

Mouthpiece
A breathing loop starts with the mouthpiece, which is reminiscent of the old twin hose regulators. There is a mouth bite and a one-way check valve on either side of the mouthpiece block so that gas flow is unidirectional. This allows the passage of inhaled and exhaled gas via separate paths. Unlike twin hose open-circuit regulators, rebreather mouthpieces usually incorporate some type of shut-off valve to the outside world. This valve is necessary to prevent the accidental ingress of water into the loop when underwater it is also to prevent collapse of the counter-lung when the diver is partially submerged with the mouthpiece above water (in some systems, this could result in purging the loop with diluent. This might in turn lead to hypoxia if the diluent contains insufficient oxygen for breathing at the surface). More sophisticated rebreather designs also incorporate an integral open-circuit bailout regulator into the rebreather mouthpiece.

Counter-lung
The counter-lung, or 'breathing bag', can take many forms in a rebreather. It is made of a flexible material which expands and contracts as the diver breathes. Different rebreather designs mount the counter-lung in different positions. Oxygen rebreathers tend to have chest-mounted counter-lungs. The USN MK15 has a single back-mounted counter-lung, and the 'Buddy Inspiration' unit employs double counter-lungs, one upstream from the mouthpiece and one downstream. The positioning of the counter-lung(s) relative to the diver's lungs can be critical to the breathing characteristics of the unit, due primarily to hydrostatic effects.

There is a theoretical point within the lungs known as the 'centroid'". At this point, the net pressure due to the gas in the lungs is assumed to be zero. The centroid is approximately 19 cm below and 7 cm behind the sternal notch in an upright position in the average person[69]. Breathing is easiest when gas pressures are balanced to this pressure point. When a rebreather diver is in the normal horizontal swimming position, a chest-mounted counter-lung will be exposed to slightly greater hydrostatic pressure than a back-mounted counter-lung. Consequently, a chest-mounted counter-lung design requires less effort on inhale and more effort on exhale than a back-mounted counter-lung design. The reverse is true for a back-mounted counter-lung.

As mentioned earlier, some rebreather designs incorporate twin or 'split' counter-lungs in the rebreather loop, one upstream of the mouthpiece and one downstream. The primary function of dual counter-lungs is to minimise the amount of diver effort required to push the gas past the CO_2 absorbent. When a diver inhales, the upstream counter-lung collapses. This establishes a hydrostatic pressure gradient between the two counter-lungs, causing gas to move from the downstream counter-lung, through the CO_2 absorbent into the upstream counter-lung. When a diver exhales, the downstream counter-lung inflates, maintaining the same hydrostatic pressure gradient and flow of gas through the CO_2 absorbent. By the time a diver is ready to inhale the next breath, the upstream counter lung is already full of gas that has been cleaned of CO_2.

[69] Taylor and Morrisson, 1989.

Carbon Dioxide Absorbent and Canister

As mentioned above, the design of a CO_2 absorbent canister greatly affects gas flow and breathing resistance. Canister designs are with two primary categories:

1. **Axial**, where the gas flow is through a 'block' of absorbent in a linear direction.
2. **Radial**, where gas enters the centre of a 'donought' cross section and radiates outward through the absorbent material.

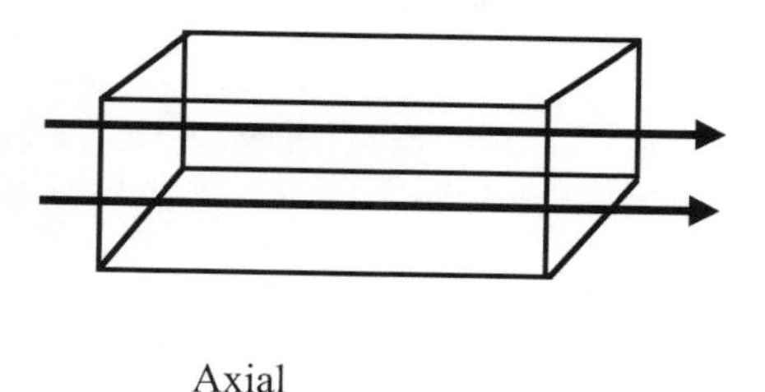

Axial

Radial

Primary concerns of any canister design are:

1. to ensure gas is exposed to enough surface area of the absorbent to remove CO_2.
2. to ensure gas flow rates across the absorbent allow sufficient exposure time (often referred to as 'dwell time') for the chemical process of binding CO_2 to take place.
3. to allow simple and correct packing of the absorbent such that gas 'channelling' does not occur.
4. to prevent excess moisture from reaching the absorbent material.

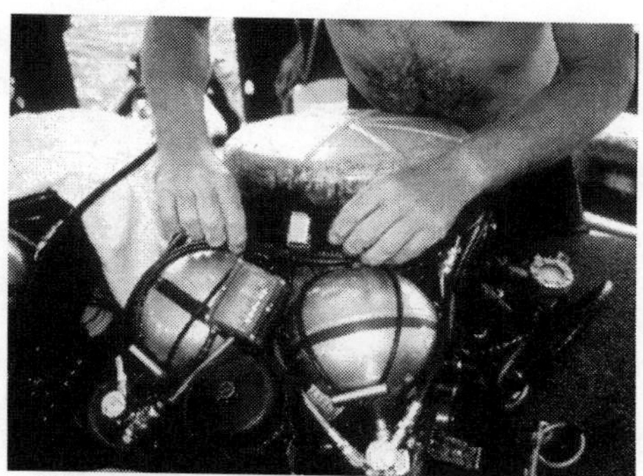

Changing a Mk15.5 absorbent cannister

The quantity and type of absorbent used directly affects the duration of the canister. Temperature, work load and excess humidity of the absorbent also have an affect on the canister duration; colder and more humid conditions can dramatically shorten the life of the absorbent. The addition of more absorbent in the gas path lengthens the life of the canister but also can increase the flow resistance. Most rebreathers use between 2 and 8 kg of absorbent material.

The process of CO_2 removal encompasses a series of exothermic chemical reactions which starts with the uptake of water and the final formation of alkali carbonates. Typical CO_2 absorbents used in rebreathers are derived from alkali metal hydroxides and include barium hydroxide, soda lime and lithium hydroxide. These three absorbents are available under various trade names.

Forms of soda lime are the most commonly used scrubbing agent in rebreathers, as well as in deep sea submersibles. soda lime is relatively inexpensive and fairly easy to work with and handle. Lithium hydroxide is the most efficient absorbent and can provide about twice the CO_2 absorbing capacity as an equivalent quantity of soda lime. However, lithium hydroxide is more expensive than other types of absorbent materials and it reacts violently with water, so must be handled carefully, even in air.

In addition to absorbent type, particle-size is also an important consideration. Large particles cause less breathing resistance (because gaps between particles are relatively large), but they are less efficient due to lower surface area to volume ratio (the chemical at the centre of the particle is often not used even though the outside material may have been exhausted). Some absorbents have colour indicators which change from white to purple (or pink) as the absorbent is used up. These indicators are not always reliable, however and some absorbent manufacturers have stopped incorporating them.

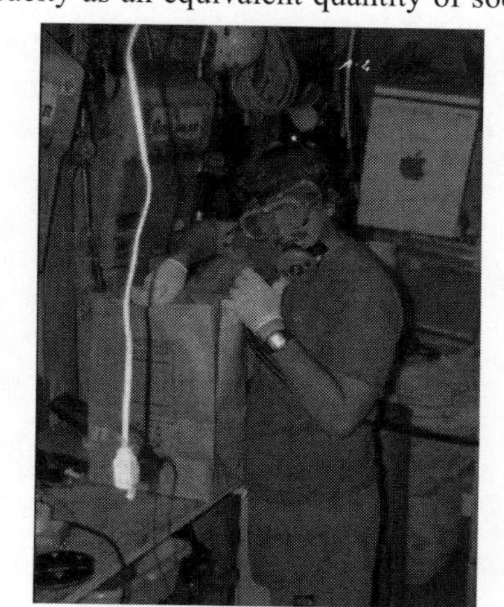

Rich Pyle taking lithium hydroxide seriously

Absorbent materials do not mix well with water. Obviously, this poses a significant problem for rebreathers designed to be used underwater. Indeed, problems associated with flooding the absorbent canister have historically been among the most significant obstacles for safe and reliable rebreather operation. Water can enter the breathing loop not only through accidental flooding in the mouthpiece or damaged loop, but also in the form of condensation. In most cases, surrounding water is considerably cooler than gas leaving lungs. When the warm, moist exhaled gas passes over the cool breathing hoses and counter-lungs, water condenses on the inner walls of the loop (just as water condenses on the outside of a cold bottle of beer or soft drink). Over the course of long dives, an alarming amount of condensed water can accumulate inside the breathing loop. Apart from the fact that water can clog the absorbent (thereby increasing breathing resistance), the potential for the notorious 'caustic cocktail' is still present with all absorbent types. A derivative of soda lime called 'sofnolime'" is popular among current users due to its resistance to water. Most rebreather designs incorporate some form of safeguard to prevent water in the breathing loop from reaching the absorbent material. Whilst a small amount of water build up as a result of saliva or condensation may on occasion generate an unpleasant taste in the mouth, a salt water flood will almost instantly produce a very obnoxious odour and taste and probably disintegrate any water absorbent sponges with which it comes into contact. Over long dives in saltwater even poor mouthpiece control can produce this effect.

Cold is also an enemy of absorbent efficiency. Certain rebreather designs (mainly commercial and military) may employ canister heating systems to improve absorbent life. Reductions in life as great as 75% have been noted in some military applications with water temperatures down to 4 degrees centigrade. Lithium hydroxide (LiOH) is better than most other kinds of CO_2 absorbent materials for maintaining effectiveness during dives in cold water due to its in-built exothermic (heat producing) reaction.

Gas Injection Systems

The gas injection system of pure oxygen and semi-closed circuit rebreathers is an entirely mechanical process, not requiring electronics. Pure oxygen rebreathers use either a constant-mass flow of oxygen into the loop, or a volume-compensating mechanism that replenishes oxygen as the volume of the counter-lung decreases (as oxygen is metabolised and carbon dioxide is bound to the absorbent material the gas volume drops). Most semi-closed circuit systems use a constant-mass flow valve calibrated to replenish the oxygen consumed during metabolism. In dual-gas semi-closed circuit units (both oxygen and diluent supplies) there is normally a manual oxygen injection valve as well.

The majority of closed-circuit systems have an electronic control module which regulates the amount of oxygen injected. These systems typically include a series of galvanic oxygen sensors within the breathing loop. The sensors are connected to a computer which activates an electrical oxygen injection valve whenever the PO_2 drops below a pre-defined level (i.e., the **set point**). Diluent is added mechanically by means of an automatic volume-compensating addition valve in response to a decreasing counter-lung volume (or manually). Some semi-closed circuit systems also employ one or more oxygen sensors to give an indication of the oxygen level, but not to control gas injection.

Closed-circuit systems also have manual gas injection valves accessible by the diver in case the computer malfunctions. Most electronic closed-circuit rebreathers also have a secondary, totally 'passive' oxygen monitoring system which is not connected to the main computer or battery system in any way. In the event of a computer failure, this secondary system will continue to provide information on the PO_2 within the breathing loop. In the case of the MK15 range of units the secondary display is actually powered by the cells themselves requiring no extra battery as they can provide sufficient current to drive a small metre. With this information, a diver can safely complete a dive using manual gas addition valves.

Electrical Oxygen Sensors

Of all the components of a closed-circuit rebreather, perhaps the most critical are the oxygen sensors. With the exception of a few, very expensive kinds of electronic oxygen sensing devices[70], almost all oxygen sensors used for rebreathers are galvanic fuel cells. The basic elements of a sensor consist of a lead anode, a gold plated cathode with a solution of potassium hydroxide as an electrolyte. The cathode is a convex metal disc plated with a noble metal e.g. gold, silver etc. with numerous perforations. It is designed to facilitate continuous wetting of the upper surface and contains a small amount of electrolyte between the membrane and the cathode. When oxygen is diffused into the sensor the lead is oxidised into lead oxide, this reaction produces a small current between anode and cathode. Galvanic oxygen sensors are, in effect, batteries that generate an electrical current that is proportional to the abundance of oxygen molecules (i.e., oxygen partial pressure) exposed to the sensor. An increase in the exposed PO_2 results in a proportional increase in the current generated by the sensor. This is measured by a rebreather computer and converted to a PO_2 value.

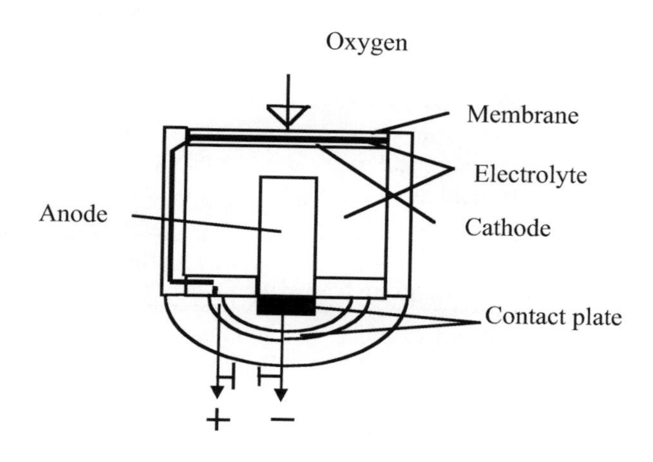

Oxygen Cell Cross-Section

For reasons that should be obvious, careful and accurate monitoring of the PO_2 within the breathing loop of a closed-circuit rebreather is fundamental to the well-being of the diver. Not only is this information vitally important to ensure PO_2 levels do not drift into hypoxic or hyperoxic levels, it is also critical for determining decompression obligation. Decompression requirements depend on the partial pressure of inert gas in the breathing loop. Rebreather computers determine the inert gas partial pressure by subtracting the PO_2 from the total ambient pressure. Because no two oxygen sensors are exactly alike, they each need to be individually calibrated.

An incorrect calibration routine can be disastrous.

> When you have the unit calibrated as per the manufacturers instructions, flush the loop (evacuating it prior to each flush) three times with pure oxygen. Do not let exhaled gas back into the loop. On the third count, when the loop is full, momentarily open and shut the mouthpiece to pressure equalise the loop to ambient. Now (assuming 1 bar absolute) the sensors should read 1 bar + or – 0.05. If not recalibrate until they do. Most units benefit from the manual oxygen flush routine prior to doing any automatic calibration.

In addition to individual sensor differences, there are different brands, models, and types of oxygen sensors as well. Not all of them are equally suited for use in rebreathers. Of paramount importance is that the sensor is capable of being pressure-balanced (most are). This means that the front and rear of the sensing diaphragms must be pressure-equalised at all points of the dive for accurate measurement of the counter-lung PO_2, irrespective of depth. Response time is also critical, especially with multi-level profile diving. Sensors with fast response times (20-40 seconds full scale) will be better-suited for use in rebreathers.

Regardless of what kind of oxygen sensor is used it also represents a potential weak point. The current generated and thus the registered PO_2, can be affected by both temperature and humidity. Most oxygen sensors are designed to automatically compensate for temperature changes within certain tolerances and most sensor manufacturers quote an operating range from 0 to 50 degrees centigrade degrees Fahrenheit. Although generally oxygen sensors are

---

[70] Paramagnetic cells

designed to operate at in as much as 95% humidity, the humidity in a rebreather loop may exceed this. Droplets of water directly on the sensor can lead to a variety of errors in registered PO_2.

If a sensor drifts, reacts slowly or becomes 'stuck' on a dive, suspect water on its membrane and instigate flush routines as appropriate.

Like all batteries, galvanic oxygen sensors do not last forever. Over time, the sensors gradually lose their ability to generate electricity. For this reason, sensors need to be recalibrated on a regular basis to ensure PO_2 conversions are accurate.

It is wise to keep a log of the sensors milli-volt output in order to estimate change-out periods.

Eventually, the output drops enough that the sensors can no longer be recalibrated to give reliable readings, at which time they must be replaced. The effective life of an oxygen sensor is determined in part by the amount of oxygen to which it is exposed. Most sensors will last up to 2-3 years in air (21% oxygen) but the effective lifespan will be reduced if exposed to higher concentrations of oxygen. Thus, the effective life of oxygen sensors in a rebreather may be extended by flushing an oxygen-rich mixture out of the breathing loop after a dive. To further extend their life, sensors can be removed from a rebreather and placed in a container devoid of oxygen altogether (pure nitrogen, for example). However, if this technique is used, sensors must be allowed a 'recovery period' (usually about 15 minutes) before they can be used or recalibrated.

The effective life of oxygen sensors in a rebreather may be extended by flushing an oxygen-rich mixture out of the breathing loop after a dive.

Humidity also affects the lifespan of oxygen sensors. Thus, not only is it important to keep sensors dry during rebreather operation, it is also important to keep them dry between dives. This is one of the reasons why rebreathers should never be stored with the breathing loop intact and sealed.

Because even the best galvanic oxygen sensors are prone to failure, most rebreathers incorporate several sensors to provide a level of redundancy. Two oxygen sensors are not much better than one, because if they do not give the same reading, there is no way to determine which one is correct, and which one is in error. For this reason, most closed-circuit rebreathers are equipped with at least three oxygen sensors. With three sensors, there is a 'democracy' of sorts, in that 'voting logic' may be used to isolate an erroneous sensor reading. This, of course, does not work if two sensors simultaneously fail in the same direction and magnitude, but at least the probability of a false reading is greatly reduced. In most cases, if all three sensor readings indicate the same reading (within certain tolerances of error) an average of the three readings will be taken as the actual PO_2.

Oxygen sensors are the most critical component of a closed-circuit rebreather. Take care of your oxygen sensors or they will not take care of you!

If you are at all unsure about the readings your sensors are giving you on a dive, you should complete a verification. To do this turn off the oxygen solenoid or supply gas. Now flush the unit at least 3 times with diluent (confirming first it is breathable at that depth). Using Dalton's law, work out what the PO_2 of the diluent should be at that depth in the diluent. Now check which sensor(s) give this value. These sensors are the correct ones. If the oxygen controller appears to be using a bad value, then switch to manual control using the good sensor(s) only.

If you are at all unsure about the readings your sensors are giving you on a dive, you should complete a verification

Preparation and Diving

Pre-Dive Preparation

Prior to any rebreather dive, an assortment of variables must be considered. As with open-circuit SCUBA diving, it is important to ensure that all equipment components are functioning correctly. Quite often the most important part of any dive and especially a rebreather dive, is the pre-dive preparation.

Gas Choice.

The process of selecting a diluent gas or gases for a closed-circuit rebreather is not as straightforward as it might seem. Because the oxygen in these systems is supplied by a separate cylinder, some might be inclined to fill a diluent cylinder with pure inert gas (e.g., pure nitrogen, pure helium, or a binary mixture of the two). However, in case of an emergency bailout situation that requires a diver to breathe in open-circuit mode, or in case the oxygen supply is lost, the diluent may become[71] the emergency breathing supply. For this reason, it is critical that the diluent of a closed-circuit rebreather ***always contains a gas mixture that will sustain a diver when breathed directly.*** In other words, the oxygen partial pressure of the diluent gas mixture, when breathed at the target depth of the dive, should always be within safe levels. Because the oxygen in the diluent is added to the breathing loop, it is available for uptake by the diver, and is therefore not wasted.

In semi-closed circuit rebreathers, other factors must also be taken into consideration when choosing the oxygen rich gas supply. Specifically, it is important to ensure that the supply gas contains enough oxygen that the F_IO_2 remains above 20% (ref. shallow water hypoxia). In addition to being safe to breathe in shallow water, as with closed-circuit; at the maximum depth of the dive, the gas supply for a semi-closed circuit rebreather must not be hyperoxic.

The other important consideration of the diluent in either closed-circuit or semi-closed circuit rebreathers is the narcotic affects of the gas. Because rebreathers are functionally more complex than open-circuit SCUBA, it is even more important to maintain a clear head at all times during the dive. Ideally, the equivalent narcosis depth (END) should remain less than 40 metres. Whereas the END was once calculated by considering only the nitrogen component of the breathing gas, it is now generally believed that oxygen plays a role in narcosis.

(**NOTE:** There is some anecdotal evidence that oxygen can cause more severe narcosis than nitrogen under certain conditions. However, in such conditions, oxygen toxicity is generally a much greater concern.)

The formula for calculating the FN_2 required to provide an END value, considering nitrogen as the basis for narcosis, is:

$$\mathbf{FN2} = \frac{(\mathbf{END\ (metres)} + \mathbf{10}) \times \mathbf{0.79}}{\mathbf{D} + \mathbf{10}}$$

or,

$$\mathbf{FN2} = \frac{(\mathbf{END\ (feet)} + \mathbf{33}) \times \mathbf{0.79}}{\mathbf{D} + \mathbf{33}}$$

To find the fraction of nitrogen to give the required equivalent narcotic depth.

[71] some rebreathers attach open-circuit regulators to the diluent supply for bailout

Example:

The FN_2 required in a diluent to provide an END of 39 metres on a dive to 75 metres is;

$$FN2 = \frac{(39\ \text{metres} + 10) \times 0.79}{75 + 10} = 0.455 = 45.5\%$$

or

$$FN2 = \frac{(130\ \text{feet} + 33) \times 0.79}{250 + 33} = 0.455 = 45.5\%$$

As described, narcotic potency is at this level considered to be a function of nitrogen partial pressure and hence the above equations are true and are provided as an example to show that at deeper depths other gases such as helium need to be introduced into the loop to reduce narcosis. As a new rebreather diver, you would be concerned with air or nitrox as diluents and hence our narcotic depth is not variable once the MOD (PO_2, PN_2 combination) is defined. Helium or helium combinations as diluents and other more detailed END maths will be covered later.

Decompression

Decompression diving with rebreathers involves many complexities and logistical considerations. A basic understanding of decompression principles as they apply to various kinds of rebreathers is a crucial component of any rebreather training.

As discussed earlier, Pure oxygen rebreathers do not incorporate any inert gas in the breathing loop and are limited to very shallow diving applications, so decompression issues are not a consideration. Closed-circuit and semi-closed circuit rebreathers incorporate inert gases in the breathing loop, thereby enabling deeper dives where decompression limitations do become a concern. It is important to understand how decompression issues differ between closed-circuit and semi-closed circuit rebreathers.

As discussed, semi-closed circuit rebreathers generally maintain a constant *fraction* of oxygen (**F_IO_2**) in the breathing gas, just as open-circuit SCUBA systems do. Therefore, semi-closed circuit rebreather divers should follow decompression tables and computers designed for open-circuit SCUBA. However, the **F_IO_2** in the breathing loop of a semi-closed circuit rebreather is only 'constant' with respect to depth changes. Other variables such as gas supply flow rates and diver metabolic rates can affect the **F_IO_2**, and unless multiple oxygen sensors are incorporated into the system, the actual **F_IO_2** cannot be known with any degree of certainty[72]. For this reason, it is important to assume the minimum possible **F_IO_2** when calculating decompression schedules for a semi-closed rebreather dive.

[72] See chapter on Active vs Passive semi-closed systems.

Example:

A diver using a semi-closed circuit rebreather chooses EAN-40 as the supply gas (**F_SO_2** = 0.40) and the flow rate (**Q_S**) is set to 10 litres/min. The diver experiences a fairly heavy work load during the dive, such that the rate of metabolic oxygen consumption is 1.5 litres/min. The maximum depth of the dive is 25 metres.

a) What is the actual inspired fraction of oxygen?

Using Equation 1, the actual inspired oxygen fraction can be calculated:

$$F_IO_2 = \frac{(10 \times 0.40) - 1}{(10 - 1)} = 0.333 \text{ or } 33.3\%$$

b) What equivalent air depth (EAD) should be used for decompression calculations?

From basic nitrox training, the EAD of EAN-33.3 at a depth of 25 metres can be calculated as:

$$\frac{(1 - 0.333) \times (25 + 10)}{0.79} - 10 = 19.5 \text{ metres}$$

For decompression calculations, an EAD of 19.5 metres or a 21 metres table should be used.

(**NOTE:** Even though the **F_IO_2** is less than 0.40, and thus the inspired PO_2 at a depth of 25 metres is less than 1.4 bar, the maximum PO_2 exposure for Semi-closed-circuit rebreather dives should be calculated based on the **F_SO_2**, not the **F_IO_2**.)

In closed-circuit rebreathers, inert gas dynamics are different from what they are with semi-closed-circuit rebreathers or open-circuit SCUBA. Because the oxygen *partial pressure* remains constant, the **F_IO_2** changes with depth. Therefore, standard decompression tables and computers cannot be used to calculate decompression schedules for closed-circuit rebreathers. No-decompression limits (NDL) of dives using nitrox closed-circuit rebreathers may be calculated for various depths by calculating the EAD at each depth. However, the formula for calculating the EAD must be rearranged for closed-circuit rebreather dives, for which the PO_2 is known, but the **F_IO_2** is dependant on depth:

$$\text{EAD (in metres)} = \left(\frac{(P - PO_2)}{0.79} - 1\right) \times 10$$

or

$$\text{EAD (in feet)} = \left(\frac{(P - PO_2)}{0.79} - 1\right) \times 33$$

where **P** = the absolute ambient pressure at the target depth (in bar).

Example:

A diver using a closed-circuit rebreather with an oxygen set point of 1.4 bar (the same PO_2 as the semi-closed example) makes a dive to 25 metres. What is the EAD for decompression purposes?

The absolute pressure (**P**) at a depth of 25 metres is 3.5 bar:

$$\mathbf{EAD\,(in\ msw)} = \left(\frac{(3.5 - 1.4)}{0.79} - 1 \right) \times 10 = 16.6\ \mathbf{msw}$$

Thus, the EAD is 16.6 metres and the NDL for an 18 metres may be obtained from standard open-circuit SCUBA decompression tables. From these examples it can be seen that a further decompression advantage of 3 metres is obtained over the use of semi-closed.

NOTE: The concept of EAD for closed-circuit rebreathers applies only to calculating the NDL at a given depth; schedules for decompression dives will be different.

Decompression dives with closed-circuit rebreathers require special schedules based on a constant oxygen partial pressure. Some closed-circuit rebreather manufacturers will provide either integrated computers capable of calculating real-time decompression requirements or the necessary computer software to generate decompression tables[73]. In an emergency situation where a closed-circuit rebreather diver who has exceeded the NDL must abort to open-circuit bailout, decompression considerations become even more complex.

Because of potential fluctuations in the breathing gas composition when using either closed-circuit and semi-closed circuit rebreathers, decompression limits should be treated with extra conservatism. This, combined with the fact that the scenario could occur where at the end of a NDL[74] closed-circuit dive, an open-circuit bailout may be required to the surface. **It is therefore recommended that at least one minute of NDL time be deducted for each 10 metres of depth, and that 'safety decompression stops' of several minutes at 3-6 metres be incorporated into *all* rebreather dives.**

Other gas considerations

Oxygen and on-board diluent are not the only gases we carry. As with extended range in open-circuit we choose to back up our primary life support system with another unit i.e. a second regulator and cylinder. In a rebreather the actual loop its self and the absorbent it contains are our life-support system. If something occurs that means we can no longer use them, like in the open circuit system, we must switch to our backup or 'bailout' (in the case of the rebreather). What we bailout to becomes important for the following reasons:

1. like the rebreather carried diluent, the bailout must be breathable at the target depth (we may elect to use the rebreather diluent for a short period prior to switching to a larger 'off-board' supply).
2. it must be of a sufficient volume to ensure a safe exit to the surface or the next gas supply
3. it must provide an adequate decompression profile
4. it must not be excessively narcotic

The diluent of any rebreather (if available in open-circuit mode) must always be safe to breathe at the maximum depth of the dive.

In the air range the choice should be kept simple and ideally a sufficient quantity of air carried 'off-board' (as an extra cylinder) to facilitate an ascent and decompression. On getting to shallow water an emergency buoy can be sent up to request additional decompression gases if required. Custom mixes of various nitrox's for bailout only negate the idea of rebreathers in the first place- keep it simple.

It should be noted however that a switch to open-circuit air for one minute at depth prior to ascent may significantly modify the planned decompression profile and should be catered for.

[73] Also available now are mixed gas dive computers which have a link to an independent oxygen cell for online decompression calculations.
[74] No decompression limit

If you are not sure how much volume to carry then complete a test. Try an open circuit ascent from a typical dive and add at least 15% stress reserve. If the cylinder is almost empty on surfacing, that is acceptable as long as you make it. Standard 'rule of thirds' need not apply.

Heliox and Trimix as Diluents

By their nature, rebreathers waste much less gas than open-circuit SCUBA systems. Therefore, the cost of more expensive inert gases (such as helium) becomes much less of an issue with rebreathers. Consequently, helium is often incorporated into the diluent gas mixtures of rebreathers in the form of either heliox or trimix. There are many issues involved with using multiple-constituent diluents in rebreathers, a large number of which may not be obvious.

First lets look at a simple one gas trimix dive. This type of configuration is suitable down to 80 metres for limited bottom times (30 minutes max). As there need to be no diluent switches involved here, we can keep it simple. Make the on-board diluent the same as the off-board initial trimix bailout. This fits the previous rules i.e. it is breathable, it will not modify the initial decompression profile significantly (at the target depth the PO_2 and PN_2/Phe's etc are similar) and it will not be excessively narcotic for the same reason. There are two other advantages to this:

1. it is possible to decant from an off-board bailout to a small on-board rebreather cylinder to top up diluent (assuming bailout volumes allow) for subsequent dives
2. assuming a PO_2 of 1.2 to 1.3 in a closed circuit unit, a very similar ascent profile can be maintained, if a bailout is required. The closed circuit ascent time (whilst remaining on the single trimix in the loop and maintaining the PO_2) will be almost the same as bailing out to open-circuit (diluent matched) trimix and then switching to nitrox 36 and oxygen in open-circuit during the ascent. Hence, a simple backup open-circuit set of tables can be used to cover both situations. This means, on a normal dive the diver will stay in closed-circuit right up to 6 metres and either switch to open-circuit oxygen (preferred) or do the decompression on the rebreather at a high set point, remembering to flush the unit every 20 minutes or so. In the event of a bailout to open circuit, switching to EAN36 at its MOD and oxygen at 6 metres will enable you to follow the same schedule as the closed circuit profile.

Once past 80 metres or so, the rules change a little, as they do in open-circuit diving and more detailed bailout procedures need to be analysed for each specific dive. The main problem occurs because often on open circuit dives at this depth, three or more decompression gases may be required and hence the rebreather must also be capable of switching diluents. The big question here is narcosis. If the dive starts on an air diluent and then switches to a trimix, one advantage of the rebreather is that at whatever depth you switch from air to trimix will set your narcotic depth for the rest of the dive no matter how deep you go (within the limits of the final diluent). In other words if you switch at 30 metres you do not increase the loop PN_2 (number of nitrogen molecules) anymore until the trimix diluent PN_2 at depth exceeds it.

Obviously, exactly where you switch will also affect your decompression strategy.

Inert gas shifts
Another less considered problem with trimix diluents is the varying makeup of the inert gas ratio as the PO_2 changes. For instance:

You dive a trimix diluent of 10/52 the balance being 38% nitrogen. You are at 70 metres with a set point of 1.4. From Dalton's Law we know that the oxygen fraction is now 17.5%. What has happened to the ratios of the other two gases? They cannot be the equivalent partial pressures of 52% and 38% at 70 metres because those partial pressured added together (with the 1.4 oxygen) will not make 8 bar (70m).

We normalise the ratio. The remaining gas in the bag is still in the ratio 52 helium to 38 parts nitrogen. Therefore, with 82.5% inert gas (100-17.5), the helium content is:

$$\frac{82.5 \times 52}{52 + 38} = 47.67\%$$

The nitrogen content is now:

$$\frac{82.5 \times 38}{52 + 38} = 34.83\%$$

This is another good reason to match trimix diluents more closely with the target depth.

Decompression planning software is a vital tool when planning rebreather bailouts.

Maintaining PO_2
Even with sophisticated electronic control it is sometimes difficult for the rebreather to maintain PO_2 especially during descents and in particular ascents. Descents are difficult because if we allow the unit to get up to set point on the surface, once we are at the target depth we will potentially have a high PO_2 (as the absolute pressure has increased) and diluent flushing may be required to reduce it. One option is to set a low PO_2 of 0.7 (which is still breathable at the surface) and allow the system to 'catch-up' during the descent. On extremely deep dives, this may still give a problem dependant on the speed of descent. What ever the system employed, this should be taken into account in the decompression strategy especially on deeper dives. An assumption of a low descent PO_2 should be planned for.

Ascents are worse. As you rise the gas expands, the unit vents and subsequently PO_2 drops. The oxygen controller fights to maintain it by adding more gas and it may vent again creating a vicious circle. One technique here is to vent prior to moving to the next stop. Manually add oxygen and move up. This will allow the loop to stabilise much more quickly. During long closed circuit decompressions where a diluent switch (change of inert gas) has been conducted, a simple flush should be performed at the switch point (not unlike the gas switch on open-circuit) to remove all the previous diluent from the loop. Every 15-20 minutes this should be repeated to flush from the loop any inert gas which we'off-gas' from our bodies. The PO_2 will then again need time to stabilise and may need to be assisted manually.

Another area that can be a problem for units with automatic diluent addition is if too much venting takes place and diluent is inadvertently added thus reducing the PO_2. The only real solution to this is to shut off diluent at the start of the ascent. This is potentially dangerous because if the depth suddenly increases the bag volume will drop and you may not be able to breathe and also the PO_2 will rise quickly. **This level of PO_2 control should only be used by very experienced users.**

Rebreather Gas Rules
Unlike open circuit it is not required to maintain one third of your gas supply for reserve. The 'rule of thirds' in open-circuit has historically been proven to provide just enough gas for an exit if a failure occurs at the worst point on a dive. Assuming that on-board gas will not be used for bailout then any carried external gas to be used in an emergency must have a sufficient volume to get you to a safe exit or in cave diving, back to the next staged safety gas. Whilst it is prudent to build in a stress reserve of approximately 15%, you need not calculate the gas volume to have one third left on a normal exit on open-circuit.

One major advantage of rebreathers in penetration diving such as cave exploration, (where multiple days of diving to extend a line may be the plan) is that you will set the stage/bailout cylinders only once. Providing they are not used (they should be checked at every swim past) they can stay in position throughout the trip, unlike in an open circuit expedition where they will need to be used on every dive.

Weight

To determine the proper amount of weight to wear for a particular rebreather model, follow these steps:

1. enter shallow water with the rebreather and more than enough weight to sink you and your typical equipment configuration (exposure suit, etc.)
2. purge gas from the loop until a normal full inhalation just activates the automatic diluent addition system or in manual system where you feel a tightness of breath.
3. incrementally remove weights until you become slightly positively buoyant.
4. add an additional 20% of the remaining weight to your weight belt to allow for buoyancy shifts

Now practice a series of controlled ascents until the weight\buoyancy ratio feels comfortable

Masks

With the small supply of diluent gas carried with most rebreathers, it is imperative that the diver use a well-fitted mask that does not leak. Repeated mask clearing will quickly deplete the gas source, be sure to use a good fog-preventing agent. Full-face masks are also an option with rebreathers. One advantage of using a full-face mask is that electronic communications systems can be used. The quality of wireless ‘comm gear’ is greatly improved by using a rebreather, as there is no bubble noise to acoustically interfere with the signal. The choice of which kind of full face mask to use depends on a variety of factors, but it is important that only those with an oral/nasal cavity should be used to avoid CO_2 build-up.

CO_2 Absorbent Management

The main enemy of all CO_2 absorbents is water. It is important that the canister housing containing the absorbent is inspected between dives and allowed to vent to the atmosphere when stored. If canisters are to be stored for several weeks prior to use, it is recommended that they are placed in dry air-tight containers. Certain absorbents are more volatile than others and may require special handling. If the rebreather model is designed such that the user packs the absorbent canister, packing instructions from the manufacturer must be followed precisely. Some of the key points include:

- remove and thoroughly dry the canister and housing.
- wearing suitable mouth, hand and eye protection as defined by the manufacturer of the absorbent. Remove the canister top and take out all of the used absorbent material.
- any absorbent material stuck to the canister should be carefully removed with an appropriate tool until the canister is completely empty.
- inspect the canister and any water traps for damage.
- inspect and replace any faulty ‘O’ rings.
- dispose of the absorbent according to the manufacturer’s guidelines.
- wear suitable protection, re-pack the canister with fresh absorbent, ensuring that there are no air gaps. A simple check is to shake the canister and listen for movement of the particles. A well-packed canister may require several ‘tap down’ routines before final sealing.
- replace the canister, checking and re-lubricating any ‘O’ rings.

Careful time logging of absorbent use is critical. Some systems have electronic absorbent timers to cope with this. **Where multiple rebreathers of the same type are at the site, it is wise to actually write your name on your canister and the absorbent life used so far.**

If you are uncertain about the actual remaining absorbent life, then change it!

Cylinder Configurations

Cylinder configurations are especially important for mixed-gas and decompression dives using rebreathers. However, some important cylinder configuration considerations must be taken into account on all rebreather dives. For example, BCD and drysuit inflation gas usage may significantly affect the duration of the unit. It is therefore important that different diving requirements are discussed and planned for and that appropriate volumes of gas for different purposes are available.

Having established the gas source for a semi-closed circuit system it is important to choose a cylinder volume based on the depth of the dive, the dive time planned (hence flow rate) and predicted inflation usage. At the end of this no dive time a direct ascent should be possible at a high (stressed) breathing rate allowing a minimum of 15% reserve for emergency ascents in open-circuit bailout mode. With closed-circuit rebreathers, diluent is usually only used during descents. In most cases, very little diluent will be expended. Especially on decompression dives or dives past 20 metres, it is recommended that independent bailout cylinders be used. The primary bailout should (as with open-circuit systems) have a neck-tie for the bailout (backup) regulator. These cylinders will often double as bailout and suit/BCD inflation.

Checklists

In any life support situation checklists are vital. As an example, the airline pilot, even though he has flown the plane 1000 times, still runs a written checklist. This is not just because there are lots of things to remember, it is because we all have bad days when we forget things or become distracted. During rebreather training you should be asked to generate a checklist for your unit. Whenever you work on the unit you should use the written checklist as a reminder of what to do. This is especially important when a complete strip-down and rebuild has been performed or the loop integrity has been broken such as in an absorbent change. In field operations it is wise to make a waterproof list and fix it to the inside of the units cover. In addition to this, have an acronym based verbal list for final pre-dive checks. One such acronym I made up years ago was **FLAGS** which is used as a check just before jumping in the water. You can adapt this to most rebreathers. For my closed circuit unit it goes like this:

Flow Ensure the flow valves in the mouthpiece are working and do negative and positive pressure tests. Check addition valves and bailout.

Loop Go on the breathing loop and start a pre-breathe, having ensured there is sufficient oxygen in the loop.

Analyse Inject oxygen and check all PO_2 displays rise (having done a calibration during the build this is a final verification that the sensors are working). Now inject diluent and watch the PO_2 fall. A flush with oxygen and then diluent is a further check that the cylinders have been installed the right way around.

Gauge Check gauge press are sufficient to perform the dive. This includes bailout.

Stack Confirm stack (canister) duration is sufficient for the dive. Continue breathing for 3-5 minutes and note any signs of hypercapnia.

Pre-dive Checks

The following is a guide to pre-dive checks on any (all) rebreather systems:

- analyse diluent/enriched O_2 cylinder
- check diluent/enriched O_2 supply and oxygen cylinder pressures and assemble into the unit
- assemble breathing hoses and mouthpiece, checking for any leaks
- check operation of mouthpiece (mushroom valve function)
- turn on gas supply and check function of valves and bailout regulator systems
- verify correct calibration of O_2 sensors (where applicable)
- inflate counter-lung and check overpressure relief valve
- check automatic addition valve (if fitted)
- verify sufficient absorbent time remaining
- check battery time remaining (closed-circuit only)
- verify proper computer function (closed-circuit only)
- verify proper function and calibration of backup PO_2 display (where applicable)
- confirm PO_2 set point (closed-circuit only)
- set flow valve (semi-closed circuit only)
- after any rebuild do a immersion test with all gases on.

Pre-breathe Sequence

Prior to immersion, a pre-breathe sequence should be completed on all rebreathers, especially closed-circuit units. Specific procedures differ from one rebreather model to another, but key points include:

Closed-circuit rebreathers

- with all gases off perform negative and positive pressure tests
- select an oxygen set point (select a relatively low value so as not to 'pre-charge' the loop with a rich nitrox mixture), 0.7 bar is sufficient
- activate electronic oxygen control system
- put mouthpiece in closed-circuit mode and begin breathing normally
- confirm oxygen control system properly maintains the set point for a minimum of 3 minutes
- verify PO_2 values using backup display
- confirm CO_2 absorbent is functioning properly (pay attention for symptoms of hypercapnia)
- confirm operation of diluent addition system
- confirm operation of bailout system

Semi-closed circuit rebreathers

- perform negative and positive pressure tests
- confirm flow valve/injection setting
- operate bypass mechanism
- operate mouthpiece and begin breathing normally
- confirm CO_2 absorbent is functioning properly (pay attention for symptoms of hypercapnia)
- confirm operation of bailout system

Dive Procedures

Once all appropriate steps have been taken to ensure that the rig is functioning correctly and is configured in a manner appropriate for the planned dive, you are ready to enter the water. Rebreather dive procedures differ in many respects from open-circuit SCUBA diving procedures. Although extensive experience with open-circuit SCUBA is useful for a basic understanding of diving physics and physiology, specific dive procedures are quite different with a rebreather.

Initial In-water Verification

There are several procedures that must be performed immediately when entering the water with a rebreather. These should occur at no deeper than 6 metres:

- check to see if any gas is leaking from the system
- verify oxygen control system is working (closed-circuit)
- verify backup PO_2 display is working (closed-circuit)
- verify gas supply flow rate is appropriate (semi-closed circuit)
- adjust buoyancy
- re-check bailout regulator

Descents

There are several important variables associated with descents when using rebreathers that differ from open-circuit SCUBA. With any kind of rebreather, the increasing ambient pressure experienced during descents will lead to compression of the counter-lung. In addition to buoyancy characteristics associated with counter-lung compression (see '*Buoyancy Control*' section below) breathing characteristics and inspired oxygen partial-pressure are also affected. When a rebreather counter-lung is fully collapsed, there is no excess gas volume in the breathing loop from which a diver can inhale. Most rebreather designs compensate for counter-lung collapse by automatically adding additional gas to the loop. Depending on the mechanism of automatic volume compensation, the rate of gas addition may not be sufficient to supply an inhaling diver's needs. Manual gas injection may therefore be necessary to supplement automatic gas injection during rapid descents.

Another consequence of rapid descents when using rebreathers is increasing oxygen partial pressure in the breathing loop. This is generally not a problem when diving with semi-closed circuit rebreathers, because these units maintain a relatively constant fraction of oxygen and the maximum depth of the dive is determined by the oxygen fraction in the supply gas. Therefore, as along as this maximum depth is not violated, the PO_2 should not rise to dangerous levels in a semi-closed circuit rebreather loop, regardless of descent rates. With closed-circuit systems, however, it is possible to achieve excessively high PO_2 values during rapid descents. In most cases, diluent will be injected into the loop during descents. Because the diluent composition must be chosen such that the PO_2 does not exceed maximum safe levels when breathed in open-circuit mode at the maximum depth of the dive, the addition of diluent into the breathing loop will minimise this problem. However, unless the counter-lung is maintained at minimum volume, there will be a short time lag between the initial descent and automatic diluent addition. During this time lag, the PO_2 may 'spike' to dangerously high levels, especially near the maximum depth of a dive, where the diluent is least effective at reducing PO_2. For this reason, it is important when diving with a closed-circuit rebreather to maintain counter-lung volume close to minimum, use a diluent with a relatively low oxygen fraction (e.g., air) and maintain a conservative PO_2 set point to allow for a broad margin of error. In systems with a selectable PO_2 whilst diving, it may be prudent to select a low PO_2 for the start of the dive (descent) and increase this once the unit has stabilised on the bottom.

Buoyancy Control

Almost all experienced open-circuit SCUBA divers have considerable difficulty controlling buoyancy when first entering the water with a rebreather. There are two reasons for this and both are associated with the counter-lung.

The first reason involves fine-tune buoyancy adjustments. Most divers rely on the change in volume of their lungs during the breathing cycle to make subtle buoyancy adjustments (i.e., inhale to ascend, exhale to descend). When using a rebreather, however, the counter-lung expands and contracts in opposition to the diver's lungs, so buoyancy does not change during the breathing cycle. Experienced open-circuit SCUBA divers may find this disorienting at first, but, with practice, fine-tune buoyancy control through subtle adjustments to loop volume is easily mastered.

The second reason involves buoyancy changes with depth. In order to contract and expand in opposition to a diver's lungs, a rebreather counter-lung must be some sort of collapsible bag, much like a BCD. Also like a BCD, the counter-lung will expand or contract with depth changes as the gas within the loop expands and compresses due to changes in ambient pressure. The counter-lung will collapse with increasing ambient pressure during descent and will typically activate an automatic addition system that injects gas to compensate. On ascent, the counter-lung will expand until completely filled and excess gas will be vented either by the diver or through some sort of over-pressure relief valve in the loop. Because rebreathers must be designed to accommodate a variety of people with different lung volumes (among other reasons), the total loop volume change from fully collapsed counter-lung to fully inflated counter-lung may be substantial. The corresponding change in buoyancy, therefore, may also be considerable. Because it is usually advisable to maintain total loop volume at a minimum, this variable buoyancy characteristic becomes most evident during ascents. Although most rebreathers are designed to vent excess gas automatically when the counter-lung is fully expanded, it is usually better if the diver manually vents excess gas during ascents, either by exhaling through the nose when using a standard mask or half-mask. If careful attention is not paid to buoyancy control during ascents, an uncontrolled rapid ascent may result.

Breathing Characteristics

Breathing on a rebreather is different from breathing on open-circuit SCUBA. Several factors affect the breathing resistance of a rebreather and in most cases, the resistance will be equal to or less than the breathing resistance in typical SCUBA regulators. Various hydrostatic effects play a role in determining the effort required to ventilate the lungs. In most rebreather designs, there will be mild to moderate differences in the breathing characteristics, depending on the orientation of the diver. For example, a diver using a rebreather with a back-mounted counter-lung will expend more effort on inhalation when in a prone position than when upright or lying back. The reverse would be true for a diver using a rebreather with a front-mounted counter-lung. A well-designed rebreather will minimise the effect of body orientation on breathing characteristics. Other factors that affect breathing resistance include hose diametre and absorbent canister design.

Another consideration of rebreather breathing characteristics is the fact that the same gas is recirculated through repeated breaths. Two of the benefits of this are that the breathing gas remains humid (reducing dehydration problems) and the breathing gas tends to remain warm (reducing heat loss). The latter is especially true when the selected absorbent binds with CO_2 in an exothermic reaction. For obvious reasons, it may also be of some importance what food a diver eats immediately preceding a rebreather dive!

Monitoring Oxygen Partial Pressure

The importance of maintaining safe inspired oxygen partial pressure levels ***cannot be overemphasised!*** With closed-circuit rebreathers, both hypoxia and hyperoxia are very real dangers. The only way a diver can monitor the PO_2 in a closed-circuit rebreather is via the electronic oxygen sensors. Ensuring safe PO_2 limits within a closed-circuit rebreather loop requires both intelligent rebreather design (e.g., multiple oxygen sensors, backup display systems, etc), as well as proper monitoring procedures on the part of the diver. Good practices include frequent cross-checking of primary and backup oxygen sensor displays to verify consistency, and periodic tests to verify accuracy of the sensor readings (diluent flushes).

With semi-closed rebreathers, hyperoxia should not be a concern if the proper supply gas mixture has been selected; however, hypoxia can be a problem if the gas flow rate is not sufficient to meet the metabolic needs of the diver or during ascents in shallow water.

Andy Matroci and myself, working with a water dredge at 75 metres but still watching the PO_2!

Monitoring Gas Supplies

Although divers using rebreathers consume gas supplies at a much lower rate than divers using open-circuit SCUBA, careful monitoring of gas supplies is still an important part of safe rebreather diving protocol. In the case of semi-closed-circuit rebreathers, the gas supply declines at a steady rate, just as it does with open-circuit SCUBA. Consequently, semi-closed rebreather divers must carefully monitor gas supply levels and reserve enough to allow completion of the dive, with adequate margins for error.

With closed-circuit rebreathers (used at a static depth) it is usually the oxygen supply, not the diluent supply, that limits the duration of the dive. Consumption rates will depend on the level of exertion, as well as the extent of gas loss from mask clearings, loop leakage and extent of ascents/descents during the dive. Again, adequate margins for error must be allowed for.

Regardless of rebreather type, if the same gas supply used for the rebreather diluent is also relied upon for emergency open-circuit bailout, then the dive *must* be terminated when the remaining supply is not sufficient to allow a safe return to the surface in open-circuit mode. This issue is especially important on decompression dives. For this reason most rebreathers carry insufficient in-board bailout for even short duration dives past 20 metres. It is recommended separate bailout cylinders are used.

Ascents
The two most important considerations during ascents from rebreather dives are changes in buoyancy due to expansion of the counter-lung, and drops in the oxygen partial pressure within the breathing loop to hypoxic levels. Buoyancy considerations were discussed in detail above. The main concern for dives within the dive parametres covered in this is to avoid hypoxia during ascents. Specifically, the PO_2 within the breathing loop must not be allowed to drop below 0.20 bar. At a maximum depth of 40 metres, where the ambient pressure is 5 bar, this should not be a problem as long as the loop PO_2 at depth is at least 1.0 bar. The reason is, even with a direct ascent from this maximum depth, the PO_2 would be 0.20 upon arriving at the surface. On deeper dives and on dives where the target/set point PO_2 is less than 1.0 bar (generally not recommended), the possibility of hypoxic blackout when approaching the surface can be a real hazard and care must be taken to avoid this problem.

With semi-closed units it is recommended that the breathing bag is flushed prior to any direct ascent to the surface to ensure maximum F_iO_2 is available.

Post-Dive Breakdown

Post dive:
- wash and disinfect as per the defined schedule
- ventilate the unit and deflate counter-lungs
- refill absorbent as required
- always refill diluent\oxygen enriched supply cylinders
- refill any other bailout cylinders
- refill the oxygen cylinder as required

Storing:
- wash and disinfect
- vent
- remove oxygen sensors (long periods)
- remove absorbent and store in a dry place
- leave cylinders partially filled
- lubricate 'O' rings
- log sensor and battery values

Failure Modes
Although basic rebreather skills are relatively easy and can be learned in a short period of time, preparing for and dealing with problems that may come up requires considerably more practice and skill. The danger with learning to become a rebreather diver is one of overconfidence. Because experienced divers can feel comfortable diving with a rebreather without much effort, they often make the false assumption that they are experienced rebreather divers before they are truly ready. All problems that may occur on an open-circuit SCUBA dive can also occur when using a rebreather. However, because of their inherent complexity, there are many more problems that are specific to rebreathers.

Our first line of defence is proper pre-dive checks

One of the major drawbacks with rebreathers when compared with open-circuit SCUBA is that potentially fatal problems are more insidious. In particular, hypoxia and hyperoxia can render a diver unconscious without any warning at all. It is absolutely imperative that rebreather divers learn how to recognise problems *before* they become life-threatening and to be able to intelligently cope with these problems as they arise. The only way to ensure that a diver is prepared to deal with such problems is through repetitive practise drills.

In an emergency, it is the poorly learned survival skills that are lost first.

A good thing about most rebreather malfunctions is that the diver normally has far more time to take corrective action than with open-circuit (provided a diver does not become unconscious before a problem is recognised). Furthermore, many problems may be completely reversible so the dive does not always have to be aborted.

Flooded Loop
Unfortunately, most carbon dioxide absorbent materials do not react well with water. In fact, some absorbent materials (e.g., lithium hydroxide) react vigorously with water and may produce the dreaded 'caustic cocktail'. For obvious reasons, divers using rebreathers underwater are at risk of exposing CO_2 absorbent material to water. Although some sophisticated rebreather designs incorporate systems that virtually prevent water from reaching the absorbent even with a total loop flood, it is still important to minimise the volume of water introduced into the breathing loop and to know how to purge any water that does get in from the loop.

All rebreathers will get some water in the loop as a result of condensation. A diver's exhaled breath is warm and highly saturated with water vapour. The volume of water vapour that can remain in a given gas volume is affected by the temperature: the warmer the gas, the more water vapour it can hold. Gas passing over absorbent material is warmed even more by the exothermic reaction of the absorbent with CO_2. When this gas comes in to contact with the breathing hose, which may be cooled by the surrounding water, it cools and water vapour condenses on the walls of the hose. (This is similar to water vapour condensing on the side of a cold can of beer or soft drink in a warm, humid room.) The total volume of accumulated condensation may be upwards of several millilitres per hour and even more in cold water.

The next most common source of water in the breathing loop is from accidental removal of the mouthpiece underwater. All rebreather designs include a shut-off valve on the mouthpiece block, that allows the diver to safely remove the mouthpiece underwater without introducing water into the loop. Nevertheless, unexpected or accidental mouthpiece removal may result in the introduction of considerable quantities of water into the loop.

Other sources of water in the breathing loop include leaky hose connections, damages hoses, punctured counter-lungs, and other damaged loop components.

In most cases, it will be obvious to the diver that water has entered the loop because there will usually be a gurgling sound, or breathing resistance will increase significantly. Different rebreather models will deal with flooded loops in different ways and recovery methods will be specific to each rebreather model.

Absorbent Failures
The worst form of absorbent failure is a flooded canister. There is almost no method of recovery once the absorbent material has been flooded. At best, breathing resistance will sky-rocket and CO_2 absorption will fall off. At worst, the loop will be filled with a caustic and dangerous 'cocktail'. In either case, virtually the only option is open-circuit bailout.

Another form of absorbent failure is ineffective absorption efficiency. This can be caused by several things, such as:

- improperly packed absorbent canister (channelling)
- overuse of absorbent by excessive exertion and/or individual metabolic variation
- contaminated absorbent material
- mismanagement of absorbent usage and remaining life
- incorrect absorbent material

Whatever the cause of an absorbent failure, the result is generally the same - hypercapnia (excess CO_2 in the breathing loop). Fortunately, the symptoms of hypercapnia are usually detectable before they reach dangerous levels. Unfortunately, excess CO_2 has been linked to other, more insidious problems such as oxygen toxicity convulsions, so hypercapnia should be carefully avoided.

Initial symptoms of hypercapnia include a 'stale' taste to the breathing gas and shortness of breath during periods of exertion. As CO_2 levels rise, shortness of breath becomes more obvious, even at low exertion levels and other symptoms such as headaches, dizziness, tingling, etc. may become evident. The rate of symptom severity increase depends on several factors, including the type of absorbent material, cause of the absorbent failure, level of exertion, individual metabolic characteristics, among others.

Whenever symptoms of hypercapnia are detected, the dive should be aborted. If symptoms increase rapidly in severity, then an open-circuit bailout should be engaged.

Gas Supply Failures
Although rebreather gas supplies are depleted at much slower rates than open-circuit SCUBA gas supplies, it is still important to carefully monitor gas supplies and terminate the dive with a reasonable margin of error. Gas supply failures on rebreathers generally fall into three categories:

- gas mismanagement
- rapid gas loss
- gas delivery failure

Gas mismanagement failures can only be avoided by careful planning and diligence, allowing satisfactory margins for error. Rapid gas loss may be in the form of a burst supply hose, blown 'O' ring, or gas delivery valve failure. If such a failure occurs in the oxygen injection solenoid of a closed-circuit rebreather, a rapid rise in the PO_2 could be disastrous if not quickly corrected by shutting off the oxygen supply and reducing the PO_2 by injection of diluent. A gas delivery failure involves an inability to inject gas into the breathing loop. Failures of this type in a semi-closed circuit rebreather generally requires an open-circuit bailout unless manual injection is feasible.

In the case of semi-closed circuit rebreathers, if only one gas supply is available for both the rebreather and the open-circuit bailout supply, then a gas supply failure could be extremely dangerous. For this reason, at least two independent gas supplies are recommended for semi-closed circuit rebreather dives. In the case of closed-circuit rebreathers, diluent gas supply failure is relatively minor, as long as an immediate abort is engaged. As the diver ascends, no additional diluent is needed as the gas in the loop expands. An oxygen supply failure, however, can be devastating for a closed-circuit rebreather diver, since the diluent supply generally does not provide sufficient oxygen to maintain a diver in while in closed-circuit mode. Consequently, an oxygen supply failure on a closed-circuit rebreather usually leads to an open-circuit bailout, unless a backup oxygen supply is available or a diluent of air or nitrox can be flushed through the bag.

Electronics Failures (closed-circuit)
With all rebreather systems, and in particular closed-circuit systems, it is imperative that the diver has a full understanding of the bypass or manual controls associated with the unit. Electronics are notoriously prone to failure when taken underwater, so skills associated with manual control to perform a safe egress from the water are mandatory regardless of how reliable electronic systems may be. Even though electronic failures may be rare in a modern closed-circuit rebreather, manual control of the unit must be practised with regularity. Specific procedures will be covered in the manufacturer-specific portion of this course.

Manual control of the unit must be practised with regularity

Oxygen Sensor Failures (closed-circuit)
Electrical oxygen sensors can fail for a variety of reasons, including water on the sensing membrane, pressure disequilibrium, incorrect calibration, over-charging, broken electrical connections, drastic temperature fluctuations and numerous other causes. A vitally important aspect of rebreather training is the recognition of oxygen sensor malfunctions before inspired PO_2 reaches dangerous levels. Most closed-circuit systems incorporate at least three oxygen sensors to allow for 'voting logic'. In cases where two sensors give similar readings, but the third sensor gives a drastically different reading, it is often (though not always) the case that the third sensor is incorrect.

Whenever an oxygen sensor failure is suspected, it is important to perform specific tests to determine which of the sensors are yielding reliable readings and which are not. The most obvious test is to inject diluent into the loop and observe the relative responsiveness of each of the three oxygen sensors. In cases where two sensors have simultaneously failed in the same way, it is possible that the computer system will take the incorrect reading as correct and attempt to adjust the PO_2 accordingly. In such cases, the diver must disable the automatic oxygen control system and operate the unit manually. Specific oxygen sensor tests and recovery procedures will be different for different rebreather models and should be investigated and practised.

Failure Modes and Bailout Scenarios - Summary

The following is a typical (but not all-encompassing) list of potential problems and possible remedies:

Symptom(s)	Failure	Semi-Closed Recovery	Closed-Circuit Recovery
Water movement noises (gurgling)	Flooded hoses or counter-lung	Perform flood recovery drill[1]	Perform flood recovery drill[1]
Increased breathing resistance	Flooded absorbent canister[2]	Perform flood recovery drill[1]	Perform flood recovery drill[1]
Unable to breathe	Unrecoverable loop failure	Open-circuit bailout	Open-circuit bailout
Desire to breathe/headaches	Absorbent failure	Continued flushing to remove excess CO_2 and ascend or immediate open-circuit bailout	Continued flushing to remove excess CO_2 and ascend or immediate open-circuit bailout
No flow/auto injection of gas	Diluent/enriched supply loss	Ascend immediately on open-circuit	Do not increase depth, ascend in closed circuit
PO_2 falls, silent solenoid	Oxygen supply loss	N/A	Ascend slowly, if the PO_2 falls to 0.2 bar, then open-circuit bailout
No supply readings/gas loss	HP gauge failure	Abort dive and ascend	Do not increase depth and ascend in closed circuit
Blank screen/erratic readings	Control computer failure[3]	N/A	Manual control abort
Drifting PO_2 readings	Oxygen sensor failure.	Maintain work/flow rates and ascend (if fitted)	Disable automatic O_2 injection. Ascend on open-circuit or use metabolic makeup drill[4]

[1]For units without flood recovery capability, or in cases where water and the absorbent may come into contact, the only option is an open-circuit bailout to the surface.

[2]Units employing certain semi-permeable membranes to prevent water from reaching the absorbent material may experience a breathing resistance increase after a flood of the membrane. The only effective remedy is to dry the membrane prior to using again.

[3]Some sophisticated systems have multiple computers which will automatically isolate a "rogue" processor and maintain control with the alternative processor(s).

[4]The metabolic makeup drill involves logging the approximate O_2 injection rate at rest (usually about 5 seconds). With the automatic injection isolated ,an ascent to the surface is made and the manual injection activated as appropriate. Most closed-circuit rebreathers will probably not generate shallow water hypoxia on a direct ascent anyway, especially in the sport diving depth ranges with PO_2 set points in excess of 1 bar on the bottom.

In Water Skills - Summary

The following is a list of minimum in-water skills to be regularly performed both during a course and during subsequent familiarisation on the units:

Skill	Semi-Closed Circuit	Closed-Circuit	Practise
Sensor monitoring	N/A (normally)	On both primary computer and backup displays	On all dives
Flow-rate bypass (bag flush)	Use manual system	N/A	Prior to every ascent
Manual injection of diluent with buoyancy control	N/A	Inject while monitoring PO_2 . Used to reduce high PO_2 levels	Initially in shallow water, then at depth to a minimum PO_2 of 0.6 bar
Adjust flow rate with buoyancy control	To determine worst case weight considerations	N/A	Initially in shallow water, then at depth (20 metres)
Manual injection of oxygen to a safe maximum PO_2 of 1.4 bar	N/A	Isolate automatic oxygen injection and add manually (solenoid failure simulation)	Initially at 6 metres, then on a typical dive during ascent
Loop-flood recovery	Initiate purge routine if possible or open-circuit bailout	Initiate purge routine if possible or open-circuit bailout	Initially 6 metres or shallower, to a maximum of 20 metres.
Open-circuit bailout	Assume loop partly intact and will fill on ascent	Assume loop partly intact and will fill on ascent	Initially from 20 metres to a maximum of 30 metres. Bailout gas usage must be monitored to confirm min. required cylinder size.

Rebreather Maintenance

Oxygen Sensors

Arguably the most important element of any mixed gas rebreather is the oxygen control/monitoring system. In automatic systems, the weakest point is the galvanic sensors. These sensors are like small batteries, the electrical output of which is generated by a chemical reaction with oxygen. Oxygen sensors degrade with time, and thus have a limited life. Commonly used sensors currently last from between one and three years, depending on their environmental usage.

Also, due to the degradation, the sensors must be regularly calibrated. Older rebreathers employed a series of potentiometres (variable resistors) to help adjust amplifiers within the electronics. The units were calibrated in 100% oxygen, and the amplifiers were then calibrated to read the equivalent of 1 bar PO_2 at sea level. Modern electronics, through advanced sampling techniques, allow the calibration to take place with 100% oxygen at any altitude. Oxygen sensors are affected by temperature and excess humidity, and a good rebreather design should take these considerations into account. Some users take time to store the sensors in an inert gas atmosphere between periods of use. Although this process does lengthen the life of the cell, care must be taken when replacing them in the rebreather, as they take time to stabilise when first reintroduced to oxygen.

Water is the enemy of oxygen sensors. It is vital that after use the breathing loop is vented to the atmosphere and the sensor membranes allowed to dry. It is generally a good idea to blow dry air over (but not into) sensor membranes to remove any accumulated moisture. House air-conditioning and ozone cleaning units are excellent for drying sensors and rebreathers in general.

Disinfecting and Cleaning

A rebreather is a warm, damp environment and ideally suited for bacterial growth. The breathing loop should be regularly disinfected with safe disinfectants (Betadyne, Dettox etc.) and thoroughly dried. Check with the manufacturer for approved methods.

Some cleaning agents may affect 'O' ring elasticity, so 'O' rings should regularly be checked for cracks and the correct amount of lubrication. As all rebreathers can be used with pure oxygen, an appropriate oxygen-compatible grease is the only acceptable lubricant.

The following is a practical disinfecting schedule:

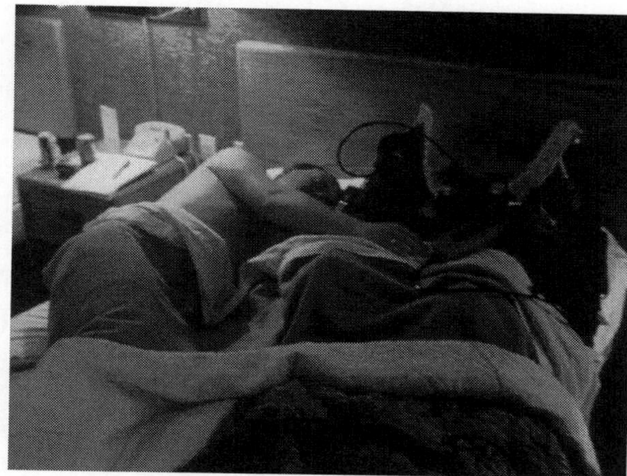

Caring for your rebreather!

After every dive:

- vent to atmosphere.
- wash the mouthpiece in fresh water.
- avoiding water ingress to the loop.

After each day of diving:

- disinfect the mouthpiece and hoses.
- use only medically approved disinfectants in the correct dilution ratios. (Product such as Betadine may be mixed 10:1 with water; Dettox may be used as a light hand spray.
- flush with warm fresh water.
- do not leave breathing parts soaking in disinfectant.

The process may be repeated for gross contamination.

After 8 total hours of diving:

- disinfect mouthpiece, hoses, water traps, counter-lungs and inside of canister housing.

O-Rings

Whenever possible, do not disturb 'O' rings unnecessarily. All 'O' rings must be carefully inspected prior to reassembly, and any damaged 'O' rings should be replaced. Excessive lubrication is usually not required, and may attract particles which could endanger the seal. A light periodic lubrication is all that is required. 'O' ring grooves should also be checked for damage.

A complete 'O' ring inspection should be undertaken a minimum of 30 hours use or less as defined by the manufacturer. Only those deemed as in *operational use* should be checked. Some units will have factory-sealed compartments. These rings will be checked during the service period and should not be tampered with. Remove and replace 'O' rings individually in order to ensure correct size replacement.

Hoses

Check for visible damage after every dive and immediately replace any worn parts. Store hoses in a hard carry case to avoid damage in transport. Be wary of other people carrying the unit by the hoses or placing heavy equipment on them.

Counter-lungs

Keep dry (vented) when not in use. Check breathing loop interface ports for damage to threads etc. Inspect the actual inner bag for damage or wear at every leak test. If counter-lungs are external to the main casing, check the external bag for damage after every dive and then the inner bag if any is found.

BCD

Especially with wetsuit diving the BCD is vital to buoyancy control and safety. Do visual inspections regularly and as a rule, fully inflate either pre or post every dive and check for leaks.

Pre-dive Check List

Check	*Semi-Closed*	*Fully Closed*
Analyse diluent/enriched O_2 cylinder		
Check diluent/enriched O_2 supply and oxygen cylinder pressures and assemble into the unit		
Assemble breathing hoses and mouthpiece, checking for any leaks		
Check operation of mouthpiece (mushroom valves)		
Perform positive and negative tests		
Turn on gas supply and check function of valves and bailout regulator systems		
Verify correct calibration of O_2 sensors (where applicable)		
Inflate counter-lung and check overpressure relief valve		
Verify sufficient absorbent time remaining		
Check battery time remaining		
Verify proper computer function		
Verify proper function of backup PO_2 display (where applicable)		
Confirm PO_2 set point		
Set flow valve		
Pre-breathe sequence Prior to immersion, a pre-breathe sequence should be completed on all rebreathers, especially closed-circuit units. Specific procedures differ from one rebreather model to another, but key points include:		
Select an oxygen set point (select a relatively low value so as not to 'pre-charge' the loop with a rich nitrox mixture), 0.7 bar is sufficient		
Activate electronic oxygen control system		
Put mouthpiece in loop mode and begin breathing normally		
Confirm oxygen control system properly maintains the set point for a minimum of 3 minutes		
Verify PO_2 values using backup display		
Confirm CO_2 absorbent is functioning properly (pay attention for symptoms of hypercapnia)		
Confirm operation of diluent addition system		
Confirm operation of bailout system		
Confirm flow valve/injection setting		
Operate bypass mechanism		

Perform checks and tick the appropriate box prior to commencing operations.

Rebreather Diving. A Survivor's Guide

Looking back, my own introduction to rebreathers was somewhat of a baptism of fire, which, with hind sight and education I would probably never do again, even though the experience was invaluable.

The author testing a prototype rebreather. Note the sticky tape!

I remember some time in 1991 someone convincing me to strap a prototype rebreather on and do a deep heliox chamber dive with it (my logbook says 100 metres). Until that point I had only done 'bench flights' with the unit and a few shallow 'air range' runs. It seemed like a good idea at the time and I lived to tell the tale. Due to a variety of system failures it became one of those character-building dives.

At that time there were no training courses and no one was using rebreathers outside the military. You couldn't even get operators manuals. After several years of 'experimenting' with a series of unreliable ex-military units I met Dr Bill Stone, the inventor of the Cis-Lunar range of rebreathers. To cut a long story short I found my self along with Richard Pyle in Bill's garage with a box full of rebreather bits covered in mud from his latest cave expedition. Richard and I badly wanted to gain education from the master and get to dive what had proven to be a reliable unit.

Bill's approach was "if you can build it, you can dive it". His philosophy being that if we understood how the system worked and had a mental picture of it we could 'see' a problem as it occurred underwater and automatically apply the corrective action. This was ***Lesson 1.*** Three days later Rich and I proudly presented our new 'children' for Bill's approval.

To our surprise Bill just smiled and asked us if we thought we had built them correctly. Of course we replied in the positive. "OK, lets see" he replied. "Lets go dive 'em".

Rich Pyle with our new children

Because we had built the units, we naturally developed our own pre-flight checklist. ***Lesson 2*.** Which through fear of the unknown we rigidly stuck to. After three hours in NASA's space-training tank in Maryland (during which we built a chess set out of space shuttle bits) we had survived! After a series of open water dives we were 'qualified' according to Bill. I still have that same MK4 rebreather today and still use it occasionally, although my main unit is a USN MK15.5.

Next came a series of brushes with the 'then' infant sport rebreathers, early Draeger Atlantis, a couple of American military derivatives and the first prototype Inspirations and MK5's, leading finally to production Inspirations. Learning all the time.

The next paradigm shift came whilst working on a contract in Guam. Billy Deans had been asked to put together a closed-circuit qualified team to work in deep-water. The end result was that six CC divers put in about 170 hours each in a four-month period at depths down to 80 metres. Minor mechanical problems aside, there were no unit failures and no diver-error problems. Quite a track record. How did we achieve it? Without wishing to sound too militaristic, simple discipline.

A typical rebreather day would include:

- assemble the units, which had been disassembled to allow them to dry out from the previous day
- canister times were checked and entered in a daily log
- sensors were checked and their voltage readings noted so that we could roughly predict when one was due to fail
- negative pressure tests were performed

- the units were then pressurised and immersed to locate any leaks. We found this to be one of the most invaluable tests and it solved many potential problems
- a pre-flight check list was rigorously adhered to and filled in during assembly
- we never broke this SOP (Standard Operating Procedure). ***Lesson 3***

The units would then be sealed and transported to the dive site.

- Prior to diving a shortened checklist would be run through in case any problems occurred during transport. ***Lesson 4***
- Each unit would spend approximately daily 4-6 hours submerged
- Post-dive the units were instantly disinfected and the loop disassembled. The log was updated for canister time, gas pressures etc.
- Back at base the units were dried and left disassembled ready to repeat the process the next day
- The main lesson learned was that RB's cannot be treated like open-circuit SCUBA and just be thrown together and dived. More importantly, they cannot just be thrown in a kit bag after diving ready for the following time. Pre-flight checklists save lives!

A generic checklist I have evolved over the years breaks down as follows:

F **Flow**. Check all things that flow gas.
Turn on HP (the oxygen valve should be just open and diluent fully open). Check manual addition buttons, wing and suit inflation and bailout regulators. Do a check on the mouthpiece-mushroom valves.

L **Loop**. Perform a negative and positive test on the breathing loop. Ideally, the positive test should be an immersion test. Take your time over this. Now start breathing the loop.

A **Analyse**. Do a visual check of the cylinder gas content tags. Are the cylinders in the right place, has the gas been analysed? Add oxygen and watch the sensors rise and then diluent and watch them drop. This again confirms the right gas is correctly connected to the right place and the sensors are responding. If a sensor is slow to respond it is either old or waterlogged. Change it! Next, calibrate the sensors. Some units have automatic calibration. I have the habit of confirming the auto-cal by filling and evacuating the counter-lungs with oxygen several times to check the auto-cal has been successful (i.e. it reads 1 bar at atmospheric pressure when purged with 100 % O_2). It is surprising how many times it's not quite right. This is the same for any unit, especially if you're decompression diving. This has to be accurate. ***Lesson 5.***

G **Gauge**. Check gauge pressures of all gas supplies. Never go in without a full diluent cylinder if it is to be used for bailout. Whilst a diluent loss on the bottom is generally no big deal providing you continue to ascend (gas expands during ascent), a lack oxygen can be fatal if sufficient bailout gas is not available. Know your oxygen consumption and plan the dive accordingly. As a rule of thumb never enter the water with less than a half fill of oxygen. As most RB's use 2-3L cylinders this is normally more than adequate.

S **Stack**. Stack is a slang term for where the absorbent canister is housed. Basically, it means check the canister life is adequate for the dive. All manufacturers have recommendations for this which vary with depth and temperature. Stick to them, don't get inventive! Personally, I not only write the stack time in the log but also on the canister its self, especially where there are other RB's on the boat. Several times I have seen people pick up the wrong canister!

This is the major assembly checklist. The pre-dive shortened version just replaces a full calibration with injecting O_2 and diluent and watching the sensors. Instead of a full pressure test, a negative test is performed followed by an in water (6 metres) bubble check by your partner.

Bailout is a RB diver's worst nightmare as it means the loop has become un-breathable. Bailing out basically means switching to open-circuit. In a no-decompression scenario the inboard diluent cylinder may have enough volume to be useful. If you're not sure, practise it. In general, past 20 metres most RB's don't carry enough in-board gas for a successful bailout. Hence, especially when decompression diving, plan for and carry sufficient bailout should the unthinkable happen - one day it will! ***Lesson 6.***

So now to training. I don't advocate training the way that was initially open to me. Several agencies currently have RB courses.

Largely rebreathers don't kill people, people kill people. They are either improperly trained in the first place or become lax after training. Complacency kills! ***Lesson 7.***

No matter how good you think you are, regularly repeat the skills you have learned. If you do not, when SFI occurs (s**t, fan, interface) you will not have the automatic response required. Muscle motor memory is the technical term.

Seek proper training. There is no such thing as a discount course. Be very aware of 'cost effective' training programmes. You pay for what you get and unless you hire a professional it may hurt later. The only way you can ensure you receive a good course is to look at the instructor's experience (not just his/her qualifications). ***Lesson 8.***

Train in the environment in which you will do the majority of your diving. A rebreather wetsuit course in the Red Sea does not prepare you for dry-suit diving the English Channel ***Lesson 9.*** The single biggest problem a student experiences is buoyancy control. With a BCD, a dry suit and a counter-lung; buoyant ascents are common in the early stages of training. Other environmental problems often ensue like, 'well I could shut the mouthpiece in the Red Sea but with these mitts on in this freezing water it's a bit different!'. If you choose to train in warmer climes, at least do a series of acclimatisation dives when you return.

A final point on training - find out about the course content. Ask for a set of the standards for the course to ensure you are receiving the dive time laid down by the accredited training association. ***Lesson 10.*** Many people fail to check this. Somewhere around 500 minutes in the water on a level 1 course is appropriate, usually over six dives.

There is no substitute for proper training, especially if you plan to decompression and/or trimix dive the units.

Post-training. Take it easy. ***Lesson 11.*** Just because you're an open-circuit trimix diver doesn't mean you can leap into 75 metres straight away on a rebreather. You should certainly never do it without additional training and in any case do a series of long, shallower dives with lots of ascents and simulated decompression before you need the real thing.

Watching your PO_2 is everything. Natural open-circuit divers monitor their gauges very occasionally, especially if they are experienced. This is the worst habit to get into with RB's. Having taught a variety of rebreather courses, I have found the single best way to get people out of this poor habit is to in effect disable the automation. Make people manually maintain their PO_2 for the majority of their training dives. This is something I still do on actual dives especially if the dive involves work which might distract me. If my mind is saying, "never mind its on automatic", I find myself paying less attention. If I know I have to push a button to live then I definitely will! Do regular manual flights. This also helps you get a better 'feel' for the systems breathing dynamics. ***Lesson 12***

Far more than open-circuit, a good understand of gas physics is also essential. This is particularly applicable to trimix diving. Never dive anything you don't completely understand. The 'safety' zone using open-circuit comes as you move towards the surface. This is totally the reverse on closed-circuit as the ascent will mean gas expansion and a associated drop in PO_2 may occur, especially when their diluent may be hypoxic. Also, divers rarely naturally monitor their gauges during descent, again another vital phase in a closed-circuit dive as the volumetric changes can greatly affect the breathing gas content. ***Lesson 13***

Without doubt rebreathers are the 'weapon of choice' especially for extended range/technical diving. As with any tool you have to fully understand it to be able to use it properly. If you don't it may cut you!

A simple summary of rebreather diving might be:

Educate gradually, prepare slowly, descend slowly, ascend slowly and watch those PO_2's.

A Standard Operation Procedure

Britannic Project 1997

Introduction
This chapter references a project which an international team of divers conducted in 1997. I was privileged to lead this expedition. The information is taken from the actual standard operating procedure (SOP) used.

The purpose of this section is to detail a simple standard operating procedure and the relevant expedition documentation for the would-be explorer. This is just one way to do it and is what worked in 1997. There are many other ways of conducting expeditions and much has moved on especially in the field of decompression thinking. What is important is that any SOP's you generate are clear and unambiguous and above all, cover all safety issues involved with your project.

Actual text from the 'Britannic' SOP and related documents is in *italics*. My additional comments for this chapter are in standard text. I have also added some project pictures.

Mission Statement

Project Purpose
All projects should have a well defined purpose within which may lie a range of mission objectives. The project purpose should be clear and unambiguous as it is this which will initially attract sponsors and potential team members. An example of such a project might be 'to complete a thorough search and subsequent excavation of the site of the Spanish Galleon "Nostromo" using free swimming divers on closed-circuit diving equipment'. In our case *it was to video and survey HMHS 'Britannic', lost in 120 metres of water off Greece in World War One.* This chapter could easily relate to a cave expedition but in the text a wreck diving expedition will be quoted as an example.

Britannic underway

Mission Objectives
Having agreed a project purpose, the individual tasks to allow the primary objective to be met can be defined. Typical tasks might include:

Research
Before any project can begin there is always an element of research. If the target of the operation is a sunken ship then dependant on the age the research may be extensive and lengthy. Research can cover the following areas:

- mechanical details of the vessel
- details of the ship's activities
- details of the ship's manifest
- details of the period of loss
- subsequent surveys and exploration
- current environmental information (depth, state and location of the wreck)

'Britannic' launching

Most of our research will be provide by the owner and Harland and Wolfe, the builders, with some information from the U- Boat archives.

Surveying
If the current position of the vessel is known then surveying can be a relatively simple exercise. If it is unknown then it is most likely that the research will have defined an 'approximate position'. Armed with this, the primary search tool is probably a proton magnetometre. This is a device which looks for disturbances in the earths magnetic field caused by ferrous objects such as a shipwreck. Sidescan sonars are also very affective, the choice is target-dependant.
Other elements to a survey can include:

- initial diver surveys
- metal detectors
- compass and line surveys
- DPV surveys
- video and still surveys

Our primary search equipment will be a side-scan sonar during the main project, although a local fisherman and an echo sounder was initially used to locate the ship during the reconnaissance dive.

Excavation

In our case there will be none. Older projects may require that official archaeologists are on site. Long-term excavation requires specialist skill outside the scope of this book.

Recovery

Again there will be none, except that the owner and the 'Titannic' Society has asked us to recover a small section of hull material for forensic analysis. We were to be prevented in doing this by the Greek government.

Preservation

This can be a very costly affair with whole cleaning laboratories being set up. *None was undertaken on Britannic '97.*

Documentation

In archaeology, specific artefact documentation is required, tagging finds with unique numbers and pinpointing their position with triangulation and photo grids. *On larger vessels the position of off-ship wreckage may be of use in establishing a cause of sinking. With the 'Britannic' a large section of wreckage was located away from the main site, probably as a result of a mine explosion.*

Diving Tactics to be Employed

Diving tactics are a function of the depth, environmental conditions which prevail on site and the duration of the submerged time required to complete primary tasks. The key element of any diving operation must be 'safety first' and this statement should never be compromised.

Working at depth will normally involve decompression diving to be able to complete the tasks efficiently. It will also often mean using gases other than air and in some instances equipment other than open-circuit.

Our dives willd put us in 100 to 120 metres regularly and will necessitate four gases mixes being used by each diver. A complete decompression/safety strategy has been worked out due to the remote location. This is detailed later.

Physiology

Due to the lack of in field data available from mixed gas diving trials, we will be data logging and using and Doppler on all the dives and will critically analyse results. This will be compared with the dive profiles stored by our Aladdin nitrox computers (set to 50% oxygen to avoid locking them out) and used to adjust decompression schedules as appropriate.

Team Selection

All team members are privately invited, based on their individual expertise. This will not be an easy project, if anything diving it is the easy bit. Within the short timescales we now have we can only pull this off with a consolidated team effort, this I am confident we can achieve.

Funding

In the main the project will be self-funded by the dive team. There will also be an element of equipment sponsorship and some private financial assistance.

Team 'Britannic 1997'

What Happens to the Money?

Initially it will be deposited in a bank account. Having read this document and agreed the terms, all of us that take part take the risk of losing all or some of this money. This is however extremely unlikely. The money will be used essentially to get us to the site and dive the wreck. We are of course seeking additional funding (see separate proposal). The purpose of this additional funding is to allow us all to purchase new equipment and complete the project in a little more comfort. It will also allow a professional film crew to take part, from which any profit return will come. However, if no other funding is forthcoming, we can complete on our £xxx each budget.

The money will initially be spent on any hardware\services needed for which we do not receive sponsorship. A full set of accounts will be retained and will be open for team scrutiny. If the project is successful and we make a profit then the first people to get paid back are ourselves. If the project cannot take place for whatever reason, then any bought items will be sold and the return evenly distributed, along with the remaining money in the account.

Any profit over and above our payback of £xxx each has to be shared between a range of interested parties. These are:

1. *the owner*
2. *the Greek contingent*
3. *the film crew*
4. *all the divers*
5. *any financial sponsors*

Actual profit percentages are as yet undefined and will remain so for some time. The bottom line is we all get a free week diving on the 'Britannic', which is why I started this in the first place and not for any money we may make. (The team actually spent nearly four weeks on the project).

Dates
The 7.5 t truck will leave the UK on 20th, so people needing kit shipped in the van should get it to me by the 19th. Everyone else will be leaving the UK the night of the 24th. I will arrange pickup for everyone in Athens and transport to Kea. Once we all arrive we will unload the van into the lockup and drive back to Athens to get gas supplies.

The actual project dates are from the 25th of October to the 8/9th of November, the second week being the actual dives on the 'Britannic'. There may, however, be some diving the first week on other wrecks in the area to test the system and I would want all divers on site by 25th October.

For the trip across Europe I need myself and two others to share the drive.

In order to get the whole thing off the ground I decided to do a reconnaissance dive earlier this year, mainly to identify the site and investigate local conditions and facilities. Below is the report for this.

Reconnaissance Dive
The following is a brief article I wrote, post-trip in June. It has some useful points and I will expand on the salient ones in the rest of this document.

'On the 22nd of June 1997 at 8.30am I dived the wreck of His Royal Majesty's Hospital Ship 'Britannic'. The team led by myself, was completed by a pair of Greek divers; Alexander Sotiriou and Kyriakos Kavalaris. To my knowledge, we were the first recreational divers to visit the wreck using open circuit trimix and non-commercial techniques. Diving it was the easy bit. Let me tell you why and how we got that far.

For several years I have been involved in what is now known as 'technical diving'. Having eventually attained the position of a trimix instructor with IANTD, this diving tool has allowed me to see and visit many places inaccessible to the average sport diver. This coupled with a love of exploring sunken liners, inevitably led me to the 'Britannic', at 48,158 tons and 852 ft 6 inches in length and larger than her sisters 'Olympic' and 'Titanic', the largest sunken liner in the world.

'Britannic' lies near the island of Kea in Greece as a result of her sinking (probably by a mine) at 9.07 am on Tuesday 21st of November, 1916. General depths are reported in the order of 110 to 120 metres.

As the 'Britannic' is in Greek waters and the Greeks have very strict policing of their dive sites (especially wrecks) the first step was to seek ministerial permission. After two years this was granted on 14th May 1997. Next, the owners. My initial inquiries drew a blank as it now transpires she was about to change hands at the time. She is now owned by Mr. Simon Mills who also strictly controls the right to dive at his end.

What was the purpose of the June 1997 visit? Basically, it was a reconnaissance and feasibility study to see if further diving on a larger scale later in 1997 was logistically and practically possible, using current non-commercial technology.

Due to the remoteness, the team's safety was logistically difficult, so three prime decisions were made:

1. keep the team small
2. use a small fast boat should medi-vac be needed, as helicopters were not an option
3. due to time constraints and lack of accurate site information (currents, depth of wreck etc.) use as much local knowledge as possible

We had to locate and find out everything about the dive-ability of the site by undertaking it ourselves.

Having spent about 5 days completing the formalities with the local Greek Port Police and equipping our 6.6m 200HP RIB to the best of our ability we were ready to conduct the search. The week was ticking away and we only had three days left to locate and dive her. Day one ended with 50% success due to the failure of some echo sounding equipment. We could not get it repaired or replaced as it was the weekend and due to local bureaucracy I had been unable to import extensive search equipment. However, we did locate a fisherman who regularly nets the site. Spurred on by this (and with the relevant formalities exchanged) we arranged to meet the next day. As he fished at night he wanted to start at 4pm. This left matters tight but manageable for the actual dive if we found the wreck quickly, as he had promised.

From the fisherman's knowledge the wreck rose to around 80 metres (which didn't sound right) and was quite tidal although we were assured the current was primarily thermal and abated at 6 metres. We mixed gas. The plan was not to go to the bottom but somewhere in the superstructure to make a positive ID. A maximum operating depth of 90 metres was chosen mainly to keep the decompression down as we were in a major shipping lane with large freighters regularly passing within 200 metres of the site and there was limited support.

Day 2. After 3 hours of searching we eventually marked the wreck (I was later informed that it took so long because the fisherman usually uses light transits at night!) The lack of a sounder on our boat made our GPS useless so we had to work a kind of data transfer between the two boats, via an interpreter of course, are you getting the picture!?

So now it is dark and we have a shot in the wreck. Our only option is to return to Kea for the night and dive at dawn. Surprise, surprise it is a holiday weekend and all the accommodation is full. So four of us get to share a RIB and one half of a fishing boat for the night. We slept 'al fresco' in our under-suits with that great smell of fish. Oh ,and did I mention Kea is 'Mosquito City'.

A little tired but carefully hydrated we woke to a perfect day. There is something magical about dawn dives on an oily calm sea. We located the wreck and due to the current, tied in with the RIB. Safety being an issue, we sank a second shot down the main line to the deepest decompression stop. On it were staged spare decompression gases at relevant depths. In the event that the tide should be too great we would disconnect this system and float with it under the boat. Although this was not ideal (as it would take us out of the pre-arranged exclusion zone around the wreck) it was the only way to comfortably decompress and provide surface support at the same time.

Hitting the water at 8.30 am before the 40-degree C sun had a chance to attack, we pulled ourselves down the bowline into a reasonable current. Six metre checks completed, we descended to the first gas switch which was to our bottom mix (trimix). Mmmm! Mental note, deep-water and still current! At about 50 metres the flow reduced to a trickle. Light and visibility were excellent, temperature had dropped from a surface 21 to 15 degrees C.

At 75 metres, I sucked in heavily. The over used simile of 'my heart stopped' is the most accurate way I can describe it, but then it started again very fast. There she was, an awesome site in the 30 metre visibility, quietly sleeping on her side. Over two years of planning generated a big sigh of relief. Our line had caught in the superstructure close to the second pair of lifeboat davits, still in their launch position. There was a short swim to the top rail, during which I really had a feeling of falling in space.

At 88 metres I touched down just inside my maximum operating depth. The wreck was over 300 metres long and the chances of finding the highest point (reportedly around 80 metres) the first time around were a million to one. Our gas just made it. We could have mixed for deeper, but time and shipping were our enemies, so we had to go with the assimilation of all the available knowledge. I bottomed at 89.6 metres with all gauges checking out.

A short scan confirmed her identity as I swan over recognisable features from the model I had kept at home. I looked the two hammer head sharks which local fishing lore believe protect the wreck. 15 minutes later we had to leave. Great liners always leave a feeling of sadness when you exit their tombs especially where there has been loss of life. We honoured the dead by touching nothing and left for the decompression.

At 30 metres the decision was made to cut loose and float with the boat due to the current. The prearranged yellow SMB went up and a few minutes later we were free. With a hand on the travel gas and an ear for propellors we spent the minutes until we surfaced. Big smiles at the 6 metre stop, a safe exit and a vow to return.

Conclusions? I wish I had a scooter! Although it was a technical dive in all aspects of the phrase, it would be definitely possible with a well equipped, motivated team. I am currently assembling a larger project for late 1997 with more detailed logistics and support to allow us to extensively explore, document and film the wreck.

Legal Issues

Contracts and Licences

It has taken the best part of two years to secure a licence to dive the site from the Greek authorities. This has been largely dealt with by our Greek team members and myself. It would appear that having opened the door, other teams have also been granted the licence. We are still however the first to organise a trip.

Technically the Greeks have control over who dives in their waters and without a license we would be in trouble with the local port police in Lavrio who control the area with gunboats. As it is, because of the work before and due to the incident free 'recon' trip, we have an 'in' with the local police, so things should go smoothly as long as we keep them informed. They have actually been given a ministerial directive to 'help us as much as possible.

The owner is the next issue. The 'Britannic' was recently sold to an individual by the name of Simon Mills who lives in the UK. Technically, he cannot stop us diving the site but could prosecute if he found evidence of tampering or artefact removal. He could, however, possibly make it awkward for us in Greece if we did not sign the contract he has presented to me. I don't see this as a major problem..

As an aside, Simon has actually asked us to look at certain parts of the wreck and I have agreed to give him copies of some of the footage. He is a useful contact and has a lot of information about the ship. His own interest is that he wants to work with Ballard in 1998 who intends to set up cameras on the site and link up to a live web site[75].

Owners' Contract and Releases

As you are all aware we (I) have had to sign a contract with the owner in order for us to dive the Britannic. The key points of this contract I will outline when we arrive on site. In summary they inhibit us from entering sealed areas and control the way in which we release images of the wreck. It also covers artefact removal. This has been fully addressed and an amicable agreement has been reached between us.

As a part of this, all team members must sign to say they understand and agree with the contract. This I will arrange on site but the draft is attached below.

---

[75] Authors note. This never happened.

Draft contract
For now, I, Kevin Gurr, take responsibility for the afore-mentioned people and confirm that only those in the attached list will be diving to the 'Britannic' and will only do so having countersigned this document.

Team Member	**Position**
Kevin Gurr	*Project leader*
Dave Thompson	*Lead Diver*
Tristran Cope	*Team Medic\Standby diver*
Alan Wright	*Lead Diver*
Dan Burton	*Lead Diver\Senior Cameraman*
Uffe Ericksson	*Lead Diver*
Richard Lundgren	*Lead Diver\Cameraman*
Ingmar Lundgren	*Lead Diver*
John Thornton	*Lead Diver*
Kevin Denlay	*Dive Supervisor*
Gary Sharp	*Standby diver*
Alexander Sotiriou	*Lead Diver*
Kerk Kavalaris	*Lead Diver*
Ian Fuller	*Surface Cameraman\Standby diver*

Signed *Date*

In addition to this we should all sign a liability release. This is attached below.

Liability Release
I ____________________________________ am fully conversant and trained in all aspects of mixed gas diving. I understand that this activity is potentially hazardous and life-threatening. I fully appreciate that diving the wreck of HMHS Britannic as a part of the October 1997 expedition falls into the category of extreme exposure diving and hence is susceptible to all the risks associated with mixed gas diving.

By signing this release I fully accept that any liability is my own and in the event of any incident resulting in injury, death, equipment loss or any other expense incurred as a result of repatriation or medical treatment, I fully exonerate; the remainder of the team, project organisers, support personnel and their families of any blame or claims associated with said incident and the 'Britannic' 1997 Project.

Signed *Print* *Date*

Filming and Sponsorship

Film update and funding

The three key organisations we have been in touch with are NOVA Channel and Discovery in the US and the UK end of National Geographic. I have also been in contact with Gregg Bemis (the owner of the Lusitania) who has been our NOVA contact. To date National Geographic are undecided as to whether they will fund us and NOVA and Discovery have said they would like to view a 'demo' film once we shoot it and complete the project. Gregg has just agreed to give us $x,xxx. Hhe is keen to travel to Greece and see what we do. In return, he wants the right to try and sell our footage in the US for us. He may also be a useful contact for future expeditions.

Copyrighting

So that we all understand each other, I have drafted a copyright contract for everyone to sign. This basically means that every image we take is the property of the team and any profits from sales will be shared.

Images Copyright Release

I ________________________________ fully understand that all images (still, video, dive log data etc.) remain the property of the Project Britannic dive team in perpetuity.

I understand the importance of controlling the release of said images in order to attain the maximum return from the sale. To that end, I undertake that I will not sell, loan, issue for view or in any other way transmit the images without written permission from the Project Leader, Mr Kevin Gurr.

I understand that as a team member I am entitled to a share of any profits resulting from the sale of the images and by signing this agreement furthermore empower the Project Leader to act upon mine and the team's behalf when negotiating image sales contracts. I understand that my share of the proceeds will be defined by such contracts.

Signed *Print*

The stern of the 'Britannic'
The dot in the middle is a diver

One of her 6 metre diameter propellors

Web Site
One of the things I want us to do is to run a daily web site. I think I have sponsorship from 'Orange' for the phones and West Dorset Internet, Phoenix's web server is generating and sponsoring the site. Richard and Uffe please take responsibility for this and make sure you have the correct PC, digital camera and the relevant software for this. We should backup on the modem phone if possible. The site address is WWW.WDI.CO.UK/PB/WELCOME.[76]

Existing Sponsors
Below is the list of those things already promised to us.

♦ *Custom Diver primary lights*	*Minimum of 6*
♦ *Yellow and red SMB*	*Full team.*
♦ *Citizen watches*	*Will know in a week or two about 10 watches*
♦ *Poseidon*	*18 Jet streams + spares + 2 semi dry suits*
♦ *RIB*	*Supplied by Alexander Soutiriou*
♦ *Cousteau Plaque*	*Supplied by IANTD*
♦ *Side scan equipment and sub bottom profilers with crew*	*Supplied by Ultra and DRA.*

This is a major advantage for us as we will not only be able to get the first accurate pictures of the wreck, but will also be able to search for the mine anchors and possibly prove why she sank. This is essentially top secret military hardware. We just have to get it there.

♦ *Dry suits*	*Otter* *Otter have agreed to make us what ever we want. Including under suits and semi dry's. Measurement forms are in the post.*
♦ *Medical Kit.*	*Supplied through Tristran*
♦ *Nappies/diapers*	*Supplied by Dave Rigg*
♦ *Surface supplied O2 system*	*APEKS*
♦ *Need to purchase two long HP hoses*	
♦ *With male/female DIN fittings*	
♦ *Compressors*	
♦ *Promised two Greek 15cfm units.*	
♦ *Also sourcing from Hamworthy*	
♦ *Des Quigley and Gregg Bemis*	*Cash*

Post project all sponsors will be contacted and offered a selection of photos/articles etc. The information supplied and release timing of this will be formalised so as not to interfere with and film contracts.

Logistics Problems

The site
The wreck its self is a fairly simple dive. There appears to be a constant thermal tide in a southerly direction (the wreck almost lies North East /South West). This abates at about 50 metres. There appears to be little line on the wreck. However, I only saw a small portion in my 15 minutes. She is VERY intact and VERY impressive. Navigation should be relatively simple but ideally we will need scooters for some of the work.

The Kea Channel is a major shipping lane with regular cargo and tanker visits. This is a problem for long floating decompressions. Please see the initial proposals on decompression safety under that section.

The location of the wreck is approximately 2.6 miles NE of KEA, which is 13 miles off shore from the nearest mainland harbour of Lavrio. The positions given by Cousteau are probably the closest and are noted as xx.xx:xxN, xx.xx:xxE. Kea is basic, the main harbour on our coast has two small developments with limited accommodation. The team should be able to stay on the island.

Accommodation
We are accommodated at the Hotel Karthea which is the only on the island. We also have local equipment storage arranged.

[76] This site no longer exists. References to the project can be found on www.phoenixdivers.co.uk

Dive Boats

At present we have a primary deployment boat and a chase/deco/rescue RIB. The owners will be sending photos and costs after which we can meet to make a decision. The RIB belongs to the Sotirious and will mainly be used as the surface marker for the deco station, as chase boat and medi-vac vessel. The big boat will basically just take us to site, provide major surface cover and emergency gas deployment for separated team members and take us home again. The main reason for this is that we cannot anchor in with sufficient rope and weight to support a large vessel over the site. We will be using a series of strategically placed lightweight shots into which the RIB will tie.

Compressors

We have two, three-phase units which should meet us on Kea. We also have two Haskels.

Gas Filling System

All gas is coming locally from Greece at the best rate possible (see budget). Our biggest problem would appear to be the pure gas decant system. I had planned to make two triple cascade whip systems which could fill three cylinders on each system to cut down decanting times. The system will comprise 6 stainless steel whips, a metal junction block with bleed screw and a digital and analogue gauge.

Medi-Vac

Local facilities are nil, the chamber in Pavros is a long way away and there are no medi-vac heli's. Basically we have to look after ourselves. In order to minimise risk, the following arrangements are being made and the following guidelines will be discussed, refined and adhered to:

1. *we have a good contact with the local chamber and Tristran Cope our doctor will be making emergency evacuation plans with them which will form a part of this document.*
2. *we are trying to obtain a one-man recompression chamberfor transportation only*
3. *we will be taking and practising with in-water recompression equipment.*
4. *everyone will follow a strict hydration programme.*
5. *all dives will be dopplered and fitness to dive lies with Tristran and myself for a final decision.*
6. *dives will be structured and progressive in order to maximise safety and meet project objectives*
7. *decompression models used will be cross-referenced with several experts and standard tables issued to all team members.*

Medical Kit list

Item	Number
Airway Box	1
Facemask + connectors	2
Ambubag (self-inflating bag)	1
Green bubble tubing	2
Guedel airways, No 2	2
No 3	2
Nasal airways	2
Safety pins	2
Endotracheal tubes, Size 9	2
Size 8	2
Catheter mounts	2
Syringes 20ml	2
Laryngoscopes + Blades	2
Tape	2
Gum elastic bougie	1
Hudson Masks + reservoirs	2
Portable ventilator	1
Portable suction	1
IV Box	1
Cannulas 18g	4
16g	4
14g	4
Tagaderm / vecafix / tape	1
lumen central venous cannulas	1
Seldinger	2
IV Administration Sets	4
IV fluid bags N. Saline, 1l	3
Sphygmanometre	1
Otoscope / Laryngoscope	1
Tendon hammer	1
Demand valves with oronasal masks	1
and adapters	2
Continuous flow adapter	2
Medical drugs inventory	
IV/IM Injections	
Adrenaline, 1:10,000 10mls	2
Adrenaline, 1:1000 1ml	2
Chlorpheniramine, IV 10mg	2
Lignocaine 1% 10mls	3
Etomidate 20mg	2
Suxamethonium 100mg	4
Vecuronium 10mg	4
Morphine 10mg	1
Tramadol 100mg	6
Midazolam 10mg/5mls	5
Ondansetron 4mg	1 box
Methylprednisolone 2g	2
Water for injections 10mls	10
Cefotaxime 1g	6

Item	Number
5% Dextrose, 1l	1
3 way taps	3
Syringes 5ml	5
10ml	5
Needles 18g	5
16g	5
Chest Drain Kit	1
Chest Drains	2
Scalpel	2
Forceps (blunt dissection)	
Sutures 2,0 silk	
Heimlich valves	
Chlorhexidine sachets	
Gauze swabs, sterile	6 packs
Sleek tape or Elastoplast	1
Pressure bandage	2
Suture set and sutures	1
Chlorhexidine sachets	6
Sterile gauze swabs	6 packs
Wound dressings	Selection
Tape Micropore	
Elastoplast	
Plasters	Selection
Scissors	1
Urinary catheters	3
Lignocaine gel	3
Urine bags	2
Stethoscope	1
Erythromicin 500mg	40
Gentamicin ear drops	2 bottles
Oral Drugs	
Paracetamol 500mg	50
Ibuprofen 600mg	50
Tylex / Coprxamol tabs	40
Stugeron forte tabs	40
Chlorpheniramine 4mg	20
or	
Zirtek 10mg	20
Amoxycillin 500mg	30
Ciprofloxacin 500mg	20

Equipment

Sponsorship

You can all see from the attached sponsorship list that I am trying to obtain as much new equipment as possible. We will inevitably be using some our own gear. Wherever possible I would like us to standardise on primary equipment for the following reasons:

1. *common kit configurations increase team safety*
2. *we only have to carry one type of spares kit in each case.*
3. *we look professional on film*

The equipment list only includes the major components. I hope we can get sponsorship for the rest.

List 1. Individual Kit

Item	Qty
15/20 litre twin set and manifold	1
Wing and harness	1
Primary torch	1
Back up torch	1
Jon-line	1
Strobe	1
Primary reel (100 metres)	1
Back up reel (35 metres)	1
Communication slate	1
Depth/timers	2
Deco tables	2
Mask/fins	1
Gloves	1
Dry suit + thermals	1
Semi dry suits	1
Delayed SMB's	2
Primary regs (1 x long hose)	2
Decompression regulators	3
10 litre decompression cylinders	3
Net/line cutters	2
DAN medical insurance	1
DPV if you have one please advise	1

List 2. *Things we need to beg/steal or borrow.*

Item	Qty	Supplied by
Surface-supplied O2 system	2	
Emergency drop cylinders (10l) and regulators	4	
Mechanical tool kit	1	
Regulator service tools	1	
Booster pump	2	
LP compressor for boosters	1	
240v 10a petrol generator	1	
Greek mains power plugs	6	
HP compressors	2	
Water tanks for filling	1 / 2	
Dive trackers	4	
RIB	1	
Medical kit	1	
Diver comms kit	1	
In-water recompression harness/mask	1	
Hire (4 weeks) 7.5t van	1	
Cousteau commemorative plaque	1	
Citizen watches	10	
Triple decant system	2	
Lap top (486 minimum) and modem	1	
GSM phone for Greece with modem link	1	
25kg shot weights	8	
8mm polypropylene rope	1000m	
50mm brass rings	10	
Large snap shackles	8	
600mm inflatable buoys	8	
Small pill buoys	8	
Tie wraps	500	
6mm surgical tubing	5m	
10mm bungee	10m	
Diapers/nappies	100	
Oxygen grease	2	
Silicone grease	2	
Saltex	1L	
Doppler	1	
Ratchet straps	4	
Outboard engine oil	10l	
Fuel can	2	
Spare LP hoses (suit wing inflate)	4	
25mm diametre. 9m long aluminium tube	6	
DPV Camera mounts	2	
Spare HP hoses (gauge)	4	
Scaffolding bar clamps	10	
Helium and oxygen valve converters	3 each	
Oxygen analysers	2	

Diving

Mission Plan

We want to explore as much as possible and especially the blast area. Precise lightweight shot lines will be located by the RIB and finally fixed by two man dive teams with the aid of a sidescan sonar and hopefully a military accuracy GPS. Any additional lines will be coded, biodegradable bottom lines run by dive teams to key landmarks. Much of the early dives will be spent installing this system.

Diving Philosophy

We have 10 bottom divers and two permanent standby divers. When you are not diving on the wreck you are surface cover only.

We could have 7-10 days diving. I currently propose we have a shift system of 'one day on' and 'one off' in two teams of 5. This is a decision based around safety and the need to film/explore[77]*. The team format will be:*

- *scooter camera*
- *scooter tender*
- *main diver camera*
- *diver camera tender*
- *free swimming diver*

Scooter teams arriving on 'Britannics' bow

Obviously the scooters will stay together and the 3 non-scooter divers will also act as a team. Aside from the two standby divers there will be a mid water cameraman who can assist as required. I suggest we leave this for now as it will probably change from day to day for a variety of reasons and can be amended within these safe parametres on site.

Decompression

I have generated the deco tables on Proplanner and have had them validated by Max Hann and Jean Pierre Imbert. We will be carrying two deco gases with a third surface-supplied source. Profiles are yet to be computed but basically we will probably spend a maximum of 25 minutes on the wreck in a multi-profile mode, although the worst case profile is probably 25 minutes at 120 metres. This is the limit of our open-circuit gas supply.

This scenario will involve us carrying two deco cylinders 21% and 40% with the final 80% being surface supplied from the RIB, with two emergency drop stations (40/21%) to cover lost divers. On the main boat will also be a spare 80% for each team member in case of station loss. **With today's decompression knowledge intermediate trimix's would have been a better choice. 80% was used because of the low pressure supply of local oxygen. We mixed our own 80% by adding air to these large oxygen cylinders to obtain the required volume.**

Current allowing, we will decompress under the stern of the RIB on a series of fixed bars using Jon-lines. This allows the surface supplied gas to be easily deployed and judging on past experience should be quite comfortable. If the flow is too strong or larger ships are a hazard (we do have a prearranged exclusion zone) then we can disconnect the RIB with the station and divers safely underneath. In an emergency should the RIB have to depart, a similar gas system and rope station can be deployed from the primary boat and we can all transfer.

Decompression System

We have two problems here - thermal tide and shipping. We will have an exclusion zone to cover shipping problems but just in case any ships ignore this I propose the following:

---

[77] In reality we found our decompression stress to very acceptable and several of us dived for 3 or 4 days at a time.

Basically, we need to stay in one place whilst decompressing. This will be achieved using Jon-llines on a tethered decompression station, as we also need surface-supplied gas for the final phase of deco. (the two work well together). The deco station will be attached to the RIB with the surface-supplied bottles in situ. The RIB will be tethered to the relevant working down line for that day (a maximum of 4 lines will be staged at key points on the wreck). In the event of any emergency the RIB can disconnect from the down line taking with it the deco station (slowly) or if the RIB has to depart then the station can be completely disconnected (having its own buoys) and the surface O_2 dumped over board on buoys.

The whole system needs to support a maximum of five divers although we will stagger the two teams to lighten the load a little. Gas is supplied by APEKS Sentinel regulators on 4m whips, four off on each of two first stages. Each second stage has a shutoff in the event of a free flow. First stages are kept at 6m with HP lines to the surface.

The bar system will float on its own buoys but be tethered on quick releases to the rear of the RIB. It comprises two down bars (9m long) and three cross bars (6m long) at 9m, 6m and 4.5m depths. The base will be weighted and tethered at the base via a quick release to the main down line. With the constant thermal tide this should make for a good rigid system to Jon-line onto. The whole thing can disconnect and float on its own if need be.

Data logging

General

If at all possible the dives will be logged on wrist computers with a backup master paper log. nitrox computers are preferred as we can set them to 50% 0_2 to prevent them 'bending'.

Post each dive a visual picture of the wreck will be drawn by each team member and compared against ships plans.

Video and film footage will also be taken and reviewed every evening.

Thank you for accepting to join the project.

Below is a sample of the decompression tables we used. Because of the range of attainable depths on the wreck, we grouped possible dives into sets and by using a look-up table were able to select the correct table for the dive. A range of dives could fall within one set. Sets were labelled A through F.

Profiles

Main Tables

Case *105/23*		Set *B*	D1 *21*	D2 *40*	D3 *80*
M	T	RT	M	T	RT
4.5	60	202	33	2	40
6	34	142	36	1	38
9	19	108	39	1	37
12	14	89	42	1	36
15	10	75	45	1	35
18	7	65	48	1	34
21	5	58	51	3	33
24	4	53	54	1	30
27	3	49			
30	6	46	70	1	28

Case *108/10*		Set *F*	D1 *21*	D2 *40*	D3 *80*
M	T	RT	M	T	RT
4.5	25	90	33	1	23
6	14	65	36	1	22
9	9	51	39	3	21
12	6	43			
15	4	37			
18	4	33			
21	2	29			
24	1	27			
27	1	26			
30	2	25	60	1	16

Case *108/25*		Set *A*	D1 *21*	D2 *40*	D3 *80*
M	T	RT	M	T	RT
4.5	69	232	33	2	45
6	40	163	36	2	43
9	22	123	39	2	41
12	17	101	42	1	39
15	10	84	45	1	38
18	9	74	48	1	37
21	6	65	51	3	36
24	4	59	54	1	33
27	4	55	57	1	32
30	6	51	70	1	30

Case *93/20*		Set *D*	D1 *21*	D2 *40*	D3 *80*
M	T	RT	M	T	RT
4.5	42	147	33	1	35
6	24	105	36	1	34
9	13	81	39	1	33
12	11	68	42	1	32
15	6	57	45	3	31
18	5	51			
21	3	46			
24	3	43			
27	2	40			
30	3	38	70	1	25

Case *96/23*		Set *C*	D1 *21*	D2 *40*	D3 *80*
M	T	RT	M	T	RT
4.5	52	180	33	1	37
6	30	128	36	1	36
9	16	98	39	1	35
12	11	82	42	1	34
15	9	71	45	1	33
18	5	62	48	3	32
21	5	57			
24	3	52			
27	3	49			
30	6	43	70	1	27

Case *99/15*		Set *E*	D1 *21*	D2 *40*	D3 *80*
M	T	RT	M	T	RT
4.5	32	116	33	1	28
6	19	84	36	1	27
9	11	65	39	1	26
12	7	54	42	3	25
15	6	47			
18	4	41			
21	3	37			
24	2	33			
27	1	31			
30	2	30	70	1	19

Lookup Tables

Set A		Set B		Set C	
D	BT	D	BT	D	BT
102	25	114	18	96	20
108	23	108	20	114	15
117	20	93	25	117	15
105	25	99	23	99	20
111	23	117	18	90	23
120	20	96	25	120	15
108	*25*	102	23	102	20
		111	20	93	23
		120	18	90	25
		99	25	105	20
		114	20	*96*	*23*
		105	*23*		

Set D		Set E		Set F	
D	BT	D	BT	D	BT
102	15	111	10	90	10
105	15	90	15	93	10
90	20	114	10	96	10
108	15	93	15	99	10
111	15	117	10	102	10
93	*20*	96	15	105	10
		120	10	*108*	*10*
		99	*15*		

Key:
M = stop depth
T = time at stop
RT = runtime
D1-3 = decompression gases
Case = depth/time

Initial Site 'To do' list

The following is a list of primary tasks which have to be completed in the first few days of our arrival (I have no doubt there will be others).

I have put some provisional names against the list so that we are not standing around with our thumbs up our backsides when we arrive. If any of the team are delayed in arriving, will others please take over any undone tasks?

- *check out equipment storage area (power, light, water for fill tanks etc.)* — *Uffe/Alex*
- *check compressors* — *Uffe/Alex/Gary*
- *check hotel team conference room* — *Kerk/Kev D*
- *fit winch to boat* — *All*
- *fit electronics to boat* — *All (Kev M to supervise)*
- *kit RIB with GPS etc.* — *KG/Alex*
- *make 2 x 150m shots for initial location* — *John*
- *set bow and stern shots with RIB* — *KG/Alex/John*
- *start sidescan tests* — *All*
- *set up gas system* — *Uffe/Al*
- *drive to Athens for gas* — *Kerk/John/Gary*
- *checkout/checkout video kit* — *Richard/Dan/Ian/Kev D*
- *build deco station and drop-stations* — *DT*
- *rig safety cylinders* — *DT*
- *sort medical kit/ datalogging system* — *Tristran/Phillipa*
- *make shots for main survey* — *KG/John/Gary etc.*

This should cover the first two days and get us going. The truck will arrive on Kea by Saturday morning and the flight team should get there mid-afternoon.

Hopefull, the last team change. Kevin Denlay can no longer be a bottom diver due to a recent injury but will run standby/surface supervisor/surface camera. Ingmar Lundgren is taking his place as a deep cameraman. Ian Fuller has joined the team as a mid-water standby/cameraman and surface camera. Ian has two digital systems, one in a housing.

Primary Tasks

Date	**20**	**23**	**24**	**25**	**26**	**27**	**28**	**29**	**30**	**31**	**1**	**2**	**3**	**4**	**5**	**6**	**7**
Truck leaves UK	*																
Truck arrives Kea				*													
First Team leaves UK			*														
First team arrives Kea				*													
Boat arrives Kea				*													
Rig sidescan + test				*	*												
Rig compressors				*	*												
Initial RIB locate of 'Britannic'					*												
Main hull survey (sidescan)						*	*										
Debris field survey								*	*	*							
Set main down lines (boat)								*									
Build and test deco station							*	*									
Shakedown dives									*	*							
Set main down lines (divers)											*	*					
Start UW filming									*	*	*	*	*	*	*	*	*

Standby Diver Protocol

General

The following is offered as a guide for the standby safety system to be employed. Standby diver roles fall into the following areas:

1. *responsible for generation and checking of all non-bottom diver-carried safety cylinders. These are categorised as:*

   A. *10 off single 10/12 litre of 80%. These are to be kept on the main vessel and will only be used in the event of surface-supplied system failure. In theory they will never be used but must be checked daily. These cylinders will be rigged as diver carried stages.*

   B. *2 off single 10/12 litre with 40% and two off 10/12 litre with 21%. Each pair (21/40) will be rigged on a 50 metre drop station. A 50 metre line with a stage ring at 50m and 30m. These will only be deployed if divers become separated from the main shot lines and drift off station (see emergency signals). These drop stations will be kept on the main boat.*

   C. *1 off each 21% and 40% 10/12 litre carried by each standby diver. Only to be used if a bottom diver loses decompression gas at any point during deco.*

   D. *surface-supplied system. We basically have two, 4-man in-water systems with regulator first stages positioned at 6 metre with 4 metre whips to the divers. Each of the two surface cylinders are oxygen 50 litre J cylinders pumped to 250 to make 80%. We will complete consumption trials to see just how long these will last on shakedown dives. In the unlikely event of the RIB having to disconnect from the station these cylinders have to be deployed on floats connected to the station. We need to look at the logistics of this. (See disconnect rules).*

   E. *a 50 litre of 100% with 4 second stages for surface post-dive washouts. To be kept on the large boat.*

2. *in water support for bottom divers. The current plan is to run two five man dive teams. One team dives each day. The five-man team is organised thus:*
   a. One swimming camera diver
   b. One swimming cameraman support diver
   c. One swimming diver
   d. One scooter camera
   e. One scooter tender

This means a team of 3 and a team of 2 underwater. We should have a maximum of three scooters and be able to place two in the water each day.

In order to support this team, I want to try using one standby timed to meet us back at the first deco gas switch (usually 50 metre). On some profiles we do have deeper stops, but these are irrelevant from a standby perspective as the stops are on bottom mix. Due to the depth, standbys will not be able to spend too long there and I suggest this first standby should follow the dive team up to the 30 metre gas switch. At this point (and for the remaining shallow deco) the two standbys can rotate at leisure as long as one remains in the water at all times. Additional support may be afforded by the 'off' team if needed (I will bring a couple of spare twin sets).

Emergency Signals

The standard emergency signal from divers will be one yellow SMB or two SMB's together, preferably with a slate attached highlighting any problem. In any event, if this signal is seen and divers are' off-station' a drop-station will be deployed and a standby launched to define the problem. If possible, the existing in-water standby will be used (we need to make a simple diver recall signal). If not possible, the dry standby will transfer to the main vessel and locate the 'lost' divers. Wherever possible these will be guided back to the station if current allows.

This standby will stay with the 'lost' divers throughout their deco. One of the 'off-divers' taking his place in the RIB.

Other Emergencies
As a general rule the RIB will stay connected to the working shot. This is because of excessive shipping traffic in the area. It will only be disconnected for three reasons:

1. *excessive tide making the deco uncomfortable.*
2. *ships ignoring the arranged exclusion zone.*
3. *we have a major emergency which means the RIB has to be used as a fast rescue vessel. In this instance not only will we disconnect from the down line but the RIB will ditch the station and deploy the 80% cylinders into the water.*

One problem we may need to deal with is that Tristran, whilst being a standby diver, is also our team doctor and will not only need to be on surface in an emergency, but has to be there at the end of the dives to take the doppler results. We will have to manage the standbys accordingly but this should easily covered by intelligent rotation and employing some of the 'off'- divers as needed.

Surface Supervisor
I also intend to set up a surface supervisor/rescue co-ordinator/spare standby role. Due to a recent minor accident, this will probably be Kevin Denlay. Kev has a wealth of experience in this area. This should release some of the pressure on the standbys as he can co-ordinate all surface activities.

Emergency Procedures

All of the above will be expanded upon after the first meeting.

In-water Incidents
- *loss of partner*
- *loss of station*
- *loss of gas*

Surface Incidents
- *collision procedures*
- *in water recompression*
- *evacuation procedures*

Insurance
It is recommended everyone takes full DAN. Details are available through Kevin.

So, the project finally took off. Hampered by bad weather initially, we eventually did 36 man dives on the ship and logged over 15 hours of underwater video. It was definitely one of the most exciting things I have ever done. It was all worth it. Many things didn't quite go to plan but that's another story!

Semi-Closed Inspired FO_2 Vs Flow Rate and Supply FO_2

Oxygen Consumption in Litres/min

0.5

Supply FO2 ↓ / Flow Rate →

Supply FO2	10	15	20	25	30	35	40	45	50	55	60	65	70	75
0.25	0.211	0.224	0.231	0.235	0.237	0.239	0.241	0.242	0.242	0.243	0.244	0.244	0.245	0.245
0.28	0.242	0.255	0.262	0.265	0.268	0.270	0.271	0.272	0.273	0.273	0.274	0.274	0.275	0.275
0.3	0.263	0.276	0.282	0.286	0.288	0.290	0.291	0.292	0.293	0.294	0.294	0.295	0.295	0.295
0.32	0.284	0.297	0.303	0.306	0.308	0.310	0.311	0.312	0.313	0.314	0.314	0.315	0.315	0.315
0.34	0.305	0.317	0.323	0.327	0.329	0.330	0.332	0.333	0.333	0.334	0.334	0.335	0.335	0.336
0.36	0.326	0.338	0.344	0.347	0.349	0.351	0.352	0.353	0.354	0.354	0.355	0.355	0.355	0.356
0.38	0.347	0.359	0.364	0.367	0.369	0.371	0.372	0.373	0.374	0.374	0.375	0.375	0.376	0.376
0.4	0.368	0.379	0.385	0.388	0.390	0.391	0.392	0.393	0.394	0.394	0.395	0.395	0.396	0.396
0.42	0.389	0.400	0.405	0.408	0.410	0.412	0.413	0.413	0.414	0.415	0.415	0.416	0.416	0.416
0.44	0.411	0.421	0.426	0.429	0.431	0.432	0.433	0.434	0.434	0.435	0.435	0.436	0.436	0.436
0.46	0.432	0.441	0.446	0.449	0.451	0.452	0.453	0.454	0.455	0.455	0.455	0.456	0.456	0.456
0.48	0.453	0.462	0.467	0.469	0.471	0.472	0.473	0.474	0.475	0.475	0.476	0.476	0.476	0.477
0.5	0.474	0.483	0.487	0.490	0.492	0.493	0.494	0.494	0.495	0.495	0.496	0.496	0.496	0.497

Oxygen Consumption in Litres/min

1

Supply FO2 ↓ / Flow Rate →

Supply FO2	10	15	20	25	30	35	40	45	50	55	60	65	70	75
0.25	0.167	0.196	0.211	0.219	0.224	0.228	0.231	0.233	0.235	0.236	0.237	0.238	0.239	0.240
0.28	0.200	0.229	0.242	0.250	0.255	0.259	0.262	0.264	0.265	0.267	0.268	0.269	0.270	0.270
0.3	0.222	0.250	0.263	0.271	0.276	0.279	0.282	0.284	0.286	0.287	0.288	0.289	0.290	0.291
0.32	0.244	0.271	0.284	0.292	0.297	0.300	0.303	0.305	0.306	0.307	0.308	0.309	0.310	0.311
0.34	0.267	0.293	0.305	0.313	0.317	0.321	0.323	0.325	0.327	0.328	0.329	0.330	0.330	0.331
0.36	0.289	0.314	0.326	0.333	0.338	0.341	0.344	0.345	0.347	0.348	0.349	0.350	0.351	0.351
0.38	0.311	0.336	0.347	0.354	0.359	0.362	0.364	0.366	0.367	0.369	0.369	0.370	0.371	0.372
0.4	0.333	0.357	0.368	0.375	0.379	0.382	0.385	0.386	0.388	0.389	0.390	0.391	0.391	0.392
0.42	0.356	0.379	0.389	0.396	0.400	0.403	0.405	0.407	0.408	0.409	0.410	0.411	0.412	0.412
0.44	0.378	0.400	0.411	0.417	0.421	0.424	0.426	0.427	0.429	0.430	0.431	0.431	0.432	0.432
0.46	0.400	0.421	0.432	0.438	0.441	0.444	0.446	0.448	0.449	0.450	0.451	0.452	0.452	0.453
0.48	0.422	0.443	0.453	0.458	0.462	0.465	0.467	0.468	0.469	0.470	0.471	0.472	0.472	0.473
0.5	0.444	0.464	0.474	0.479	0.483	0.485	0.487	0.489	0.490	0.491	0.492	0.492	0.493	0.493

Oxygen Consumption in Litres/min
2

Supply FO2 ↓ / Flow Rate →	10	15	20	25	30	35	40	45	50	55	60	65	70	75
0.25	0.063	0.135	0.167	0.185	0.196	0.205	0.211	0.215	0.219	0.222	0.224	0.226	0.228	0.229
0.28	0.100	0.169	0.200	0.217	0.229	0.236	0.242	0.247	0.250	0.253	0.255	0.257	0.259	0.260
0.3	0.125	0.192	0.222	0.239	0.250	0.258	0.263	0.267	0.271	0.274	0.276	0.278	0.279	0.281
0.32	0.150	0.215	0.244	0.261	0.271	0.279	0.284	0.288	0.292	0.294	0.297	0.298	0.300	0.301
0.34	0.175	0.238	0.267	0.283	0.293	0.300	0.305	0.309	0.313	0.315	0.317	0.319	0.321	0.322
0.36	0.200	0.262	0.289	0.304	0.314	0.321	0.326	0.330	0.333	0.336	0.338	0.340	0.341	0.342
0.38	0.225	0.285	0.311	0.326	0.336	0.342	0.347	0.351	0.354	0.357	0.359	0.360	0.362	0.363
0.4	0.250	0.308	0.333	0.348	0.357	0.364	0.368	0.372	0.375	0.377	0.379	0.381	0.382	0.384
0.42	0.275	0.331	0.356	0.370	0.379	0.385	0.389	0.393	0.396	0.398	0.400	0.402	0.403	0.404
0.44	0.300	0.354	0.378	0.391	0.400	0.406	0.411	0.414	0.417	0.419	0.421	0.422	0.424	0.425
0.46	0.325	0.377	0.400	0.413	0.421	0.427	0.432	0.435	0.438	0.440	0.441	0.443	0.444	0.445
0.48	0.350	0.400	0.422	0.435	0.443	0.448	0.453	0.456	0.458	0.460	0.462	0.463	0.465	0.466
0.5	0.375	0.423	0.444	0.457	0.464	0.470	0.474	0.477	0.479	0.481	0.483	0.484	0.485	0.486

Semi-closed EAD

Nitrox mixes	Equivalent Air Depths-Metric Dive Depth 9	12	15	18	21	24	27	30	33	36	39	42
25%	8	11	14	17	19	22	25	28	31	34	37	39
28%	7	10	13	16	18	21	24	26	29	32	35	37
32%	6	9	12	14	17	19	22	24	27	30	32	35
36%	5	8	10	13	15	18	20	22	25	27	30	32
38%	5	7	10	12	14	17	19	21	24	26	28	31
40%	4	7	9	11	14	16	18	20	23	25	27	29

Nitrox mixes	Equivalent Air Depths - Imperial Dive Depth 30	40	50	60	70	80	90	100	110	120	130	140
25%	27	36	46	55	65	74	84	93	103	112	122	131
28%	24	34	43	52	61	70	79	88	97	106	116	125
32%	21	30	38	47	56	64	73	81	90	99	107	116
36%	18	26	34	42	50	59	67	75	83	91	99	107
38%	16	24	32	40	48	56	64	71	79	87	95	103
40%	15	22	30	38	45	53	60	68	76	83	91	98

CNS% and OTU's

For a one-minute exposure at each partial pressure.

PO_2	CNS% per minute	OTU per minute
0.60	0.14	0.26
0.65	0.16	0.37
0.70	0.18	0.47
0.75	0.20	0.56
0.80	0.22	0.65
0.85	0.25	0.74
0.90	0.28	0.83
0.95	0.30	0.92
1.00	0.33	1.00
1.05	0.37	1.08
1.10	0.42	1.16
1.15	0.44	1.24
1.20	0.47	1.32
1.25	0.51	1.40
1.30	0.56	1.48
1.35	0.61	1.55
1.40	0.65	1.63
1.45	0.72	1.70
1.50	0.83	1.78
1.55	1.11	1.85
1.60	2.22	1.92

Note. Time limits are extrapolated and may vary slightly compared with the NOAA Single Exposure table

Single Exposure Oxygen Limits

Partial Pressure (ata/bar)	Single Exposure (minutes)	Single Exposure (hours)
1.6	45	0.75
1.5	120	2.00
1.4	150	2.50
1.3	180	3.00
1.2	210	3.5
1.1	240	4.00
1.0	300	5.00
0.9	360	6.00
0.8	450	7.50
0.7	570	9.50
0.6	720	12.00

SOURCE: National Oceanographic and Atmospheric Administration

REPEX Maximum OTU Limits

Days in Mission	Maximum Daily OTU	Maximum Total OTU
1	850	850
2	700	1400
3	620	1860
4	525	2100
5	460	2300
6	420	2520
7	380	2660
8	350	2800
9	330	2970
10	310	3100
11	300	3300
12	300	3600
13	300	3900
14	300	4200
14-30	300	N/A

Adjusted turn pressure table

Surface gas consumption (in litres)												
Diver 2	**Diver 1**											
	8	**10**	**12**	**14**	**16**	**18**	**20**	**22**	**24**	**26**	**28**	**30**
8	0.67	0.64	0.63	0.61	0.60	0.59	0.58	0.58	0.57	0.57	0.56	0.56
10	0.69	0.67	0.65	0.63	0.62	0.61	0.60	0.59	0.59	0.58	0.58	0.57
12	0.71	0.69	0.67	0.65	0.64	0.63	0.62	0.61	0.60	0.59	0.59	0.58
14	0.73	0.71	0.68	0.67	0.65	0.64	0.63	0.62	0.61	0.61	0.60	0.59
16	0.75	0.72	0.70	0.68	0.67	0.65	0.64	0.63	0.63	0.62	0.61	0.61
18	0.76	0.74	0.71	0.70	0.68	0.67	0.66	0.65	0.64	0.63	0.62	0.62
20	0.78	0.75	0.73	0.71	0.69	0.68	0.67	0.66	0.65	0.64	0.63	0.63
22	0.79	0.76	0.74	0.72	0.70	0.69	0.68	0.67	0.66	0.65	0.64	0.63
24	0.80	0.77	0.75	0.73	0.71	0.70	0.69	0.68	0.67	0.66	0.65	0.64
26	0.81	0.78	0.76	0.74	0.72	0.71	0.70	0.69	0.68	0.67	0.66	0.65
28	0.82	0.79	0.77	0.75	0.73	0.72	0.71	0.69	0.68	0.68	0.67	0.66
30	0.83	0.80	0.78	0.76	0.74	0.73	0.71	0.70	0.69	0.68	0.67	0.67

Rules.

1. Find diver 1's breathing rate at the surface (SAC).
2. Move down the column until you meet diver 2's SAC
3. Now multiply the correction factor by diver 1's fill pressure to calculate the adjusted turn pressure for diver 1
4. Check by changing diver 2's rates and fill pressure for diver 1's. Which ever is the higher corrected turn pressure turns the dive
5. To convert these SAC rates to Cubic feet, multiply by 28

Heliair Top-Off Table (air - 13/38)

		Fill pressure in bar																					
O2	He	40	50	60	70	80	90	100	110	120	130	140	150	160	170	180	190	200	210	220	230	240	250
20.9	0	0	0	0	0	0	0	0	0	0	0	0	0	0	0	0	0	0	0	0	0	0	0
20.7	1	0	0	0	0	0	0	1	1	1	1	1	1	1	1	1	1	2	2	2	2	2	2
20.5	2	0	1	1	1	1	1	2	2	2	2	2	3	3	3	3	3	4	4	4	4	4	5
20.3	3	1	1	1	2	2	2	3	3	3	3	4	4	4	5	5	5	6	6	6	6	7	7
20.1	4	1	2	2	2	3	3	4	4	4	5	5	6	6	6	7	7	8	8	8	9	9	10
19.9	5	2	2	3	3	4	4	5	5	6	6	7	7	8	8	9	9	10	10	11	11	12	12
19.6	6	2	3	3	4	4	5	6	6	7	7	8	9	9	10	10	11	12	12	13	13	14	15
19.4	7	2	3	4	4	5	6	7	7	8	9	9	10	11	11	12	13	14	14	15	16	16	17
19.2	8	3	4	4	5	6	7	8	8	9	10	11	12	12	13	14	15	16	16	17	18	19	20
19.0	9	3	4	5	6	7	8	9	9	10	11	12	13	14	15	16	17	18	18	19	20	21	22
18.8	10	4	5	6	7	8	9	10	11	12	13	14	15	16	17	18	19	20	21	22	23	24	25
18.6	11	4	5	6	7	8	9	11	12	13	14	15	16	17	18	19	20	22	23	24	25	26	27
18.4	12	4	6	7	8	9	10	12	13	14	15	16	18	19	20	21	22	24	25	26	27	28	30
18.2	13	5	6	7	9	10	11	13	14	15	16	18	19	20	22	23	24	26	27	28	29	31	32
18.0	14	5	7	8	9	11	12	14	15	16	18	19	21	22	23	25	26	28	29	30	32	33	35
17.8	15	6	7	9	10	12	13	15	16	18	19	21	22	24	25	27	28	30	31	33	34	36	37
17.6	16	6	8	9	11	12	14	16	17	19	20	22	24	25	27	28	30	32	33	35	36	38	40
17.3	17	6	8	10	11	13	15	17	18	20	22	23	25	27	28	30	32	34	35	37	39	40	42
17.1	18	7	9	10	12	14	16	18	19	21	23	25	27	28	30	32	34	36	37	39	41	43	45
16.9	19	7	9	11	13	15	17	19	20	22	24	26	28	30	32	34	36	38	39	41	43	45	47
16.7	20	8	10	12	14	16	18	20	22	24	26	28	30	32	34	36	38	40	42	44	46	48	50
16.5	21	8	10	12	14	16	18	21	23	25	27	29	31	33	35	37	39	42	44	46	48	50	52
16.3	22	8	11	13	15	17	19	22	24	26	28	30	33	35	37	39	41	44	46	48	50	52	55
16.1	23	9	11	13	16	18	20	23	25	27	29	32	34	36	39	41	43	46	48	50	52	55	57
15.9	24	9	12	14	16	19	21	24	26	28	31	33	36	38	40	43	45	48	50	52	55	57	60
15.7	25	10	12	15	17	20	22	25	27	30	32	35	37	40	42	45	47	50	52	55	57	60	62
15.5	26	10	13	15	18	20	23	26	28	31	33	36	39	41	44	46	49	52	54	57	59	62	65
15.3	27	10	13	16	18	21	24	27	29	32	35	37	40	43	45	48	51	54	56	59	62	64	67
15.0	28	11	14	16	19	22	25	28	30	33	36	39	42	44	47	50	53	56	58	61	64	67	70
14.8	29	11	14	17	20	23	26	29	31	34	37	40	43	46	49	52	55	58	60	63	66	69	72
14.6	30	12	15	18	21	24	27	30	33	36	39	42	45	48	51	54	57	60	63	66	69	72	75
14.4	31	12	15	18	21	24	27	31	34	37	40	43	46	49	52	55	58	62	65	68	71	74	77
14.2	32	12	16	19	22	25	28	32	35	38	41	44	48	51	54	57	60	64	67	70	73	76	80
14.0	33	13	16	19	23	26	29	33	36	39	42	46	49	52	56	59	62	66	69	72	75	79	82
13.8	34	13	17	20	23	27	30	34	37	40	44	47	51	54	57	61	64	68	71	74	78	81	85
13.6	35	14	17	21	24	28	31	35	38	42	45	49	52	56	59	63	66	70	73	77	80	84	87
13.4	36	14	18	21	25	28	32	36	39	43	46	50	54	57	61	64	68	72	75	79	82	86	90
13.2	37	14	18	22	25	29	33	37	40	44	48	51	55	59	62	66	70	74	77	81	85	88	92
13.0	38	15	19	22	26	30	34	38	41	45	49	53	57	60	64	68	72	76	79	83	87	91	95

Heliair Top-Off Table (13/38 - 5/76)

Fill prssure in bar

O2	He	40	50	60	70	80	90	100	110	120	130	140	150	160	170	180	190	200	210	220	230	240	250
13.0	38	15	19	22	26	30	34	38	41	45	49	53	57	60	64	68	72	76	79	83	87	91	95
12.7	39	15	19	23	27	31	35	39	42	46	50	54	58	62	66	70	74	78	81	85	89	93	97
12.5	40	16	20	24	28	32	36	40	44	48	52	56	60	64	68	72	76	80	84	88	92	96	100
12.3	41	16	20	24	28	32	36	41	45	49	53	57	61	65	69	73	77	82	86	90	94	98	102
12.1	42	16	21	25	29	33	37	42	46	50	54	58	63	67	71	75	79	84	88	92	96	100	105
11.9	43	17	21	25	30	34	38	43	47	51	55	60	64	68	73	77	81	86	90	94	98	103	107
11.7	44	17	22	26	30	35	39	44	48	52	57	61	66	70	74	79	83	88	92	96	101	105	110
11.5	45	18	22	27	31	36	40	45	49	54	58	63	67	72	76	81	85	90	94	99	103	108	112
11.3	46	18	23	27	32	36	41	46	50	55	59	64	69	73	78	82	87	92	96	101	105	110	115
11.1	47	18	23	28	32	37	42	47	51	56	61	65	70	75	79	84	89	94	98	103	108	112	117
10.9	48	19	24	28	33	38	43	48	52	57	62	67	72	76	81	86	91	96	100	105	110	115	120
10.7	49	19	24	29	34	39	44	49	53	58	63	68	73	78	83	88	93	98	102	107	112	117	122
10.5	50	20	25	30	35	40	45	50	55	60	65	70	75	80	85	90	95	100	105	110	115	120	125
10.2	51	20	25	30	35	40	45	51	56	61	66	71	76	81	86	91	96	102	107	112	117	122	127
10.0	52	20	26	31	36	41	46	52	57	62	67	72	78	83	88	93	98	104	109	114	119	124	130
9.8	53	21	26	31	37	42	47	53	58	63	68	74	79	84	90	95	100	106	111	116	121	127	132
9.6	54	21	27	32	37	43	48	54	59	64	70	75	81	86	91	97	102	108	113	118	124	129	135
9.4	55	22	27	33	38	44	49	55	60	66	71	77	82	88	93	99	104	110	115	121	126	132	137
9.2	56	22	28	33	39	44	50	56	61	67	72	78	84	89	95	100	106	112	117	123	128	134	140
9.0	57	22	28	34	39	45	51	57	62	68	74	79	85	91	96	102	108	114	119	125	131	136	142
8.8	58	23	29	34	40	46	52	58	63	69	75	81	87	92	98	104	110	116	121	127	133	139	145
8.6	59	23	29	35	41	47	53	59	64	70	76	82	88	94	100	106	112	118	123	129	135	141	147
8.4	60	24	30	36	42	48	54	60	66	72	78	84	90	96	102	108	114	120	126	132	138	144	150
8.2	61	24	30	36	42	48	54	61	67	73	79	85	91	97	103	109	115	122	128	134	140	146	152
7.9	62	24	31	37	43	49	55	62	68	74	80	86	93	99	105	111	117	124	130	136	142	148	155
7.7	63	25	31	37	44	50	56	63	69	75	81	88	94	100	107	113	119	126	132	138	144	151	157
7.5	64	25	32	38	44	51	57	64	70	76	83	89	96	102	108	115	121	128	134	140	147	153	160
7.3	65	26	32	39	45	52	58	65	71	78	84	91	97	104	110	117	123	130	136	143	149	156	162
7.1	66	26	33	39	46	52	59	66	72	79	85	92	99	105	112	118	125	132	138	145	151	158	165
6.9	67	26	33	40	46	53	60	67	73	80	87	93	100	107	113	120	127	134	140	147	154	160	167
6.7	68	27	34	40	47	54	61	68	74	81	88	95	102	108	115	122	129	136	142	149	156	163	170
6.5	69	27	34	41	48	55	62	69	75	82	89	96	103	110	117	124	131	138	144	151	158	165	172
6.3	70	28	35	42	49	56	62	70	77	84	91	98	105	112	118	125	133	140	147	154	161	168	175
6.1	71	28	35	42	49	56	63	71	78	85	92	99	106	113	120	127	134	142	149	156	163	170	177
5.9	72	28	36	43	50	57	64	72	79	86	93	100	108	115	122	129	136	144	151	158	165	172	180
5.6	73	29	36	43	51	58	65	73	80	87	94	102	109	116	124	131	138	146	153	160	167	175	182
5.4	74	29	37	44	51	59	66	74	81	88	96	103	111	118	125	133	140	148	155	162	170	177	185
5.2	75	30	37	45	52	60	67	75	82	90	97	105	112	120	127	135	142	150	157	165	172	180	187
5.0	76	30	38	45	53	60	68	76	83	91	98	106	114	121	129	136	144	152	159	167	174	182	190

Helium and oxygen fractions are shown in the left hand columns with fill pressures in bar along the top. This chart calculates the pure helium required to make the mix. 1 bar = 14.7 psi.

Nitrox Top-Off Table (21% - 60%)

Fill pressure in bar

FO_2	30	40	50	60	70	80	90	100	110	120	130	140	150	160	170	180	190	200	210	220	230	240	250
21%	0	0	0	0	0	0	0	0	0	0	0	0	0	0	0	0	0	0	0	0	0	0	0
22%	0	1	1	1	1	1	1	1	2	2	2	2	2	2	2	3	3	3	3	3	3	3	3
23%	1	1	1	2	2	2	2	3	3	3	3	4	4	4	5	5	5	5	6	6	6	6	7
24%	1	2	2	2	3	3	4	4	4	5	5	5	6	6	7	7	7	8	8	9	9	9	10
25%	2	2	3	3	4	4	5	5	6	6	7	7	8	8	9	9	10	10	11	11	12	12	13
26%	2	3	3	4	5	5	6	6	7	8	8	9	10	10	11	12	12	13	14	14	15	15	16
27%	2	3	4	5	5	6	7	8	8	9	10	11	12	12	13	14	15	15	16	17	18	19	19
28%	3	4	4	5	6	7	8	9	10	11	12	13	13	14	15	16	17	18	19	20	21	22	22
29%	3	4	5	6	7	8	9	10	11	12	13	14	15	16	17	18	19	20	22	23	24	25	26
30%	3	5	6	7	8	9	10	12	13	14	15	16	17	18	20	21	22	23	24	25	26	28	29
31%	4	5	6	8	9	10	11	13	14	15	17	18	19	20	22	23	24	26	27	28	29	31	32
32%	4	6	7	8	10	11	13	14	15	17	18	20	21	22	24	25	27	28	29	31	32	34	35
33%	5	6	8	9	11	12	14	15	17	18	20	21	23	24	26	28	29	31	32	34	35	37	38
34%	5	7	8	10	12	13	15	17	18	20	22	23	25	26	28	30	31	33	35	36	38	40	41
35%	5	7	9	11	12	14	16	18	20	21	23	25	27	29	30	32	34	36	37	39	41	43	45
36%	6	8	10	11	13	15	17	19	21	23	25	27	29	31	32	34	36	38	40	42	44	46	48
37%	6	8	10	12	14	16	18	20	22	24	26	28	31	33	35	37	39	41	43	45	47	49	51
38%	6	9	11	13	15	17	19	22	24	26	28	30	32	35	37	39	41	43	45	48	50	52	54
39%	7	9	11	14	16	18	21	23	25	27	30	32	34	37	39	41	43	46	48	50	53	55	57
40%	7	10	12	14	17	19	22	24	27	29	31	34	36	39	41	43	46	48	51	53	56	58	60
41%	8	10	13	15	18	20	23	25	28	30	33	36	38	41	43	46	48	51	53	56	58	61	64
42%	8	11	13	16	19	21	24	27	29	32	35	37	40	43	45	48	51	53	56	59	61	64	67
43%	8	11	14	17	20	22	25	28	31	34	36	39	42	45	47	50	53	56	59	61	64	67	70
44%	9	12	15	18	20	23	26	29	32	35	38	41	44	47	50	53	55	58	61	64	67	70	73
45%	9	12	15	18	21	24	27	30	34	37	40	43	46	49	52	55	58	61	64	67	70	73	76
46%	10	13	16	19	22	25	29	32	35	38	41	44	48	51	54	57	60	63	67	70	73	76	79
47%	10	13	16	20	23	26	30	33	36	40	43	46	49	53	56	59	63	66	69	73	76	79	82
48%	10	14	17	21	24	27	31	34	38	41	45	48	51	55	58	62	65	69	72	75	79	82	86
49%	11	14	18	21	25	28	32	36	39	43	46	50	53	57	60	64	67	71	75	78	82	85	89
50%	11	15	18	22	26	29	33	37	40	44	48	52	55	59	63	66	70	74	77	81	85	88	92
51%	11	15	19	23	27	30	34	38	42	46	49	53	57	61	65	68	72	76	80	84	88	91	95
52%	12	16	20	24	28	31	35	39	43	47	51	55	59	63	67	71	75	79	83	86	90	94	98
53%	12	16	20	24	28	32	37	41	45	49	53	57	61	65	69	73	77	81	85	89	93	97	101
54%	13	17	21	25	29	33	38	42	46	50	54	59	63	67	71	75	80	84	88	92	96	100	105
55%	13	17	22	26	30	34	39	43	47	52	56	60	65	69	73	78	82	86	91	95	99	103	108
56%	13	18	22	27	31	35	40	44	49	53	58	62	67	71	75	80	84	89	93	98	102	106	111
57%	14	18	23	27	32	37	41	46	50	55	59	64	68	73	78	82	87	91	96	100	105	110	114
58%	14	19	23	28	33	38	42	47	52	56	61	66	70	75	80	84	89	94	98	103	108	113	117
59%	14	19	24	29	34	39	43	48	53	58	63	67	72	77	82	87	92	96	101	106	111	116	120
60%	15	20	25	30	35	40	44	49	54	59	64	69	74	79	84	89	94	99	104	109	114	119	124

Oxygen fractions are in the left column with fill pressures in bar along the top row. To cross mix find the pressure (from the chart) of what you need in the new fill and take away the pressure (from the chart) of the old fill. The difference is the oxygen to add to the old fill. Then fill to the final pressure with air. 1 bar = 14.7 psi.

Nitrox Top-Off Table (60% - 100%)

Fill pressure in bar

FO_2	30	40	50	60	70	80	90	100	110	120	130	140	150	160	170	180	190	200	210	220	230	240	250
60%	15	20	25	30	35	40	44	49	54	59	64	69	74	79	84	89	94	99	104	109	114	119	124
61%	15	20	25	30	35	41	46	51	56	61	66	71	76	81	86	91	96	101	106	112	117	122	127
62%	16	21	26	31	36	42	47	52	57	62	68	73	78	83	88	94	99	104	109	114	120	125	130
63%	16	21	27	32	37	43	48	53	59	64	69	75	80	85	90	96	101	106	112	117	122	128	133
64%	16	22	27	33	38	44	49	54	60	65	71	76	82	87	93	98	104	109	114	120	125	131	136
65%	17	22	28	33	39	45	50	56	61	67	72	78	84	89	95	100	106	112	117	123	128	134	139
66%	17	23	29	34	40	46	51	57	63	68	74	80	86	91	97	103	108	114	120	125	131	137	143
67%	17	23	29	35	41	47	52	58	64	70	76	82	87	93	99	105	111	117	122	128	134	140	146
68%	18	24	30	36	42	48	54	60	65	71	77	83	89	95	101	107	113	119	125	131	137	143	149
69%	18	24	30	36	43	49	55	61	67	73	79	85	91	97	103	109	116	122	128	134	140	146	152
70%	19	25	31	37	43	50	56	62	68	74	81	87	93	99	106	112	118	124	130	137	143	149	155
71%	19	25	32	38	44	51	57	63	70	76	82	89	95	101	108	114	120	127	133	139	146	152	158
72%	19	26	32	39	45	52	58	65	71	78	84	90	97	103	110	116	123	129	136	142	149	155	162
73%	20	26	33	40	46	53	59	66	72	79	86	92	99	105	112	119	125	132	138	145	151	158	165
74%	20	27	34	40	47	54	60	67	74	81	87	94	101	107	114	121	128	134	141	148	154	161	168
75%	21	27	34	41	48	55	62	68	75	82	89	96	103	109	116	123	130	137	144	150	157	164	171
76%	21	28	35	42	49	56	63	70	77	84	91	98	104	111	118	125	132	139	146	153	160	167	174
77%	21	28	35	43	50	57	64	71	78	85	92	99	106	113	121	128	135	142	149	156	163	170	177
78%	22	29	36	43	51	58	65	72	79	87	94	101	108	115	123	130	137	144	152	159	166	173	180
79%	22	29	37	44	51	59	66	73	81	88	95	103	110	118	125	132	140	147	154	162	169	176	184
80%	22	30	37	45	52	60	67	75	82	90	97	105	112	120	127	134	142	149	157	164	172	179	187
81%	23	30	38	46	53	61	68	76	84	91	99	106	114	122	129	137	144	152	160	167	175	182	190
82%	23	31	39	46	54	62	70	77	85	93	100	108	116	124	131	139	147	154	162	170	178	185	193
83%	24	31	39	47	55	63	71	79	86	94	102	110	118	126	133	141	149	157	165	173	181	188	196
84%	24	32	40	48	56	64	72	80	88	96	104	112	120	128	136	144	152	160	168	175	183	191	199
85%	24	32	41	49	57	65	73	81	89	97	105	113	122	130	138	146	154	162	170	178	186	194	203
86%	25	33	41	49	58	66	74	82	91	99	107	115	123	132	140	148	156	165	173	181	189	198	206
87%	25	33	42	50	58	67	75	84	92	100	109	117	125	134	142	150	159	167	175	184	192	201	209
88%	25	34	42	51	59	68	76	85	93	102	110	119	127	136	144	153	161	170	178	187	195	204	212
89%	26	34	43	52	60	69	77	86	95	103	112	121	129	138	146	155	164	172	181	189	198	207	215
90%	26	35	44	52	61	70	79	87	96	105	114	122	131	140	149	157	166	175	183	192	201	210	218
91%	27	35	44	53	62	71	80	89	97	106	115	124	133	142	151	160	168	177	186	195	204	213	222
92%	27	36	45	54	63	72	81	90	99	108	117	126	135	144	153	162	171	180	189	198	207	216	225
93%	27	36	46	55	64	73	82	91	100	109	118	128	137	146	155	164	173	182	191	201	210	219	228
94%	28	37	46	55	65	74	83	92	102	111	120	129	139	148	157	166	176	185	194	203	213	222	231
95%	28	37	47	56	66	75	84	94	103	112	122	131	141	150	159	169	178	187	197	206	215	225	234
96%	28	38	47	57	66	76	85	95	104	114	123	133	142	152	161	171	180	190	199	209	218	228	237
97%	29	38	48	58	67	77	87	96	106	115	125	135	144	154	164	173	183	192	202	212	221	231	241
98%	29	39	49	58	68	78	88	97	107	117	127	136	146	156	166	175	185	195	205	214	224	234	244
99%	30	39	49	59	69	79	89	99	109	118	128	138	148	158	168	178	188	197	207	217	227	237	247
100%	30	40	50	60	70	80	90	100	110	120	130	140	150	160	170	180	190	200	210	220	230	240	250

Conversions

One of these..	Equals..	Equals..	Equals..
1 atmosphere	14.7 pounds/sq inch	33.07 feet of sea water	33.9 feet of fresh water
1 atmosphere	1.0133 bar	10.13 metres of sea water	10.38 metres of fresh water
1 bar	0.987 atmospheres	10.20 metres of fresh water	10.455 metres of sea water
1 bar		33.47 feet of fresh water	32.634 feet of sea water
1 foot of sea water	0.0295 atmospheres	0.0306 bar	
1 foot	0.3048 metres		
1 metre	39.37 inches	3.281 feet	
1 Imperial gallon	1.20095 US gallons	3.785 litres	
1 Litre	0.264 Imperial gallons	0.317 US Gallons	
1 ft^3	28.3 liters		
1 mile per hour	0.8684 knots	1.609 km per hour	
1 Kilogram	2.205 pounds		
1 Pound	0.4536 Kilograms		
1 mile (statute)	1.609 kilometres		
1 mile (Nautical)	1.853 kilometres		
1 Kilometre	0.539 Miles (Nautical)		

To convert degrees Centigrade to degrees Fahrenheit and vice versa.

$$Degrees\ F = Degrees\ C \times (9 \div 5) + 32$$

$$Degrees\ C = Degrees\ F - 32 \times (5 \div 9)$$

Specific Gravity

Material	Weight /kg in m^3	Weight/lb in ft^3
Salt water	1026	64.04
Fresh water	999	62.36
Aluminium	2691	168
Brass	8394	524
Bronze	8715	544
Cement (set)	2483	155
Iron (cast)	7209	450
Lead	11342	708
Steel	7769	485
Silver	10493	655
Gold	19304	1205

Gas Management - Definitions

Bottom Time.	**This is actual Time at Target Depth calculated by Decompression Bottom Time (from tables) - Descent Time.** **N.B. This is different to Decompression Bottom Time which runs from the surface and stops having left the bottom.**
Descent\Ascent Time.	**Time spent travelling to and from the Target Depth.**
Descent\Ascent Rate.	**Speed of Descent\Ascent in metres\min.**
Absolute Pressure.	**Depth in metres divided by 10. Then add 1 bar for surface Ambient Pressure at sea level.** **i.e. 60m = (60/10) + 1 = 7 bar.**
RMV.	**Respiratory Minute Volume. Breathing rate in litres / minute at the surface.**
Breathing rate at depth.	**RMV multiplied by Absolute Pressure at depth.**
Cylinder size (WC).	**Cylinder Water Capacity in litres.**
Cylinder Working Pressure.	**Cylinder maximum fill pressure in bar.**
Turnaround Time.	**Time in the dive when 1/3rd of the gas supply is exhausted. This includes the Descent Time and normally 1/2 of the Time at Target Depth.** **This would only be modified if there is a strong current\outflow.** ◆ **Where the diver intends to return to the shot to ascend, this point dictates the maximum time\distance from the shot. This is the recommended system.** ◆ **Where the diver does not return to the shot and intends to free ascend on a buoy at the end of the Decompression Bottom Time. At this 1/3rd gas point, 1/2 of the actual Time at Target Depth should have elapsed. Having completed the remaining half, they must ascend.** **(NB. Current on a site will affect swim and breathing rates and should be catered for. A rule of thumb is make the out leg against the tide and the home leg with it).**
Turnaround Pressure.	**When there is 2/3rd's of the gas remaining. (See Turnaround Time).**
Swim Rate.	**Speed of swim on bottom in metres\min.**

Gas management Work Sheet

		Units	*Formulae*
A.	RMV	= ____ Litres\min	
B.	Depth	= ____ Metres	
C.	Absolute Pressure	= ____ ATA	(B\10) + 1
c.	Hydrostatic pressure	= ____ ATA	B\10
D.	Breathing rate at depth	= ____ Litres\min	A x C
E.	Planned Decompression Bottom Time (includes descent time).	= ____ Min	From Deco. tables.
F.	Descent Rate	= ____ Metres\min	
G.	Descent Time	= ____ Min	B\F
H.	Time at Target Depth	= ____ Min.	E - G
I.	Descent gas used	= ____ Litres.	((0.5 x c) +1) x G x A
J.	Bottom gas used	= ____ Litres	H x C x A
K.	1/3 rd of gas used or Turnaround Pressure.	= ____ Litres.	I + (J\2)
L.	Total gas required	= ____ Litres.	K x 3
M.	Maximum Working Pressure of your cylinders.	= ____ Bar.	
N.	Calculated Water Capacity of cylinders for this dive.	= ____ Litres.	L\M.

N.B. If using a twin cylinders, divide N by 2. If the answer is greater than your nearest standard size, you must either use cylinders with a greater WC or decrease your dive time.

To calculate Turnaround Time and Distance.

			Units	*Formulae*
O.	**Swim Rate**	= ____	**Metres\min.**	
P.	**Turnaround Time (From surface to 1/3rd point).**	= ____	**Min.**	**E\2**

N.B. On a dive, if either K or P is reached first, this should be the turnaround point. To extend K would deplete the gas reserve and to extend P would increase the decompression penalty. Both, unless planned for, are unacceptable.

As ascent rates will be slower than descent rates, the return leg may use slightly more gas. This and increased breathing rates is why the 1/3rd rule is not excessive in an emergency situation.

Q.	**Turnaround Distance. (Maximum excursion, when returning to the shot).**	= ____	**Metres.**	**(H\2) x O**

Stage and Decompression Gas Management.

N.B. This applies to the definition of a stage as a cylinder used to extend bottom time such as in a cave dive. Items D and E would follow the 1/3rd's Rule when used as a decompression cylinder. In other words the total decompression gas used would be 2/3rd's of that you carried.

		Metres	ATA	Time	RMV	Litres required
A.	**Stops =**	____	____	____	____	____
	=	____	____	____	____	____
	=	____	____	____	____	____
	=	____	____	____	____	____
	=	____	____	____	____	____

			Units	*Formulae*
B.	**Litres for cylinder 1**	= ____	**Litres**	**(Add stops on same gas mix\cylinder from above.**
C.	**Litres for cylinder 2**	= ____	**Litres**	**As above.**

Stage cylinder rule (for decompression cylinder rule use (B/2) x 3 and (C/2) x 3).

D.	**Total Litres for cylinder 1**	= ____	**Litres + 15 bar**	**(B x 2) + 15 bar.**
E.	**Total Litres for cylinder 2**	= ____	**Litres + 15 bar**	**(C x 2) + 15 bar.**

At this point an assumption must be made on cylinder size.

F.	**WC of cylinder 1**	= ____	**Litres**	
G.	**WC of cylinder 2**	= ____	**Litres**	
H.	**WP of cylinder 1**	= ____	**Bar**	
I	**WP of cylinder 2**	= ____	**Bar**	
J.	**15 bar x F**	= ____	**Litres**	
K.	**15 bar x G**	= ____	**Litres**	
L.	**Calculated litres for cylinder 1**	= ____	**Litres**	**D + J**
M.	**Calculated Litres for cylinder 2**	= ____	**Litres**	**E + K**

Check.

F x H must be greater or equal to L.	___ **F x H**	___ **L**
G x I must be greater or equal to M.	___ **G x I**	___ **M**

If not, F and G must increase or the time at stops (hence bottom time) must decrease.

Cylinder Filling Worksheet

To calculate the pressures required to generate a trimix fill:

		Units	Formulae
A. Target Depth	= ____	**Metres**	
B. Absolute Pressure	= ____	**Bar**	**(A\10) + 1**
C. Target PPO_2	= ____	**PPO_2**	**Check CNS Clock!!**
D. Target FO_2 as a %	=	**%**	**(C\B) x 100**
E. Air Narcosis Depth	= ____	**Metres**	**Depth, on air at which Narcosis is apparent.**
F. Air Narcosis depth Absolute Pressure	= ____	**ATA**	**(E\10) +1**
f. PPN_2 at depth E	= ____	**PPN_2**	**0.79 x F**
G. Percent of nitrogen in mix	=	**%**	**(f\B) x 100**
H. PPN_2 at FN_2 in G	= ____	**PPN_2**	**(G\100) x B**

Check for END. (H\0.79) -1 x 10 should = E.

I. Percentage of helium in mix.	=	**%**	**100-(D+G)**
J. Working pressure of your cylinder	= ____	**Bar**	
K. Helium pressure	=	**Bar**	**J x (I\100)**
L. Nitrogen pressure	= _____	**Bar**	**J x (G\100)**
M. Total oxygen pressure	= ____	**Bar**	**J x (D\100)**
N. Total air pressure	=	**Bar**	**L\0.79**
O. Pure oxygen pressure	=	**Bar**	**J -(N+K)**

Now fill helium to pressure in K, oxygen to pressure in O + K and air to pressure in J

Date 2/2/2	Mix 1 Pressure start	Mix 2 Pressure start	Mix 3 Pressure start	Latitude 50.35.34	Longitude 01. 54.00	Notes Wind Ne F. 3. Sea slight. Pilar Project.			Cannister start	
Divers Name	Presure end	Presure end	Presure end	Tables/Profile	Planned Run-time	Enter time	Exit time	Actual Run-time	Total	Dive supervisor
A. Diver	Mix 18/40	Mix 36	Mix 100	Po2 1.3 cc table 70m/20 mins Proplanner	90 mins	120.00	13.35	95 mins	100	KG
	Ps 232	Ps 200	Ps 200							
	Pe 200	Pe 190	Pe 100							
Eqp. Mk 15.5									195	
	Mix	Mix	Mix							
	Ps	Ps	Ps							
	Pe	Pe	Pe							
Eqp.										
	Mix	Mix	Mix							
	Ps	Ps	Ps							
	Pe	Pe	Pe							
Eqp.										
	Mix	Mix	Mix							
	Ps	Ps	Ps							
	Pe	Pe	Pe							
Eqp.										
	Mix	Mix	Mix							
	Ps	Ps	Ps							
	Pe	Pe	Pe							
Eqp.										

Expedition Dive Log

Bibliography

The following is a list of the 'must read' books and 'must visit' websites for the serious diver. Some are good reference books and some are just a good read.

Books

Name	Author	Publisher
Aquarius	Tailliez	Harrap
Basic Cave Diving	Sheck Exley	NSSCDS
Basic Decompression Theory	Wienke	Best Publishing
Bismark, Titanic etc.	Ballard. Various books	Hodder & Stougton
Caves & Cave Diving	Lavar	Hale
Cave Diving	Cave Diving Group	Mendip Publishing
Caves Measureless to Man	Sheck Exley	Exley
Comex Medical Book	Comex	Comex
Decompression & Decompression Sickness	Bühlman	Springer Verlag
Deep Diving	Gilliam/Von Maier/Crea/Webb	Watersport Books
Deeper Into Diving	Lipman	J L Publications
Diving Physiology in Plain English	Bookspan	Undersea & Hyperbaric Medical Soc.
Few Survived	Gray	Cooper
HMHS Britannic. The last Titan	Mills	Shipping Books Press
Mixed Gas Diving	Mount/Gilliam	Watersport Books
Monitor	Tertius dekay	Ballantine Books
My Mystery Ships	Gordon-Campbel	Hodder & Stoughton
NOAA Diving Manual	Miller	NOAA
NSS Cave Diving Manual	Prosser/Grey	NSSCDS
Oxygen and the Diver	Donald	The Spa Ltd.
Oxygen Measurement for Divers	J. Lamb	Best Publishing
Raiders of the Deep	Thomas	Heinemann
Sharks	Readers Digest	Readers Digest
Stars Beneath the Sea	Norton	Century
Stress & Performance in Diving	Bachrach/Egstrom	Best Publishing
The Darkness Beckons	Martin Farr	Diadem
The Frogmen	Waldron/Gleeson	Evans
The Grand Scuttle	Van Der Vat	Grafton Books
The Infernal Diver	Bevan	Submex
The Last Corsair	Van Der Vat	Panther
The Professional Divers Handbook	Sisman	Submex
The Sea Remembers	Throckmorton	Smithmark
The Search for the Atocha	Lyon	Florida Classics Library
The Silent World	Cousteau	Hamish Hamilton
The Spanish Treasure Fleets	Walton	Pineapple Press
The Terrible Hours	Maas	Perenial
The Wakulla Springs Project	Stone	USDCT
Trimix Diving Manual	Mount/Gurr	IANTD
Technical Diver Manual	Mount	IANTD
Various AquaCorp Journals	Mike Menduno	AquaCorp
Workshop on Enriched Air Nitrox	Hamilton\Crossen\Hubert	NOAA

Useful Websites

URL (WWW.)	Subject
Bestpub.com	Diving books
Caves.org	Cave diving
Cavedivers.com	Cave diving
Cavedivinggroup.org	Cave diving
Deep-Tech.com	Technical magazine
Divenet.com	General diving links
Hammerheadpress.com	Diving books
Immersed.com	Technical magazine
Safecavediving.com	Cave diving
990mag.com	Technical magazine
Sidemount.com	Equipment configuration
Phoenixdivers.com	Technical training

Index

NOTES:

LIFELINE
JETSTREAM
THE ULTRA HIGH PERFORMANCE REGULATOR OFFERING EXTREME BREATHABILITY REGARDLESS OF DEPTH AND PHYSICAL DEMAND. NUMBER ONE WITH SCIENTIFIC, MILITARY, CAVE AND TECHNICAL DIVERS .
CYKLON 5000
THE REGULATOR THAT BUILT POSEIDON'S REPUTATION FOR RELIABILITY - A REAL WORK HORSE. USED BY COMMERCIAL OPERATIONS AND MANY OF THE WORLD'S NAVIES.
DIN & A-CLAMP
FULL 300 BAR CAPABILITY. ALL REGULATORS COME WITH DIN FITTING AND A-CLAMP.
POSEIDON
DIVING SYSTEMS

WHATEVER YOU WANT
Open Circuit
Nitrox
2 mix Nitrox
Closed Circuit
BUDDY
NEXUS
Nexus technology will take you all the way
SRP £349.00
Ambient Pressure Diving Ltd.
Water-ma-Trout Industrial Estate,
Helston, Cornwall UK TR13 0LW
Telephone: 01326 563 834
Email: info@ambientpressurediving.com
Web: www.ambientpressurediving.com
Photo courtesy of Danah Diver, Red Sea